COMMERCIAL DISPUTE RESOLUTION

The University of Law
Braboeuf Manor
Portsmouth Road
Guildford
Surrey GU3 1HA

COMMERCIAL DISPUTE RESOLUTION

Michael Waring LLB, Solicitor

The University of Law
Braboeuf Manor
Portsmouth Road, Guildford
Surrey GU3 1HA

Published by

College of Law Publishing,
Braboeuf Manor, Portsmouth Road, St Catherines, Guildford GU3 1HA

British Library Cataloguing-in-Publication Data

A catalogue record for this book is available from the British Library.

ISBN 978 1 914219 64 1

Typeset by Style Photosetting Ltd, Mayfield, East Sussex

Tables and index by Moira Greenhalgh, Arnside, Cumbria

Preface

This book has been written as a guide to students taking an Advanced Dispute Resolution elective.

Although I am responsible for this edition, I remain indebted to the late Graham Beecher who was primarily responsible for earlier versions of this book.

In the interest of brevity, the masculine pronoun has been used to include the feminine.

MIKE WARING

The University of Law
Manchester

Contents

Table of Cases

Table of Statutes

Table of Secondary Legislation and Court Guides

Table of Abbreviations

AA 1996	Arbitration Act 1996
ADR	alternative dispute resolution
AJA 1920	Administration of Justice Act 1920
ATE	after the event (insurance)
B&PCs	Business and Property Courts of England and Wales
CDR	commercial dispute resolution
CEDR	Centre for Effective Dispute Resolution
CFA	conditional fee agreement
CJJA 1982	Civil Jurisdiction and Judgments Act 1982
CMC	case management conference
CMO	costs management order
CPR 1998	Civil Procedure Rules 1998
DBA	damages-based agreement
ECJ	European Court of Justice
EEO	European Enforcement Order
EFTA	European Free Trade Association
ENE	early neutral evaluation
EU	European Union
FJ(RE)A 1933	Foreign Judgments (Reciprocal Enforcement) Act 1933
GLO	Group Litigation Order
ICC	International Chamber of Commerce
LA 1980	Limitation Act 1980
LASPO 2012	Legal Aid, Sentencing and Punishment of Offenders Act 2012
PD	Practice Direction
SRA	Solicitors Regulation Authority
TCC	Technology and Construction Court
UNCITRAL	United Nations Commission on International Trade Law
WFO	worldwide freezing order

PART I

COMMERCIAL DISPUTE RESOLUTION

CHAPTER 1

THE NATURE OF COMMERCIAL DISPUTE RESOLUTION

LEARNING OUTCOMES

After reading this chapter you will understand:

- the approach of business clients to commercial dispute resolution
- the specialist courts available in commercial litigation
- the main alternatives to commercial litigation as methods of resolving commercial disputes
- the importance of being able to advise the client on appropriate methods of dispute resolution.

1.1 INTRODUCTION

This chapter introduces the factors which need to be taken into account in the field of commercial dispute resolution (CDR) and the different methods of dispute resolution available. Every lawyer working in this field must be aware of all the available options to resolve the client's problem. Commercial disputes come in all shapes and sizes of course, ranging from fairly straightforward debt collection cases to extremely complex international disputes involving a multitude of parties.

This book deals with the three main types of CDR:

(a) commercial litigation;

(b) arbitration (the most well-established form of alternative dispute resolution (ADR));

(c) other methods of ADR, with particular emphasis on mediation.

Whilst this book concentrates on commercial litigation, the alternatives to litigation, particularly ADR in all its manifestations, are becoming increasingly important.

It is important to realise that in considering how to resolve any dispute, a businessperson is making a commercial decision. They therefore need a solicitor who is aware of the constraints of business on the conduct of whichever method of dispute resolution is chosen. These constraints are mainly time and money. There is a limit to the amount of time that a businessperson can devote to the resolution of the dispute. There is a limit to the amount of money they can afford, or wish, to spend on legal costs. They want a satisfactory resolution of the dispute at reasonable and proportionate expense.

In view of this, the solicitor needs to keep numerous points in mind, including the following:

(a) What is the appropriate method of dispute resolution to best achieve the client's aims?

(b)   Is the client's priority a quick settlement – possibly to avoid incurring legal costs 'unnecessarily'?

(c)   Does the client want to preserve the business relationship with the other party?

(d)   How will the dispute, and possibly the chosen method of resolution, affect relationships with other customers or suppliers? Clients will not generally want to be seen as a 'soft touch'.

(e)   Will the knowledge that your client is willing to resort to litigation in order to enforce or preserve his rights deter others from attempting to infringe those rights?

(f)   Is the other party involved in the dispute solvent?

(g)   Does the client want the legally correct solution to the dispute, the cheapest solution, the quickest solution, or the best combination of the three?

These are matters which a dispute resolution lawyer must consider with the client at the beginning of the case. They also have to be kept under review as the case progresses. As more is known about the opponent's strengths and weaknesses, the strategy and tactics may have to be changed.

1.2   COMMERCIAL LITIGATION

The term 'commercial litigation' is a very broad term and not easy to define. This book uses it in the context of the resolution of commercial disputes by litigation or the threat of litigation. Litigation to resolve business disputes is carried out in county courts and the Queen's Bench Division of the High Court throughout England and Wales, but the following courts may be said to provide specifically for the resolution of such disputes:

(a)   The Commercial Court. The Commercial Court in London was established in 1895, intended as a court which would have a great familiarity with the subject matter of commercial and mercantile disputes, and to provide procedures which would enable those disputes to be determined justly, expeditiously and efficiently. The practices of the court are discussed in **Chapter 3**.

(b)   The Admiralty Court. Based in London, this deals with shipping and maritime disputes.

(c)   The London Circuit Commercial Court. This was established to deal effectively with commercial claims where the most convenient venue is London, but which are less complex or of smaller value than those claims dealt with in the Commercial Court.

(d)   The regional equivalents of the Commercial Court are the Circuit Commercial Courts in the High Court district registries of Birmingham, Bristol, Cardiff, Leeds, Liverpool, Manchester and Newcastle.

(e)   The Technology and Construction Court (TCC) (formerly known as the Official Referee's Court), as its name suggests, is the appropriate venue for construction and engineering disputes as well as those of a 'technical' nature such as computer disputes. The TCC is part of the High Court and sits in London. Outside London, TCC claims should be issued in one of the following District Registries in which a TCC judge will usually be available – Birmingham, Bristol, Cardiff, Chester, Exeter, Leeds, Liverpool, Manchester, Newcastle upon Tyne and Nottingham.

The practices of the court are discussed in **Chapter 5**.

(f)   The Chancery Division. The specialist parts of the High Court referred to above are part of the Queen's Bench Division. Many commercial claims are, however, of a nature which makes them suitable for trial in the Chancery Division (eg claims relating to commercial property or intellectual property). The particular rules and procedures applicable to the Chancery Division are considered in **Chapter 4**.

From 2 October 2017, all of these courts have operated under the single umbrella of the Business and Property Courts of England and Wales (B&PCs). Those courts in London are all housed at the Rolls Building in Fetter Lane, making it the largest specialist centre for financial, business and property litigation in the world.

On 13 October 2017, an advisory note about issuing proceedings in the B&PCs was produced. This gives detailed guidance about which particular court or list in which to issue proceedings. There are 10 of these as follows:

(1) Admiralty Court (QBD)

(2) Business List (Chancery Division)

(3) Commercial Court (QBD). This includes the option to issue in the London Circuit Commercial Court or those outside London

(4) Competition List (ChD)

(5) Financial List (ChD/QBD)

(6) Insolvency and Companies List (ChD)

(7) Intellectual Property List (ChD)

(8) Property, Trusts and Probate List (ChD)

(9) Revenue List (ChD)

(10) Technology and Construction Court (QBD)

The Advisory Note appears in full at **Appendix 19** and the Practice Direction for the B&PCs is at **Appendix 20**.

The B&PCs are also the venue for recent and forthcoming innovation under the Civil Procedure Rules. From 1 October 2018 two new schemes, the Shorter Trials Scheme and the Flexible Trials Scheme, have operated in all of these courts. This follows a three-year pilot in the Rolls Building courts. Details of these schemes and the types of case suitable for them can be found in PD 57AB.

From 1 January 2019 radical changes to the disclosure process are being piloted for a three-year period in all of the B&PCs. Further details about this can be found in **Chapter 10**.

1.3 ALTERNATIVES TO LITIGATION AS A METHOD OF DISPUTE RESOLUTION

It is important to appreciate that litigation is not always the appropriate solution to a client's problems.

Many disputes are resolved without the need to commence proceedings and, where litigation is used, most proceedings are settled before trial. Alternatives to litigation, such as ADR and arbitration, are becoming increasingly popular.

1.3.1 Alternative dispute resolution

Litigation can be very expensive, very slow and it causes antagonism. Often, the business client will need to continue to deal with the person with whom he is in dispute. Such dealings are unlikely to be happy while litigation continues between the two of them.

The most common type of ADR is mediation, the principal feature of which is that it enables a neutral third party to discuss the problem and possible solutions with both parties. This may lead to a quick and painless solution. Disputes are often caused by misunderstanding rather than bad faith, and when the parties come to realise how the problem came about, they may find it easier to see the other side's point of view and to reach agreement. The different forms of ADR are considered later on in this book (see **Chapter 12**).

Courts have become increasingly supportive of using ADR as a means of resolving disputes even after litigation has commenced. Rule 1.4(2)(e) of the Civil Procedure Rules 1998 (CPR 1998) identifies one of the court's case management powers as

> encouraging the parties to use an alternative dispute resolution procedure if the court considers that appropriate and facilitating the use of such procedure …

A solicitor who fails to advise about the availability of ADR may be negligent. It could also amount to a breach of Principle 7 of the SRA Code of Conduct 2019 if a solicitor does not act in the best interests of their client.

1.3.2 Arbitration

Many business contracts contain an arbitration clause requiring the parties to refer their disputes to arbitration rather than litigation. Even if there is no arbitration agreement, after the dispute arises the parties will often agree to refer the matter to arbitration, in preference to litigation.

In arbitration, a dispute is decided by one or more arbitrators who are usually experts chosen from a particular field or professional body. The decision of the arbitrator(s), called the arbitration 'award', is binding on the parties and enforceable through the courts.

Arbitration has many advantages over litigation:

(a)   The parties can choose their own arbitrator (or arbitrators). This means that they can choose an expert from within their own trade or profession to resolve the dispute. The arbitrator will have personal experience of the matters in question and (unlike a judge) they will not have to be educated by the parties and their experts on the subject matter of the dispute. For example, an engineer who is a member of the Institute of Civil Engineers might be chosen as an arbitrator for a large construction dispute. As a result, there is little risk of a wrong decision on the facts and there is less need for the parties to call their own expert evidence. There is also a saving of time and a corresponding saving of cost.

(b)   The arbitration can be conducted with the convenience of the parties in mind. There are no fixed rules of procedure like CPR 1998 (although many standard form contracts incorporate arbitration rules which are quite detailed). Instead, the parties may have a preliminary meeting with the arbitrator, when they will work out the timetable for the arbitration and the procedure they want to follow.

(c)   The arbitration can take place at a time and place which suits the parties rather than being fixed by the dictates of the court listing system (although other calls on the arbitrator's time may sometimes limit the parties' freedom of choice).

(d)   The dispute can be resolved in total privacy so that, for example, trade secrets can be protected.

(e)   Arbitration is binding on the parties. If the arbitrator's award is not complied with, it can be enforced through the courts.

(f)   Arbitration offers a range of procedures. The parties may opt for a formal hearing, an informal site meeting, or for the case to be resolved on documents only.

(g)   There is greater finality because there is no appeal on questions of fact.

(h)   It can be easier to enforce an arbitration award in a different jurisdiction than it is to enforce a court judgment in a different jurisdiction – certainly outside the EU. This is because many countries are signatories to the New York Convention – see **13.1**.

Not all cases are suited to arbitration, however. If the dispute is about a point of law, it is best resolved in the courts. In some cases, the claimant may need remedies which only a court can give (eg assistance in the enforcement of an injunction). Section 44(2) of the Arbitration Act 1996 (AA 1996) enables the court to supplement the arbitrator's powers in such cases, but they are usually best dealt with by litigation.

Arbitration is not cheap. Lawyers are usually instructed by each party and charge as much for their services in an arbitration as they do in a court case. In litigation, the State provides the judge and the courtroom in return for a relatively nominal fee (although this may change in the future). In an arbitration, the parties have to hire a room for the hearing and they have to pay the arbitrator's fee. Because the arbitrator is an experienced professional, their time will not come cheaply.

1.4 WHICH METHOD OF DISPUTE RESOLUTION?

The most appropriate method of resolution for a particular dispute will depend on all the circumstances and, ultimately, the client's wishes – assuming that there is indeed a choice. Sometimes the best option will be clear-cut – for example, if the client needs an injunction then court proceedings must be taken. If the client wants as quick a resolution as possible, then some form of ADR will clearly be the best option. An arbitration clause in the contract may mean that arbitration must be pursued. The essential attribute for the commercial dispute resolution lawyer is that they understand the scope and characteristics of the available options and can advise the client accordingly.

CHAPTER 2

EARLY CONSIDERATIONS IN COMMERCIAL LITIGATION CASES

LEARNING OUTCOMES

After reading this chapter you will understand:

- the methods of funding commercial litigation
- the changes to funding introduced by the Jackson reforms in April 2013
- limitation issues which may arise in commercial litigation
- the scope of pre-action disclosure and when it may be appropriate to apply for a *Norwich Pharmacal* order
- how the rules provide for the conduct of complex actions involving more than two parties
- the difference in approaches when acting for an insurer client or a trade union
- the ways in which the court can impose sanctions for failing to comply with the Practice Direction on Pre-action Conduct
- basic jurisdiction issues
- the changes in the approach of the courts to case management following the introduction of the Jackson reforms in April 2013.

2.1 INTRODUCTION

When the solicitor is first instructed in relation to any dispute or potential dispute, there are a number of factors which they must explore with their client at a very early stage (during or shortly after instructions are received) in order to protect their client's position.

This chapter seeks to introduce in checklist form some of the more important of those factors and to act as a summary of points which the solicitor must run through or discuss with their client. It does not attempt to do more than raise points which may be applicable. Some of the topics, such as jurisdiction, are dealt with in detail in later chapters of this book; others are only mentioned here. In practice, the onus is then upon the individual solicitor to explore the issue in the required depth and to determine whether any action is in fact appropriate. (The more basic considerations which apply in relation to all litigation are examined on the Civil Litigation course, and a good understanding of Chapter 2 of the Legal Practice Guide, *Civil Litigation* has therefore been assumed for the purposes of this chapter.)

In all cases of course the solicitor needs to identify the client's objective in the matter. In particular, does the client want the best business solution (usually yes) or the 'correct' legal outcome? The solicitor and client must then agree on a strategy to achieve that objective.

2.2 FUNDING THE ACTION

2.2.1 The position prior to April 2013

Conditional fee agreements (CFAs) have traditionally been used almost exclusively in personal injury actions. However, they are of course available for use in commercial litigation, although the potential risk and level of costs in such cases undoubtedly makes them less attractive to solicitors. It is one thing to lose a case, and therefore your costs, in a fast track personal injury case; it is rather different to face the prospect of losing your costs of, say, £100,000 in a substantial commercial case. A solicitor is, however, under a duty to discuss all possible methods of funding the case with a client, and in certain situations a CFA may be the best option.

The House of Lords confirmed in *Cambell v MGN Ltd* [2005] UKHL 61 that CFAs can be used by clients who would be able to fund the litigation themselves. Lord Hoffman stated:

> There is in my opinion nothing in the relevant legislation or practice directions which suggests that a solicitor, before entering into a CFA, must inquire into his client's means and satisfy himself that he could not fund the litigation himself. ... And if the solicitor is not expected to make such inquiries in advance, it would be most unfair for the success fee to be afterwards disallowed on the ground that his client had sufficient means.

Similarly, the possibility of obtaining after the event (ATE) insurance should also be discussed with the client. Again, ATE insurance is most commonly used in personal injury cases but is available from various insurers for commercial litigation. The cover required – ie the amount of the indemnity for the other side's costs – may well run into hundreds of thousands of pounds in commercial litigation, which will be reflected in the size of premium.

In 2015 the Supreme Court, in *Coventry and Others v Lawrence and Another* [2015] UKSC 50, considered a further challenge to the compatibility of the system of the recovery of costs in this country, including the success fee and ATE insurance premium, with the European Convention on Human Rights. The case itself concerned proceedings brought by the claimants against a local speedway track situated some 800 metres away from their house. They claimed the noise emanating from the track constituted a nuisance. After an 11-day trial in the High Court, the judge found in favour of the claimants and awarded them damages totalling £20,750, together with an injunction limiting noise emanating from the track. The judge also ordered the defendants to pay 60% of the claimants' costs. The claimants' base costs were £307,642 and therefore the defendants were liable for £184,585, representing 60% of that figure. However, in addition, as the claimants had instructed their solicitors under a conditional fee agreement, the defendants were also liable for 60% of the success fee of £215,007, ie £129,004. In addition, the defendants were also liable for 60% of the ATE insurance premium of £305,000, ie £183,000. The defendants argued that their liability for payments of these sums infringed their rights under Article 6 of the Convention.

The Supreme Court, by a 5:2 majority, decided that such rights had not been infringed. It would have caused many problems for the Government if the Court had found otherwise, as that would have meant unravelling thousands of earlier decisions relating to the recoverability of those success fees and ATE insurance premiums. (This issue can no longer arise in relation to any post-April 2013 CFA agreements – see **2.2.2** below.)

2.2.2 The Jackson Report

In January 2010 Jackson LJ, who had been appointed by the Master of the Rolls to review the costs of civil litigation, published his final Report, *Review of Civil Litigation Costs*. Amongst his key proposals were:

(a) the abolition of the recovery of success fees and ATE insurance premiums;

(b) the banning of referral fees in personal injury cases;

(c) allowing the use of contingency fees in contentious work;

(d) fixed pre-trial costs in fast track cases;

(e) qualified one-way costs shifting in personal injury, clinical negligence, judicial review and defamation cases (whereby an unsuccessful claimant would not be required to pay the successful defendant's costs);

(f) a voluntary code of conduct for third party litigation funders;

(g) greater case management powers for courts, in particular in relation to costs management. Specific recommendations included allocating judges who have relevant experience to a particular case for the duration of that case (docketing), as indeed already happens in the Commercial Court and TCC, the power to limit the content or length of witness statements and experts' reports, and 'hot tubbing' experts (whereby the expert evidence of both sides is heard concurrently on an issue-by-issue basis). As far as costs management is concerned, Jackson LJ suggested that parties be required to provide budgets at the outset of a claim, to be updated throughout;

(h) greater incentives to accept offers of settlement. Jackson LJ suggested an automatic 10% increase of the damages awarded where a defendant fails to beat a claimant's Part 36 offer at trial;

(i) more encouragement for the use of ADR, ensuring that all lawyers and judges fully understand how the various forms work and their benefits. However, Jackson LJ did not suggest that it should be mandatory.

In March 2011 the Government published its response to the Report, stating that its aim was to implement most of the recommendations in full 'as soon as Parliamentary time allows'.

The Legal Aid, Sentencing and Punishment of Offenders Act 2012 (LASPO 2012) was then passed, and the provisions in Part 2 of the Act implementing the Jackson reforms came into force in April 2013, as did the associated changes to the CPR 1998:

- s 44 abolishes the recovery of the success fee from the losing party;

- s 46 abolishes the recovery of any ATE insurance premium from the losing party;

- s 45 in effect allows the use of contingency fees in civil litigation – these will be known as 'damages-based agreements' (DBAs), which are already permitted in employment tribunal cases (see **2.2.3** below);

- s 55 implements the sanction against defendants referred to at (h) above, allowing the court to provide that a defendant be ordered to pay an additional 10% of damages where the defendant fails to 'beat' a claimant's Part 36 offer.

So far as proposal (g) above is concerned, see **2.12** below.

2.2.3 Damages-based agreements

Section 45 of LASPO 2012 amended s 58AA of the Courts and Legal Services Act 1990 to allow for DBAs in civil litigation. This therefore allows a solicitor to enter into a fee agreement with the client, where the solicitor can take an agreed percentage of the monies recovered for costs.

To be enforceable the DBA must comply with the requirements of s 58AA and the Damages-Based Agreements Regulations 2013 (SI 2013/609), which came into force on 1 April 2013. Under reg 3 of the Regulations, the agreement (which must be in writing) must specify:

(a)   the claim or proceedings or parts of them to which the agreement relates;

(b)   the circumstances in which the representative's payment, expenses and costs, or part of them, are payable; and

(c)   the reason for setting the amount of the payment at the level agreed.

In non-personal injury cases the maximum percentage permitted is 50% of the sums recovered. This must include VAT and counsel's fees but does not include other disbursements.

As costs under a DBA are recoverable only from monies recovered, this means that the case has been successful, at least in part. Usually, therefore, there will also be a costs order in favour of the client. Credit must be given for costs recovered from the losing party.

EXAMPLE

Claimant enters into a 40% DBA with solicitor.

Claimant recovers £500,000 in damages.

Claimant recovers £100,000 in costs. This figure includes disbursements incurred (eg court fees and expert fees).

40% of £500,000 is £200,000.

Credit is given for the £100,000 costs recovered.

Solicitor is entitled to a further £100,000 out of the damages.

Client receives £400,000.

Of course if the case had been lost the solicitor would receive nothing. The client would be liable to pay the defendant's costs (subject to having the benefit of any ATE insurance). The risk for the solicitor in running a commercial case on a DBA is therefore similar to running it on a CFA – perhaps even higher, because they will be paid only from monies recovered from the other party. For that reason acting on a DBA may not be very popular, except where the potential rewards justify the risk taken. It also seems that a DBA can be used only when acting for a party who may recover money in the action, ie the claimant.

The fact that a solicitor is acting under a DBA does not excuse them from the requirement to file a costs budget in appropriate cases (see **2.12**).

2.2.4   Third party funding

Another type of funding which may be available in commercial litigation is 'third party funding' or 'litigation funding'. This is where a third party – usually a specialist litigation funding company – agrees to finance all or part of the legal costs of the litigation. In return, it will take a fee from any money recovered in the litigation – often expressed as a percentage. This can be used in conjunction with a solicitor acting under a CFA or DBA. This type of funding is becoming increasingly common in England and Wales, and there are now a large number of such companies operating in the market. Whilst this is an expensive method of funding the claim for the client, they may well be attracted to the idea of sharing the risk with the third party.

2.3   LIMITATION ISSUES

This topic is raised in the Legal Practice Guide, **Civil Litigation** as one of the considerations to be borne in mind at the first interview with the client, and the basic limitation rules are set out there. Limitation is a complex area of the law, and this section seeks only to remind the solicitor of its importance in the litigation process and to ring some warning bells. If there is a potential limitation problem, the solicitor should refer to specialist texts such as McGee (see **2.13**) so that they may be sure that all possible arguments are pursued. The principal statutory authority is the Limitation Act 1980 (LA 1980).

In the majority of cases, the limitation period commences on the date the cause of action arises. The basic rule for claims founded on contract or tort is that the claimant has six years from the date of the cause of action to commence proceedings.

In *Law Society v Sephton* [2006] UKHL 22 the House of Lords considered the issue of when the cause of action arose where there was a contingent liability. The case arose out of the activities of a solicitor who stole £750,000 from his client account over a period of six years ending in March 1995. The defendants in the case were the accountants who certified the dishonest solicitor's accounts. There was no doubt the accountants had been negligent in doing so. The clients who had lost money made claims on The Law Society Compensation Fund – the first claim was made on 8 July 1996 and the first payment was made in October 1996. The fund paid out a total of £245,764.11.

At the time there was some doubt as to whether The Law Society could recover damages from an accountant in these circumstances. That point was resolved in The Law Society's favour in *Law Society v KPMG Peat Marwick* [2000] 1 WLR 1921.

In the *Sephton* case the claim form was issued on 16 May 2002. This date was clearly more than six years after the negligent acts of the defendant, but less than six years after the first claim made on the Compensation Fund. The defendants pleaded the issue of limitation in their defence. The issue for the court to decide therefore was when the cause of action arose – was it the date of the act of negligence or the date claims were made on the Compensation Fund?

After losing on this issue at trial, The Law Society was successful in both the Court of Appeal and House of Lords. Lord Hoffman stated that 'a contingent liability is not as such damage until the contingency occurs'. The contingent liability here was that of The Law Society to pay compensation to the clients of the dishonest solicitor. That did not occur until (at the earliest) July 1996. That was the date The Law Society suffered damage as a result of the accountants' negligence and was therefore the date of the cause of action. The claim form had therefore been issued within the six-year limitation period.

In commercial litigation, issues of limitation may arise because the limitation period is about to end; because the time the cause of action arose is not clear-cut; or because some of the extensions and/or exceptions to the basic limitation rule may apply. A number of those extensions/exceptions are considered briefly below.

2.3.1 Initial considerations

Failure to issue proceedings or take other steps within the limitation period has always been a major source of negligence claims against solicitors and should therefore remain foremost in the solicitor's mind. All necessary checks must be put in place to ensure that any time limits are not missed (eg a duplicate diary system), and also that any relevant exceptions to the basic rule are claimed on behalf of the client. (Remember that limitation must be specifically claimed, whether as a defence or as an extension to the basic rule.) If there is any doubt as to whether the limitation period has expired, or if the time period left is short, a solicitor should issue proceedings to protect the client's position. The solicitor must look at the problem from all angles to establish what type of claim they are dealing with, whether more than one claim (and thus potentially more than one limitation period) is involved, and what points on limitation might be raised by the other side. Even if the most obvious claim is time-barred, an alternative claim might be available. Solicitors acting for potential defendants should pay equal attention to this consideration when first approached by their client. If limitation can be pleaded as a defence, it is a very effective tool for a defendant.

2.3.2 Exceptions

There are a number of exceptions to the basic limitation periods. The extension of the period in respect of minors (until they attain majority) has already been encountered on the Civil Litigation course, as has the latent damage exception for a claim in negligence. On the latter point, remember that the initial time limit can be extended under s 14A of the LA 1980 to the date three years after the claimant first had knowledge of all the facts relevant to the cause of action, with an ultimate longstop date of 15 years from the alleged breach of duty. Section 14A applies only to negligence claims in tort and not to claims which can only be framed in contract (see *Société Commerciale de Reassurance v Eras International (formerly Eras (UK)); The Eras Eil Actions (Note)* [1992] 2 All ER 82).

Some other points are worthy of a brief mention:

(a)   *Fraud.* Section 32 of the LA 1980 contains a similar exception to that contained in s 14A, namely that in the event of fraud, concealment or mistake, the limitation period is postponed until six years from the claimant discovering the fraud, etc.

(b)   *Consumer.* Claims under the Consumer Protection Act 1987 are subject to a statutory 10-year longstop date after which claims cannot be brought.

(c)   *Contribution.* Where a claim for contribution is brought by way of separate proceedings (ie not by way of an additional claim under Part 20), under the Civil Liability Contribution Act 1978 the limitation period is two years from the date of judgment or, if none, from the date of any agreement to settle reached between the parties. The court has the power to apportion liability between two or more persons who are liable for the same damage (whether in tort, contract or otherwise).

(d)   *Pending actions.* Lastly, s 35 of the LA 1980 and r 19.5 of CPR 1998 restrict the ability of a party to defeat the rules on limitation by adding a new claim to existing proceedings when it would be too late to start a separate action (whether a Part 20 counterclaim, new party or new cause of action etc – see further **2.7.1** and **2.7.2**).

2.3.3   Other time limits

There are other time limits of which a solicitor needs to be aware. These include those applicable under the Companies Act 2006, the Insolvency Act 1986, and the Financial Services and Markets Act 2000.

Very often, commercial contracts alter the limitation period by specifying very short periods for notifying the other party of claims. If, for example, a contract between A and B says that any party must notify the other within six months of any dispute or potential dispute, the courts are likely to enforce that contract. If A complains even a day late about an alleged breach of contract by B, he will probably find that he will be unable to sue B. It is vitally important for solicitors acting for a party to a potential dispute to check the contract and related documents to make sure that there are no such time limits. It is equally important to comply with those time limits, even if the limitation period under the LA 1980 has not expired. As you will see in **Chapter 13**, a similar issue arises in arbitration agreements.

2.3.4   Agreeing to extend limitation periods

In some cases, it may not be desirable to commence proceedings against another party or to join another party at the outset of the action. This may, for example, be because the claim against such parties is not strong or because, for commercial reasons, it is preferable to sue another person. The danger, however, is that due to problems of limitation, it may not be possible to take steps at a later stage to sue or to join that other party. In such circumstances, the parties will often in practice try to agree a stay of the limitation period. The agreement will stop time running as between the parties for a specific purpose, dispute or case as set out in the agreement. If either party then wishes to bring a claim (because the original defendant is held not liable or because further facts emerge changing the whole face of the litigation), he is not prevented from doing so. It is therefore essential for a solicitor to be aware of all persons against whom such a potential claim might be made. They must consider whether any other parties should be sued or joined to the main action and, if not, whether a stay should be agreed (see **2.7**).

2.3.5 Foreign element

Another area which should always be borne in mind in commercial litigation is the question of whether any foreign limitation period might apply. If so, foreign legal advice should be taken as early as possible to ensure that any claim is not time-barred as a result of a foreign time limit. Where (eg as a result of a contractual choice of law clause) the English courts apply foreign law, then under the Foreign Limitation Periods Act 1984 the limitation period will be that governed by the foreign law. The foreign limitation period will be determined by the judge as a matter of fact on hearing expert evidence on the question from the parties.

2.4 CAPACITY

A solicitor must be satisfied, before bringing any claim, that their client has legal capacity under English law to sue and, equally importantly, that the intended defendant can be sued. The same consideration will of course apply if acting for the defendant; the solicitor should immediately check that the claimant has the right to sue and that their client can be sued. The solicitor should never make any assumptions, particularly where the limitation period is about to expire or where a foreign party is involved. A foreign party may well be recognised under foreign law but not have the right to sue in England and Wales.

When acting for or against individuals, remember that special rules exist to protect children and patients, and that they must be followed strictly where such persons are sued or intend to sue. Equally, if the client or intended other party is dead, the solicitor should consider whether the claim will survive (it does not, eg, in relation to a potential defamation claim) and should also check that any necessary approvals have been correctly obtained from the representatives of the deceased.

The question of legal capacity is equally important when dealing with some other form of legal body (which will be far more common in commercial litigation). In cases involving partnerships, make sure that all the relevant partners involved at the time of the cause of action are named in the action. If a party is neither a company nor a partnership, the solicitor will need to determine whether the body constitutes an unincorporated body (eg a trade union) for the purposes of English law. If not, then it cannot sue or be sued.

Finally, the solicitor should confirm whether the approval of any third person is required before litigation can be brought either by or against the intended party. The approval of a liquidator or an administrator (or possibly the permission of the court) would normally be required, for example, for an insolvent person to commence court proceedings. Alternatively, the approval of a trustee (eg for a charity) might be required. If any approval is required, it should be obtained at the outset. Do not make any assumptions and do not wait until the limitation period has almost expired in the hope that there will be no problem.

2.5 IN-HOUSE LEGAL DEPARTMENTS

Many large commercial clients will have their own legal departments. In this situation, instructions to a firm to act for the company will usually come from its lawyer. The in-house lawyer may well deal with the initial stage of the dispute before taking the decision to instruct an outside firm.

2.6 DISCLOSURE OBLIGATIONS AND PRE-ACTION DISCLOSURE

2.6.1 Advising the client

Bearing in mind a party's obligations in relation to disclosure under Part 31 of CPR 1998, it is vital to warn the client right at the outset of these obligations and the requirement to preserve any documents which may be relevant. This is particularly important in relation to documents held in electronic form, a point emphasised in PD 31B (see **10.5.2.2**).

2.6.2 Pre-action disclosure

Rule 31.16 of the CPR 1998 gives the court the power to make an order for disclosure before proceedings are issued where the respondent is likely to be a party to the subsequent proceedings (see Legal Practice Guide, *Civil Litigation* at **3.9**). However, where a party needs an order for disclosure against a respondent who is unlikely to be a party to the potential proceedings then it can make use of what is generally known as a *Norwich Pharmacal* order. The ability of the court to make such an order was established by the House of Lords in *Norwich Pharmacal v Commissioners of Customs & Excise* [1974] AC 133. In that case the applicant, Norwich Pharmacal, wanted to obtain information from Customs & Excise about the importation of a particular chemical compound (patented by Norwich Pharmacal) that had been imported into the country without a licence from Norwich Pharmacal. Norwich Pharmacal had no cause of action against Customs & Excise but sought disclosure of the names of the wrongdoers who had imported the chemical compound. The House of Lords held that Customs & Excise was indeed under a duty to disclose the information sought. In order to obtain a *Norwich Pharmacal* order, the party will generally have to show:

(a)   there are no other relevant CPR 1998 provisions;

(b)   the respondent is likely to have relevant documents or information;

(c)   the respondent is involved in the wrongdoing;

(d)   the respondent is not merely a witness who could be called to give evidence or produce documents;

(e)   the order is necessary in the interests of justice.

The court may also require the applicant to provide a cross-undertaking in damages.

Applications for *Norwich Pharmacal* orders should be made by issuing a claim form in accordance with CPR 1998, r 8 with the respondent as the defendant. The application must be supported by evidence which will usually be in the form of a witness statement. The applicant should give full and frank disclosure of all material facts. The application will usually be made on notice unless there is a need for secrecy or urgency. That might apply, for example, where the respondent is likely to be under a duty to inform the intended defendant (in the proposed main action) of the application. Where the application is going to be made on notice then it would be sensible for the applicant to contact the respondent asking for voluntary disclosure of the information requested to save the costs of the application to the court.

2.7 COMPLEX ACTIONS

It is commonplace for commercial litigation disputes to involve a number of different parties and/or causes of action. The Legal Practice Guide, *Civil Litigation* introduces the provisions in Part 20 of CPR 1998 which govern the circumstances in which a defendant may bring a claim against:

(a)   the claimant (a counterclaim);

(b)   another defendant (a claim for a contribution or indemnity); or

(c)   someone who is not already a party (a Part 20 'Third Party' claim).

This section considers the rules other than those in Part 20 by which the court manages disputes involving a number of parties or causes of action. As a starting point, it is worth remembering that the aim of the court is to have as few actions as possible, with as few parties as possible. This reduces duplication of work, ensuring that the dispute is resolved as quickly as possible and without incurring unnecessary costs, all of which is in accordance with the overriding objective. It also avoids the risk of inconsistent judgments on related matters. On the other hand, there is a limit to what can appropriately be dealt with in a single action. The purpose of the court rules is to enable the court to strike a sensible balance.

2.7.1   Causes of action

It is not at all unusual for a number of causes of action to be dealt with in a single action. Under r 7.3 of CPR 1998, the claimant may use a single claim form to start all claims which can be conveniently disposed of in the same proceedings.

However, the claimant may run into difficulties if he wishes to introduce a new cause of action after he has served his particulars of claim. He cannot amend the particulars of claim without obtaining either the written consent of all the other parties or the permission of the court. Broadly, the court is likely to allow the amendment, provided the new cause of action can conveniently be dealt with as part of the original proceedings. Important factors are whether the amendment would necessitate an alteration in the arrangements for trial and whether it is fair for the defendant to face a new claim given the stage the proceedings have reached.

More stringent considerations apply where the claimant is seeking to introduce a cause of action after the expiry of the limitation period. The court has a discretion to allow the amendment if the new claim arises out of the same facts or substantially the same facts as an existing claim.

EXAMPLE

C sues D for breach of contract, issuing the claim form on 1 March. In December, he decides he also wishes to bring a claim against D for negligence, but the limitation period for this expired in June. If C issued a separate claim form, D would have an impregnable defence. If, however, C is allowed to amend his original claim form and particulars of claim, the negligence claim will be treated as having been made on the date the original claim form was issued. The court may allow the amendment only if the negligence and contract claims arise out of the same or substantially the same facts.

2.7.2   Addition, substitution and removal of parties

Part 19 of CPR 1998 states that once a claim form has been served, the court's permission is required to remove, add or substitute a party. An application to the court may be made, either by an existing party or by a person who wishes to be added as a party.

2.7.2.1   Adding a party

The court may add a new party to the proceedings if:

(a)   it is desirable for resolving the matters in dispute; or

(b)   there is an issue involving the new party and an existing party which is connected to the matters in dispute in the existing proceedings, and it is desirable to add the new party so that the court can resolve that issue.

A party cannot be added as a claimant unless their written consent has been filed at court. The court may, however, require such a party to be joined as a defendant.

2.7.2.2   Removing a party

The court can order any person to cease to be a party to proceedings if it is not desirable that they should be one.

2.7.2.3   Substituting a party

The court may order the substitution of one party for another, provided this is desirable and the original party's interest or liability has passed to the new party.

Where the court makes an order removing, substituting or adding a party, it may also make any consequential directions that are necessary, such as the serving of relevant documents on a new party.

2.7.2.4   Limitation

Special considerations apply where a party wishes to add or substitute after the expiration of a limitation period.

The court may add or substitute a party if the relevant limitation period was current when the proceedings were started and the addition or substitution is necessary. Rule 19.5(3) provides that it is only necessary if the court is satisfied that:

(a)   the new party is to be substituted for a party who was named in the claim form in mistake for the new party; or

(b)   the claim cannot properly be carried on by or against the original party unless the new party is added or substituted as claimant or defendant; or

(c)   the original party has died or has had a bankruptcy order made against him and his interest or liability has passed to the new party.

There are further provisions relating to personal injuries claims which are not within the scope of this book.

2.7.3   Consolidation

As part of its general management powers (see further **2.12.1**), the court may direct that two or more actions shall be consolidated into a single action (r 3.1(2)(g)). The purpose of consolidation is to save costs by avoiding unnecessary duplication of work during the interim stages and by holding a single trial. Alternatively, the court may leave the actions as separate proceedings but order that they be tried together (r 3.1(2)(h)).

In both cases, the court can make the order on its own initiative or on the application of a party. The claims must be pending in the same court, but where they have been started in different courts, they can be transferred so that the order can be made.

2.7.4   Multi-party actions

This is intended only as a brief introduction to this topic. The solicitor handling a case should consider at the outset of a dispute whether a multi-party approach is appropriate. If so, specialist advice, or at least further research into CPR 1998 will be required.

Part 19 identifies two categories of proceedings that can be described as multi-party:

(a)   proceedings taken or defended by representative parties; and

(b)   group litigation.

2.7.4.1   Representative parties (r 19.6)

Where more than one person has the same interest in a claim, one of them may, with the permission of the court, pursue or defend the claim as representative for the others. In *National Bank of Greece SA v RM Outhwaite 317 Syndicate at Lloyds* [2001] Lloyd's Rep IR 652, the court held that 'same interest in a claim' was to be interpreted with a view to giving effect to the overriding objective in CPR 1998. Specifically, it should be interpreted in a way that made the representative proceedings machinery available in cases where its use would save expense and enable a matter to be dealt with expeditiously.

Unless the court directs otherwise, any judgment or order that is made against the representative party is binding on all the persons represented in the claim. However, the judgment or order may be enforced by or against anyone other than the representative only with the permission of the court.

2.7.4.2   Group litigation (r 19.10–r 19.15)

Where there are a number of claims that give rise to common or related issues of fact or law, the court may make a Group Litigation Order (GLO). Such orders are intended for large-scale litigation involving multiple parties. Their purpose is to ensure that all the claims which fall within the scope of the group litigation are properly coordinated. For example, a GLO might be suitable where a large number of individuals and/or businesses have been damaged by an environmental disaster caused by a particular company, or, alternatively, where a pharmaceutical company faces hundreds of claims as the result of the alleged ill-effects of one of their drugs. In both instances, it is advantageous to both the claimants and the defendant(s) to ensure that the mass of claims is effectively managed and that work is not duplicated.

Where a GLO is made, a register is established of all the claims that form part of it and a direction may be made as to how the GLO should be publicised. The court will set a date by which those wishing to take part in the group litigation should register. Anyone wishing to register after the cut-off date will be permitted to do so only with the permission of the court.

All the claims within the GLO will be allocated to the multi-track. They are managed by a single court, which has the power to make directions to ensure that the litigation is handled effectively. To assist in this, a managing judge is appointed with overall responsibility for the claim. A single solicitor may be appointed as the 'lead' solicitor. Practice Direction (PD) 19B of CPR 1998 recommends that their role and their relationship with the solicitors representing the other group litigants should be carefully defined in writing.

In order to reduce duplication, the court may order group particulars of claim to be prepared. The allegations common to all the claimants are set out in the main body of the document, with the facts relating to individual claimants being contained in a schedule. Another way the court can reduce costs is by ordering one or more claims to proceed as test cases.

A judgment or an order that is made in relation to any claim in the register will be binding on all the parties to all the claims which are on the register at the time it is made. It is for the court to direct whether and how the order or judgment should affect claims that join the register after it was made. A party who is affected by an order or judgment may apply for an order that he should not be bound by it.

2.8 DERIVATIVE CLAIMS (CPR 1998, r 19.9)

This is the name for a claim made by one or more members of a company, other incorporated body or trade union for a remedy to which the company, body or union claims to be entitled. The company, body or union for whose benefit the remedy is sought must be a defendant to the claim.

For example, if the minority shareholders in a company want to sue the directors for breach of the duties that they owe to the company, the minority shareholders would issue a derivative claim against the directors. The company would also be named as a defendant.

After the claim has been issued, the claimant is obliged to apply to the court for permission to continue the proceedings.

2.9 ACTING FOR INSURERS OR TRADE UNIONS

Throughout the course of any proceedings, whether they take place in court or elsewhere, a solicitor acting for insurers or trade unions (on behalf of their insured and members respectively) will have a number of additional factors to bear in mind. Similarly, there are different considerations if acting against such bodies.

The essential thing to remember is that insurers and trade unions have interests other than those of the actual party itself and are keen to keep costs to a minimum. They are in business and have relatively large sums of money at their disposal with which to fight a case if necessary. They will not hesitate to use those advantages in order to force favourable settlements and they will negotiate hard. Solicitors need to be alert to those interests whichever side they are acting for.

Most insurance policies contain a 'control of defence' clause. This means in simple terms that the insurer is entitled to bring or defend an action in the name of the insured. (The action must still be brought by or against the insured by name and not against the insurer but the insurer is usually entitled to enforce this result under the insurance contract, ie make the insured lend his name to the action.)

Solicitors need to be alive to the possibility of a conflict of interest between the client (insurer) and the insured. The solicitor owes many of the same duties to the insured but their primary responsibility is to the insurer. If there is likely to be a conflict of interests, it may well be that the solicitor cannot represent the insured, and they must bear this consideration in mind throughout the life of the litigation. Depending on the circumstances, it may also be the case that it is inappropriate for them to continue acting for *either* party, ie for either the insurer or the insured.

2.10 PRE-ACTION CONDUCT

The general principles governing pre-action conduct are set out in Practice Direction – Pre-action conduct and protocols, which applies where there is no specific pre-action protocol.

The objectives are set out in para 3:

3. Before commencing proceedings, the court will expect the parties to have exchanged sufficient information to—

    (a) understand each other's position;

    (b) make decisions about how to proceed;

    (c) try to settle the issues without proceedings;

    (d) consider a form of Alternative Dispute Resolution (ADR) to assist with settlement;

    (e) support the efficient management of those proceedings; and

    (f) reduce the costs of resolving the dispute.

Proportionality is dealt with in paras 4 and 5:

4. A pre-action protocol or this Practice Direction must not be used by a party as a tactical device to secure an unfair advantage over another party. Only reasonable and proportionate steps should be taken by the parties to identify, narrow and resolve the legal, factual or expert issues.

5. The costs incurred in complying with a pre-action protocol or this Practice Direction should be proportionate (CPR 44.3(5)). Where parties incur disproportionate costs in complying with any pre-action protocol or this Practice Direction, those costs will not be recoverable as part of the costs of the proceedings.

Settlement and ADR are dealt with in paras 8–11:

8. Litigation should be a last resort. As part of a relevant pre-action protocol or this Practice Direction, the parties should consider whether negotiation or some other form of ADR might enable them to settle their dispute without commencing proceedings.

9. Parties should continue to consider the possibility of reaching a settlement at all times, including after proceedings have been started. Part 36 offers may be made before proceedings are issued.

10. Parties may negotiate to settle a dispute or may use a form of ADR including—

    (a) mediation, a third party facilitating a resolution;

    (b) arbitration, a third party deciding the dispute;

    (c) early neutral evaluation, a third party giving an informed opinion on the dispute; and

    (d) Ombudsmen schemes.

    (Information on mediation and other forms of ADR is available in the Jackson ADR Handbook (available from Oxford University Press) or at—

    • http://www.civilmediation.justice.gov.uk/

    • http://www.adviceguide.org.uk/england/law_e/law_legal_system_e/law_taking_legal_action_e/alternatives_to_court.htm)

11.   If proceedings are issued, the parties may be required by the court to provide evidence that ADR has been considered. A party's silence in response to an invitation to participate or a refusal to participate in ADR might be considered unreasonable by the court and could lead to the court ordering that party to pay additional court costs.

The approach of the courts towards compliance is dealt with in paras 13–16.

13.   If a dispute proceeds to litigation, the court will expect the parties to have complied with a relevant pre-action protocol or this Practice Direction. The court will take into account non-compliance when giving directions for the management of proceedings (see CPR 3.1(4) to (6)) and when making orders for costs (see CPR 44.3(5)(a)). The court will consider whether all parties have complied in substance with the terms of the relevant pre-action protocol or this Practice Direction and is not likely to be concerned with minor or technical infringements, especially when the matter is urgent (for example an application for an injunction).

14.   The court may decide that there has been a failure of compliance when a party has—

(a)   not provided sufficient information to enable the objectives in paragraph 3 to be met;

(b)   not acted within a time limit set out in a relevant protocol, or within a reasonable period; or

(c)   unreasonably refused to use a form of ADR, or failed to respond at all to an invitation to do so.

15.   Where there has been non-compliance with a pre-action protocol or this Practice Direction, the court may order that

(a)   the parties are relieved of the obligation to comply or further comply with the pre-action protocol or this Practice Direction;

(b)   the proceedings are stayed while particular steps are taken to comply with the pre-action protocol or this Practice Direction;

(c)   sanctions are to be applied.

16.   The court will consider the effect of any non-compliance when deciding whether to impose any sanctions which may include—

(a)   an order that the party at fault pays the costs of the proceedings, or part of the costs of the other party or parties;

(b)   an order that the party at fault pay those costs on an indemnity basis;

(c)   if the party at fault is a claimant who has been awarded a sum of money, an order depriving that party of interest on that sum for a specified period, and/or awarding interest at a lower rate than would otherwise have been awarded;

(d)   if the party at fault is a defendant, and the claimant has been awarded a sum of money, an order awarding interest on that sum for a specified period at a higher rate, (not exceeding 10% above base rate), than the rate which would otherwise have been awarded.

An example of the imposition of sanctions came in *Digicel v Cable and Wireless* [2010] EWHC 888 (Ch) (see **10.5.1**) where the court ordered the unsuccessful claimant to pay the defendant's costs on the indemnity rather than standard basis. One of the reasons for the court's decision was the failure by the claimant to comply with the Practice Direction, in particular by failing to send a letter of claim before issuing proceedings.

It is important to note, however, that the Practice Direction accepts that in certain situations the general principles cannot or should not apply. An example of this is freezing injunctions (see **Chapter 8**), where telling the other party in advance of your intentions would defeat the whole purpose of the application.

Similarly, if the limitation period is about to expire, proceedings must be issued without delay. In that situation, following the issue of proceedings, the parties should seek to agree to apply to the court for an order staying the proceedings whilst the parties take steps to comply.

2.11   JURISDICTION

One of the most important tactical considerations to bear in mind at the outset of any dispute is the choice of forum of any proceedings (whether they are to take place in court or elsewhere).

In commercial litigation, there is very often some foreign element involved and thus, since the forum can be very important to the client and to the outcome of the action, it is essential, at the outset, to take all necessary steps to try to ensure that the chosen forum is the best for the client. Such steps may involve issuing proceedings before another party takes the initiative to sue elsewhere, or indeed making a challenge to jurisdiction, where appropriate. Considerations of cost and practicality will of course have to be borne in mind and discussed with the client. It may be necessary to obtain foreign legal advice. (This topic is dealt with in more detail in **Chapters 16** and **17**.)

If a claim is brought within an EU country, remember that there are many differences between the various legal systems of the Member States. For example, many European countries' judicial authorities have a far more inquisitorial role, and more may be determined by the consideration of written submissions rather than oral evidence. The economics of pursuing the case also have to be considered. It may be necessary to warn the client that in certain countries costs are not recoverable from the losing party. Remember also that limitation periods differ between the EU Member States, ranging from one year to 30 years.

Sometimes it may be possible to bring a claim in the US. Claimants are often attracted to the US courts as a result of the high levels of damages in certain cases which have attracted media coverage.

2.12   CASE MANAGEMENT

Closer control of cases through the exercise of the court's management powers is a very important feature of CPR 1998.

In today's climate of commercially aware clients and in an increasingly competitive market place, solicitors need to be prepared to 'manage' the litigation for the client as if it were any other business project. The more the solicitor can plan up front, the better prepared the solicitor and their client will be for all eventualities. This means that the solicitor will need to spend an additional amount of time at the outset planning the expected life of the litigation, discovering exactly what the client wishes to do and anticipating the likely moves by the other side, rather than simply waiting to react later. Steps can then be taken to avoid or frustrate likely action by the other side, for example to issue proceedings first in a location convenient for the client.

Costs are always an overriding concern of the client (and rightly so, given the average price of commercial litigation today). It is essential to determine what price the client is prepared to pay in respect of the claim or dispute. Obtaining justice or proving a principle may seem less important to the client as the costs of litigation spiral. The client is running a business and the litigation is merely one element of it. The solicitor must be prepared to discuss this 'costs/benefit analysis' with the client on a regular basis. A realistic costs estimate may result in the client deciding not to proceed with the claim, but that client is far more likely to return in the future than a dissatisfied client who has been faced with a series of 'unpleasant surprises' by way of costs.

Under para 8.7 of the SRA Code of Conduct, clients must receive the best possible information, both at the time of engagement and when appropriate as their matter progresses, about the likely overall cost of their matter. To what extent is a solicitor bound by any estimate of the likely overall costs? In *Mastercigars v Withers LLP* [2007] EWHC 2733 (Ch) the defendant solicitors had given their client an estimate of just over £206,000 to take the case through to trial. This was not updated. The final costs were in the region of £1 million.

The court held that although the estimate was an important factor to take into account on the assessment of costs as between solicitor and client, it did not bind the solicitor absolutely.

However, in *Reynolds v Stone Rowe Brewer* [2008] EWHC 497 the court came to a rather different conclusion, holding that the solicitor was bound by the original estimate even though he had updated it from time to time. The basis for this was that the client had relied upon the original estimate in deciding how to approach the litigation.

As was seen at **2.2.2**, one of the key recommendations of the Jackson Report was to give the courts greater case management powers and to introduce a requirement for the parties to provide costs budgets. The changes introduced to the CPR 1998 in April 2013 were intended to encourage judges to be more proactive in their case management, in relation both to the general conduct of the claim and to the control of costs – particularly in the context of proportionality (hence the amendment of the wording of the overriding objective to include 'and at proportionate cost').

The general provisions about costs management and costs budgets are set out in the Legal Practice Guide **Civil Litigation** at **9.7**. As stated there, the budget must be in the form of Precedent H, which is annexed to PD 3E of CPR 1998. It must be filed with the court and served on the other side either with their directions questionnaire if the value of the claim is less than £50,000, or at least 21 days before the first case management conference (CMC). Failure to do so can result in very severe sanctions – CPR 1998, r 3.14 states that unless the court orders otherwise, any party which fails to file a budget despite being required to do so will be treated as having filed a budget comprising only the applicable court fees (see the case of *Mitchell v News Group Newspapers Ltd* discussed at **2.12.1** below).

Following the filing of the budgets, the parties must file an agreed budget discussion report (usually in the form of Precedent R) no later than seven days before the CMC. In most cases the court will then make a costs management order (CMO) pursuant to CPR 1998, r 3.15. This will record the extent to which the budgets are agreed between the parties, and, in respect of budgets which are not agreed, record the court's approval after making appropriate revisions. If a CMO is made, the court will thereafter control the parties' budgets in respect of recoverable costs.

What if a party wants to increase its budget? In *Henry v News Group Newspapers Ltd* [2013] EWCA Civ 19, the Court of Appeal, in what it described as 'the rather unusual circumstances of the case', allowed the successful claimant to depart from the approved budget. However, the Court clearly did not want to give the impression that such departures would be tolerated in most cases, and Moore-Bick LJ said (at [24]), 'it will rarely, if ever, be appropriate to depart from the budget if to do so would undermine the essential object of the scheme'.

In *Elvanite Full Circle Ltd v AMEC Earth & Environmental (UK) Ltd* [2013] EWHC 1643 (TCC), the successful defendant's approved budget was in the sum of £268,488. On 7 February 2013, a month before trial, the defendant sent a revised budget of £531,946 to the claimant. The defendant failed to obtain either the claimant's agreement or the court's approval for this revised figure before the trial. At trial the defendant won. At a subsequent costs hearing the trial judge, Coulson J, refused to increase the budget figure. He stated that a formal application to the court for approval of the revised budget should have been made as soon as it became apparent that the original budget costs had been exceeded by more than a minimal amount. He stated (at [39]):

> Furthermore, in my judgment, an application to amend an approved costs budget after judgment is a contradiction in terms. First, it would mean that the exercise would no longer be a budgeting exercise, and would instead be based on the actual costs that have been incurred. Secondly, it would encourage parties to 'wait and see'; only applying to increase the budget costs if it was in their interests. Thirdly, it would make a nonsense of the costs management regime if, at the end of the trial, a party could apply to double the amount of its costs budget. The certainty provided by the new rules would be lost entirely

if the parties thought that, after the trial, the successful party could seek retrospective approval for costs incurred far beyond the level approved in the costs management order.

Under CPR 1998, r 3.18 it is still possible for the judge carrying out any assessment of costs to depart from an approved or agreed budget if satisfied that there is good reason to do so. However, it seems likely that a costs judge will need to hear some very good reasons to depart significantly from a budget.

Cost-capping orders, now dealt with in CPR 1998, rr 3.19–3.21 , are likely to be fairly rare now.

2.12.1   Case management under CPR 1998

Part 26 of CPR 1998 deals with the first aspect of case management. This is the allocation of a case to the appropriate track, which is dealt with in the Legal Practice Guide, **Civil Litigation**.

Once a case has been allocated to the correct track, Part 3 of CPR 1998 sets out the court's case management powers. The general powers of the court are set out in r 3.1(2) which provides that the court may:

(a)   extend or shorten the time for compliance with any rule, practice direction or court order (even if an application for extension is made after the time for compliance has expired);

(b)   adjourn or bring forward a hearing;

(c)   require a party or a party's legal representative to attend the court;

(d)   hold a hearing and receive evidence by telephone or by using any other method of direct oral communication;

(e)   direct that part of any proceedings (such as a counterclaim) be dealt with as separate proceedings;

(f)   stay the whole or part of any proceedings either generally or until a specified date or event;

(g)   consolidate proceedings;

(h)   try two or more claims on the same occasion;

(i)   direct a separate trial of any issue;

(j)   decide the order in which issues are to be tried;

(k)   exclude an issue from consideration;

(l)   dismiss or give judgment on a claim after a decision on a preliminary issue;

(ll)   order any party to file and exchange a costs budget;

(m)   take any other step or make any other order for the purpose of managing the case and furthering the overriding objective.

Rule 3.3 makes it clear that the court can exercise any of its case management powers on its own initiative without waiting for an application by one of the parties. Before doing so, however, it must give any person likely to be affected an opportunity to make representations. They are normally entitled to three days' notice of any hearing, but if the matter is urgent, r 3.3(4) enables the court to make a provisional order without giving the parties any opportunity to make representations.

Under r 3.4, the court has the usual power to order that all or part of a statement of case should be struck out if it 'discloses no reasonable grounds for bringing or defending the claim' or if it 'is an abuse of the court's process or is otherwise likely to obstruct the just disposal of the proceedings'. Rule 3.4(2) also gives the court power to strike out a statement of case if 'there has been a failure to comply with a rule, practice direction or a court order'.

Where a party who has been struck out during the limitation period commences fresh proceedings based on the same cause of action as the original proceedings, r 3.4(4) makes it clear that if (as will usually be the case) a struck-out claimant has been ordered to pay the defendant's costs of the original action, any new action by the claimant can be stayed until the claimant has paid the costs of the first action.

Rule 3.5 deals with what are commonly known as 'unless orders'. If the court does make an order which says that a statement of case will be struck out if the order is not complied with then, in the event of non-compliance by that party, the other party can apply for judgment and costs. The party seeking judgment simply has to file a request for judgment stating that the right to enter judgment has arisen through non-compliance with a court order.

The onus now shifts to the party who has been struck out. He has 14 days from service of the judgment on him to apply to set the judgment aside. If he can show that the judgment had been entered prematurely, the judgment must be set aside. Otherwise he will have to persuade the court that it is appropriate to grant relief from sanctions (see below).

Rule 3.1(3) states that, when the court makes any order, it may specify the consequences of non-compliance. Under r 3.8, any sanction for failing to comply with any rule, practice direction or court order takes effect automatically unless the party in default applies for and obtains relief from that sanction. Where the court has set a deadline for complying with an order, it is possible for the parties to agree to extend such a deadline for up to a maximum of 28 days, provided always that any such extension does not put at risk any hearing date – r 3.8(4).

Rule 3.9 requires all applications for relief to be supported by evidence, which will usually be witness statements from the parties and their lawyers. An oral application merely supported by an apology from the party's lawyers will no longer suffice.

Rule 3.9(1) also lists the matters the court will take into account in deciding whether or not to grant relief from sanctions. Prior to 1 April 2013, the list set out nine matters the court would take into account. As part of the Jackson reforms (see 2.2.2) the list was reduced to two:

(a)   for litigation to be conducted efficiently and at proportionate cost; and

(b)   to enforce compliance with rules, practice directions and orders.

The change to CPR 1998, r 3.9(1) was intended to demonstrate a hardening of the court's approach to parties who do not comply with rules or orders. It was intended to make it far more difficult for parties to be given a 'second chance'. In para 6.5 of his Report, Jackson LJ discussed case management decisions and stated:

> Courts at all levels have become far too tolerant of delays and non-compliance with orders. In so doing they have lost sight of the damage which the culture of delay and non-compliance is inflicting on the civil justice system. The balance therefore needs to be addressed.

In para 7.2 of the same section of the Report, he made it clear that he regarded it as vital that the Court of Appeal support first instance judges who make robust but fair case management decisions.

Even before the changes of 1 April 2013 to r 3.9, the Court of Appeal in *Fred Perry (Holdings) Ltd v Brands Plaza Trading* [2012] EWCA Civ 224 gave an indication of this new approach. The defendants had failed to comply with an 'unless order' for disclosure. As a result, the defence was struck out and judgment entered for the claimants. The defendants applied for relief from sanctions under the former r 3.9(1). The application was unsuccessful, as was the appeal to the Court of Appeal. Jackson LJ stated (at [48]):

> Non-compliance with the CPR and orders of the court on the scale that has occurred in this case cannot possibly be tolerated. Any further grant of indulgence to the defendants in this case would be a denial of justice to the claimants and a denial of justice to other litigants whose cases await resolution by the court.

Since April 2013 the courts have consistently stated that far less tolerance will be shown to parties who fail to comply with rules and orders.

In *Venulum Property Investments Ltd v Space Architecture Ltd and others* [2013] EWHC 1242 (TCC), the issue before the court was whether it should extend the time for service of the particulars of claim. The claim form was issued on 12 November 2012. It was not served until 12 March 2013 – the last day for service permitted by CPR 1998, r 7.5(1). However, the claimant's solicitors did not serve the particulars of claim at the same time, mistakenly believing that they had a further 14 days in which to serve them. The solicitors for two of the 10 defendants objected to the application to extend the time for service since, so far as their clients were concerned, if the application was refused, the claim against them would be statute barred as being outside the limitation period.

As the application was made before 1 April, the judge, Mr Justice Edwards-Stuart, did still consider the factors under the old r 3.9(1) of the CPR 1998, but in the end he dismissed the application. He stated (at [58]):

> In my judgment, when the circumstances are considered as a whole, particularly in the light of the stricter approach that must now be taken by the courts towards those who fail to comply with rules following the new changes to the CPR, this is a case where the court should refuse permission to extend time. The Claimant has taken quite long enough to bring these proceedings and enough is now enough. I therefore refuse this application.

In *Fons HS v Corporal Ltd and Pillar Securitisation* [2013] EWHC 1278 (Ch), the parties applied for an extension of time to serve witness statements. Judge Pilling granted the application (although only to the extent of giving the parties until 4 pm on the following day), but in so doing stated (at [10]):

> However, all parties and the wider litigation world should be aware that all courts at all levels are now required to take a much stricter view of the failure by parties to comply with directions, particularly where the failure to comply is likely to lead into a waste of the limited resources made available to those with cases to litigate.

The Court of Appeal gave its first decision on the post-April 2013 regime in *Mitchell v News Group Newspapers Ltd* [2013] EWCA Civ 1537. This was the civil case arising out of the 'Plebgate' affair. Andrew Mitchell MP sued the *Sun* newspaper for defamation following its reporting of what he was alleged to have said to police officers in Downing Street.

Proceedings were issued on 7 March 2013 – before the new rules came into force. However, there was already a pilot costs budget scheme running in defamation cases under PD 51D, requiring the filing of costs budgets not less than seven days before the date of the hearing for which the costs budgets are required (usually the case management conference (CMC)). The background facts are set out in paras 5–8 of Lord Dyson's judgment in the Court of Appeal:

5.   On 5 June 2013, the court issued an order (which was delivered to the claimant's solicitors on 6 June) that there would be a case management and costs budget hearing on Monday 10 June. As a result of the late notification of the date to the parties, the hearing was relisted for 18 June. The defendant used outside costs lawyers to prepare its costs budget which it filed on 11 June. Its budget figure was £589,558. The claimant's solicitors prepared their costs budget in-house. At 12.14 pm on 17 June, Master McCloud sent an email to the parties' solicitors noting that there was no budget from the claimant on the court file and asking whether the parties' budgets were agreed. The defendant's solicitor replied at 12.27 pm the same day saying: '... despite a number of written promptings from me to exchange costs budgets the Claimant's solicitors have not replied or provided us with a copy of their Costs Budget'. At 12.44 pm, the claimant's solicitors emailed the Master saying:

> 'Apologies, we have yet to be able to finalise the Claimant's Precedent H budget as we have been delayed in receiving Counsel's figures despite chasing for these daily since the middle of last week. We aim to file the document in the next two hours and exchange with the Defendant.'

6.   In the event, the claimant's solicitors filed their budget during the afternoon of 17 June.

7.   The parties attended before the Master on 18 June. The claimant was represented by counsel and the defendant by its solicitor. The defendant's solicitor said that there had not been sufficient time to consider the claimant's budget. The Master had to decide what to do in view of the fact that the claimant's costs budget had not been lodged with the court at least 7 days

before 18 June. She was told by the claimant's counsel on instructions that the reason why the budget had not been filed until the previous day was 'to do with pressure of litigation elsewhere in the firm on another case'. She noted that this explanation was at odds with what she had been told in the email. At para 9 of her judgment, she said: 'So what we have here is a position where a defendant has attempted to comply with the rules and has produced a budget and has engaged with the process and the claimant has not produced a budget and has not engaged until the very last minute in response to prompting from myself dealing with the costs management in the afternoon of the day before. On any basis that is a breach of the Practice Direction 51D and of the overriding objective in my judgment.'

8. She said that there were 'really no adequate excuses for this breach' (para 12). There needed to be a case plan agreed if possible by the parties as to how the litigation would proceed and how it would be costed throughout. She then said: '... that process has simply died in this case. It has simply failed notwithstanding the defendant's compliance, and attempts by it to engage the claimant in budget discussion and exchange' (para 14).

Due to the lack of compliance, the Master made an order that the claimant should be treated as having filed a costs budget comprising only the applicable court fees. (The costs budget that had eventually been filed had been for £506,425.)

The application for relief from sanctions was heard on 25 July 2013 by the same Master and was refused. The appeal from that decision was then fast-tracked to the Court of Appeal pursuant to the provisions of CPR 1998, r 52.14(1) (see **11.3.1** below).

In giving the judgment of the Court of Appeal, the Master of the Rolls, Lord Dyson, took the opportunity to lay down guidelines on the interpretation of the new rules:

40. We hope that it may be useful to give some guidance as to how the new approach should be applied in practice. It will usually be appropriate to start by considering the nature of the non-compliance with the relevant rule, practice direction or court order. If this can properly be regarded as trivial, the court will usually grant relief provided that an application is made promptly. The principle 'de minimis non curat lex' (the law is not concerned with trivial things) applies here as it applies in most areas of the law. Thus, the court will usually grant relief if there has been no more than an insignificant failure to comply with an order: for example, where there has been a failure of form rather than substance; or where the party has narrowly missed the deadline imposed by the order, but has otherwise fully complied with its terms. We acknowledge that even the question of whether a default is insignificant may give rise to dispute and therefore to contested applications. But that possibility cannot be entirely excluded from any regime which does not impose rigid rules from which no departure, however minor, is permitted.

41. If the non-compliance cannot be characterised as trivial, then the burden is on the defaulting party to persuade the court to grant relief. The court will want to consider why the default occurred. If there is a good reason for it, the court will be likely to decide that relief should be granted. For example, if the reason why a document was not filed with the court was that the party or his solicitor suffered from a debilitating illness or was involved in an accident, then, depending on the circumstances, that may constitute a good reason. Later developments in the course of the litigation process are likely to be a good reason if they show that the period for compliance originally imposed was unreasonable, although the period seemed to be reasonable at the time and could not realistically have been the subject of an appeal. But mere overlooking a deadline, whether on account of overwork or otherwise, is unlikely to be a good reason. We understand that solicitors may be under pressure and have too much work. It may be that this is what occurred in the present case. But that will rarely be a good reason. Solicitors cannot take on too much work and expect to be able to persuade a court that this is a good reason for their failure to meet deadlines. They should either delegate the work to others in their firm or, if they are unable to do this, they should not take on the work at all. This may seem harsh especially at a time when some solicitors are facing serious financial pressures. But the need to comply with rules, practice directions and court orders is essential if litigation is to be conducted in an efficient manner. If departures are tolerated, then the relaxed approach to civil litigation which the *Jackson* reforms were intended to change will continue. We should add that applications for

an extension of time made before time has expired will be looked upon more favourably than applications for relief from sanction made after the event.

The decision in *Mitchell* was controversial to say the least and was heavily criticised by many practitioners, who considered that it led to an increase in uncooperative behaviour by litigants and their legal representatives. Many felt that the 'trivial' test referred to in para 40 (see above) was too narrow. It generated precisely the type of 'satellite' litigation that the Jackson reforms sought to stop.

Perhaps inevitably therefore these issues came back before the Court of Appeal in the case of *Denton v TH White Ltd* [2014] EWCA Civ 906. Lord Dyson and Vos LJ gave the majority judgment. Jackson LJ (the author of course of the Jackson reforms) gave a separate judgment, although he agreed with much of the content of the majority judgment. After reviewing the *Mitchell* decision (and referring specifically to paras 40 and 41 therein) and then considering some of the post-*Mitchell* decisions, Lord Dyson and Vos LJ then gave fresh guidance in relation to r 3.9 as follows:

> 24.   We consider that the guidance given at paras 40 and 41 of *Mitchell* remains substantially sound. However, in view of the way in which it has been interpreted, we propose to restate the approach that should be applied in a little more detail. A judge should address an application for relief from sanctions in three stages. The first stage is to identify and assess the seriousness and significance of the 'failure to comply with any rule, practice direction or court order' which engages rule 3.9(1). If the breach is neither serious nor significant, the court is unlikely to need to spend much time on the second and third stages. The second stage is to consider why the default occurred. The third stage is to evaluate 'all the circumstances of the case, so as to enable [the court] to deal justly with the application including [factors (a) and (b)]'. We shall consider each of these stages in turn identifying how they should be applied in practice. We recognise that hard-pressed first instance judges need a clear exposition of how the provisions of rule 3.9(1) should be given effect. We hope that what follows will avoid the need in future to resort to the earlier authorities.

Detailed guidance on how to go through the three stages set out in para 24 is then given in paras 25–38. The key stage is really the third stage, where the court has to 'consider all the circumstances of the case, so as to enable it to deal justly with the application'. In para 31 the judges stated:

> 31.   The important misunderstanding that has occurred is that, if (i) there is a non-trivial (now serious or significant) breach and (ii) there is no good reason for the breach, the application for relief from sanctions will automatically fail. That is not so and is not what the court said in *Mitchell*: see para 37. Rule 3.9(1) requires that, in every case, the court will consider 'all the circumstances of the case, so as to enable it to deal justly with the application'. We regard this as the third stage.

After dealing in some detail with the 'third stage', Lord Dyson and Vos LJ then spent some time dealing with the 'fallout' from *Mitchell* – satellite litigation and non-cooperation – and what should happen in the future. They went on:

> 39.   Justifiable concern has been expressed by the legal profession about the satellite litigation and the non-cooperation between lawyers that *Mitchell* has generated. We believe that this has been caused by a failure to apply *Mitchell* correctly and in the manner now more fully explained above.
>
> 40.   Litigation cannot be conducted efficiently and at proportionate cost without (a) fostering a culture of compliance with rules, practice directions and court orders, and (b) cooperation between the parties and their lawyers. This applies as much to litigation undertaken by litigants in person as it does to others. This was part of the foundation of the Jackson report. Nor should it be overlooked that CPR rule 1.3 provides that 'the parties are required to help the court to further the overriding objective'. Parties who opportunistically and unreasonably oppose applications for relief from sanctions take up court time and act in breach of this obligation.
>
> 41.   We think we should make it plain that it is wholly inappropriate for litigants or their lawyers to take advantage of mistakes made by opposing parties in the hope that relief from sanctions will

be denied and that they will obtain a windfall strike out or other litigation advantage. In a case where (a) the failure can be seen to be neither serious nor significant, (b) where a good reason is demonstrated, or (c) where it is otherwise obvious that relief from sanctions is appropriate, parties should agree that relief from sanctions be granted without the need for further costs to be expended in satellite litigation. The parties should in any event be ready to agree limited but reasonable extensions of time up to 28 days as envisaged by the new rule 3.8(4).

42.   It should be very much the exceptional case where a contested application for relief from sanctions is necessary. This is for two reasons: first because compliance should become the norm, rather than the exception as it was in the past, and secondly, because the parties should work together to make sure that, in all but the most serious cases, satellite litigation is avoided even where a breach has occurred.

43.   The court will be more ready in the future to penalise opportunism. The duty of care owed by a legal representative to his client takes account of the fact that litigants are required to help the court to further the overriding objective. Representatives should bear this important obligation to the court in mind when considering whether to advise their clients to adopt an uncooperative attitude in unreasonably refusing to agree extensions of time and in unreasonably opposing applications for relief from sanctions. It is as unacceptable for a party to try to take advantage of a minor inadvertent error, as it is for rules, orders and practice directions to be breached in the first place. Heavy costs sanctions should, therefore, be imposed on parties who behave unreasonably in refusing to agree extensions of time or unreasonably oppose applications for relief from sanctions. An order to pay the costs of the application under rule 3.9 may not always be sufficient. The court can, in an appropriate case, also record in its order that the opposition to the relief application was unreasonable conduct to be taken into account under CPR rule 44.11 when costs are dealt with at the end of the case. If the offending party ultimately wins, the court may make a substantial reduction in its costs recovery on grounds of conduct under rule 44.11. If the offending party ultimately loses, then its conduct may be a good reason to order it to pay indemnity costs. Such an order would free the winning party from the operation of CPR rule 3.18 in relation to its costs budget.

Although in some sense *Denton* can be considered as a qualification of what was perceived as the harshness of the *Mitchell* decision, it is still clearly incumbent upon litigation lawyers to ensure that court orders and deadlines are complied with. Following *Denton* there is also a clear requirement to cooperate with your opponents and not seek to take advantage of 'minor inadvertent errors'.

In *Caliendo v Mishcon De Reya* [2015] EWCA Civ 1029, the Court of Appeal upheld a judge's decision to grant relief from sanctions where the claimant's solicitors were three-and-and-a-half months late in notifying the defendant of the existence of a CFA and ATE insurance policy. (This was prior to April 2013 so the success fee and ATE insurance premium were potentially recoverable.) They had failed to comply with the requirements of CPR 1998, r 44.15(1) as it then stood which required notification within seven days. The Court of Appeal felt that the judge had correctly applied the *Denton* guidelines.

2.13   SUMMARY

When the solicitor first receives instructions from their client in relation to a commercial dispute, there are a number of preliminary considerations, which it is essential for them to run through, before they can think about issuing proceedings. In general, any time (within reason) which the solicitor spends planning the litigation is time well spent and should help achieve the client's aims, reduce the chance of unwelcome surprises and result in a satisfied client.

As a result of the changes introduced in April 2013, in most cases a costs budget must be prepared, and the solicitor should ensure that during the conduct of litigation all rules and orders are complied with.

To conclude, the solicitor needs to be prepared to discuss the realistic level of costs and to show a plan for the litigation in order to prepare their client. The client's objectives need to be aired in full at the outset and a strategy agreed. This plan and the level of costs must be kept under constant review throughout the life of the litigation.

2.14 FURTHER READING

A McGee, *Limitation Periods* (8th edn, 2018).

J O'Hare and K Browne, *Civil Litigation* (20th edn, 2021).

CHAPTER 3

THE COMMERCIAL COURT

LEARNING OUTCOMES

After reading this chapter you will understand:

- the nature of the Commercial Court
- the importance of the Commercial Court Guide
- case management in the Commercial Court
- the disclosure process in the Commercial Court
- interim applications in the Commercial Court
- trial in the Commercial Court
- the role of the Circuit Commercial Courts.

3.1 INTRODUCTION

As stated at **1.2**, much commercial litigation is conducted in the Commercial Court. This chapter explains the role of the Commercial Court and its special practices and procedures.

3.1.1 The Commercial Court

The Commercial Court is part of the Admiralty and Commercial Registry which is itself part of the Queen's Bench Division of the High Court. The Commercial Court was established in 1895 to provide a court which was familiar with commercial disputes and which would have procedures to enable such disputes to be resolved quickly and efficiently. It was restructured in its present form in 1970. Since October 2017, it has been a key part of the Business and Property Courts of England and Wales.

The Commercial Court provides a specialised service for businesspersons. The judges of the Commercial Court are specifically assigned to that court. They practised in the Commercial Court before they became judges and are experts in the types of cases dealt with by the Commercial Court. Although the court can be, and is, used for relatively straightforward matters, it also attracts cases which are highly complex and involve vast sums of money. Much of the court's specialised practice arises from the need to prevent these 'heavy' cases from becoming 'bogged down' by the weight of the evidence. Slow progress to a lengthy trial is discouraged.

3.1.2 The Commercial Court Guide

Part 58 of CPR 1998 and the accompanying Practice Direction deal specifically with the Commercial Court. These set out the basic differences of procedure in the Commercial Court as compared with the 'general' courts. By r 58.3:

> These Rules [ie CPR 1998 as a whole] and their practice directions apply to claims in the commercial list unless this Part or a practice direction provides otherwise.

However, that does not reflect the whole picture because practitioners in the Commercial Court must also be fully acquainted with, and follow, the provisions of the Commercial Court Guide (or, to give it its full title, the Admiralty and Commercial Courts Guide).

The Guide is prepared by the Commercial Court Committee ('the Committee'). The Committee is made up of judges and representatives of practitioners and users of the court. It receives and discusses suggestions for improving Commercial Court practice and makes recommendations to the judges, who approve the final version of the Guide.

The 10th edition of the Guide, published in 2017, is some 135 pages long and is divided into 16 sections dealing with the various stages of a Commercial Court action. It also has 14 appendices dealing with various aspects of litigation in the Commercial Court. The Guide can be found online at the Ministry of Justice website.

This chapter will concentrate on those aspects of practice in the Commercial Court which depart from the norm of CPR 1998.

3.1.3 The practice of the court

Proceedings in the Commercial Court follow the same order of events as other court actions. All the usual interim steps (eg security for costs, disclosure, interim payments, etc) can be taken in the Commercial Court in the same way as in any other case. This chapter simply highlights the extent to which proceedings in the Commercial Court differ from other civil proceedings.

The court's practice places great emphasis on cooperation between the parties' lawyers (many of whom are specialists in commercial litigation). They are expected to show a sense of realism in their handling of the case. This applies to dealings (including correspondence) between the parties' legal representatives, as well as to their dealings with the court. For example, the court encourages them to give advance disclosure of information and to provide written summaries which can be read by the judge before the hearing of an application or during the course of a trial in order to save time.

Many practices which originated in the Commercial Court have been incorporated into CPR 1998 – a recent example is that of disclosure of electronic data and documents (see **3.6.2** below).

3.2 COMMENCEMENT

A case should be commenced in the Commercial Court only if it fulfils the characteristics of a 'commercial claim'. Rule 58.1(2) states that a 'commercial claim' means any claim arising out of the transaction of trade and commerce, and includes any claim relating to:

(a)   a business document or contract;

(b)   the export or import of goods;

(c)   the carriage of goods by land, sea, air or pipeline;

(d)   the exploitation of oil and gas reserves or other natural resources;

(e)   insurance and re-insurance;

(f) banking and financial services;

(g) the operation of markets and exchanges;

(h) the purchase and sale of commodities;

(i) the construction of ships;

(j) business agency; and

(k) arbitration.

Apart from arbitration claims, proceedings in the Commercial Court will be commenced by either a Part 7 or Part 8 claim form. Practice form N1(CC) must be used for Part 7 claims and practice form N208(CC) for Part 8 claims.

3.3 TRANSFER

Cases which have not been commenced in the Commercial Court may be transferred there, if appropriate. Alternatively, an action started in the Commercial Court may be transferred to another court, if it is found to be an unsuitable case for the Commercial Court. Rule 30.5(3) states that an application for the transfer of proceedings to or from a specialist list must be made to a judge dealing with claims in that list.

3.3.1 Transfer into the Commercial Court

A case can be transferred to the Commercial Court by an application to a judge of that court. The judge considers whether the case is a suitable matter for the Commercial Court. The judge has a virtually unfettered discretion. At the same time, if appropriate, the judge can also give case management directions.

3.3.2 Transfer out of the Commercial Court

If the claimant commences proceedings in the Commercial Court when it is inappropriate to do so, the action can be removed from the court by the judge on their own initiative or on the application of another party. Such an application should be made promptly and normally not later than the first case management conference.

Although there is no rigid financial limit, a claim for less than £200,000 is likely to be transferred out of the Commercial Court unless it involves a point of special commercial interest.

Cases transferred out of the Commercial Court are likely to be transferred to the London Circuit Commercial Court or, if a venue outside London is more appropriate, to one of the other Circuit Commercial Courts (see **Chapter 1**). Guidance on practical steps for transferring cases to the Circuit Commercial Courts is set out in Appendix 19 to the Guide.

3.4 STATEMENTS OF CASE

Guidance as to drafting statements of case in the Commercial Court is set out in Section C of the Guide. Generally speaking, these guidelines do not depart significantly from Part 16 of CPR 1998 and the accompanying Practice Direction, but there is one significant departure from normal practice in para C1.1(e) of the Guide. This specifically says that 'evidence should not be included' in statements of case in the Commercial Court.

3.4.1 Content

Paragraph C1.2(a) of the Guide states that statements of case should be limited to 25 pages in length. The court will only exceptionally give permission for a longer statement of case to be served where a party shows good reason for doing so. In that situation, the court may require that a summary of the statement of case is also served.

3.4.2 Service

By para 9 of PD 58, unless the court orders otherwise, the Commercial Court will not serve documents or orders and service must be effected by the parties.

The normal rules for service of the particulars of claim under r 7.4 (particulars of claim to be served with the claim form or within 14 days of service of the claim form) are significantly different in the Commercial Court. Although a claimant can do so if he wishes, there is no obligation to serve the particulars of claim as provided by r 7.4. Instead, by rr 58.5 and 58.6, the defendant is obliged to file an acknowledgement of service in *every* case, within 14 days of service of the *claim form*, rather than within 14 days of service of the particulars of claim. Failure to do so entitles the claimant to enter a default judgment. For this reason, details of any claim for interest must be set out in the claim form.

If an acknowledgement of service is filed indicating an intention to defend, the claimant must then serve the particulars of claim within 28 days of the filing of the acknowledgement.

By para C2.1 of the Guide, the parties may agree extensions of the period for serving the particulars of claim. Any such agreement and brief reasons must be evidenced in writing and notified to the court, addressed to the Listing Office. The court may make an order overriding any agreement by the parties varying a time limit.

3.4.3   The defence

Where the defendant has filed an acknowledgement of service indicating an intention to defend, the time limit for serving and filing the defence is 28 days after service of the particulars of claim. By para C3.2 of the Guide, that period can be extended, by agreement between the parties, by up to 28 days. Again, any such agreement and brief reasons must be evidenced in writting and notified to the court. An application to the court is required for any further extension, although if the parties are in agreement a consent order should be lodged.

3.4.4   The reply

Under CPR 1998, r 58.10, the time for filing and serving a reply is 21 days after service of the defence. If a longer period is necessary, the claimant should make a written application to the court for an extension of time because an extension will almost inevitably result in the postponement of the case management conference (see **3.5.5**). The details of the procedure can be found in para F.4 of the Guide.

3.4.5   Amendments

All amendments to a statement of case in the Commercial Court must be verified by a statement of truth.

Instead of colour-coded amendments, the amendments can be made by footnotes or marginal notes. In such cases the statement of case should retain the original text. Paragraph C5.1(d) of the Guide does, however, recommend that, if the amendments are extensive, the document should be retyped and accompanied by a copy showing where and when the amendments were made.

3.5   CASE MANAGEMENT

3.5.1   Allocation

By r 58.13, all proceedings in the Commercial Court are treated as being allocated to the multi-track. Part 26 does not apply and so the parties do not file directions questionnaires.

3.5.2   The approach of the court

Paragraph 10 of PD 58 and Section D of the Guide deal with case management, and CPR 1998, Part 29 is almost entirely excluded.

Paragraph D.2 of the Guide identifies 13 key features of case management in the Commercial Court:

(a)   statements of case will be exchanged within fixed or monitored time periods;

(b)   a case memorandum, a List of Common Ground and Issues and a case management bundle will be produced at an early point in the case. The parties will be expected to agree the case memorandum and the List of Common Ground and Issues;

(c)   the case memorandum, List of Common Ground and Issues and case management bundle will be amended and updated or revised on a running basis throughout the life of the case and will be used by the Court at every stage of the case. In particular the List of Common Ground and Issues will be used as a tool to define what factual and expert evidence is necessary and the scope of disclosure;

(d)   the Court itself will approve the List of Common Ground and Issues and may require the further assistance of the parties and their legal representatives in order to do so;

(e)   a mandatory Case Management Conference will be held shortly after statements of case have been served, if not before (and preceded by the parties filing case management information sheets identifying their views on the requirements of the case);

(f)   at the Case Management Conference the Court will (as necessary) discuss the issues in the case and the requirements of the case with the advocates retained in the case. In a case where expert evidence is proposed the Court will consider whether to grant permission for that evidence and how that evidence should be controlled. The court will set a pre-trial timetable and give any other directions as may be appropriate;

(g)   after statements of case have been served, each of the parties may serve a disclosure schedule (see further E2.3). At the first Case Management Conference, the Court will discuss with the advocates retained in the case, and by reference to the List of Common Ground and Issues, the strategy for disclosure with a view to ensuring that disclosure is addressed in accordance with section E;

(h)   before the progress monitoring date the parties will report to the Court, using a progress monitoring information sheet, the extent of their compliance with the pre-trial timetable;

(i)   on or shortly after the progress monitoring date a Judge may (without a hearing) consider progress and give such further directions as she or he thinks appropriate;

(j)   if at the progress monitoring date all parties have indicated that they will be ready for trial, all parties will complete a pre-trial checklist;

(k)   in appropriate cases the Case Management Conference will be restored and/or there will be a pre-trial review;

(l)   the parties will be required to prepare a trial timetable for consideration by the Court;

(m)   throughout the case there must be regular reviews of the estimated length of trial, including how much pre-trial reading should be undertaken by the Judge.

If a party needs to apply for a direction which has not been included in the pre-trial timetable, or to vary any direction in that timetable, he must do so as soon as possible.

An outline chart of the typical case management sequence for cases in the Commercial Court is reproduced in **Appendix 1** to this book.

3.5.3   The case memorandum and List of Common Ground and Issues

Once a defence (and any reply) has been served, the parties' lawyers should agree a case memorandum and a List of Common Ground and Issues.

According to para D5.2 of the Guide, the case memorandum should contain:

(a)   a short and uncontroversial description of what the case is about;

(b)   a very short and uncontroversial summary of the material procedural history of the case.

The List of Common Ground and Issues should include the main issues of fact and law in the case. The list should identify the principal issues in a structured manner, such as by reference to headings or chapters. The beginning section of the document should specify what is Common Ground between the parties.

The claimant's solicitors will normally be responsible for the preparation of both documents.

After the case management conference, the parties must cooperate in ensuring that both these documents are kept up to date.

3.5.4 The case management bundle

The claimant's solicitors must prepare a case management bundle before the case management conference. It should contain the claim form, all statements of case, the case memorandum, the List of Common Ground and Issues, the case management information sheets and the pre-trial timetable if one has already been established, all principal orders made in the case, and any written agreement relating to disclosure of documents.

They must lodge this with the court at least seven days before the case management conference. They must then update the court's bundle as follows:

(a)   within 10 days of the case management conference, add the pre-trial timetable and any other order made at the case management conference, along with a revised case memorandum;

(b)   within 10 days of the making of any significant order, add a copy of that order or revise the case memorandum;

(c)   within 14 days of the service of any amended statement of case, replace the original statement with the new statement and revise the case memorandum and the List of Common Ground and Issues;

(d)   if the case memorandum or List of Common Ground and Issues is revised for any other reason, do so within 10 days.

3.5.5 The case management conference

By para 10.2 of PD 58, the claimant must apply for a case management conference (CMC) within 14 days of the date when all defendants who intend to file and serve a defence have done so, although any party may apply for a CMC earlier than then if they wish to do so.

If the claimant does not apply within the 14-day time limit, any other party may apply for a CMC. If none of the parties has applied for a CMC within 28 days, the Listing Office at the court will inform the judge in charge of the list, and a date for the CMC will then be fixed without further reference to the parties.

The court also has the power to fix a CMC at any time on its own initiative. If it does, it must give the parties at least seven days' notice, unless there are compelling reasons for a shorter period of notice.

The CMC will normally take place on the first available date six weeks after all defendants who intend to serve a defence have done so. This allows time for the preparation and service of any reply.

If any party wishes to postpone the conference (eg because of the late service of a reply), he should apply to the court in writing. There will not be an oral hearing of the application unless any other party requests one or the court feels that such a hearing would be helpful.

At the conference, each party should be represented by a solicitor with conduct of the case and an advocate retained in the case. There is no need for any of the clients to attend unless the court orders to the contrary.

Each party must file and serve a completed case management information sheet at least seven days before the conference. This information sheet takes the place of the directions questionnaire used in mainstream litigation. An example of a case management information sheet appears in **Appendix 2** at the end of this book.

According to para D8.7 of the Guide, the judge will, at the hearing of the conference:

(a)   discuss the issues in the case by reference to the draft List of Common Ground and Issues, and approve a List of Common Ground and Issues;

(b)   discuss the requirements of the case (including disclosure), with the advocates retained in the case;

(c)   fix the entire pre-trial timetable or, if that is not practicable, fix as much of the pre-trial timetable as possible;

(d)   in appropriate cases make an ADR order;

(e)   in appropriate cases, consider whether the case is suitable for the Shorter Trials Scheme or the Flexible Trials Scheme in the interests of reducing the length and cost of trial.

3.5.6   Security for costs

Where the defendant (or defendant to a counterclaim) intends to apply for security for costs, he should do so no later than the case management conference. Guidance is provided by Appendix 10 to the Guide. This states that any delay which is prejudicial to the claimant or to the administration of justice will probably cause the application to fail. Similarly, if the court forms the view that the application is motivated by a desire to harass the claimant, it is likely to be refused.

The Commercial Court is reluctant to investigate the merits when considering the application. The merits will be taken into account only in cases where it is clear that without any detailed examination of the facts or the law that the claim is certain or almost certain to fail.

As a condition of the grant of security, the defendant may be required to give an undertaking to the court to comply with any subsequent order to compensate the claimant for any loss suffered as a result of giving security. This would be appropriate where no costs order was ultimately made in the defendant's favour.

Where security is granted, this will usually be on the basis that if the claimant fails to comply with the order, it is for the defendant to apply to the court for an order to stay the proceedings or to strike out the particulars of claim. Unless the defendant does so, the case will continue in accordance with the pre-trial timetable. The aim is to prevent any unnecessary delay in the proceedings pending a decision by the court about the claimant's default.

3.5.7   Alternative dispute resolution

Paragraph D8.9 of the Guide indicates that the court will consider applications for an adjournment of the case at the case management conference stage to enable the parties to negotiate a settlement or to use some form of ADR. The parties can use the case management information sheet to indicate that such an adjournment may be appropriate.

The Guide then goes on to say:

> In an appropriate case, an ADR order may be made without a stay of proceedings. The parties should consider carefully whether it may be possible to provide for ADR in the pre-trial timetable without affecting the date of trial.

If the court does adjourn the case and all parties want an extension to the adjournment, one of the parties should write to the court before the end of the adjournment period confirming that all parties consent to the further adjournment. The letter should also explain what steps are being taken to settle the case and identify any mediator or other third party who is seeking to help the parties to settle the case. As under CPR 1998, any further adjournment is likely to be for no more than four weeks, but the court can then grant further adjournments if it sees fit.

Section G of the Guide deals specifically with ADR. Paragraph G1.2 states:

> Whilst the Commercial Court remains an entirely appropriate forum for resolving most of the disputes which are issued in the Commercial Court, the view of the Commercial Court is that the settlement of disputes by means of ADR:

(a)   significantly helps parties to save costs;

(b)   saves parties the delay of litigation in reaching finality in their disputes;

(c)   enables parties to achieve settlement of their disputes while preserving their existing commercial relationships and market reputation;

(d)   provides parties with a wider range of solutions that those offered by litigation; and

(e)   is likely to make a substantial contribution to the more efficient use of judicial resources.

In an appropriate case the judge may consider making an ADR order in the terms set out in Appendix 3 to the Guide.

The Commercial Court also provides parties with the option of taking advantage of its early neutral evaluation (ENE) service. If all parties agree, the court will provide a without prejudice, non-binding ENE of the dispute or of particular issues. The judge who conducts the ENE will take no further part in the case, unless the parties agree otherwise. Details of this service are set out in para G.2 of the Guide.

3.5.8   The pre-trial timetable

This will include a progress monitoring date (see **3.5.10** below) and a direction that the parties attend upon the Clerk to the Commercial Court to obtain a fixed date for trial.

A standard form of pre-trial timetable is set out in Appendix 4 to the Guide, which is reproduced in **Appendix 3** at the end of this book.

The parties can agree minor variations to the timetable as long as the overall structure is not affected and the variation will not affect the trial date or the progress monitoring date.

If more significant variations to the timetable are needed, the parties should apply to the court for a further case management conference rather than waiting until the progress monitoring date.

3.5.9   Special cases

There are minor variations to the rules on case management conferences for Part 8 and Part 20 claims in paras D.9 and D.10 of the Guide. Students need not concern themselves with this level of detail.

3.5.10   Progress monitoring

At the case management conference, the court will fix a progress monitoring date which will usually be after the time for exchanging witness statements and expert reports has expired.

The parties must serve and file a progress monitoring information sheet at least three days before the progress monitoring date. This will tell the court:

(a)   the extent to which they have been able to comply with the pre-trial timetable to date; and

(b)   whether they will be ready for trial on time and, if not, when they will be ready for trial.

A standard form of progress monitoring sheet is set out in Appendix 2 to the Guide and is reproduced in **Appendix 4** at the end of this book.

3.5.11   Reconvening the case management conference

If the progress monitoring information sheets show that one or more of the parties will not, or may not, be ready in time for the trial, the court can reconvene the case management conference. It can rewrite the pre-trial timetable by giving further directions and may make any appropriate orders for costs. It can also stipulate that a statement of case will be automatically struck out unless the party concerned complies with certain directions by certain specified dates.

3.5.12 Pre-trial checklist

Not later than three weeks before the date fixed for trial, each party must send to the Listing Office (with a copy to all other parties) a completed checklist confirming final details for trial (a 'pre-trial checklist') in the form set out in Appendix 2. This is reproduced in **Appendix 5** to this book.

3.5.13 Requests for further information

The court can make orders requiring a party to provide further information under Part 18 of CPR 1998 at the case management conference. Under para D15.1(a) of the Guide, the parties must communicate directly with each other in an attempt to reach agreement before any application is made to the court. If an application is then made, it will not be listed for hearing unless the applicant has confirmed in writing that the requirements of para D15.1(a) have been complied with.

3.5.14 The trial date

The normal practice of the Commercial Court is to fix the trial date immediately after the pre-trial timetable has been set at the case management conference. The Guide recognises that there may be some cases where, through matters outside the court's control, the trial may be delayed by a few days. If this might 'cause particular inconvenience', the Clerk to the Commercial Court should be given plenty of notice so that they can take steps to avoid the problem.

3.5.15 Provisional estimates of the length of the trial

As in all courts, accurate estimates of the likely length of the trial are essential to the efficient running of the court. Provisional estimates of the minimum and maximum duration of the trial will be made at the case management conference and will become part of the pre-trial timetable. These will then be confirmed or revised by the advocates when the pre-trial checklist is filed. It is the duty of all advocates who are to appear at the trial to seek agreement, if possible, on the estimated minimum and maximum lengths of trial. As soon as one of the advocates realises that the provisional or confirmed estimate may be inaccurate, they must contact the other advocates with a view to agreeing a revised estimate which can be filed with the court.

3.5.16 The pre-trial review

The Guide, in para D18.1, states that the court will order a pre-trial review in any case in which it considers it appropriate to do so. This will usually be some two to eight weeks before the trial begins and should be attended by the advocates who will appear at the trial.

The claimant's advocate should prepare a timetable for the trial in consultation with the other advocates, and they should indicate any areas of disagreement about this timetable. The judge will finalise the timetable at the pre-trial review.

3.6 DISCLOSURE

3.6.1 General

Paragraph E1.1 of the Guide states that: 'The purpose of disclosure is to assist in achieving the fair disposal and trial of a claim; the underlying principle is the promotion of the administration of justice. Regard must however be had to the overriding objective and the need to limit disclosure to that which is necessary to deal with the case justly: rule 31.5(7).'

Standard disclosure

Specific guidance on disclosure of electronic data and documents is given in para E.4 of the Guide. This also deals with the extent of the reasonable search for documents required by r 31.7 of CPR 1998.

The parties should, prior to the case management conference, discuss any issues that may arise regarding searches for and the preservation of electronic documents. This may involve the parties providing information about the categories of electronic documents within their control, the computer systems, electronic devices and media on which any relevant documents may be held, the storage systems maintained by the parties and their document retention policies. In the case of difficulty or disagreement, the matter should be referred to a judge for directions at the earliest practical date, if possible at the case management conference.

By para E3.2 of the Guide, a party who contends that to search for a category or class of document would be unreasonable should indicate this in his case management information sheet so that the court can, at the case management conference, decide what is and what is not a reasonable search.

An adapted version of the list of documents has been approved for use in the Commercial Court (Form N265(CC)) and a copy is reproduced at **Appendix 6**.

Under r 31.10(7)(b) of CPR 1998, where the party making a disclosure statement is a company, firm, association or other organisation, the statement must explain why the person making it is considered an appropriate person to do so. Paragraph 4.3 of PD 31A indicates that the person making the statement will have an office or position in the disclosing party – for example a director of a company.

Paragraph E5.8 of the Guide recognises that in the Commercial Court where, for example, effective control over the conduct of litigation may be in the hands of insurers, an officer of the disclosing party may not be the best person to make the disclosure statement. Paragraph E5.8 states:

(a)   For the purposes of PD31 section 4.3 the court will normally regard as an appropriate person any person who is in a position responsibly and authoritatively to search for the documents required to be disclosed by that party and to make the statements contained in the disclosure statement concerning the documents which must be disclosed by that party.

(b)   A legal representative may in certain cases be an appropriate person.

(c)   An explanation why the person is considered an appropriate person must still be given in the disclosure statement.

(d)   A person holding an office or position in the disclosing party but who is not in a position responsibly and authoritatively to make the statements contained in the disclosure statement will not be regarded as an appropriate person to make the disclosure statement of the party.

(e)   The Court may of its own initiative or on application require that a disclosure statement also be signed by another appropriate person.

From 1 January 2019 new rules on disclosure are being introduced in all of the Business and Property Courts, including the Commercial Court, as a two-year pilot. Further details about this can be found in **Chapter 10**.

3.7   INTERIM APPLICATIONS

3.7.1   General

Although Section F of the Guide confirms that Part 23 of CPR 1998 applies to proceedings in the Commercial Court along with its supplementary Practice Direction, it does exclude certain parts of the Practice Direction and impose qualifications on other parts of the Practice Direction. This book merely deals with the main differences between the Guide and PD 23. In practice, it is important to consult the exact wording of the Guide and PD 23.

Except for orders made by the court on its own initiative (rather than on application by a party), orders are not drawn up by the court but by the parties. The party who made the application is responsible for drafting the order, which is usually required to be signed by all the parties or (more usually) their legal representatives and lodged at court for sealing within three days of the relevant decision. The draft order should be lodged in hard copy rather than on disk. The parties are expected to cooperate to ensure that the draft order is prepared promptly and accurately reflects the decision of the court.

On most occasions, where the parties are able to agree the terms of the order they wish to make, they need not attend a hearing but may submit a draft consent order for approval. The exceptions are the case management conference and pre-trial review, where the consent order procedure cannot be used. Although the parties are encouraged to agree the directions they wish the court to make prior to these hearings, they must attend even if agreement is reached.

3.7.2 Service

In accordance with the usual procedure in the Commercial Court, application notices must be served by the parties. The court will not effect service.

3.7.3 Hearings

Although most applications will be heard in public, this does not apply to applications for freezing injunctions or search orders, neither does it apply to most arbitration applications (see CPR 1998, r 62.10(3)(b)).

Although PD 23 refers to applications being heard by telephone or by a video conference, para F1.9 of the Guide indicates that it will normally be preferable for hearings to be dealt with by personal attendance.

3.7.4 Expedited applications

Where an urgent application has to be made, but the case is not one which justifies an application without notice, the Commercial Court is able to offer an expedited application with an earlier hearing than would otherwise be the case. The Clerk should be asked to make expedited arrangements, but all other parties must be notified of this request.

3.7.5 Ordinary applications

The Guide defines ordinary applications as 'applications on notice expected to involve an oral hearing lasting half a day or less'. Such applications will normally be listed for hearing on a Friday. The timetable for such applications will be that:

(a)   the supporting evidence should be served with the application;

(b)   the respondent should serve his evidence within 14 days;

(c)   the applicant should serve any evidence in reply within 7 days (PD 58, para 13.1).

In the Commercial Court, the evidence may take the form of either a witness statement or an affidavit (unless an affidavit is specifically required).

This timetable can be abridged by agreement of the parties or by order of the court.

The applicant should lodge an application bundle by 1 pm one clear day before the date of the hearing (ie if the application is to be heard on a Friday it must be lodged by 1 pm on Wednesday). The application bundle must include copies of the following documents:

(a)   the application notice;

(b)   the draft order sought;

(c)   statements of case;

(d)   any relevant previous order;

(e)   witness statements and affidavits in support of/opposition to the application together with any exhibits.

Skeleton arguments must be lodged and served by 1 pm on the day before the hearing (ie in the case of a hearing on a Friday, by 1 pm on Thursday).

Failure to lodge documents on time may result in the court refusing to hear the application.

3.7.6 Heavy applications

Hearings which are likely to last longer than half a day are regarded as 'heavy applications'. Because there is likely to be a lot more evidence in such applications, which may involve more documents and more extensive issues than ordinary applications, the timetable is extended. Evidence in support of the application should still be lodged with the application, but:

(a)   the respondent has 28 days to serve his evidence; and

(b)   the applicant has 14 days in which to serve any evidence in reply (PD 58, para 13.2).

Such applications will not usually be dealt with on a Friday. If, for example, the application is to be heard on a Thursday, the applicant must lodge an application bundle with the court by 4 pm two clear days before the hearing (ie by 4 pm on Monday).

The applicant's skeleton argument should be served and lodged with the application bundle. The respondent's skeleton argument should be served and lodged within the next 24 hours (ie in our example, by 4 pm on Tuesday). Guidelines on the preparation of such arguments are set out in Appendix 5 to the Guide. An example of a skeleton argument can be found in **Appendix 7** at the end of this book.

The parties must also inform the court of the reading time (by the judge) required in order to enable the judge to dispose of the application within the time allowed for the hearing.

In heavy applications and others where the reading time is likely to exceed one hour, each party must lodge with the Listing Office, not later than 1 pm, two clear days before the hearing of the application, a reading list (identifying those documents the judge needs to read before the hearing) with an estimate of the likely reading time.

In all other applications, this must be lodged not later than 1 pm on the day before the hearing.

It will usually be useful to include a chronology or timetable of events; a cast list (referred to in the Guide as *dramatis personae*) explaining who the principal people in the case are; and indices identifying the relevant pages for each piece of evidence. Further guidance can be found in Appendix 6 to the Guide.

Failure to lodge the appropriate documents at the appropriate time may result in the court refusing to hear the application.

3.7.7 Time estimates and time limits

Paragraph F10.3 of the Guide indicates the normal maximum time for certain types of application (eg applications for summary judgment should not normally exceed four hours). A longer time estimate will be accepted by the court only if the advocate in question makes a written application to the judge in charge of the Commercial List explaining why extra time is needed.

Time estimates can assume that the judge will have read the skeleton arguments and the documents in the reading list before the hearing. The time estimate for an ordinary application should allow for judgment to be given. In a heavy application, the judge is likely to reserve judgment to a later date.

3.8 EXPERT EVIDENCE

3.8.1 Single joint experts

Although CPR 1998 emphasise the need to use single joint experts where appropriate, and the Guide recognises the need to avoid unnecessary expenditure on expert witnesses, para H2.6 of the Guide goes on to say:

> In many cases the use of single joint experts is not appropriate and each party will generally be given permission to call one expert in each field requiring expert evidence. These are referred to in the Guide as 'separate experts'.

3.8.2 The expert's duty to the court

Appendix 8 to the Guide sets out useful guidance to experts about their duty to the court. It is set out in full in **Appendix 8** at the end of this book. It is the solicitor's responsibility to ensure that Appendix 8 is drawn to the attention of their party's expert(s) as early as possible.

3.8.3 Request for directions

If an expert wishes to file a written request to the court for directions as to how they should fulfil their duties as an expert, they must normally give the party who instructed them seven days' notice of their intention to make such an application, and four days' notice of their intention to make such an application to all other parties. This ensures that one or other party can approach the court first if the request prepared by the expert would result in the expert informing the court about, or about matters connected with, communications or potential communications between the parties that are without prejudice or privileged.

3.8.4 Sequential exchange

When fixing the pre-trial timetable, the court will consider whether experts' reports should be exchanged sequentially rather than simultaneously. This would be appropriate where, for example, it would be difficult for the defendant's expert to comment fully without sight of the claimant's expert evidence. A simultaneous exchange in such circumstances is likely to result in the defendant applying for permission for his expert to file a supplemental report, and sequential exchange may be more cost- and time-effective. The claimant, on the other hand, may perceive an order for sequential exchange as giving the defendant an unfair advantage.

3.9 THE TRIAL

3.9.1 The documents

Appendix 7 to the Guide sets out the requirements for the trial bundle. The trial bundle should normally be agreed with the other parties at least 14 days before the trial date and lodged with the court at least seven days before the trial date. It is for the claimant's representatives to compile and lodge the bundle.

3.9.2 Information technology

By para J.3 of the Guide:

J3.1   The use of IT at trial is strongly encouraged where it is likely to save time and cost or to increase accuracy. Paperless trials in particular are strongly encouraged, except where the cost would be too great for a party (in this connection, see further J3.4).

J3.2   If any party considers that it would be advantageous to make use of IT in preparation for, or at, trial, the matter should be raised at the first Case Management Conference. This is particularly important if it is considered that document handling systems would assist disclosure and inspection of documents or the use of documents at trial. In any event, at the first Case Management Conference or subsequently, even if neither party itself raises the use of IT, the parties must expect the Court to consider its use, including its use at trial.

J3.3   Where IT is to be used for the purposes of presenting the case at trial the same system must be used by all parties and must be made available to the Court.

J3.4   In deciding whether and to what extent IT should be used at the trial the Court will have regard to the financial resources of the parties and where those resources are unequal it will consider whether it is appropriate that, having regard to the parties' unequal financial resources, the party applying for the use of such IT should initially bear the cost subject to the Court's ultimate orders as to the overall costs of the case following judgment.

3.9.3 Trial documentation

A single reading list approved by all advocates must be lodged by 1 pm on the earlier of either the day before the reading period for the trial (set out in the CMC order or as subsequently amended by pre-trial order/checklist or otherwise) commences or two clear days before the start of the trial. At the same time, the claimant should also lodge a trial timetable, prepared by the advocate for the claimant after consultation with the advocates for all other parties. This will provide for oral submissions, witness evidence and expert evidence over the course of the trial.

Each party must prepare written skeleton arguments. The claimant should serve and lodge his skeleton argument by the same deadline as for the reading list, and the defendant should do the same not later than 1 pm on the following day. In 'heavier' cases, the parties should try to serve and lodge their skeleton arguments earlier than the normal deadlines. Indeed, the court may impose an earlier deadline in the pre-trial timetable or at any pre-trial review.

When the claimant provides his skeleton argument, he should also provide a chronology and consider whether it will be helpful to supply indices and a list of dramatis personae.

As soon as possible after skeleton arguments have been exchanged, the claimant must provide the Listing Office with a bundle of the authorities referred to in the skeleton arguments.

3.9.4 Trial and costs

The trial will proceed in much the same way as in any other court, but in the more substantial cases, once the court has heard all the evidence, it will adjourn to enable the advocates to prepare written closing submissions before making their oral closing submissions.

The rules governing the award and assessment of costs are the same as in other courts.

3.10 POST-TRIAL MATTERS

Even after the case has been tried, any application to continue, vary or set aside interim remedies or undertakings must be made to a commercial judge. Paragraphs 1.2 and 1.4 of PD 25 – Interim Injunctions, which enable such applications to be made to a Master, do not apply in the Commercial Court.

Enforcement, on the other hand, will automatically be referred to a Master of the Queen's Bench Division or a district judge (PD 58, para 1.2(2)).

3.11 THE CIRCUIT COMMERCIAL COURTS

These regional equivalents of the Commercial Court (see **3.1**) are part of the Business and Property Courts of England and Wales and generally follow the practice and procedure of the Commercial Court Guide, save to the extent that Part 58 and PD 58 differ from Part 59 (Circuit Commercial Courts) and PD 59. By r 59.1(2) a claim may only be started in a Circuit Commercial Court if it relates to a commercial or business matter in a broad sense and is not required to proceed in another specialist list of the Business and Property Courts. There is a Circuit Commercial Court Guide providing detailed guidance on how to conduct a claim in the court. It is similar to, but considerably shorter than, the Commercial Court Guide. Provisions as to case management in the Circuit Commercial Court are set out in para 6 of the Guide. These are similar, thought not identical, to those in the Commercial Court.

As with the Commercial Court, all interim matters are dealt with by a Circuit Commercial Court judge, rather than by a District Judge or Master. Appendix B to the Guide contains the Circuit Commercial Court Case Management Information Sheet, which has to be filed by all parties at least seven days before the Case Management Conference (CMC). Appendix C to the Guide contains a set of specimen directions for use at the CMC. Appendix D to the Guide is the pre-trial checklist. Appendix E is a useful table of cross-references to the equivalent provisions in both CPR 1998 and the Commercial Court Guide.

3.12 SUMMARY

The Commercial Court provides a specialised service for business organisations in cases worth a minimum of £200,000. It sits in London and many of its cases have an international element.

Specialist Commercial Court judges deal with all interim applications as well as trials.

Procedure in the Commercial Court is governed by CPR 1998, Part 58 and PD 58, together with the Commercial Court Guide.

The regional equivalents of the Commercial Court are the Circuit Commercial Courts sitting in Birmingham, Bristol, Cardiff, Leeds, Liverpool, Manchester and Newcastle.

THE CHANCERY DIVISION

> **LEARNING OUTCOMES**
>
> After reading this chapter you will understand:
>
> - which types of proceedings are suitable for the Chancery Division
> - use of Part 8 claim forms.

4.1 INTRODUCTION

Whilst most High Court civil claims are commenced in the Queen's Bench Division, certain types of case are better suited to the Chancery Division. Chancery business involves specialist knowledge of, for example, land law and trusts, intellectual property, insolvency and company law, and although procedure in the Chancery Division will generally follow CPR 1998, litigants will continue to commence proceedings in the Chancery Division to take advantage of the specialist skills of the Chancery judges, should the case come to trial.

There is a Chancery Guide (the latest version was published in February 2016 and last updated in August 2019) which notifies areas where practice in the Chancery Division will depart from the normal CPR 1998. These differences are by no means as significant as in the Commercial Court and, for the purposes of this book, readers can assume that practice in the Chancery Division will follow CPR 1998. In practice, however, it will be necessary to check the details of the Chancery Guide for any proceedings commenced in the Chancery Division.

Certain types of 'commercial' actions will be started in the Chancery Division rather than in the Commercial Court. These include disputes involving land, probate, trusts and intellectual property. If the claim is a 'commercial claim' as defined by r 58.1(2), the procedure adopted in the Chancery Division will generally be that used in the Commercial Court, save that the case management of the case will be handled by a Master (or district judge) rather than by a High Court judge.

The Chancery Division and its specialist lists (**see 1.2**) are now all part of the Business and Property Courts of England and Wales. As such the new disclosure rules apply in the Chancery Division from 1 January 2019 – for further details see **Chapter 10**.

4.1.1 Allocation of business

Although the Chancery Division deals with land, trusts, probate actions and other property disputes, the Senior Courts Act 1981, Sch 1, para 1 also allocates some other commercial matters to the Chancery Division. These include the following proceedings which should be commenced in the Chancery Division:

(a)   bankruptcy;

(b)   dissolution of partnerships and taking partnership or other accounts;

(c)   patents, trade marks, registered designs and copyright;

(d)   matters affecting the affairs of a company.

4.1.2   Personnel

The head of the Chancery Division is the Chancellor of the High Court ('the Chancellor'). There are currently 16 High Court judges attached to the Division.

4.1.3   Procedure

There are special procedures for certain types of actions (eg probate actions are governed by CPR 1998, Part 57, and possession claims by CPR 1998, Part 55). This book does not deal with these specialist Rules.

Further, as mentioned in **4.1**, the Chancery Division has its own guide to practice in this Division, just as there is the Guide to Commercial Court Practice. The Chancery Guide sets out, for example, the steps taken before a hearing, including the preparation of bundles of documents, skeleton arguments, witness statements and expert evidence, and the use of pre-trial reviews and checklists.

4.2   ALTERNATIVE PROCEDURE FOR CLAIMS

Whilst most civil claims are commenced with a Part 7 claim form, that standard procedure is not appropriate for cases where the principal issues are legal or interpretative rather than factual. Part 8 of CPR 1998 sets out an alternative procedure for such claims, which will always be allocated to the multi-track. That procedure is dealt with in this chapter because it is more likely to be used in the sort of cases which are dealt with in the Chancery Division. It may, however, be used by any claimant if the claim is 'unlikely to involve a substantial dispute of fact' (r 8.1(2)). There is a summary of the procedure at **Appendix 9** to this book.

The claimant will file a claim form indicating that the claim is being made under Part 8. The claim form must indicate what questions the claimant wants the court to decide, the remedy the claimant is seeking and the legal basis for the claim (r 8.2(b)). At the same time, he must file his written evidence. The court will then serve the claim form and the claimant's evidence on the defendant.

A defendant who wishes to contest the claimant's application should file an acknowledgement of service. If he fails to do so, the claimant will not be able to enter a default judgment. However, although the defendant may attend the hearing of the claim, he will not be able to take part in the hearing without the court's permission.

A defendant who acknowledges service must state whether or not he contests the claim, and any remedy he is seeking. At the same time, he must file and serve any written evidence he intends to rely on. The claimant then has 14 days in which to file and serve further written evidence.

No further evidence is allowed without permission of the court. The court does have a discretion to require or permit additional oral evidence and/or to require the maker of a statement to be cross-examined on that statement.

A defendant who wishes to raise an additional claim under Part 20 in a Part 8 case will always need the permission of the court to do so. If the court grants permission it will give directions regarding the conduct of the additional claim.

A defendant who believes that the Part 8 procedure is not appropriate should state his objections and the reasons for them when he files his acknowledgement of service. The court will then have to give directions as to the future management of the case, and these could include an order that the claim continue as if the Part 8 procedure had not been used.

4.3 SUMMARY

The Chancery Division deals with cases involving specialist knowledge of areas of the law such as land law, trusts, intellectual property, insolvency and company law.

Procedure is governed by the Chancery Guide as well as the CPR 1998.

Most cases in the Chancery Division are commenced with a Part 8 claim form as the principal issues in Chancery cases are legal or interpretive rather than factual.

4.4 FURTHER READING

The Chancery Guide (available from the Ministry of Justice website at www.justice.gov.uk and in hard copy in vol 2 of *Civil Procedure* (Sweet & Maxwell, 2021)).

CHAPTER 5

THE TECHNOLOGY AND CONSTRUCTION COURT

LEARNING OUTCOMES

After reading this chapter you will understand:

- which types of proceedings are suitable for the TCC
- the procedure in the TCC
- the use of Scott Schedules.

5.1 INTRODUCTION

The Technology and Construction Court (TCC) is a specialist court which deals with cases which are technically complex or for which a trial by a judge of the TCC is for any other reason desirable. Cases involving the construction industry are the most common cases in the TCC, but many cases involving complex documentary or expert evidence are appropriate for the court. The types of actions normally dealt with in the TCC include:

(a) building or other construction disputes, including claims for the enforcement of the decisions of adjudicators under the Housing Grants, Construction and Regeneration Act 1996;

(b) engineering disputes;

(c) claims by and against engineers, architects, surveyors, accountants and other specialised advisers relating to the services they provide;

(d) claims by and against local authorities relating to their statutory duties concerning the development of land or the construction of buildings;

(e) claims relating to the design, supply and installation of computers, computer software and related network systems;

(f) claims relating to the quality of goods sold or hired, and work done, materials supplied or services rendered;

(g) claims between landlord and tenant for breach of a repairing covenant;

(h) claims between neighbours, owners and occupiers of land in trespass, nuisance, etc;

(i)   claims relating to the environment (for example, pollution cases);

(j)   claims arising out of fires;

(k)   claims involving taking of accounts where these are complicated; and

(l)   challenges to decisions of arbitrators in construction and engineering disputes including applications for permission to appeal and appeals.

The TCC is similar to the Commercial Court in that CPR 1998 apply to proceedings in the court, but subject to the provisions of Part 60 and its Practice Direction. As with the Commercial Court, the TCC has its own Guide. The second edition of the Guide (much expanded from the first) was introduced on 3 October 2005 and the latest revision was in February 2015. This chapter will identify some of the differences in procedure in the TCC from the mainstream courts.

The website of the Technology and Construction Solicitors Association (www.tecsa.org.uk) is a very useful source of information on the TCC.

As it is part of the Business and Property Courts of England and Wales, the new disclosure rules are being piloted in the TCC from 1 January 2019 – for further details see **Chapter 10**.

5.2   PRE-ACTION MATTERS

Many cases which are suitable for the TCC are covered by the Pre-Action Protocol for Construction and Engineering Disputes (reproduced in **Appendix 10** to this book). Where the dispute involves a claim against architects, engineers or quantity surveyors, this Protocol prevails over the Pre-Action Protocol for Professional Negligence.

If the Protocol applies, the TCC will expect all parties to have complied with its provisions. Even if a dispute is not covered by the Protocol, for example a claim relating to computers, the court would normally expect its provisions to be followed.

Paragraph 2.3 of the TCC Guide sets out six situations where the Protocol does not have to be followed. These are where the claim:

(a)   is to enforce the decision of an adjudicator;

(b)   is to seek an urgent declaration or injunction in relation to adjudication (whether ongoing or concluded);

(c)   includes a claim for interim injunctive relief;

(d)   will be subject of a claim for summary judgment pursuant to Part 24 of CPR 1998;

(e)   relates to the same or substantially the same issues as have been the subject of a recent adjudication or some other formal alternative dispute resolution procedure;

(f)   relates to a public procurement dispute.

Apart from these exceptions, failure to comply with the Protocol can result in the usual costs sanctions (TCC Guide, para 2.6).

5.3   COMMENCEMENT

Many TCC claims are dealt with in the High Court. In London, as part of the Business and Property Courts of England and Wales, the TCC is based at the Rolls Building, Fetter Lane, London EC4A 1HD. There, the TCC has its own judges (presently six) who deal only with TCC work. In the High Court outside London, TCC claims can be issued in any District Registry. However, para 3.3 of the Practice Direction – Technology and Construction Court Claims – states that wherever possible such claims should be issued in one of the following District Registries, in which a TCC judge will usually be available: Birmingham, Bristol, Cardiff, Chester, Exeter, Leeds, Liverpool, Manchester, Newcastle upon Tyne and Nottingham. There are full-time TCC judges in Birmingham, Leeds and Manchester.

5.4   TRANSFER

If, in a case started in the usual way, either party considers that the matter is now more suitable for the TCC, they may apply for a transfer to that court. The court can also order a transfer of its own motion if the parties consent or have been given an opportunity to object.

The court may also transfer TCC proceedings back into the High Court mainstream, if it considers that the case may be tried more appropriately in that court.

5.5   CASE MANAGEMENT

As with the Commercial Court, all TCC claims are treated as being allocated to the multi-track and CPR 1998, Part 26 does not apply (r 60.6). However, CPR 1998, Part 29 and its PD do apply to the case management of TCC claims, except where varied by or inconsistent with the Practice Direction to Part 60.

When a TCC claim is issued, or a case is transferred to the TCC, the court will assign the claim to a TCC judge who will have the primary responsibility for the case management of that claim. Again, this is similar to the position in the Commercial Court. Normally, all applications in the case will be heard by the assigned TCC judge.

Paragraph 8 of the Practice Direction to Part 60 deals with the case management conference (CMC). Much more detailed guidance is given in Section 5 of the TCC Guide. The court will fix a CMC within 14 days of the earliest of:

(a)   the filing of an acknowledgement of service;

(b)   the filing of a defence;

(c)   the date of an order transferring the claim to a TCC.

When the court notifies the parties of the date and time of the CMC, it will send them a case management information sheet and a case management directions form. (These forms are set out in Appendices A and B to the Practice Direction.) All parties must file and serve completed copies of these forms at least two days before the CMC. As usual, the parties are encouraged to agree directions. Failure to file or serve the forms can lead to sanctions.

The directions given at the CMC will normally include the fixing of dates for:

(a)   any further CMCs;

(b)   a pre-trial review;

(c)   the trial of any preliminary issues that the court orders to be tried;

(d)   the trial.

When the court fixes the date for a pre-trial review it will send each party a pre-trial review questionnaire. (This form is set out in Appendix C to the Practice Direction.) All parties must file and serve a completed copy of this form at least two days before the pre-trial review. Again, the parties are encouraged to agree directions, and failure to file or serve the form may lead to sanctions.

At the pre-trial review the court will give such directions for the conduct of the trial as it sees fit.

The provisions about pre-trial checklists and listing in CPR 1998, Part 29 and its Practice Direction do not apply to TCC claims.

Whenever possible the trial will be heard by the assigned TCC judge.

5.6   EXPERT EVIDENCE

Section 13 of the TCC Guide deals with the use of expert evidence in the TCC. The Guide reflects the problems regarding expert evidence that may arise in TCC cases. Paragraph 13.3.1

refers to the 'unresolved tension arising from the need for parties to instruct and rely on expert opinions from an early pre-action stage and the need for the court to seek, wherever possible, to reduce the costs of expert evidence by dispensing with it altogether or by encouraging the appointment of jointly instructed experts'.

As in the Commercial Court (see **3.8.1**) the TCC Guide reflects the fact that single joint experts are not usually appropriate for the principal liability disputes in large cases, or in cases where considerable sums have been spent on an expert in the pre-action stage (para 13.4.2). The Guide goes on to say that single joint experts are generally inappropriate where the issue involves questions of risk assessment or professional competence.

At para 13.4.3, however, the Guide states that single joint experts may often be appropriate:

(a)   in low value cases, where technical evidence is required but the cost of adversarial expert evidence may be prohibitive;

(b)   where the topic with which the single joint expert's report deals is a separate and self-contained part of the case, such as the valuation of particular heads of claim;

(c)   where there is a subsidiary issue, which requires particular expertise of a relatively uncontroversial nature to resolve;

(d)   where testing or analysis is required, and this can conveniently be done by one laboratory or firm on behalf of all parties.

5.7   SCOTT SCHEDULES

Apart from the usual statements of case in an action, it will be common for the judge to order additional statements of case in the form of a 'Scott Schedule'. (GA Scott, who was a judge in the 1920s, devised this document, although it is no longer peculiar to the TCC.) An example of a Scott Schedule appears in **Appendix 11** to this book. Paragraph 5.6 of the Guide explains when the use of a Scott Schedule is appropriate.

A Scott Schedule sets out the issues in tabular form so that they are clearly stated in one source rather than being scattered through the statements of case. Such a Schedule is especially appropriate where there are a large number of disputed issues or the case is very detailed. There is no fixed form which has to be followed. In the example in **Appendix 11**, column 1 gives the item's number for ease of reference at the trial. Column 2 gives the claimant's allegations on each issue, and his estimate of the loss he has suffered on each point appears in column 3. Columns 4 and 5 are for the defendant's side of the story. He gives his specific response to the claimant's allegations. He also gives, on a without prejudice basis, his estimate of the actual loss suffered by the claimant should the court accept the claimant's allegation. The final column is left blank. The judge uses it for their findings at the trial.

Where there are a number of parties there will be additional columns so that the court can see a summary of each party's views on every issue affecting them. The Schedule is normally settled by counsel.

The order requiring a Scott Schedule is normally made at the case management conference. The claimant is usually required to draw it up. The order specifies when the Schedule must be delivered to the other parties who will have to complete their parts of the Schedule and return it to the claimant within a specified time. If a party gives insufficient information in the Schedule, he can be ordered to give further information.

The claimant must lodge the court copy with the court clerk well in advance of the trial so that it can be read by the judge. Each party needs a copy for counsel, a copy for the solicitor, and a copy for each expert witness.

5.8   PREPARATION FOR TRIAL

5.8.1   The documents

A case proceeding in the TCC will often have a large number of documents and, as always, it will be necessary to produce an agreed bundle. It will usually be helpful to have separate bundles for the statements of case, correspondence, contracts, etc. If the parties cannot agree on whether a particular document is relevant, they can prepare a supplementary bundle of each party's additional documents. It is usually easier, however, to have just one bundle containing every document any party wants to have included.

The documents should be arranged chronologically and given consecutive page numbers. In addition to the court bundle, each lawyer and the witness who is giving evidence will need a copy of the bundle. If there are a large number of documents, the court clerk should be consulted about what should be filed in advance. It is likely that the judge in such cases will read the statements of case and any Scott Schedule in advance, but will expect counsel to take them through the remainder of the documents at the trial.

5.8.2   The pre-trial review

Before the pre-trial review, every party must complete a pre-trial review questionnaire. This takes the place of the pre-trial checklist used in mainstream litigation. The judge is likely to ask the claimant's counsel to circulate a list of issues beforehand, together with proposals for the conduct of the trial, so that the other parties can comment. At the pre-trial review, the judge will check that their directions have been complied with and settle the arrangements for the preparation of the bundles and the trial (eg whether facilities are needed to show evidence on video or by computer graphics). Counsel who are going to attend the trial should also attend the pre-trial review.

5.9   THE TRIAL

The trial will proceed in substantially the same way as any trial elsewhere in the High Court. In longer cases and the more difficult short cases, the judge will often want to inspect the subject matter of the action, accompanied by an expert appointed by each party. The parties do not have to pay the expenses of this inspection unless it takes place abroad.

5.10   ALTERNATIVE DISPUTE RESOLUTION

Section 7 of the TCC Guide gives guidance on the use of ADR in TCC cases. As with other courts, the TCC will encourage the parties to make use of any appropriate form of ADR. At the first CMC, the TCC will want to be addressed on the parties' views as to the likely efficacy of ADR, the appropriate timing of ADR, and the advantages and disadvantages of a short stay of proceedings to allow ADR to take place.

5.11   SUMMARY

The TCC will deal with many transactions of a business nature, especially where there is a need for an exhaustive investigation of matters of technical detail.

Cases can be commenced in the TCC or transferred to that court at a later date.

Scott Schedules will frequently be used in the TCC.

CHAPTER 6

INJUNCTIONS: THE LAW

LEARNING OUTCOMES

After reading this chapter you will understand:

- the types of injunction available
- the background law relating to the grant of an interim injunction
- the importance of the claimant's undertaking as to damages
- the importance of the *American Cyanamid* guidelines in interim prohibitory injunctions
- exceptions to the *American Cyanamid* guidelines
- the role of undertakings
- how to vary or set aside an interim injunction.

6.1 INTRODUCTION

This chapter explains the various types of injunction the courts can grant. It discusses the factors the court takes into account in deciding whether or not to grant an injunction pending trial (an interim injunction) or at the trial (a final injunction). It also explains why the claimant may have to compensate the defendant for any harm caused by the injunction if the injunction is varied or set aside later on in the case. Lastly, it explains how the defendant may avoid an injunction by giving a promise (known as an undertaking) to the court.

Injunctions are common in commercial cases because they can be used to protect confidential and commercially sensitive information, and to guard against the dissipation of assets. They are generally available only to claimants.

6.2 TYPES OF INJUNCTION

An injunction is a court order, breach of which is punishable as a contempt of court.

A party may seek an injunction at any time after proceedings have been commenced (and in exceptional cases, even before proceedings have been commenced). Such injunctions, made before trial, are known as interim injunctions. They remain in force until the case comes to trial (or until further order). At the trial, the court will decide whether or not to make a final or perpetual injunction. Both interim and final injunctions can take various forms.

There are three types of interim and final injunction, which all have a different effect. The normal type of injunction is a prohibitory or negative injunction. It prevents the defendant from taking certain steps (eg soliciting customers of the claimant). There are also mandatory injunctions which require the defendant to do something (eg to remove an obstruction to the claimant's light) and quia timet injunctions which require the defendant to take steps to prevent harm occurring (eg to provide support for the claimant's adjoining land in order to prevent subsidence).

Interim injunctions are normally obtained on notice (ie the defendant is given notice of the injunction hearing). They last until the trial of the claimant's action unless they are set aside earlier by the court (eg because of a change of circumstances). However, by r 25.3(1) of CPR 1998, the court may grant an interim remedy on an application made without notice if it appears to the court that there are good reasons for not giving notice (eg there is insufficient time to give notice, or giving notice would enable the defendant to harm the claimant in some way, such as destroying evidence which would support the claimant's case).

An injunction without notice takes one of two forms. It may fix a date for a further hearing, with all parties present, in which case it lasts until the date specified for that hearing. At the hearing, the defendant may argue that the injunction should not be granted. If he succeeds, the injunction will be set aside. Alternatively, rather than fixing a hearing date, an injunction without notice may simply tell the defendant that he can apply, if he wishes (on notice), for the order to be varied or set aside. In the meantime, the injunction remains in force until trial or further order.

6.3   GENERAL PRINCIPLES

The general principles which usually apply to all injunctions are that:

(a)   the claimant must have locus standi;

(b)   they are a discretionary remedy; and

(c)   damages must be an inadequate remedy.

These principles are discussed in more detail at **6.3.2–6.3.4**. In the case of mandatory and quia timet injunctions, there are certain other factors considered by the courts, and these are set out at **6.3.5** and **6.3.6**. In addition, the requirements and guidelines which normally apply to applications for an interim injunction are discussed at **6.4–6.7**.

First, however, it is necessary to consider the court's general jurisdiction to grant an injunction.

6.3.1   The court's powers

Under s 37 of the Senior Courts Act 1981 an injunction can be granted 'in all cases in which it appears to the court to be just and convenient to do so'. It may be granted either unconditionally or on such terms and conditions as the court thinks fit.

Although the county court generally cannot grant specialised injunctions called freezing injunctions or search orders (see **Chapters 8** and **9**), s 38 of the County Courts Act 1984 gives the county court the same power to grant any other injunctions as that possessed by the High Court.

6.3.2   Locus standi

The claimant cannot obtain an injunction unless he can show that he has a substantive cause of action in English law. The House of Lords stated in *South Carolina Insurance Co v Assurantie*

Maatschappij 'De Zeven Provincien' NV [1987] AC 24 that he must show that the defendant is either:

(a)   threatening to invade (or has invaded) the claimant's legal or equitable rights; or

(b)   threatening to behave (or has behaved) in an unconscionable manner.

Cases where an injunction was refused for lack of locus standi include *Siskina (Cargo Owners) v Distos Compania Naviera SA, The Siskina* [1979] AC 210. In that case, cargo had been loaded onto a ship which had later sunk. The subsequent dispute between the shipowners and the owners of the cargo had nothing to do with the English courts. The ship was insured in England, however. When the shipowners claimed on their insurance policy, the cargo owners sought an injunction to prevent the money from being removed from the jurisdiction. The House of Lords refused their application because the owners of the cargo had no legitimate interest in those monies.

In *Veracruz Transportation Inc v VC Shipping Co Inc and Den Norske Bank A/S, The Veracruz* [1992] 1 Lloyd's Rep 353, the claimants had paid for a ship and were awaiting delivery. Fearing that the ship might be defective, they sought an injunction preventing the defendants from taking the purchase money out of the country. The Court of Appeal refused the injunction because, even if the ship was defective, the claimants had no cause of action until the ship had been delivered to them.

6.3.2.1   Criminal offences

Sometimes a person chooses to break the criminal law because the profits he can make by so doing exceed the penalties which may be imposed by the criminal courts. In such cases the only effective way of enforcing the law is to obtain an injunction. If the defendant breaks the injunction, he can be punished by imprisonment or by severe financial penalties.

A private individual cannot usually obtain an injunction to enforce the criminal law. Usually, the Attorney-General seeks the injunction, although some laws (eg planning law) are enforced by local authorities acting under s 222 of the Local Government Act 1972.

An individual can get an injunction restraining criminal acts only if he can show that:

(a)   the offence was created to protect a particular class of people; and

(b)   he is a member of that class; and

(c)   he has suffered special damage as a result of the defendant's crimes.

For example, in *Ex parte Island Records Ltd* [1978] Ch 122, a record company obtained an injunction preventing 'bootleggers' from making and selling pirate copies of its records contrary to the Dramatic and Musical Performers Protection Act 1958 (now repealed).

6.3.2.2   Breaches of the Treaty of Rome

The House of Lords, in *Garden Cottage Foods Ltd v Milk Marketing Board* [1984] AC 130, assumed that any person who would be harmed by a breach of the Treaty of Rome would be entitled to an injunction restraining the breach.

6.3.3   Injunctions are a discretionary remedy

A claimant may have a good claim in law but still fail to get an injunction (eg because the matter is too trivial). This is because, as an injunction is an equitable remedy, it is discretionary and the claimant must comply with the usual 'equitable maxims'. Matters which might persuade the court to refuse an injunction include the following.

6.3.3.1   He who comes to equity must come with clean hands

In *Hubbard v Vosper* [1972] 2 QB 84, the Court of Appeal refused to grant an injunction preventing the publication of information criticising a religious cult because, according to

Megaw LJ, the claimants had been 'protecting their secrets by deplorable means'. If the claimant has behaved dishonestly or spitefully, he may be refused an injunction.

On the other hand, the defendant's behaviour and motivation is also a factor. If he has been harming the claimant out of malice, this may persuade the court to grant an injunction in a borderline case.

6.3.3.2 Acquiescence

If the claimant knew that the defendant was infringing his rights and failed to object, he may be refused an injunction because he led the defendant to believe that he did not object to the defendant's behaviour. In *Sayers v Collyer* (1885) 28 Ch D 103, the defendant was selling beer in breach of a restrictive covenant. The claimant owned the land with the benefit of that covenant. He sought to enforce the covenant but failed when it was proved that he had, for the past three years, been a regular customer of the defendant.

Delay of itself does not amount to acquiescence. The claim for an injunction will only fail if the delay has led the defendant to believe that he has not done any wrong; that, as a result of that belief, he has acted to his detriment and that it would now be unfair to allow the claimant to obtain an injunction (*Jones v Stones* [1999] 1 WLR 1739).

In *Church of Scientology of California v Miller* (1987) The Times, 23 October, the claimants sought an injunction to restrain publication of confidential information. They had known for some time of the defendant's plans. The defendant's preparations for publication were well advanced. An injunction was refused because, although it would have been appropriate earlier, it would now cause excessive damage and inconvenience.

6.3.4 No injunction will be granted if damages would be an adequate remedy

Under s 50 of the Senior Courts Act 1981, the court can award damages instead of (as well as in addition to) an injunction, whether or not the claimant applied for damages in his statement of case. An injunction will be granted where:

(a)   there is serious harm which is likely to continue; or

(b)   the harm is irreparable or cannot be quantified in financial terms; or

(c)   the defendant does not have the means to pay damages.

Damages were awarded instead of an injunction in *Proctor v Bayley* (1889) 42 Ch D 390 (the harm was over and unlikely to recur) and *Lyme Valley Squash Club Ltd v Newcastle-under-Lyme Borough Council* [1985] 2 All ER 405 (the harm to the claimant was only slight).

Cases where damages were not sufficient to prevent the grant of an injunction include *Evans Marshall & Co v Bertola SA* [1973] 1 WLR 349 (the alleged breach of contract would disrupt the claimant's business); *League Against Cruel Sports Ltd v Scott* [1986] QB 240 (the defendant had repeated his conduct on several occasions); and *Radley Gowns Ltd v Costas Spyrou (t/a Touch of Class and Fiesta Girl)* [1975] FSR 455 (limited lifespan of new styles and damage to goodwill). Damages are rarely seen as adequate compensation where the claimant is seeking to enforce a valid restrictive covenant relating to land.

6.3.5 Mandatory injunctions

A mandatory injunction must specify exactly what the defendant has to do and the time within which he must do it. Such orders are granted much less frequently than prohibitory injunctions. They will be granted only if the claimant will suffer serious harm if an injunction is not granted. The court will not require the defendant to incur expenditure which is disproportionate to the harm the claimant will otherwise suffer.

The approach of the courts can be illustrated by comparing two cases. In *Wrotham Park Estate Co v Parkside Homes Ltd* [1974] 2 All ER 321, the defendant had built houses in breach of a restrictive covenant. The claimant sought an injunction ordering the defendant to demolish the houses. The court refused the order as this would have involved 'an unpardonable waste of much needed houses'.

On the other hand, in *Pugh v Howells* (1984) 48 P & CR 298, the defendant built an extension to his property which interfered with the claimant's right to light. The claimant had warned the defendant that he would seek an injunction. The defendant's own surveyor had advised against the extension. The court ordered the defendant to demolish the extension.

6.3.6 Quia timet injunctions

Quia timet injunctions are a particular type of prohibitory injunction and, as stated by Lord Upjohn in *Redland Bricks Ltd v Morris* [1970] AC 652 at 655, are applicable to the following types of cases:

(a) where the respondent has as yet done no hurt to the applicant but is threatening and intending (as the applicant alleges) to do works which will cause irreparable harm to him or his property if carried to completion;

(b) where the applicant has been fully recompensed, both at law and in equity, for the damage he has suffered, but where he alleges that the earlier action of the respondent may lead to future causes of action (eg where the respondent has withdrawn support from his neighbour's land, or where he has so acted in depositing his soil from his mining operation as to constitute a menace to the applicant's land).

A quia timet injunction will be granted to restrain an apprehended or threatened injury only where the injury is certain or imminent, or where mischief of an overwhelming nature is likely to be done.

6.3.7 Special cases

In some types of cases, the courts apply special criteria before granting an injunction.

6.3.7.1 Banking

An injunction will not be granted to interfere with a banker's irrevocable letter of credit unless there is clear evidence of fraud: *Bolivinter Oil SA v Chase Manhattan Bank NA* [1984] 1 WLR 392.

6.3.7.2 Employment

By s 236 of the Trade Union and Labour Relations (Consolidation) Act 1992, a court cannot grant an order for specific performance of a contract of employment or an injunction to prevent a breach of such a contract where to do so would compel an employee to do any work or attend a place in order to do work. The courts are also reluctant to enforce restrictive covenants in a contract of employment by granting an interim injunction. They prefer to deal with the matter by ordering an early trial.

The courts also rarely grant injunctions requiring an employer to perform a contract of employment.

6.4 THE CLAIMANT'S UNDERTAKING AS TO DAMAGES

The court decides whether to grant an interim injunction based on the evidence presented at the interim hearing. It therefore grants such an injunction before there is an opportunity to investigate liability fully. At the final trial of the case, the defendant may win and the interim injunction may have caused loss to the defendant in the meantime. If so, he needs compensation for any loss he has suffered as a result of the injunction. Therefore, the court will usually grant an interim injunction only if the claimant gives an undertaking to compensate the defendant for any harm caused by the injunction if it is discharged at a later date. The normal wording of the undertaking is:

If the Court later finds that this Order has caused loss to the Respondent, and decides that the Respondent should be compensated for that loss, the Applicant will comply with any Order the Court may make.

This undertaking is often referred to as the 'claimant's cross-undertaking'.

The claimant's ability to meet his potential liability under this undertaking is taken into account in deciding whether or not to grant an injunction. He will usually have to give evidence of his financial circumstances, for example, in the case of a business, by producing recent accounts. Further, the court can order the claimant to pay money into court or to provide some other form of security to show that the undertaking is not worthless. However, the claimant will not be deprived of an injunction simply because he is short of money. In *Allen v Jambo Holdings Ltd* [1980] 2 All ER 502, the Court of Appeal held that even a legally-aided claimant can obtain an injunction in appropriate cases, in spite of the fact that his undertaking as to damages is of little value.

The cross-undertaking is not required where the injunction is sought to enforce the law by an agency such as a department of State (*Hoffman-La Roche & Co AG v Secretary of State for Trade and Industry* [1975] AC 295) or a local authority (*Kirklees Metropolitan Borough Council v Wickes Building Supplies Ltd* [1993] AC 227) or the Securities and Investments Board (*Securities and Investments Board v Lloyd-Wright* [1993] 4 All ER 210).

If the defendant subsequently wins the case at trial or establishes that the injunction should not have been granted, he can enforce the claimant's undertaking as to damages by applying for a court inquiry, by a Master or District Judge, into the damage caused to the defendant by the injunction. He will have to prove his loss. If he can, the claimant will have to compensate him even though the claimant acted in good faith throughout. It is possible for exemplary damages to be awarded if the claimant was not acting in good faith.

Even defendants who were not subject to the injunction may be able to claim damages against the claimant under this undertaking (*Berkeley Administration Inc v McClelland* (1996) *The Times*, 13 August).

EXAMPLE

A has commenced proceedings against B and C, alleging that B has infringed A's copyright by producing copies of A's work, and that C is also guilty of infringing A's copyright by selling B's copies. A obtains an interim injunction preventing B from producing any alleged copies of A's work. When the action comes to trial, B proves that he was not infringing A's copyright. B can claim damages for his loss of profits arising from his inability to make his products during the period between the injunction and the trial. C can claim damages from A for the loss of profits arising from his inability to sell B's products during the same period, even though A had not sought an injunction against C.

A solicitor should give specific warnings to their client about the potential liability the client may incur as a result of this undertaking when seeking an injunction.

6.5   INTERIM PROHIBITORY INJUNCTIONS AND THE AMERICAN CYANAMID GUIDELINES

As mentioned in **6.4**, when the court hears an application for an interim injunction, it does not know all the facts. As a result, the court is most reluctant to grant interim injunctions which require the defendant to take positive action (ie mandatory injunctions and quia timet injunctions – see **6.7.4**).

The court is more readily prepared to grant interim injunctions which merely restrain the defendant from doing something (prohibitory injunctions). In these circumstances, however, because it does not have all the facts, the court will not usually investigate the merits of the case. Instead, it applies the guidelines laid down by the House of Lords in *American Cyanamid Co v Ethicon Ltd* [1975] AC 396. Broadly, these guidelines divide into the following parts:

(a)   whether there is a serious question to be tried;

(b)   whether damages are an adequate remedy for either side;

(c)   whether the balance of convenience lies in favour of granting or refusing the injunction; and

(d)   whether there are any special factors.

These are considered below.

6.5.1   Serious question to be tried

Although the court does not generally investigate the full merits of the case in deciding whether or not to grant an interim prohibitory injunction, the claimant does have to establish that there is a serious question to be tried before he can get such an injunction.

This does not mean that he has to prove that he is more likely to win than to lose. Nevertheless he has to show that he has real prospects of success. If he cannot do this, he cannot get an injunction.

Thus, if it is clear that he has no right to an injunction under the general principles discussed above (see **6.3.2** and **6.3.3**), he will not get the injunction. Nevertheless, if the claimant does establish that there is a serious question to be tried, the defendant must then show that there is an arguable defence. If he does not, then, subject to damages not being an adequate remedy for the claimant, the court can grant an injunction without further ado. If, however, both parties have arguable cases, the court will have to consider the second factor, the adequacy of damages as a remedy for either side.

6.5.2   Adequacy of damages

The court will usually consider whether it would be possible to compensate either party financially for the consequences of its decision. So adequacy of damages as compensation must be considered from both the claimant's and the defendant's points of view.

If damages would be an adequate remedy for the claimant in any event, the claimant will not get a final injunction (see **6.3.4**) and the court will refuse to grant an interim injunction.

If damages would not be adequate compensation for the claimant if the court were to refuse the injunction, the court will usually go on to consider the impact of the claimant's undertaking as to damages (see **6.4**). If it is clear that the claimant will be able to provide adequate financial compensation to the defendant for any harm caused by the injunction, 'there would be no reason upon this ground to refuse an [interim] injunction' (Lord Diplock in *American Cyanamid*). Therefore, in practice, the court is more likely to grant an interim prohibitory injunction if it is satisfied that it would later be possible to compensate the defendant for any harm caused by the injunction, by ordering the claimant to pay damages. However, in many cases damages will not be an adequate remedy for either side, and the court then has to consider the third factor, the balance of convenience.

6.5.3   Balance of convenience

The court will now consider what course of action will cause the least damage to the parties, ie where the balance of convenience lies. If granting an injunction would clearly cause less harm to the defendant than the harm the claimant would suffer from the refusal of an injunction, the court will grant the injunction. If, on the other hand, refusing the injunction would cause little harm to the claimant but granting it would cause great harm to the defendant, the court will refuse the injunction. Most injunction applications are determined on the balance of convenience.

> **EXAMPLE**
>
> A is seeking an injunction against B. If the injunction is granted, B will go out of business. If the injunction is refused, both parties will stay in business, although A will suffer financial losses. The consequences for B of granting the injunction are much more serious than the consequences for A if an injunction is refused. The court would usually decline to grant an injunction to A.

Where all other factors are equal, the court will prefer to uphold the status quo (*Garden Cottage Foods Ltd v Milk Marketing Board* [1984] AC 130). If the claimant delayed in applying for the injunction, the status quo is the position as it was just before the application was issued. If there was no delay, the status quo is the position as it was before the start of the conduct which is the subject matter of the application. However, where there has been an alleged breach of a restrictive covenant, the status quo will be the position prior to the alleged breach (*Unigate Dairies Ltd v Bruce* (1988) *The Times*, 2 March).

> **EXAMPLE**
>
> Until recently, B was employed by A in a senior management post. B has resigned and set up in competition with A. A alleges that B is about to harm him by using trade secrets B acquired while working for A and is seeking an injunction restraining B from making use of the alleged confidential information. If the matter cannot be resolved by an award of damages (including damages paid by A under the cross-undertaking), the court is likely to preserve the 'status quo' by granting an injunction unless A has delayed seeking an injunction until B is well established in business, when the court will uphold the 'status quo' by refusing an injunction.

A couple of cases may help to illustrate the court's approach in deciding the balance of convenience. In *Dalgety Spillers Foods Ltd v Food Brokers Ltd* [1994] FSR 504, the defendants had plans to market a range of food products in competition with the claimants' established range of food products. They were aware that the claimants might try to prevent this by a passing off action and that the claimants might seek an injunction restraining them from marketing this particular product. The defendants therefore wrote to the claimants in October 1992 advising the claimants of their plans. The claimants acknowledged this letter but took no further action. The defendants put their products on the market in September 1993. The claimants then issued a claim form alleging 'passing off' and applied for an injunction. The court refused the injunction because the claimants' failure to respond to the original letter had caused the defendants to expend time, trouble and cost which they might not have incurred if the claimants had given an earlier indication of their objections.

In *News Group Newspapers Ltd v Mirror Group Newspapers Ltd* [1989] FSR 126, the defendants had advertised their newspaper by using the 'masthead' of the *Sun* which was a newspaper published by the claimants. The claimants sought an injunction to prevent this and succeeded because the injunction would cause little or no harm to the defendants, whereas the claimants could suffer significant harm if the defendants were allowed to continue what they were doing.

Finally, although the whole object of the *American Cyanamid* guidelines is to avoid a detailed investigation of the facts at this stage, if the above approach does not produce a solution, the court can be influenced by the fact that one party seems clearly to have the stronger case. Under this guideline, the court will take into account the relative strengths of a party's case only if there is no significant difference in the harm each party will suffer if the application goes against them, and the witness statements clearly show that one party has a disproportionately stronger case.

6.5.4 Special factors

When setting out the *American Cyanamid* guidelines, Lord Diplock stated:

> I would reiterate that, in addition to those to which I have referred, there may be many other special factors to be taken into consideration in the particular circumstances of individual cases.

There is no definition of what may amount to special factors, but case law since *American Cyanamid* gives various examples, such as injunctions to thwart winding-up petitions and defamation. Other special cases are considered in **6.7.5**.

6.5.5 Approach of the courts in practice

Cases since *American Cyanamid* have stressed that the guidelines 'must never be used as a rule of thumb, let alone as a straitjacket' (Kerr LJ in *Cambridge Nutrition Ltd v BBC* [1990] 3 All ER 523). The courts are mindful that this is a flexible remedy and it is a matter of discretion, taking into account all the facts. In his judgment in *Series 5 Software v Clarke* [1996] 1 All ER 853, Laddie J discussed whether the courts are just paying 'lip-service' to *American Cyanamid* as, in practice, they still seem to consider the strengths of the parties' cases when reaching their decision. It was Laddie J's view that the House of Lords in *American Cyanamid* was trying to stop mini-trials, with detailed analysis of evidence at the interim injunction stage. However, this did not prevent the courts from looking at the strengths of a party's case at this stage, and this certainly seemed to be the practice prior to *American Cyanamid*. In *Series 5 Software*, Laddie J acknowledged that the courts should not try to solve complex issues of law and fact at this interim stage. Nevertheless, he suggested that if it is apparent from the material available that one party's case is stronger than another, this should not be ignored.

In *Talaris (Sweden) AB v Network Controls International Limited* [2008] EWHC 2930 (TCC) the court considered to what extent its case management powers, and in particular its ability to order a speedy trial of the underlying issues, might affect the balance of convenience. The court held that the fact that it would be possible for the issues to be finally resolved within six to seven weeks (as the issues in dispute were narrow, and limited evidence would be required) was a factor that led the court to exercise its discretion to grant an injunction to remain in force until such trial.

6.6 INTERIM INJUNCTIONS CHECKLIST

1. Do the *American Cyanamid* guidelines apply?
2. Is the court satisfied that there is a serious question to be tried?
3. Would damages be an adequate remedy for the claimant?
4. How far are damages (under the claimant's cross-undertaking) an adequate remedy for the defendant?
5. Where does the balance of convenience lie?
   - Whether the claimant or the defendant will suffer the *greater harm* if the decision goes against him, eg consider:
     - Whether either will suffer irreparable harm, eg to reputation?
     - What is the course of action which would cause the least harm?
   - If the balance of the relative harm does not clearly favour one party, the court will uphold the *status quo*.
     - If the claimant delayed in applying for the injunction, the status quo is the position as it was just before the application was issued.
     - If there was no delay, the status quo is the position as it was before the start of the conduct which is the subject matter of the application.
6. Can the court make a decision after considering the above? If not, does one party clearly have the stronger case?

7.   If an injunction is granted, consider an early trial.

8.   Reach a conclusion.

6.7   INJUNCTIONS WHERE AMERICAN CYANAMID DOES NOT APPLY

In some special cases, set out below, the courts have varied or not applied the *American Cyanamid* guidelines.

6.7.1   There is unlikely to be a trial

The *American Cyanamid* approach assumes that the case will proceed to trial and that the claimant will either win his case and get a final injunction, or will lose and the defendant will be compensated for the harm caused by the earlier interim injunction. There are many cases, however, where the result of the interim application will be decisive and the action will never go to trial. The case of *Fulwell v Bragg* (1983) *The Times*, 6 January is an example. A firm of solicitors had expelled one of its partners. He considered that his expulsion was improper and wanted to persuade former clients of the firm to take their business away from the firm and to deal with him. He sought an order requiring the firm to allow him to do this. It was common ground that, whether an injunction was granted or refused, the matter would end there. The court, therefore, felt obliged to do what it could to investigate the merits of both parties' claims.

This illustrates that where there is unlikely to be a trial, the *American Cyanamid* guidelines do not apply and the claimant must show that he is likely to succeed at trial before an injunction will be granted.

6.7.2   Applications to prevent court proceedings

If a claimant wants to prevent someone from bringing proceedings in this country, he will have to show that those proceedings will be an abuse of process (*Bryanstone Finance Ltd v De Vries (No 2)* [1976] Ch 63).

If a claimant wants an order preventing someone from taking legal proceedings in another country, he must establish:

(a)   that there are equivalent proceedings which could be taken in this country; and

(b)   that the English proceedings would be much less vexatious and oppressive than the foreign proceedings (*Arab Monetary Fund v Hashim (No 6)* (1992) *The Times*, 24 July).

As stated in *Bankers Trust Co v PT Jakarta International Hotels & Development* [1999] 1 All ER 785:

> Similarly the courts will enforce an arbitration agreement governed by English law by granting an injunction restraining the respondent from bringing foreign proceedings in breach of that agreement.

6.7.3   Public interest

The courts will usually grant an injunction preventing publication of confidential information if it is in the public interest that confidentiality should be preserved. They do recognise, however, that there are cases where the public interest requires the truth to be revealed. Two examples of cases where an injunction against publication was refused on this ground are *Lion Laboratories Ltd v Evans* [1985] QB 526 (former employee seeking to disclose information about the reliability of a breath-test machine) and *In re a Company's Application* [1989] Ch 477 (reports of alleged infringements of the tax laws and the Financial Services Act 1986). In such public interest cases, the courts are not afraid to investigate the merits of the case before deciding whether to grant an injunction.

6.7.4   Mandatory injunctions

It is very difficult to get a mandatory interim injunction since the court usually requires clear evidence that the claimant is likely to succeed at trial and the *American Cyanamid* guidelines do not apply. Thus, in *Jakeman v South West Thames Regional Health Authority* [1990] IRLR 62, an employee failed to obtain an interim order for the payment of allegedly withheld wages.

However, the presumption against granting interim mandatory injunctions may be overridden if refusal of an injunction would clearly cause undue hardship. For example, in *Films Rover International Ltd v Cannon Film Sales Ltd* [1986] 3 All ER 772, the defendant was the claimant's only supplier and the claimant would go out of business if an injunction was not granted. In *Nikitenko v Leboeuf Lamb Greene & MacRea* (1996) *The Times*, 26 January, the court ordered the defendant to disclose documents to the claimant even though it was not sure that the claimant was entitled to see those documents. It did so because disclosure was unlikely to harm the defendant, whereas if the claimant was entitled to see the documents it was vital that he did so then. The case is, however, exceptional. The balance of convenience is generally not a relevant issue when considering an interim mandatory injunction.

Mandatory injunctions should not be confused with orders pursuant to s 99 of the Copyright, Designs and Patents Act 1988 for delivery up of copies or articles where the claimant alleges breach of copyright.

6.7.5   Other cases

6.7.5.1   Freezing injunctions and search orders

The *American Cyanamid* principles are not appropriate for freezing injunctions and search orders. These are dealt with in **Chapters 8** and **9**.

6.7.5.2   Land

The court will always grant an injunction to restrain breach of an enforceable restrictive covenant relating to land. As the defendant has already promised not to behave in a particular way, the court will enforce his promise (*Hampstead & Suburban Properties Ltd v Diomedous* [1969] 1 Ch 248). Similarly, if the defendant is clearly trespassing on the claimant's land, the claimant will usually be entitled to an injunction to restrain the trespass even if the trespass did not harm him.

6.7.5.3   Trade disputes

Section 221(2) of the Trade Union and Labour Relations (Consolidation) Act 1992 specifically states that where an injunction is sought against a defendant who claims that he is acting 'in contemplation or furtherance of a trade dispute' (as defined by the Act), the court must 'have regard to the likelihood of [the defendant's] succeeding at the trial'. The defendant may raise the defence of immunity from certain tort liabilities or peaceful picketing under ss 219 and 220 of the 1992 Act respectively. If the defence is likely to succeed at the trial, an injunction will be refused unless this would be disastrous for the claimant or other people. In such a case the defendant will have to show that his defence is almost certain to succeed before an injunction will be refused (*NWL Ltd v Woods* [1979] 3 All ER 614).

6.8   INJUNCTIONS WITHOUT NOTICE

Orders are made without notice if the matter is so urgent that the claimant does not have time to tell the defendant that he intends to seek an injunction. They are also made if secrecy is needed because, if the defendant learns of the claimant's plans, he will try to cause irreparable harm to the claimant before the claimant gets an injunction.

> **EXAMPLE**
>
> B has just been sacked by A. B is about to set up in business in competition with A. A has evidence that B is going to use confidential information belonging to A to compete with A. A also has evidence that B will conceal or destroy any confidential papers if he knows that A is taking court proceedings. A would be entitled to apply for an injunction without notice restraining B from using such information.

To proceed without notice, the claimant must also show that he has a strong enough case to justify the court not hearing the defendant's case. This is a departure from the rules of natural justice that all parties should be heard. Therefore, in the interests of fairness, the claimant must disclose all relevant facts, including any matters favourable to the defendant. Failure to do this will result in the injunction being set aside with orders for costs against the claimant who may also have to pay damages to the defendant for any harm caused by the injunction.

Section 221(1) of the Trade Union and Labour Relations (Consolidation) Act 1992 prohibits injunctions without notice where the defendant is likely to claim that he is acting 'in contemplation or furtherance of a trade dispute' (as defined by the Act) unless 'satisfied that all steps which in the circumstances were reasonable have been taken with a view to securing that notice of the application and an opportunity of being heard ... have been given to that party'.

6.9   UNDERTAKINGS IN PLACE OF AN INJUNCTION

A defendant who:

(a)   denies the claimant's allegations; or

(b)   is prepared to wait until the trial before challenging them; or

(c)   concedes that the claimant is likely to succeed,

may save costs by giving an undertaking to the court to avoid the need for an injunction. This will usually be in the same terms as the injunction the claimant is seeking. Such an undertaking has the same effect as an injunction and non-compliance is punishable as a contempt of court.

Sometimes the defendant is not prepared to give an undertaking until the court has found in the claimant's favour at an interim hearing. He will then offer an undertaking (which may be 'without prejudice to an appeal') so that, at any subsequent hearing, he is not at a psychological disadvantage in being regarded by the judge as a person who has had to be restrained by an injunction.

6.10   VARYING AND SETTING ASIDE INJUNCTIONS

As mentioned at **6.2**, an interim injunction on notice lasts 'until trial or further order'. It will usually contain a clause giving either party liberty to apply to vary or set aside the order. Even if it does not expressly do so, either party can apply to vary or set aside the order if circumstances change. The defendant is more likely to apply for this than the claimant. For example, he may do this because the burden of the injunction has become too onerous, as in *Jordan v Norfolk County Council* [1994] 1 WLR 1353. In that case, the defendant council had caused damage to the claimant's land by an admitted trespass. The claimant obtained an injunction requiring the defendant to make good that damage. Everyone assumed that this would cost about £12,000. The defendant then learned that the cost of complying with the order would be over £250,000. The claimant's land was worth only £25,000. The court varied the injunction.

A defendant may combine an application to set aside the injunction with an application to dismiss the claimant's action for want of prosecution. This is appropriate if the claimant does not proceed with his case with all proper speed. For instance, he may try to delay proceedings because he realises there is a risk that he will be unsuccessful at trial and fail to obtain a permanent injunction. By delaying, he ensures that he benefits from the interim injunction for as long as possible prior to trial.

A defendant may also apply to vary or set aside an undertaking. However, it is more difficult to do this because the defendant gave the original undertaking voluntarily. In *Chanel Ltd v F W Woolworth* [1981] 1 WLR 485, the Court of Appeal held that the defendants could vary their undertaking only if there had been a significant change of circumstances or they had become aware of new facts which they could not possibly have known about when they gave their undertaking.

As regards orders without notice, these can also be varied or set aside by the defendant, either on the return date fixed by the order, or on the defendant's application at any time (see **6.2**). Non-disclosure of material facts by the claimant is often the principal ground for setting aside an order without notice. Thus, on an application to set aside an interim prohibitory injunction on this ground, the court will again apply the *American Cyanamid* guidelines and decide whether, in the light of the defendant's new evidence, the injunction should have been granted in the first place. Non-disclosure is discussed in more detail at **8.9**.

Whenever an injunction is set aside, the defendant may have a claim for damages under the claimant's undertaking as to damages. As explained in *Cheltenham and Gloucester Building Society v Ricketts* [1993] 4 All ER 276, unless it is obvious what loss the defendant has suffered (or it is obvious that no loss has been suffered), there will have to be a separate hearing to investigate the amount of the defendant's loss. This will usually be at or after the trial of the claimant's main action.

6.11 HUMAN RIGHTS

As with civil litigation generally, it is likely that Article 6(1) of the European Convention for the Protection of Human Rights and Fundamental Freedoms (Rome, 4 November 1950) ('the European Convention on Human Rights') will be most relevant to commercial litigation:

> In the determination of his civil rights and obligations or of any criminal charge against him, everyone is entitled to a fair and public hearing within a reasonable time by an independent and impartial tribunal established by law. ...

The reference to 'everyone' in Article 6(1) includes companies as well as individuals.

It may be considered that an injunction granted without the defendant having any notice of the application does not comply with Article 6(1). On the other hand, there are circumstances where it might defeat the whole purpose of the injunction if notice were given to the other party, and therefore less harm is done by making the order in the absence of one party (see **Chapters 8** and **9**). The absent party does, of course, have some protection in relation to the disclosure requirements imposed on the applicant and the possible sanctions which may be levied by the court (see **6.8**).

6.12 SUMMARY

The court can grant injunctions to maintain the status quo pending the final trial of the claimant's action against the defendant. Such injunctions (known as interim injunctions) will be granted only where it is just and equitable to do so. There are guidelines (known as the *American Cyanamid* guidelines) which help the court to decide whether or not to grant such interim prohibitory injunctions. Under these guidelines, the court will balance the risk of injustice by considering whether it would be more convenient to grant or to refuse an injunction at this stage of the case. The court can always vary or set aside an injunction at a later date. If it does, the claimant will usually have to compensate the defendant for any harm suffered by the defendant as a result of the injunction.

Although the *American Cyanamid* guidelines represent the usual approach of the court in deciding whether or not to grant an interim injunction, there are cases (see **6.7**) where the court adopts a different approach.

A defendant can avoid being subject to an injunction by giving an undertaking to the court.

The court may also grant a final injunction at the trial of the claimant's action. In such cases (as opposed to interim injunctions), it will consider the merits of the case in detail.

6.13 FURTHER READING

I Goldrein, *Commercial Litigation: Pre-emptive Remedies* (looseleaf).

CHAPTER 7

INTERIM INJUNCTIONS: THE PROCEDURE

LEARNING OUTCOMES

After reading this chapter you will understand:

- how Part 25 of CPR 1998 applies to interim injunctions
- how to obtain an in interim injunction
- how to serve an interim injunction
- how to enforce an interim injunction.

7.1 INTRODUCTION

This chapter deals with the procedure for obtaining interim injunctions. It also explains how to enforce injunctions and undertakings in the courts.

The general procedure for applying for interim remedies is covered by Parts 23 and 25 of CPR 1998. This chapter will outline that general procedure as interpreted by PD 25A to CPR 1998 – Interim Injunctions (PD 25A). Although it will usually be the claimant who is seeking the injunction, it is also possible for defendants to apply for injunctions. The Rules and PD 25A therefore refer to the person seeking the injunction as the applicant and to the other party as the respondent. That is the terminology we shall use in this chapter and the following two chapters.

7.2 THE PROCEDURE FOR OBTAINING INJUNCTIONS

Final or permanent injunctions are granted when the applicant's action comes to trial and generally cause few procedural problems. This chapter deals solely with the procedure for obtaining interim injunctions.

7.2.1 When an injunction can be granted

Interim remedies are governed by Part 25 of CPR 1998, and r 25.1 confirms that an interim injunction is one of the remedies to which Part 25 applies. The court can grant an interim injunction whether or not the applicant has made a claim for a final injunction (r 25.1(4)).

Normally, an interim remedy will be sought at some time between the court issuing the claim form and the trial. However, r 25.2 confirms that, subject to any practice direction or other rule, the court can grant any interim remedy before the start of proceedings, but only if the matter is urgent or 'it is otherwise necessary to do so in the interests of justice' (r 25.2(2)(b)).

Thus, if the applicant can, for example, satisfy the court that the respondent will attempt to destroy evidence as soon as he knows that he is being sued, the court will grant an interim injunction enabling the applicant to preserve the evidence before the claim form is issued by the court.

Under r 25.2(3), a court which grants an interim injunction before the claim has been commenced 'may give directions requiring a claim to be commenced'. This will normally involve the applicant undertaking to issue a claim form immediately. By para 5.1(5) of PD 25A, this will usually be on the same or the next working day. The courts have, in the past, imposed heavy penalties on applicants and their solicitors for failing to comply with this undertaking. They have even discharged the original injunction, as in *Siporex Trade SA v Comdel Commodities Ltd* [1986] 2 Lloyd's Rep 428.

The court's directions will probably also require the applicant's solicitor to inform the issuing department of the court of the urgency of the situation and to ensure that the claim form is issued on the day it is filed. Practice Direction 25A does say that, where possible, this claim form should be served with the injunction.

Where an injunction is granted before the claim form has been issued, the title to the action should describe the parties as 'the Claimant and Defendant in a Intended Action'.

The court requires the solicitors acting for an applicant who has obtained an injunction before a claim form has been issued to continue to show a sense of urgency in their conduct of the case. If the applicant does not pursue his claim once he has obtained his injunction, the court could use its case management powers under Part 3 to dismiss this case.

Rule 25.2(1) also confirms that there is power to grant an injunction after the court has granted a final judgment (eg for the payment of damages). This would normally be sought in aid of attempts to enforce the judgment.

A defendant who intends to apply for an injunction, as part of his counterclaim, can do so after filing either an acknowledgement of service or a defence (r 25.2(2)(c)).

7.2.2 The normal procedure

The application for the injunction will, if the main action is also proceeding in this country, be made to the court which is currently dealing with the main action (or, if proceedings have not yet been commenced, to the court where the main action will be commenced).

Generally, the application must be made by an application notice, although r 23.3(2)(b) allows the court to dispense with this requirement. The cases where this will be done will usually be very urgent cases where the respondent is not being given advance notice of the application (see **7.2.3**).

Under r 23.6 the application notice must state:

(a)   what order the applicant is seeking; and

(b)   briefly, why the applicant is seeking the order.

Paragraph 2 of PD 25A says that the notice must also state the date, time and place of this hearing.

Rule 22.1(3) states that, if the applicant wishes to rely on anything in the application notice as evidence, it must be verified by a statement of truth.

Rule 25.3(2) says that an application for an interim remedy must be supported by evidence unless the court orders otherwise. This will usually be in the form of a witness statement including all material facts of which the court should be made aware.

Rule 23.7(1) requires the application notice to be served as soon as practicable after it has been issued and, in any event, at least three days before the hearing of the application. The court may, however, allow a shorter period of notice, or even dispense with service if this will help achieve the overriding objective.

The application must, when it is served, be accompanied by any supporting witness statements and copies of any draft order the applicant is seeking. Rule 23.7(2) says that the supporting witness statements must be filed with the court along with the application notice.

Under r 23.11, the court has power to proceed if the applicant or the respondent fails to attend the hearing. If the applicant fails to attend, the court will almost certainly dismiss the application. If the respondent fails to attend, the court will grant the application, but only if it is satisfied that the respondent had sufficient notice of the application to be able to attend. It will be easier to satisfy the court on this point if the papers were served on the respondent in person.

If the court does make an order on an application for an interim injunction in the absence of one of the parties, it may re-list the application under r 23.11(2). This would be appropriate if, for example, a party were able to show that he was unable, through no fault of his own, to attend the original hearing.

Practice Direction 25A does not contain a standard form of interim injunction. It merely states that the injunction must contain an undertaking as to damages (see **6.4**) and that, if the injunction is granted in the presence of all respondents, or at a hearing of which they all had notice, it may (and usually will) state that it is effective until trial or further order. A suggested specimen interim injunction is set out in **Appendix 12** to this book. Whenever possible, the applicant should file a draft injunction on disk.

Some general points to note about the contents of the standard form order, as set out in **Appendix 12**, are:

(a) The injunction usually lasts until after final judgment. Nevertheless, the respondent may apply to court at any time to vary or set aside the order, provided he gives the necessary prior notice to the applicant. He may wish to make this application if circumstances change prior to trial.

(b) The respondent is injuncted from doing something himself 'or in any other way'. The wording of the order makes it clear that not only is the respondent prevented from performing the prohibited acts, but he cannot use others to do them on his behalf.

(c) Schedule 2 to the order contains the standard undertaking as to damages given by the applicant (see **6.4**).

(d) The front of the order must also include a penal notice, in a prominent position, warning of the consequences of disobeying the order. The standard wording of the notice is:

If you the within named **AB DISOBEY** this order you may be held to be in contempt of court and **LIABLE TO IMPRISONMENT OR FINED OR YOUR ASSETS SEIZED.**

The standard form order also begins with a warning to the respondent of the effect of breaking the order, but this is not a substitute for a penal notice in the above form. If the injunction does not contain such a penal notice, it generally cannot be enforced if broken by the respondent.

7.2.2.1 Costs

If an interim injunction is granted on the balance of convenience, the court should usually reserve the costs of the application to the trial judge (*Richardson v Desquenne et Giral UK Ltd* (1999) LTL, 23 November). However, this is not an absolute rule, and it could be right to depart from the general approach if, on the balance of convenience, it was so clearly a case in favour of the claimant that the defendant should have a costs order against him for not conceding to the application. If a defendant waits until just prior to the hearing of the application before deciding not to contest it, he runs the risk of being ordered to pay the costs of the hearing (*Picnic at Ascot Inc v Derigs* [2001] FSR 2).

7.2.3   Applications made without notice

Rule 25.3(1) states that the court may grant an interim remedy without notice to the respondent if the court thinks that there are good reasons for not giving notice but, by para (3), the evidence in support of the application must explain why notice has not been given. No application can be made without notice unless this is permitted by a rule, or a Practice Direction or a court order. The usual reasons for seeking an interim injunction without notice will be either:

(a)   that the matter is too urgent to allow for notice to be given; or

(b)   that the respondent would take steps to harm the applicant if he was forewarned of the application.

Sometimes there will have been insufficient time for the application to be made in writing. In such cases, the application may be made orally, but the court will require undertakings from the applicant or his solicitor to file and serve written evidence forthwith. Paragraph 4.3 of PD 25A states that if a claim form has been issued:

(1)   the application notice, evidence in support and a draft order (as in 2.4 above) should be filed with the court two hours before the hearing wherever possible,

(2)   if an application is made before the application notice has been issued, a draft order (as in 2.4 above) should be provided at the hearing, and the application notice and evidence in support must be filed with the court on the same or next working day or as ordered by the court, and

(3)   except in cases where secrecy is essential, the applicant should take steps to notify the respondent informally of the application.

The procedure where no claim form has yet been issued is described at **7.2.1**.

The evidence in support of the application should state:

(a)   the facts giving rise to the applicant's action;

(b)   the facts justifying an interim injunction;

(c)   the facts justifying an application without notice to the respondent;

(d)   any answer which is likely to be raised by the respondent;

(e)   any facts known to the applicant which might make a without notice remedy inappropriate; and

(f)   the precise order being sought.

The applicant therefore must inform the court of any points he believes the respondent would have made if he had had the opportunity to be heard. Indeed, this duty extends to facts of which the applicant would have known if he had made proper enquiries. If the court subsequently considers that the applicant had not made proper enquiries or full disclosure, it will set aside the injunction. This will expose the applicant to a damages claim under his cross-undertaking.

When the court grants an application for an injunction made without notice, the applicant will have to serve the injunction on the respondent. At the same time, unless the court directs otherwise, he must serve the application and the supporting evidence on all respondents against whom the order was sought (even if it was not made in respect of all of those respondents).

He should also provide full notes of the hearing (*Interoute Telecommunications (UK) Ltd v Fashion Group Ltd* (1999) *The Times*, 10 November).

When the order has been served on the respondent, he can apply to the court to set aside or vary the injunction. He will normally have to do so within seven days of the order being served on him. The order will contain a statement reminding the respondent of this right and the time limit (r 23.9(3)).

The usual ground for applying to set aside an injunction made without notice is likely to be that the applicant did not disclose all relevant information to the court. This is dealt with in more detail in **Chapter 8.**

7.2.3.1 Applications outside normal court hours

Cases of extreme urgency may be dealt with by telephone. The detail is set out in para 4.5 of PD 25A:

(a) the judge is likely to require a draft order to be faxed to them;

(b) the application notice and supporting evidence must be filed in court on the same day (or the next working day if so ordered) together with two copies of the order for sealing;

(c) the applicant must be legally represented.

If the court office is closed, the claimant's solicitor will first have to contact the court's security officer. They will put the claimant's solicitor in contact with the duty judge's clerk who will then, if they consider it appropriate, give the claimant's solicitor a telephone number for the duty judge.

7.2.3.2 Costs

A judge who hears an application for an injunction without notice is unlikely to make any final order for the payment of costs. They are likely to leave the issue of costs open until the return date.

7.2.3.3 Contents of the order without notice

An injunction made without notice will, in addition to the usual undertaking as to damages, contain the following undertakings:

(a) an undertaking by the applicant to serve the application notice, supporting evidence, and the injunction on the respondent as soon as practicable;

(b) (where relevant) an undertaking to file the application notice and pay the court fee on the same day or the next working day; and

(c) (where relevant) an undertaking to issue the claim form and pay the court fee on the same day or the next working day (unless the court gives other directions for the commencement of the claim).

It will also contain a return date, which is a hearing where the respondent will have the opportunity to argue that the injunction should be set aside.

A suggested form of injunction without notice is set out in **Appendix 13** to this book.

7.3 SERVICE

The rules relating to service and enforcement of injunctions are contained in Part 81 of CPR 1998, which states that an injunction must be served personally on the defendant before the claimant can take any steps to enforce it. It also states that a mandatory injunction must be served on the defendant before the time stated in the injunction for compliance with the order has expired.

On a practical note, as personal service is required, it is important to have a process server on standby so that the injunction may be served as soon as it has been granted.

Rule 6.16 of CPR 1998 gives the court power to dispense with service, and r 6.15 enables the court to authorise service by some alternative method if the usual methods are impracticable.

The court is only likely to exercise these powers in injunction cases when the defendant is trying to evade service.

By r 81.8 of CPR 1998, the court may enforce a purely prohibitory injunction before it has been served if the respondent was present when the injunction was granted or has subsequently been informed of its terms (eg by telephone).

7.4   ENFORCEMENT

7.4.1   Methods of enforcement

Injunctions are enforced strictly. Even if the respondent believed that his actions did not break the injunction, he will be in contempt of court if the court rules that he has broken the injunction (In re Mileage Conference Group of the Tyre Manufacturers' Conference Ltd's Agreement [1966] 1 WLR 1137).

If the respondent does not comply with the injunction then, under Part 81 of CPR 1998, the two principal methods of enforcing an injunction are sequestration (seizure of property) and committal to prison. Alternatively, the court may:

(a)   impose a fine; or

(b)   take security to be of good behaviour; or

(c)   under CPR 1998, r 70.2A, order that the acts required to remedy the breach be done by some person appointed by the court, at the respondent's expense.

The court's role is to ensure future compliance. Punishment is a secondary consideration. As a result, the first enforcement order is often suspended. It will affect the respondent only if he breaks the injunction again.

Sequestration is usually used where the respondent is a limited company or an unincorporated association like a trade union (although it may also be used against the property of any director or officer of such an organisation if he was party to the breach). If the court grants leave for a writ of sequestration to be issued, it appoints four commissioners to handle the respondent's finances and to extract a financial penalty for breaking the injunction. The amount of the penalty is fixed by the court. Companies may be vicariously liable for the acts of their employees (Re Supply of Ready Mixed Concrete (No 2) [1994] 3 WLR 1249).

Individual respondents can be committed to prison for contempt of court. This penalty is also used against the individual officers of a defendant company who were responsible for the breach (Attorney-General for Tuvalu v Philatelic Distribution Corp Ltd [1990] 2 All ER 216).

Many of the authorities on committal proceedings are matrimonial cases. The principles are, however, the same for all types of cases.

7.4.2   The penal notice

By r 81.9 of CPR 1998, if there is no penal notice on the injunction it cannot be enforced. The notice must be prominently displayed on the front of the order and must be pointed out to the respondent when the order is served. The process server should explain the consequences of failing to comply with the order.

7.4.3   Third parties

Anyone who knowingly assists the respondent to break the injunction is also in contempt of court (Acrow (Automation) Ltd v Rex Chainbelt Inc [1971] 3 All ER 1175).

It is also a criminal contempt of court for a person who knows of an interim injunction to act in a way which will affect the applicant's prospects of making that injunction permanent. In Attorney-General v Times Newspapers Ltd [1992] 1 AC 191, the Government had obtained an interim injunction against some newspapers preventing the publication of extracts from a book which had allegedly been written in breach of confidence. Other newspapers then published other extracts from the same book. This meant that it would be more difficult for the Government to succeed at the trial in making the injunction permanent. The House of Lords confirmed that these later publications were a contempt of court.

7.4.4　Procedure for committal

Rule 81.10 of CPR 1998 sets out the procedure for committal. The applicant applies by a claim form or an application notice. This must fully describe the alleged breaches (*Chiltern District Council v Keane* [1985] 2 All ER 118). It must be supported by an affidavit explaining how the respondent is alleged to have broken the injunction.

Both documents have to be served personally on the respondent at least three working days before the committal hearing. If the papers have not been served then, unless the court has dispensed with service (see the next paragraph), the court will not hear the application, even though the applicant can prove that the respondent knew of the application.

By r 81.10(5) of CPR 1998, the court has power to dispense with service. The court exercises its power to do this only in exceptional circumstances. An example is *Wright v Jess* [1987] 2 All ER 1067. In that case, the court dispensed with service of the committal papers and committed the respondent for contempt where he had been committed for contempt on three previous occasions. An attempt had been made to serve the present papers on him and he had broken the injunction again on the day of the committal hearing.

The application is heard in public unless, for example, the original proceedings related to a secret process, discovery or invention. Even if the application is heard in private, the decision to commit must be announced in public.

The applicant has to prove the breach beyond reasonable doubt. The parties can give oral evidence, but the applicant will not normally be allowed to give evidence of matters which have happened since his affidavit or witness statement was served.

The application may be dealt with in the respondent's absence on proof that he had received the committal papers. If the court does decide to adjourn because it is not satisfied that the respondent had received the committal papers, notice of the new hearing date must be served on the respondent personally.

The committal order, if made, must be in the correct form and state what breaches have been proved. If the committal order does not do this, it is invalid and will be quashed on appeal. Technical defects which do not cause prejudice or injustice will not affect the validity of the order (*Nicholls v Nicholls* [1997] 1 WLR 314). The order must specify a fixed term of imprisonment not exceeding two years (Contempt of Court Act 1981, s 14). If a committal order is made (even in the respondent's absence), the court tipstaff is directed to arrest the respondent.

In *Delaney v Delaney* [1996] 2 WLR 74, the Court of Appeal quashed a decision to commit a respondent to prison for an unspecified period of time while the judge decided what the sentence would ultimately be.

If the applicant does not follow the rules exactly, his application to commit the respondent for contempt may fail or the committal order may be quashed on appeal. The applicant can, however, make a fresh application to commit based on the same facts as the original application (*Jelson (Estates) Ltd v Harvey* [1984] 1 All ER 12), but only if the application to commit was dismissed on a technicality as opposed to on the merits.

7.4.5　Procedure for sequestration

The procedure for sequestration is set out in r 81.26 of CPR 1998. The applicant applies to a judge by an application notice for permission to issue a writ of sequestration. The application must be served personally on the respondent unless the judge dispenses with service. The application notice will state the grounds of the application. It is supported by an affidavit or witness statement explaining why sequestration is needed.

7.4.6 Enforcement of undertakings

An undertaking given in lieu of an injunction should be indorsed with a penal notice and a copy should be served on the defendant (*Hussain v Hussain* [1986] Fam 134).

An undertaking to the court is enforceable in the same way as an injunction. Further, in *Midlands Marts Ltd v Hobday* [1989] 3 All ER 246, the court treated the respondent's undertaking as a contract, and instead of committing the respondent, it awarded the applicant damages.

7.5   SUMMARY

The normal procedure for obtaining an interim injunction is to give notice of the application to the respondent. In exceptional circumstances, however, the application may be made without notice to the respondent. An applicant who intends to apply without notice to the respondent must make a thorough investigation of the facts of the case before he makes his application. He must then disclose all relevant facts to the court. The consequences of failing to do either of these things are explained in more detail in the following chapter (see **8.9**).

Solicitors seeking injunctions need to be fully familiar with the relevant rules and the Practice Directions referred to in this chapter.

An injunction may be enforced by committal proceedings only if it contains a penal notice. The applicant's solicitor has to serve the injunction before any enforcement steps can be taken. However, if the injunction is purely prohibitory, it may still be possible to enforce it if the applicant can prove that the respondent knew of the injunction.

Anyone seeking to enforce an injunction must follow the rules to the letter. An application to commit may fail if there has been any procedural irregularity.

Undertakings can be enforced in the same way as injunctions.

7.6   FURTHER READING

I Goldrein, *Commercial Litigation: Pre-emptive Remedies* (looseleaf).

FREEZING INJUNCTIONS

LEARNING OUTCOMES

After reading this chapter you will understand:

- the nature of a freezing injunction
- the grounds for applying for a freezing injunction
- the provision of undertakings by the claimant
- the usual terms of a freezing injunction
- the meaning of the privilege against self-incrimination
- how to set aside or vary a freezing injunction
- the availability of worldwide freezing injunctions.

8.1 INTRODUCTION

This chapter explains how it is possible for a claimant to get an order 'freezing' the defendant's assets. Broadly, the claimant can do so where there is a real risk that if the injunction is not granted, the defendant will dispose of his property to avoid enforcement of any judgment subsequently obtained by the claimant. The chapter explains the exceptional circumstances which have to be proved to obtain such an order and the undertakings the claimant will have to give. Further, it details various provisions in the order which are designed to protect the interests of all parties to the action and anyone who is in possession of the defendant's property when the order is made.

The power of the court to make freezing injunctions was first established by the Court of Appeal in the case of *Mareva Compania Naviera SA v International Bulk Carriers SA, The Mareva* [1980] 1 All ER 213, which was actually decided in 1976. For a generation, such injunctions were referred to by lawyers as *Mareva* injunctions. But CPR 1998 introduced the term 'freezing injunction' because that was easier for the general public to understand. Readers of cases decided before 1999 will, however, come across the term '*Mareva* injunction' frequently.

This jurisdiction has thrown up various problems about the privilege against self-incrimination and the claimant's disclosure obligations when seeking an injunction without notice. This chapter deals with these problems, which may also occur in any application for an injunction or a search order. The relevant sections (**8.7** and **8.9**) should therefore also be borne in mind when considering the materials dealt with in **Chapters 6**, **7** and **9** of this book.

Lastly, there are various problems involved in seeking a freezing injunction where there is a foreign element in the case, and this is dealt with in **8.10** below.

8.2   THE NATURE OF THE REMEDY

A freezing injunction is an order which prevents the defendant from disposing of his property pending the trial of the claimant's action against him. It is usually restricted to the defendant's property within the jurisdiction and limited in value to the likely amount of the judgment.

Such injunctions are not granted lightly. The effect of the order on the defendant is very harsh. The court will grant it only if there is clear evidence that the defendant would otherwise dispose of his property to prevent the claimant enforcing any later judgment. The court will not make the order simply to protect the claimant against the risk that the defendant might subsequently become insolvent.

As it is usually necessary to obtain the injunction urgently and secretly, it is normal to apply without notice. The claimant must give the usual undertaking as to damages (see **6.4**). If the injunction is subsequently discharged, the defendant will be able to claim substantial damages as a result of this undertaking. Therefore, solicitors should warn clients who want a freezing injunction of the risks involved.

A freezing injunction also affects third parties who have possession or control of the defendant's property (eg the defendant's bank). They are told that the order has been made and they have to 'police' the order on the claimant's behalf. If they allow the defendant to break the terms of the order, they are at risk of being in contempt of court themselves (see **7.4.3**).

8.2.1   Related remedies

Sometimes, a freezing injunction is not the complete solution to the claimant's problems. The court does have additional powers which the claimant can use. If the defendant is a shareholder in a company, the court can make orders preventing him from using his shares, or the voting rights they give him, in a way which might harm the claimant, as in *Standard Chartered Bank v Walker* [1992] 1 WLR 561. If the defendant has already disposed of property, s 423 of the Insolvency Act 1986 enables the court, in certain circumstances, to set aside that disposition in aid of the freezing injunction, as was done in *Moon v Franklin* [1996] BPIR 196.

8.2.2   Innocent third parties

The claimant may consider that the freezing injunction will be completely effective only if other people involved with the defendant are covered by the order, even though these other people are innocent of any fraud. The courts have confirmed in *TSB Private Bank International SA v Chabra* [1992] 1 WLR 231 that this can be done. However, they have also said that freezing injunctions should not usually be used against banks as defendants (*Polly Peck International plc v Nadir (No 2)* [1992] 4 All ER 769) or in respect of routine banking transactions (*Lewis and Peat (Produce) v Almatu Properties* (1992) The Times, 14 May).

This can cause problems for such co-defendants. If it becomes public knowledge that they are subject to a freezing injunction, public confidence in their business may be affected. If the claimant is aware of potential damage to such a defendant's business reputation, he should ask for the application for the freezing injunction to be held in private (*Polly Peck v Nadir* (1991) The Times, 11 November).

8.3 THE GROUNDS FOR THE INJUNCTION

The claimant must satisfy the court on two points. First, he must show that he has a good arguable case against the defendant. Secondly, he must show that the defendant has property within the jurisdiction and that there is a real risk that if no order is made the defendant will dispose of his property in order to frustrate the enforcement of any judgment.

8.3.1 The strength of the claimant's case

As is the case for all interim injunctions, the claimant must have a good arguable claim. Since the application is made without notice, he is subject to the usual obligations to make detailed investigations before seeking the order and to make full disclosure of all relevant facts (both for and against his case) when seeking the order (see **6.8**). Failure to do so will inevitably result in the defendant applying to have the order set aside for non-disclosure. He will also seek costs and substantial damages under the claimant's undertaking as to damages. The claimant's obligation to make full disclosure extends to facts discovered after the making of the order. If there is any material change in the facts, the claimant must inform the court so that it may decide whether to continue the injunction (see *Commercial Bank of the Near East plc v A, B, C & D* [1989] 2 Lloyd's Rep 319 and *O'Regan v Iambic Productions Ltd* (1989) 139 New LJ 1378).

8.3.2 The risk that the property will disappear

The claimant must show that the defendant has property within the jurisdiction and that he may deal with that property in a way that will hinder the enforcement of any judgment the claimant subsequently obtains. The courts will not allow the claimant to use a freezing injunction to rewrite the insolvency laws and jump the queue ahead of other legitimate creditors of the defendant. Neither will they allow him to use it as a means of putting unfair pressure on a defendant to settle a disputed debt.

There usually needs to be clear evidence that the defendant is a 'debt dodger' and that the removal of assets will be done with a corrupt or dishonest purpose. This might take the form of evidence of his dishonesty vis-à-vis the claimant or other creditors. Other relevant factors will include the ease with which assets could be moved out of the claimant's reach and any subsequent difficulties in enforcement. In the case of foreign defendants the courts will take account of the fact that, if a defendant is able to remove his property from the jurisdiction, it may be very difficult for the claimant to enforce a later judgment. In such cases, evidence about the general trading reputation of businesses from the defendant's country, and information about the difficulties of enforcing English judgments in that country, is very helpful.

8.4 OBTAINING THE INJUNCTION

The claimant applies, without giving notice, with supporting affidavit evidence (a witness statement will not suffice). The application is often made before a claim form has been issued and is often supported by draft evidence only. Subject to **8.5**, the procedure is the same as for any injunction made without giving notice (see **7.2.3**). The application can also be made at any time during the proceedings, or indeed after judgment has been obtained.

Under CPR 1998, PD 25A, para 1.1, only High Court judges and other 'duly authorised' judges may grant a freezing injunction before the claimant has obtained judgment. Outside London, a party who wishes to apply for a freezing injunction should commence proceedings in the High Court, irrespective of the value of his claim. In reality, the cost of obtaining a freezing injunction will usually make it an inappropriate remedy in a low-value claim.

8.5 THE CLAIMANT'S UNDERTAKINGS

The standard form order used for a freezing injunction is set out in CPR 1998, PD 25A. It states that the claimant should normally give the following undertakings:

SCHEDULE B
UNDERTAKINGS GIVEN TO THE COURT BY THE APPLICANT

(1)   If the court later finds that this order has caused loss to the Respondent, and decides that the Respondent should be compensated for that loss, the Applicant will comply with any order the court may make.

[(2)   The Applicant will—

(a)   on or before [date] cause a written guarantee in the sum of £ to be issued from a bank with a place of business within England or Wales, in respect of any order the court may make pursuant to paragraph (1) above; and

(b)   immediately upon issue of the guarantee, cause a copy of it to be served on the Respondent.]

(3)   As soon as practicable the Applicant will issue and serve a claim form [in the form of the draft produced to the court] [claiming the appropriate relief].

(4)   The Applicant will [swear and file an affidavit] [cause an affidavit to be sworn and filed] [substantially in the terms of the draft affidavit produced to the court] [confirming the substance of what was said to the court by the Applicant's counsel/solicitors].

(5)   The Applicant will serve upon the Respondent [together with this order] [as soon as practicable]—

(i)   copies of the affidavits and exhibits containing the evidence relied upon by the Applicant, and any other documents provided to the court on the making of the application;

(ii)   the claim form; and

(iii)   an application notice for continuation of the order.

[(6)   Anyone notified of this order will be given a copy of it by the Applicant's legal representatives.]

(7)   The Applicant will pay the reasonable costs of anyone other than the Respondent which have been incurred as a result of this order including the costs of finding out whether that person holds any of the Respondent's assets and if the court later finds that this order has caused such person loss, and decides that such person should be compensated for that loss, the Applicant will comply with any order the court may make.

(8)   If this order ceases to have effect (for example, if the Respondent provides security or the Applicant does not provide a bank guarantee as provided for above) the Applicant will immediately take all reasonable steps to inform in writing anyone to whom he has given notice of this order, or who he has reasonable grounds for supposing may act upon this order, that it has ceased to have effect.

[(9)   The Applicant will not without the permission of the court use any information obtained as a result of this order for the purpose of any civil or criminal proceedings, either in England and Wales or in any other jurisdiction, other than this claim.]

[(10)   The Applicant will not without the permission of the court seek to enforce this order in any country outside England and Wales [or seek an order of a similar nature including orders conferring a charge or other security against the Respondent or the Respondent's assets].]

The first undertaking is the usual undertaking as to damages. However, the claimant also has to undertake to provide a written bank guarantee for a fixed sum of money. This is to provide security for his liability under the undertaking as to damages. The claimant has to serve a copy of the guarantee on the defendant and the freezing injunction will automatically lapse if he does not provide the guarantee within the time specified in his undertaking.

The claimant also undertakes to serve the claim form on the defendant along with the order. The words in square brackets will be included where, as is often the case, the order has been obtained before issuing the claim form. This undertaking effectively means that the injunction cannot be served until a claim form has been issued. If that is not possible, the claimant's lawyers must try to persuade the court to accept a variation of the standard undertaking.

The fourth undertaking will be needed wherever the claimant has not had time to complete all the usual formalities regarding evidence before applying for an injunction. As undertaking (5) shows, the evidence is served with the injunction along with an application notice for continuation of the order.

As the third parties who have possession or control of the defendant's property are required to police the order, they will obviously need copies of it. The sixth undertaking deals with this.

In undertaking (7), the claimant promises to reimburse the third parties (eg, the bank with whom the defendant holds an account) for the expenses they incur in complying with the injunction. In practice, the third parties will usually pass on these costs to their customer (the defendant). If the defendant cannot meet these costs, the claimant will have to meet the bill which will cover both legal and administrative costs.

The claimant has to undertake to inform all third parties affected by the injunction if it lapses, for example because the claimant fails to provide the bank guarantee or the defendant provides security (see **8.6.3**).

8.6   THE TERMS OF THE ORDER

Practice Direction 25A contains a suggested form of freezing injunction. This is reproduced in **Appendix 14** to this book. It will need to be amended and added to, depending on the facts of the individual case. However, an injunction omitting important terms may be set aside (*Bank of Scotland v A Ltd* (2000) *The Times*, 18 July). The order must also contain the usual penal notice.

Clause 2 of the order informs the defendant that he has the right to apply to vary or discharge the order. Clause 3 of the order refers to the fact that there will be a further hearing known as the return date. This will usually be about a week after the granting of the order, and the defendant can make any application for variation or discharge on that day.

8.6.1   Freezing the assets

Clauses 5–8 of the order deal with this.

Clause 5 prevents the defendant from dealing with the assets in any way, up to a certain value, which should be the approximate value of the claim. If the defendant has assets worth more than the amount specified in the order, he remains free to use the surplus. Clause 6 gives a wide meaning to 'the defendant's assets'. They include jointly-owned assets, for example a bank account in joint names, and any asset over which he has the power, directly or indirectly, to dispose of or deal with as if it were his own. He is to be regarded as having such power if a third party holds or controls the asset in accordance with his direct or indirect instructions.

If a defendant holds assets as a bare trustee, so that he has no beneficial interest in them, then such assets will not come within the scope of a standard form freezing injunction. However, in *Federal Bank of the Middle East v Hadkinson* [2000] 1 WLR 1695 the Court of Appeal held that orders made in more specific terms might cover bank accounts in which a defendant had no beneficial interest but which were in his name and under his control.

The meaning of 'assets' in the context of a freezing order has recently been considered by the Supreme Court in *JSC BTA Bank v Ablyazov* [2015] UKSC 64. In this case the claimant (one of Kazakhstan's national banks) had obtained a number of judgments against the respondent (its former chairman and majority shareholder) amounting to $4.4 billion, none of which had been paid. A freezing order had been obtained on 12 November 2009.

Paragraph 4 read as follows:

> Until judgment or further order ... the respondent must not, except with the prior written consent of the Bank's solicitors –
>
> a.   Remove from England and Wales any of his assets which are in England and Wales ... up to the value of £451,130,000 ...

b.   In any way dispose of, deal with or diminish the value of his assets in England and Wales up to the value of ... £451,130,000 ...

c.   In any way dispose of, deal with or diminish the value of any of his assets outside England and Wales unless the total unencumbered value ... of all his assets in England and Wales ... exceeds £451,130,000 ...

Paragraph 5 of the freezing order read as follows

Paragraph 4 applies to all the respondents' assets whether or not they are in their own and whether they are solely and jointly owned and whether or not the respondent asserts a beneficial interest in them. For the purpose of this Order the respondents' assets include any asset which they have power, directly or indirectly, to dispose of, or deal with as if it were their own. The respondents are to be regarded as having such power if a third party holds or controls the assets in accordance with their direct or indirect instructions.

The wording of para 5 is in accordance with the version in Appendix 5 of the Commercial Court Guide. This is a slightly wider definition of assets than in the standard order in CPR 1998, Part 25 as it includes the phrase 'and whether or not the Respondent is interested in them legally, beneficially or otherwise'.

Paragraph 9 of the freezing order set out the exceptions to the order:

a.   Paragraph 4 of this Order does not prohibit the respondent from spending up to £10,000 a week ... towards his individual ordinary living expenses ... nor does it prohibit the respondent from spending a reasonable amount on legal advice and representation. But before spending any money on legal advice and representation the respondent must notify the Bank's legal representatives in writing where the money to be spent is to be taken from.

b.   This Order does not prohibit the respondent from dealing with or disposing of any of his assets in the ordinary and proper course of any business conducted by him personally.

The respondent had entered into a total of four binding and effective loan facility agreements dated 1 September 2009, 1 April 2010, 17 August 2010 and 1 December 2010 with two British Virgin Islands companies. Each agreement provided a loan facility of £10,000,000. Under the terms of each agreement the respondent could direct the lender to transfer funds to a third party.

The loan agreements were fully drawn down and various payments made to third parties, including $16 million to the respondent's former solicitors.

The Supreme Court had to determine three issues in relation to the construction of the freezing order.

(1)   Whether the respondent's right to draw down under certain loan agreements is an 'asset' within the meaning of the freezing order.

(2)   If so, whether the exercise of that right by directing the lender to pay the sum to a third party constitutes 'disposing of' or 'dealing with' or 'diminishing the value' of an 'asset'.

(3)   Whether the proceeds of the loan agreements were 'assets' within the meaning of the extended definition in para 5 of the freezing order on the basis that the respondent had power 'directly or indirectly to dispose of, or deal with [the proceeds] as if they were his own'.

The Supreme Court allowed the claimant's appeal on issue (3). The proceeds of loan agreements entered into by the respondent after the order had been made were 'assets' within the meaning of the extended definition in para 5 as the respondent did have power directly or indirectly to dispose or deal with them as if they were his own.

In clause 7 of the order the claimant should provide details of any information he has about the defendant's assets, such as the address of any property owned by the defendant or details of any relevant bank account.

TDK Tape Distributor (UK) Ltd v Videochoice Ltd [1985] 3 All ER 345 confirms that the order is not limited to property owned by the defendant when the order was made. The order operates like a floating charge, in the sense that any property the defendant subsequently acquires is still subject to the terms of the order (although it does not give the claimant priority as a creditor – see **8.3.2**). Indeed, *Bank Mellat v Kazmi* [1989] 1 QB 541 decided that a defendant subject to a freezing injunction would be in breach of the order if he forgave payment of a debt due to him.

If the case does go to trial and the claimant wins, he will want to continue the injunction until he has been able to enforce his judgment. *Orwell Steel (Erection and Fabrication) Ltd v Ashphalt and Tarmac (UK) Ltd* [1984] 1 WLR 1097 confirms that the trial judge has jurisdiction to continue the order in this way after judgment (see also r 25.2(1)(b) of CPR 1998).

8.6.2 Disclosure

Clause 9 of the order requires the defendant to inform the claimant's solicitor immediately of all his assets within the jurisdiction, giving their value and location. By clause 10, this information must be confirmed in an affidavit.

Nevertheless, clause 9 also informs the defendant that, in cases where the privilege against self-incrimination applies, he may be entitled to refuse to provide information on the ground that it may incriminate him (see **8.7**).

In cases where the defendant serves evidence and the claimant thinks it is incomplete, the claimant can obtain an order permitting him to cross-examine the defendant about its contents. Orders for cross-examination will, however, be made only in exceptional circumstances (see *Yukong Line Ltd of Korea v Rendsbury Investment Corp of Liberia* [1996] 2 Lloyd's Rep 604). If information is needed from a third party, a separate order will be needed (see *Arab Monetary Fund v Hashim (No 5)* [1992] 2 All ER 911).

8.6.3 Exceptions to the order

Although clause 5 of the order prevents the defendant from dealing with his assets, a defendant still needs money to meet his day-to-day living expenses. The exceptions to the order set out in clause 11 deal with this by allowing him to withdraw a specified weekly sum to meet these expenses and other recurrent bills. According to *PCW (Underwriting Agencies) Ltd v Dixon* [1983] 2 All ER 158, the amount should be a reasonable sum based on the defendant's usual lifestyle. The exceptions also allow a specified weekly amount for business expenses and payment of legal costs. In return, the defendant has to tell the claimant's solicitors where he is getting the money from.

Paragraph 3 of the exceptions enables the parties to agree in writing that the defendant can incur additional expenditure. If the parties cannot agree, the defendant can ask the court for permission to incur the additional expenditure.

The last exception gives the defendant the opportunity to bring the injunction to an end by providing security for the amount applied for by the claimant, for example by a payment into court.

8.6.4 Costs

Clause 12 states that the costs of the application to obtain the freezing injunction are reserved to the judge who deals with the case on the return date.

8.6.5 Variation or setting aside of the order

Clause 13 of the order states that a defendant or third party affected by the order may apply to court to vary or set aside the injunction, having first informed the claimant's solicitors. For the procedure and grounds for variation and setting aside, see **8.9**.

8.6.6 Third parties

Clause 16 of the order warns that anyone who has been informed of the order will be in contempt of court if he helps the defendant to break the order.

However, although the third party may be liable for contempt, he is not liable to the applicant for damages if he allows the defendant to break the order.

In *HM Commissioners of Customs and Excise v Barclays Bank plc* [2006] UKHL 28, Customs and Excise obtained freezing injunctions against Brightstar Systems Ltd and Doveblue Ltd, granted on 26 and 30 January 2001 respectively. The value of the assets restrained was £1,800,000 in the Doveblue case. Both companies held accounts with Barclays. The following sequence of events then took place.

12.33 pm, 20 January 2001	Brightstar order served on Barclays by fax
2.30 pm, 29 January 2001	Barclays allow Brightstar to withdraw £1,240,570
11.38 am, 30 January 2001	Doveblue order served on Barclays by fax
2 pm, 30 June 2001	Barclays allow Doveblue to withdraw £1,064,289

Subsequently, Customs and Excise obtained judgments against both companies who failed to pay.

Customs and Excise then brought proceedings against Barclays, claiming damages on the basis that Barclays, once served with the freezing injunctions, owed it a duty of care and had acted negligently in permitting the withdrawals to be made.

The House of Lords decided that the bank owed no such duty of care and was therefore not liable.

Where, as is usually the case, a bank is one of the third parties affected by the injunction, clause 17 of the order will allow the bank to take any money due to it from the defendant and to meet any existing liabilities under any cheque or credit card which it has issued to the defendant.

The order will allow the defendant to withdraw money for living, business and legal expenses (see **8.6.3**). There is obviously a risk that he may abuse this by purporting to withdraw money for such expenses when he is, in fact, dissipating his assets to prevent the claimant enforcing any later judgment. Clause 18 of the order makes it clear that, as far as banks are concerned, this is a matter between the claimant and the defendant, and that the bank will not be blamed for any such abuse by the defendant if he appeared to be acting under one of the permitted exceptions to the order. Other third parties are obliged to ensure that the defendant is using the money for a proper purpose.

8.7 THE PRIVILEGE AGAINST SELF-INCRIMINATION

In freezing cases and in some other injunction applications, the claimant may accuse the defendant of conduct which would amount to a criminal offence. In such cases, the defendant will try to claim the privilege against self-incrimination. If he succeeds, he can refuse to disclose information about his assets by claiming that this could lead to his prosecution. He may therefore use this as a reason for not disclosing all or part of his assets in the affidavit which he is required to swear under clause 10 of the standard form injunction order (see **8.6.2**). (He will at the same time protest that he is innocent of any crime. He will say that, if the claimant chooses to make such accusations, he cannot then ask the defendant to provide the evidence for those accusations.) This privilege was considered by the Court of Appeal in

Den Norske Bank ASA v Antonatos [1998] 3 All ER 74. It held that the privilege applies to any information which might be used as evidence at a criminal trial, or which might influence a decision whether or not to prosecute. The person claiming privilege does not need to show that the information would increase the risk of his being prosecuted.

A successful claim to privilege often prevents the claimant from obtaining the information he needs to make the injunction effective. Section 72 of the Senior Courts Act 1981 removes the privilege where it relates to intellectual property and passing-off cases, and s 31 of the Theft Act 1968 prevents claims to privilege in civil cases regarding offences under that Act. Section 13 of the Fraud Act 2006 similarly removes the right to claim privilege in 'proceedings relating to property' where the risk of incrimination relates to offences under the Fraud Act or 'related offences', including conspiracy to defraud. 'Proceedings relating to property' was given a wide meaning in the case of *Kensington International Ltd v Republic of Congo and Others* [2007] EWCA Civ 1128.

Even where the claim for privilege still exists, the House of Lords, in *AT & T Istel Ltd v Tully* [1993] AC 45, decided that it would be possible to override such a privilege claim if the Crown Prosecution Service (CPS) promised that the information disclosed by the defendant would not be used in any subsequent prosecution. In such cases, the claimant would get the information he needed. If the CPS was not able to give such a promise (or had not been asked for such a promise), the courts would not make any order overriding the defendant's claim to privilege (*Johnstone v United Norwest Co-operative Ltd* (1994) *The Times*, 24 February).

In practice, where the defendant claims privilege, the claimant's best course of action is to apply for an order under r 31.19(5) of CPR 1998 asking the court to decide whether the claim to privilege (which must be made in writing and state the grounds on which privilege is claimed – r 31.19(3)) should be upheld. The court may then require the defendant to disclose the documents in question to the court so that the court can decide whether the claim to privilege is justified (r 31.19(6)). If the court agrees that it is justified, there is nothing more the claimant can do. If the court decides that there is no claim to privilege, it will order the defendant to disclose the documents to the claimant.

8.8 AFTER THE ORDER HAS BEEN MADE

8.8.1 Service

As soon as possible after the hearing, the claimant must serve the relevant documents on the defendant and any third parties, such as banks holding assets on behalf of the defendant. It may be advisable to serve the relevant documents on the defendant's bank before the defendant, to ensure that the account is frozen by the bank before the defendant knows what has happened. The documents which must be served are the freezing injunction, the application notice and a copy of the affidavit in support with any exhibits. As with all injunctions, the defendant must be served personally. If the defendant disobeys the order, he may not be the only person liable to contempt proceedings. As already mentioned at **8.2**, the third party who allowed him to do so may also be liable.

8.8.2 Land

Where the defendant owns land, the claimant will want to give notice to potential buyers and mortgagees that the land is subject to a freezing injunction. If the land has registered title, he does this by applying for a restriction under s 42(1) of the Land Registration Act 2002. There is no equivalent protection if the title is unregistered. This is because *Stockler v Fourways Estates Ltd* [1983] 3 All ER 501 decided that a freezing injunction does not give the claimant rights over the defendant's land which can be protected by registration as a land charge.

If the title is unregistered, there are still practical steps the claimant can take. He can, for example, contact local estate agents, inform them of the order, and ask them to let him know if the property is put on the market.

8.8.3 The main action

The defendant's property is now subject to this oppressive order. If he cannot set it aside, it will continue to affect him until the case comes for trial. The courts have said on many occasions that this places the claimant under a duty to press ahead with his claim quickly so that the issues between the parties can be swiftly resolved. If he does not do so, an early application to strike out his statement of case is a real possibility.

8.9 SETTING ASIDE AND VARIATION

8.9.1 The defendant seeks to set aside the order

The principal ground for setting aside the injunction is that it should not have been made in the first place. This normally involves allegations that the claimant did not disclose all the material facts when he made his application. The defendant will argue that if the court had been aware of the full facts it would not have been satisfied that the grounds for the making of the freezing injunction were made out – ie the claimant does not have a good arguable case and/or there is no real risk of dissipation of the defendant's assets in order to avoid enforcement of any judgment.

In such cases, the court considers two matters: are the new facts material to the issues; and was the non-disclosure deliberate?

Where the court considers that it would not have granted the injunction if it had known the full facts, it will inevitably set aside the injunction. It will do this even if the claimant had acted in all good faith and was totally unaware of the new facts. The courts will normally take the view that the claimant did not make proper investigations before he applied for the order. He will therefore have to pay costs (possibly on an indemnity basis) and damages for the loss caused by the injunction.

Nevertheless, sometimes there will be cases where the court considers that it would still have granted the injunction, even if it had known the full facts. It will still want to know why those facts were not available at the first hearing. The court does not like being misled, neither does it like to have its time wasted by incompetence.

If the court considers that there was a deliberate attempt to mislead it by concealing information (or that there was incompetence), it can do the following:

(a)   it can penalise the claimant in costs;

(b)   it can set aside the original injunction and replace it with a new one. This gives the defendant the opportunity to claim damages for the harm the first injunction caused, whilst maintaining the security of the injunction should the claimant eventually win his case;

(c)   in extreme cases, it can set aside the injunction completely on the basis that, while the claimant would usually be entitled to an injunction, his deliberate attempt to mislead the court disqualifies him from such protection.

Although non-disclosure is the principal reason for setting aside freezing injunctions, it is not the only one. Sometimes they are set aside because of procedural irregularities by the claimant (eg failure to comply with one of his undertakings, such as issuing a claim form). Alternatively, property affected by the injunction may not belong to the defendant. In the latter case, even if the property belongs to the defendant's spouse, it must still be freed from the order if the spouse is not a party to the claimant's action. However, if the issue of ownership is unclear the courts may, as in *SCF Finance v Masri* [1985] 2 All ER 747, decide to leave the order in place for the time being and resolve the question of ownership when the main action comes up for trial. Inordinate delay by the claimant in pursuing his action may also be a ground for setting aside.

Courts usually prefer to deal with applications to set aside an injunction at the trial of the claimant's action. However, often such an approach is not appropriate for 'freezing' cases, as the defendant then has to 'suffer the oppression' of the injunction in the meantime (*Ali & Fahd Shobokshi Group Ltd v Moneim* [1989] 2 All ER 404). Where the freezing injunction is set aside, the judge should always consider whether it is appropriate to assess damages at once and direct immediate payment by the claimant, rather than wait until trial (*Practice Direction (Mareva Injunctions and Anton Piller Orders)* [1994] 1 WLR 1233).

8.9.2 The defendant seeks to vary the order

Even if the defendant is not in a position to apply to set aside the injunction, he may want to have it varied, for example to increase the amount he can withdraw for living expenses or to pay out other monies contrary to the claimant's wishes. The defendant may argue that the injunction in its current format is oppressive.

To save costs, and to comply with the overriding objective, the parties should try to agree any variation. If they cannot agree, the defendant will have to apply to the court.

The court will normally require evidence from the defendant dealing with his financial position so that it can see that the variation is necessary. Courts have required evidence that the expenditure cannot be financed from other sources such as foreign property or, in the case of a corporate defendant, from some associated company.

The court will also want to be satisfied that the expenditure is necessary. If it thinks that the application is an attempt to circumvent the order it will refuse it. However, if the expenditure is genuine and would have been incurred were it not for the existence of the freezing injunction, then it will be authorised. This will happen even though the defendant then has insufficient money to meet the amount of the claimant's claim.

8.9.3 Third parties

Third parties can apply to have the injunction varied or set aside if it is causing them undue difficulty. Thus, in *Galaxia Maritime SA v Mineralimportexport, The Eleftherios* [1982] 1 WLR 539 the defendant's property had already been loaded on board ship by the time the order was made. The shipowner was unable to set sail as a result of the order (apparently unloading the defendant's property did not solve the problem) so the order was discharged because it was imposing an excessive burden on the shipowner.

8.9.4 Other creditors

If the defendant will not seek to vary the injunction to pay other creditors, those creditors may (at least if they have established rights over the defendant's property) be able to take the initiative. Thus, debenture holders succeeded in varying an injunction so that they could exercise their rights over the defendant's property in *Cretanor Maritime Co Ltd v Irish Maritime Management Ltd, The Cretan Harmony* [1978] 1 WLR 966. Further, solicitors with money in client accounts were able to obtain permission to use that money to meet bills they had sent to the defendant in *Prekookeanska Plovidba v LNT Lines Srl* [1988] 3 All ER 897 (see also *Cala Cristal SA v Emran Al-Borno* (1994) *The Times*, 6 May).

8.10 CASES WITH A FOREIGN ELEMENT

Subject to the normal problems which arise when suing a defendant out of the jurisdiction (see **Chapter 16**), the court can, under s 37(3) of the Senior Courts Act 1981, grant an injunction against a defendant wherever he lives and whatever his nationality. However, there may be problems where the defendant's property or the claimant's main action are out of the jurisdiction.

8.10.1   The location of the property

Usually, English courts will only make orders (including orders for disclosure) relating to property within the jurisdiction. This principle applies before and after judgment has been obtained. However, in *Derby & Co Ltd v Weldon* [1990] Ch 48, the Court of Appeal agreed that, in exceptional cases, the English courts could make 'worldwide' freezing orders ('WFOs'). It laid down three conditions:

(a)   that a large amount of money (eg several million pounds) must be involved;

(b)   that there must be insufficient property within the jurisdiction to meet the amount sought by the claimant; and

(c)   that the risk of property being concealed, etc, must be exceptionally high.

These conditions will exist only in very few cases.

Even if these conditions are met, there is no point is making an order in this country if it is going to be ignored by the courts in the country where the property is located. Evidence on the issue of enforcement will be needed, although in *Derby & Co Ltd v Weldon (No 6)* [1990] 1 WLR 1139, the Court of Appeal said that, in appropriate cases, the defendant could be ordered to transfer the property to a country which would recognise and enforce the English court's order. If the defendant did not comply, he could be debarred from taking any further part in the English proceedings.

Where a WFO order has been made, however, the English courts will not give the claimant a blank cheque. He normally has to give undertakings that he will seek leave of the English courts before seeking to enforce the order out of the jurisdiction or commencing fresh proceedings in another country arising out of the same facts.

However, the Court of Appeal in *Derby & Co Ltd v Weldon* gave little guidance as to the circumstances in which the court would exercise its discretion to grant permission to enforce a WFO.

But in *Dadourian Group Int v Simms & Others* [2006] EWCA Civ 399, the Court of Appeal took the opportunity to lay down such guidelines, as follows:

> Guideline 1: The principle applying to the grant of permission to enforce a WFO abroad is that the grant of that permission should be just and convenient for the purpose of ensuring the effectiveness of the WFO, and in addition that it is not oppressive to the parties to the English proceedings or to third parties who may be joined to the foreign proceedings.
>
> Guideline 2: All the relevant circumstances and options need to be considered. In particular consideration should be given to granting relief on terms, for example terms as to the extension to third parties of the undertaking to compensate for costs incurred as a result of the WFO and as to the type of proceedings that may be commenced abroad. Consideration should also be given to the proportionality of the steps proposed to be taken abroad, and in addition to the form of any order.
>
> Guideline 3: The interests of the applicant should be balanced against the interests of the other parties to the proceedings and any new party likely to be joined to the foreign proceedings.
>
> Guideline 4: Permission should not normally be given in terms that would enable the applicant to obtain relief in the foreign proceedings which is superior to the relief given by the WFO.
>
> Guideline 5: The evidence in support of the application for permission should contain all the information (so far as it can reasonably be obtained in the time available) necessary to enable the judge to reach an informed decision, including evidence as to the applicable law and practice in the foreign court, evidence as to the nature of the proposed proceedings to be commenced and evidence as to the assets believed to be located in the jurisdiction of the foreign court and the names of the parties by whom such assets are held.

Guideline 6: The standard of proof as to the existence of assets that are both within the WFO and within the jurisdiction of the foreign court is a real prospect, that is the applicant must show that there is a real prospect that such assets are located within the jurisdiction of the foreign court in question.

Guideline 7: There must be evidence of a risk of dissipation of the assets in question.

Guideline 8: Normally the application should be made on notice to the respondent, but in cases of urgency, where it is just to do so, the permission may be given without notice to the party against whom relief will be sought in the foreign proceedings but that party should have the earliest practicable opportunity of having the matter reconsidered by the court at a hearing of which he is given notice.

The English courts are also concerned that WFOs should not oppress third parties who have possession or control of the defendant's property in foreign countries. The order will therefore contain a proviso which states that the third parties are not at risk of English committal proceedings.

Practice Direction 25A contains the full text of the claimant's undertakings, the proviso for third parties, and the other terms of the standard form freezing injunction prohibiting the disposal of assets worldwide.

If the claimant has obtained final judgment, the court may order a defendant to disclose his assets outside the jurisdiction, even though the conditions for granting a WFO are not satisfied (*Gidrxslme Shipping Co Ltd v Tantomar Transporters Maritimos Ltd, The Naftilos* [1995] 1 WLR 299).

8.10.2   The location of the main action

At common law, a claimant could only seek a freezing injunction in aid of proceedings that were being brought within the jurisdiction. If his main action was in some other country, at common law he could not get a freezing order from the English courts to help him with that action (*Siskina (Cargo Owners) v Distos Compania Naviera SA, The Siskina* [1979] AC 210).

However, by s 25 of the Civil Jurisdiction and Judgments Act 1982 (CJJA 1982), the English courts were enabled to grant interim relief to a claimant who was taking proceedings elsewhere in a State which was party to the Brussels or Lugano Conventions (and now Council Regulation 1215/2012 (the Brussels Regulation (recast)) – see **Chapter 16**). This can be done unless it would be inexpedient to do so. Thus, in *Republic of Haiti v Duvalier* [1990] 1 QB 202, the claimants, who were seeking to recover most of their national treasury from their former dictator, and who were suing him in France to this effect, were able to get a freezing injunction in England to assist their French proceedings.

General principles to which the court should pay heed were laid down by Neuberger J in *Ryan v Friction Dynamics Ltd* (2000) *The Times*, 14 June.

By the Civil Jurisdiction and Judgments Act 1982 (Interim Relief) Order 1997 (SI 1997/302), s 25 of the CJJA 1982 has now been extended to other non-Regulation countries. This enables the English courts to grant interim relief in aid of legal proceedings even in non-Regulation countries, and it will now usually be possible to obtain a freezing injunction in this country in aid of procedures anywhere else in the world.

8.11   SUMMARY

A freezing injunction is an exceptional remedy which enables the claimant to prevent the defendant from dealing with some of his property until the claimant's action comes to trial. The court will grant this injunction only where the claimant can demonstrate that:

(a)   he has a good arguable case after full disclosure; and

(b)   the defendant has property within the jurisdiction and intends to deal with the property so as to frustrate the enforcement of the claimant's judgment.

The claimant will apply without notice for the injunction. He will have to give undertakings to protect the position of the defendant and the third parties who have possession of the defendant's property.

The injunction prevents the defendant from dealing with his property up to a specified value, and will usually require him to disclose what assets he has and where they are. It will also, among other things, allow him to spend a certain amount of money for ordinary living expenses, legal costs and paying his business debts.

If the claimant is accusing the defendant of criminal behaviour, the defendant may be able to rely on the privilege against self-incrimination to avoid revealing information about his assets.

If the claimant has failed to reveal information relevant to the case, the injunction may be set aside and the claimant could then have to pay compensation to the defendant under the usual undertaking as to damages.

The court in very exceptional circumstances grants freezing injunctions where the bulk of the defendant's property is outside the jurisdiction.

8.12   FURTHER READING

I Goldrein, *Commercial Litigation: Pre-emptive Remedies* (looseleaf).

SEARCH ORDERS

LEARNING OUTCOMES

After reading this chapter you will understand:

- the nature of a search order
- the grounds for applying for a search order
- the role of the supervising solicitor
- how to serve and execute a search order
- the position of the respondent to a search order
- the undertakings required to be given by the applicant and supervising solicitor
- how to advise a respondent faced with the execution of a search order.

9.1 INTRODUCTION

This chapter explains how a claimant can get an order which requests the defendant to allow the claimant to enter and search the defendant's premises for property belonging to the claimant, or for evidence that the defendant has been harming the claimant. If the defendant does not comply, he may be committed to prison for contempt of court.

This chapter also explains the facts which the claimant must prove to get such an order and the dangers to the claimant in seeking such an order. The obligations created by the order are set out at **9.6**, which refers to the standard form search order contained in PD 25A, set out in **Appendix 15** to this book. It also deals with the undertakings which the claimant and other people involved in the execution of the order have to give to the court.

The chapter concludes with some tips on the advice which the defendant's solicitor should give to their client, and some practical points which might be of relevance to one or other of the parties.

9.2 THE NATURE OF THE ORDER

The court's power to grant a search order was established by the Court of Appeal in *Anton Piller KG v Manufacturing Processes Ltd* [1976] Ch 55. In the same way as freezing injunctions used to be called *Mareva* injunctions (see **8.1**), search orders used to be called *Anton Piller* orders, and readers should bear this in mind when reading pre-1999 cases. The court now has statutory authority to make such an order pursuant to s 7 of the Civil Procedure Act 1997.

A search order requires the defendant to allow the claimant's named representatives to enter and search the defendant's premises specified in the order. The claimant, however, is not permitted to use force to enter the defendant's premises.

The order is used to recover property belonging to the claimant which the defendant is using to harm the claimant. Thus, if a former employee of the claimant has wrongfully taken customer and price lists from the claimant and is using them to compete against the claimant, a search order can be used to recover the stolen lists.

Search orders are also used to obtain evidence of wrongdoing. For example, if a competitor is infringing the claimant's copyright, a search order can be used to search the defendant's premises for evidence of infringing copies, the addresses of suppliers and customers, and details of the profits made by the infringement.

The order has also been used in aid of enforcement (*Distributori Automatica Italia SpA v Holford General Trading Co Ltd* [1985] 1 WLR 1066).

A search order is often made at the same time as a freezing injunction. It may be combined with orders for disclosure and/or further information. It is even possible to obtain an order which prevents the defendant from leaving the country for a short period of time so that he remains available to comply with the search order.

As with freezing injunctions (see **8.4**) the application should be made in the High Court.

9.3   ENTITLEMENT TO THE ORDER

A search order is a fundamental interference with the defendant's civil liberties. As such, it is granted only in the most extreme cases when the order is needed to ensure that justice is done. The claimant has to show three things:

(a)   He has an extremely strong prima facie case.

(b)   He will suffer (or continue to suffer) serious harm if the order is not made.

(c)   The defendant has incriminating materials in his possession which are unobtainable by other means.

An alternative to a search order would be to apply, on notice, for an order for the delivery up of goods under s 4 of the Torts (Interference with Goods) Act 1977. This is provided for by r 25.1(i)(e) of the CPR 1998. A real possibility that the defendant may destroy or dispose of the materials, or continue to exploit the confidential information contained therein, may well satisfy this requirement. The claimant will suggest that if an application on notice was made, it would simply give the defendant the opportunity to dispose of the materials being sought. Furthermore, the court must be satisfied that the harm likely to be caused to the defendant and his business is not excessive or out of proportion to the legitimate object of the order.

To apply for a search order, the claimant will have to prepare the following documents:

(a)   application notice;

(b)   affidavit in support;

(c)   draft order;

(d)   draft claim form, if not already issued;

(e)   a second application notice for a return date, if this is not dealt with on the search order application notice. (If the search order is granted, the court will fix a return date about one week after the initial hearing to enable the defendant to make representations about the order.)

In view of the draconian nature of the order, the comments in **Chapter 8** (on freezing injunctions) about the need for detailed inquiries and full disclosure also apply here. The supporting affidavit must disclose very fully the reasons for seeking the order, including the probability that relevant material would disappear if the order was not made. It must also state the address of the premises to be searched and state whether it is a private or business address.

A search order will not be made where there is any doubt about the court's jurisdiction, unless the defendant has been given the opportunity to be heard on the question of jurisdiction (*Altertext Inc v Advanced Data Communications Ltd* [1985] 1 All ER 395). Since such a hearing would defeat the whole point of seeking a search order, it may be preferable in such cases to take proceedings in the defendant's local court. This helps ensure that jurisdiction is not challenged.

9.4 PITFALLS AND SAFEGUARDS

Universal Thermosensors Ltd v Hibben [1992] 3 All ER 257 and *Columbia Picture Industries Inc v Robinson* [1987] Ch 38 are essential reading for solicitors involved in a search order case. They both give detailed guidance on obtaining and executing a search order.

The claimant will have to give the usual undertaking as to damages (see **5.4**), and this will cover oppressive execution of the order, and damages for innocent third parties who have been harmed by the order. The *Columbia Picture* case shows that aggravated damages may be awarded against a claimant who fails to make proper disclosure or who executes an order oppressively.

It is also very easy for the solicitors involved with a search order to make mistakes. Such mistakes can put them in contempt of court, as in *VDU Installations Ltd v Integrated Computer Systems & Cybernetics* [1989] 1 FSR 378.

The standard form order in PD 25A contains provisions which may help the claimant and his solicitors to avoid such problems.

9.4.1 The supervising solicitor

The standard form order provides that it should be executed by the claimant's solicitor under the guidance of a supervising solicitor who must be experienced in the operation of search orders. The supervising solicitor will be an independent solicitor from some other firm, whose role is to help the defendant understand what is happening and to ensure that nothing unfair happens. The supervising solicitor will have to prepare a report afterwards, which they will send to the claimant's solicitor, who will then provide copies for the defendant and the court. The Law Society keeps a list of supervising solicitors (as does the London Solicitors Litigation Association). The claimant's solicitors should file an affidavit, identifying the supervising solicitor's experience in executing search orders.

The order must be served personally by the supervising solicitor.

9.4.2 Dealing with the items the claimant is searching for

The order will specify the items which are the subject of the search (Sch B to the order). Only items which are clearly covered by the terms of the order may be removed. *Columbia Picture* confirms that the claimant cannot take away everything which might be relevant in order to inspect it at his leisure. The applicant's solicitor undertakes to answer forthwith any query made by the defendant as to whether any particular document or article is within the scope of the order.

What happens to the removed items depends on who owns them. If they indisputably belong to the applicant, he can do what he likes with them. Usually, however, the position is not that clear-cut.

Often the documents which are taken as evidence belong to the defendant. The applicant's solicitor undertakes to return those originals within two working days. During that time, they will take copies. Occasionally, the applicant may fear that the defendant will be able to use those documents to cause him further harm. It is possible to modify the undertaking to take account of this, but if the documents are also relevant to the defendant's legitimate activities, he must be allowed some form of access to them.

The applicant will want to use the items seized as evidence against the defendant in this action. He may also want to use them as evidence of wrongdoing by other people, either by joining them as defendants to the present action or by commencing fresh proceedings against them.

The defendant may also be under investigation by the police, HM Revenue and Customs or the Serious Fraud Office. They will be very interested in any information the applicant has about the defendant. The undertaking given by the applicant's solicitor to keep all such items in safe custody, however, means that they cannot allow anyone else to see or use the items without the permission of the court. Such permission is rarely granted (*EMI Records Ltd v Spillane* [1986] 1 WLR 967; *General Nutrition v Pradip Pattni* [1984] FSR 403).

9.5   THE TERMS OF THE ORDER

The standard search order from PD 25A is set out in **Appendix 15** to this book. The following text explains the main provisions of the search order.

A search order made upon an application which materially departs from the requirements of the Practice Direction and the standard form of order may be set aside (*Gadget Shop Ltd v Bug.Com Ltd* (2000) *The Times*, 28 June).

9.5.1   The penal notice

The penal notice, addressed to the respondent, stipulates that if the respondent disobeys the order, he may be held in contempt of court and subjected to imprisonment or fine or seizure of assets. Anyone who knows of the order and helps or permits the respondent to breach its terms will be likewise in contempt and subject to the same range of penalties.

9.5.2   The applicant's rights

The applicant is entitled to ask for the respondent's cooperation but he cannot compel it. He cannot use force if the respondent will not comply with the order. In such circumstances, his only remedy is to apply to have the respondent committed for contempt of court.

Paragraph 6 of the order is the 'business' part of the order, ordering that entry and search of premises, and vehicles on and around the premises, be allowed. It is addressed to the respondent. Subject to what is said at **9.7**, he must allow access immediately.

This part of the order also permits a search of any premises of the respondent not mentioned in the order but discovered as a result of executing the order. In addition, it extends the power to search the respondent's vehicles to those around the premises, as well as those on the premises. However, the power is expressly limited to those vehicles on or around the respondent's premises (which are under the respondent's control).

It may be necessary to include the respondent's home in the premises to be searched. If the respondent is not there, his spouse can be required to comply with the order. If the order is to be executed on a woman on her own in a private house, the supervising solicitor serving the order must be a woman or be accompanied by one (see the footnote to the part of the order headed 'The Search').

Although the order is served by solicitors, they will need help to execute the order. Usually, they will not have the technical expertise to identify the matters covered by the order. Paragraph 6 therefore allows them to be accompanied by a specified number of representatives of the applicant, who will help them to identify the relevant materials. Sometimes, search orders are used in bad faith by applicants who simply want to gain access to the respondent's trade secrets. Because of this risk, the applicant should inform the court if any representative of the applicant will be present when the order is carried out (see **9.5.3**).

Given the likelihood that much of the material in question will be stored on computer, one of the team of searchers should be skilled in operating computers to ensure that information on the computer is not withheld by the respondent.

The order must specify the premises to be searched and the items which the applicant is looking for. These are listed in Schs A and B to the order respectively.

9.5.3 Serving and executing the order

The order must be served by the supervising solicitor, who must also supervise the execution of the order. The supervising solicitor has to explain the order to the respondent in ordinary language. This is very important. When the solicitor arrives at the respondent's premises and announces that they have a court order which entitles them to enter and search the property, they are likely to be met with a reaction of blank disbelief. The respondent's initial reaction will almost certainly be to refuse admission. If the solicitor simply turns away and applies to have the respondent committed for contempt of court, the application will probably fail. Any attempt to deal with the respondent's refusal to comply with the order is likely to involve a detailed investigation of the conduct of the supervising solicitor in carrying out the order. The court will need to be satisfied that every attempt was made to explain the following matters to the respondent:

(a) that the supervising solicitor is acting under a court order;

(b) that the respondent can be punished by imprisonment if he does not obey the order;

(c) that it can be in the respondent's own interests to cooperate if he is innocent of any wrongdoing;

(d) that the respondent is entitled to take legal advice from his own solicitor before complying with the order.

As mentioned above, it is the supervising solicitor's obligation to explain the respondent's right to legal advice. The respondent may want to exercise this right, so that his own solicitor is present when the order is executed. Alternatively, he may wish to discuss with his solicitor whether there are grounds for applying to court at once to set aside or vary the order before it is executed (see **9.7**). Whilst considering these possible courses of action, the respondent may ask the supervising solicitor to delay the search for up to two hours or such period as the latter may permit.

The respondent's right to take legal advice is, however, qualified. If the respondent wants to take legal advice, he must do so immediately. This clearly implies that the order should be executed at a time when it will be possible for the respondent to take legal advice. In *Universal Thermosensors Ltd v Hibben* (at **9.4**), the court specifically said that the order should be executed during normal working hours, and the standard form order says that normally it should be served on a weekday morning after 9.30 am. This causes no problems where the premises to be searched are business premises. It creates great difficulty if the applicant also wants to search the respondent's home. If the respondent is not going to be at home during office hours, the guidance of the judge should be sought when the order is obtained. There are a number of possible solutions available to the judge. They may be prepared to allow the order to be executed when someone other than the respondent is on the premises. Otherwise, they might allow the applicant's solicitor to arrive, for example, at breakfast time when the respondent will not have to wait very long before he can take legal advice. Another possibility is that they might stipulate that the independent supervising solicitor should act as the respondent's legal adviser. Alternatively, they could require the applicant's solicitor to give advance notice to the respondent's solicitor of the proposed time for executing the order, so that the respondent's solicitor can be available to give advice at that time.

Initially, the respondent will probably seek legal advice over the telephone. The rules on solicitor/client confidentiality mean that the other solicitor cannot be present while the respondent is talking to his own lawyer. However, before this takes place the supervising solicitor should ensure that the respondent is genuinely speaking to a lawyer and is not taking the opportunity to warn his accomplices or to tamper with the evidence.

Before allowing entry to anyone but the supervising solicitor, the respondent also has the right to gather together any documents covered by legal professional privilege or the privilege against self-incrimination (in cases where that privilege applies). He should hand these documents to the supervising solicitor who will form a view on whether or not the documents are privileged. If the supervising solicitor thinks that the documents are privileged, or of doubtful status, they will exclude them from the search and retain any documents of doubtful status until the court has had an opportunity of ruling on the matter. However, if the supervising solicitor considers that the documents are not privileged, but the respondent still withholds them from the applicant, the respondent runs the risk of being in contempt of court.

In *C plc and W v P (Secretary of State for the Home Office and the Attorney General intervening)* [2006] EWHC 1226 (Ch) proceedings were brought for breach of confidence and copyright infringement. A search order was made and during the search computer images of children were discovered. The respondent wished to rely on the privilege against self-incrimination. The court held that, in the circumstances, the offensive material could be passed on to the police.

As mentioned above, if the respondent wants to delay permitting entry while he exercises the above rights, takes legal advice, or applies to court to vary or set aside the order (see **9.5.7**), he only has to allow access to the supervising solicitor in the meantime. Nonetheless, he must keep the supervising solicitor informed of what he is doing, and he can refuse to allow the search to begin only for a short period whilst he exercises his rights. According to para 10 of the order, this delay in execution should not exceed two hours unless the supervising solicitor is prepared to agree to a longer period.

The respondent may fear (sometimes with good reason) that the applicant will use the search order as an opportunity to find out about the respondent's business and trade secrets. He will therefore want to refuse entry to the applicant in person or his employees. The footnote to the part of the order entitled 'The Search' stipulates that none of the persons accompanying the applicant's solicitor should be capable of gaining personally or commercially from the search, unless their presence is essential. However, there will be cases where the applicant's lawyers need the expertise of the applicant or his employees to identify the material they are looking for. In that case, the order may name one representative of the applicant to whom the respondent cannot deny access.

The respondent is usually entitled to a list of all the items which have been removed. He should be given an opportunity to check and sign the list before the items are removed from his premises. Items should not usually be removed in the respondent's absence. In both instances, however, the supervising solicitor can permit non-compliance if full compliance is impractical.

9.5.4 The respondent's position

The respondent is required to cooperate with the executing solicitors. He cannot merely allow them to search. Paragraph 18 of the order requires him to show them where the items referred to in the order are. If they are in locked cupboards, he must unlock those cupboards. If the information is stored on a computer, he must allow effective access to that computer, subject to the applicant's party having the necessary expertise to use the computer without damaging it. By para 16, he is required to hand over the items covered by the order. He can be required to confirm all the information supplied, or required to be supplied, under the order.

Paragraph 18 also requires the respondent to reveal the identities and whereabouts of his suppliers and customers, and the location of the items sought by the applicant which have not already been handed over under para 16. He is also required to confirm that this information is accurate.

The respondent also has entitlements, however, and these are dealt with in a separate part of the order. This makes it clear that the respondent is entitled to have the order explained to him by the supervising solicitor in everyday language.

Paragraphs 10 and 11 of this section of the order explain that the respondent may be entitled to refuse disclosure of documents protected by the privilege against self-incrimination (in cases where that privilege applies, see **8.7**) or by legal professional privilege. The order then explains the respondent's rights to legal advice and the circumstances in which he may delay complying with the order (see **9.7**).

9.5.5 Prohibited acts by the respondent

Paragraph 20 prevents the respondent from telling anybody except his lawyers about the proceedings or the search order. Although it seems harsh, it is designed to ensure that the respondent does not warn accomplices, of whom the applicant is unaware, of what is happening. The clause is of limited duration and should last only for as long as is necessary for the applicant to study the items removed under the order and to find out whether he needs to take action against any other people who are harming him by their illegal activities. This will usually be until the return date.

In para 21 the respondent is also prohibited from destroying, tampering with, cancelling or disposing of the listed items, unless permitted by the order.

9.5.6 The prohibitory injunction

The order will contain a prohibitory injunction preventing the harm the applicant is complaining about. This is contained in para 22. It continues until the trial, unless the respondent successfully applies to set aside the order before the trial.

9.5.7 Applications to set aside or vary the order

As with all injunctions, if the respondent wishes to set aside or vary the order, he may apply for this at any time. That application should be served on the applicant giving him proper notice under the procedure described in **Chapter 7**. The respondent can also apply on the return date fixed when the injunction was granted.

If the respondent does apply to set aside the order, the court will mainly be interested in considering the injunction referred to at **9.5.6** on the basis that any harm caused by the search order has already happened and that the issue of compensation for such harm can be left until the final trial of the claim. If, however, the search order is likely to have a deleterious effect on the respondent's business (see **9.7**), it would be possible to apply to set aside that order on the return date.

The respondent may be able to argue that the search order should not have been granted in the first place (ie one or more of the necessary grounds for making the order was not present), or that the applicant failed to execute the order in the correct manner.

The law relating to setting aside and varying injunctions and search orders is the same as the law for setting aside and varying freezing injunctions, and is dealt with at **8.9**.

9.6 THE UNDERTAKINGS

After the usual provisions explaining that the defendant must not arrange for other people to infringe the order on his behalf, Schs C to E to the standard form search order set out the undertakings required in a search order.

9.6.1 The applicant's undertakings (Sch C)

These are largely the same as those given in any injunction obtained without notice before proceedings have been issued (see **7.2.3**). Nevertheless, the following aspects are peculiar to a search order. The applicant gives the usual undertaking as to damages, but this also expressly covers the payment of compensation to the respondent if the execution of the order is carried out oppressively (see Sch C(1)). In para 4, he further undertakes to comply with the rules on confidentiality (see **9.4.2**). These provide that the applicant will not inform anyone else of the proceedings until after the return date unless permitted by the court.

9.6.2 The applicant's solicitor's undertakings (Sch D)

These include undertaking to retain in safe-keeping all items obtained as a result of the search until the court directs otherwise, and to return to the respondent any original documents which do not belong to the applicant within two working days of their removal in the search.

9.6.3 The supervising solicitor's undertakings (Sch E)

These relate to the supervising solicitor's duties to:

(a)   explain the effect of the order;

(b)   inform the respondent of his right to legal advice (including his entitlement to legal professional privilege and, where relevant, the privilege against self-incrimination); and

(c)   provide a report on the execution of the order to the applicant's solicitors, the respondent and the court.

9.7 ADVISING THE RESPONDENT

As already discussed, a respondent who does not comply with a search order is in contempt of court. It is no defence that the search order should never have been made in the first place (*Wardle Fabrics v Myristis* [1983] FSR 263). While it was in existence, it was a court order and had to be obeyed. Neither is it a defence that the respondent's associates might cause physical harm to the respondent if he complies with the order (*Coca Cola Co v Gilbey* [1995] 4 All ER 711).

The respondent should usually therefore be advised to obey the order. If the respondent wants his solicitor to be present when the order is executed, the applicant's solicitor should be asked to delay execution until the respondent's solicitor can attend (provided this will not cause unreasonable delay – see **9.5.3**).

Paragraph 10 of the order does contemplate the possibility of refusing to comply with the order pending an immediate application to the court to vary or set aside the order. This has to be read in conjunction with the rest of para 10, which requires the respondent to allow the supervising solicitor to enter the premises. This is to enable the supervising solicitor to assure themselves that the respondent is not just using this as a diversionary tactic while he conceals or destroys evidence.

In practice, there are unlikely to be many cases where the respondent will be in a position to make an immediate application to set aside the order, and he will usually have to comply with it.

If the respondent complies with the order and incriminating evidence is found, he may not be able to rely on the privilege against self-incrimination to withhold evidence (see **8.7**). Usually, in such a case, the respondent has no option but to settle the case on the most favourable terms available.

If the applicant's search is unsuccessful, however, the respondent is in a strong position. He will ultimately be able to apply for the injunction to be set aside and for damages for the harm caused to him by the order (see **8.9**). He may wish to make this application immediately, especially if the order is having an adverse effect on his business. Nevertheless, if, as is often the case, the respondent's grounds for setting aside are that the applicant's original application did not disclose all material facts, the court will have to investigate this allegation. This will take time and the courts prefer not to do this before the trial. In any event, in most cases any harm caused by granting and executing the search order has already finished by the time of any pre-trial hearing. Only in exceptional circumstances will the matter be dealt with prior to the trial (*Dormeuil Frères v Nicolian International (Textiles) Ltd* [1988] 1 WLR 1362). More usually, the court will investigate the matter at the trial of the action, where the appropriate remedy will be damages. However, if in the meantime the applicant delays in bringing his claim to trial, the respondent can apply to strike out the applicant's statement of case and enforce the undertaking as to damages at that stage. *Hytrac Conveyors Ltd v Conveyors International Ltd* [1982] 3 All ER 415 shows that such applications can succeed at a very early stage of the proceedings.

Nevertheless, there are a few cases where it may be appropriate to apply to set aside the order at an early stage. An example is where the applicant is an established business abusing the search order jurisdiction in an attempt to drive out an unwelcome, but legitimate, newly-arrived competitor. In such cases, the search order may starve the respondent of custom, and if it is not set aside quickly, it will put him out of business. In such cases, the court should deal with the application to set aside the order when hearing the respondent's initial application rather than waiting until the trial.

According to *Practice Direction (Mareva Injunctions and Anton Piller Orders)* [1994] 1 WLR 1233, if a search order is set aside before the trial, the judge should always consider whether it is appropriate to assess damages at once and order immediate payment by the applicant (see **8.9**). Another point to note is that even 'guilty' respondents have been able to obtain damages under a search order if the order was executed oppressively, as in *Columbia Picture*. For example, persuading a respondent to agree to the removal of additional documents not covered by the order, could well be regarded as oppressive behaviour.

9.8 PRACTICAL POINTS

If there is a risk of a breach of the peace when the order is executed, the police can be asked to attend. This should rarely be necessary and the judge should be informed of any intention to do this when the order is sought. It is common practice to inform the police of what is happening before executing a search order. However, para 8 of the order makes it clear that the order should not be carried out at the same time as a police search.

If the applicant is suing a large number of people, he will have to coordinate his raids on the different premises with military precision to ensure that the respondents do not tip each other off.

There is an inevitable risk that the solicitor's conduct during the execution of the order will be criticised by the respondent. It is important that there should be no doubt about what happened. Therefore, the solicitor should make a note at the time (eg by using a dictating machine) of what is happening and should swear an affidavit as to what happened as soon as the search is over. Similarly, the respondent's solicitor should also keep a record of what happens (or, if they cannot be present, advise the client to do so).

9.9 SUMMARY

A search order requires the respondent to allow the applicant's representatives to enter and search the respondent's premises. The applicant will be able to obtain such an order only if he can show the following:

(a)   an extremely strong prima facie case after full disclosure;

(b)   that the applicant will suffer serious harm if the order is not made; and

(c)   that the respondent has materials unobtainable by any other means.

The order contains safeguards against abuse of the procedure by the applicant, such as the requirement for the order to be executed by an independent supervising solicitor. The terms of the order should be those set out in the standard form contained in PD 25A to CPR 1998.

The respondent's solicitor should usually advise the respondent to comply with the order, even if the result will be that the claimant obtains evidence which supports the applicant's case. Non-compliance could result in an order committing the respondent (and his solicitor) to prison for contempt of court. If, however, the order is executed oppressively or unsuccessfully, the respondent may be entitled to substantial damages under the applicant's cross-undertaking as to damages.

9.10 FURTHER READING

I Goldrein, *Commercial Litigation: Pre-emptive Remedies* (looseleaf).

CHAPTER 10

HANDLING THE EVIDENCE

> **LEARNING OUTCOMES**
>
> After reading this chapter you will understand:
>
> - how to advise a client in a case requiring large-scale disclosure
> - how to advise a client about electronic disclosure
> - what constitutes a claim for legal professional privilege
> - how to carry out inspection of documents
> - how to approach the disclosure provided by the other side
> - the role of expert evidence in commercial cases.

10.1 INTRODUCTION

This chapter builds upon CPR 1998 on disclosure, expert evidence, witness statements and further information (see also the Legal Practice Guide, *Civil Litigation*). It also looks at the best tactical use of these procedures and how the overriding objective of CPR 1998 and the court's case management powers affect the ways in which evidence is handled in the build-up to the trial.

Although this chapter discusses evidence in the context of litigation, the topic is equally important in arbitration and other forms of dispute resolution. Each of the procedures described in this chapter can lead to greater knowledge of the strengths and weaknesses of the client's case. With that knowledge, it is possible to review with the client the likely outcome of the case, the cost of proceeding to the next stage and the appropriate strategy and tactics.

PART I – DISCLOSURE AND INSPECTION

10.2 PRACTICAL POINTS

10.2.1 Practical consequences for the client

Disclosure is a crucial stage in a commercial case. It is often the point at which cases are won or lost because it is the time at which information is exchanged between the parties. Although there are other weapons at the disposal of the parties to obtain information (eg further information or interim applications), disclosure remains central to the action. It is not just a matter of listing documents but requires detailed knowledge of the law, in particular regarding which documents are subject to disclosure and/or are privileged. It is an extremely complicated area of the law, which has led to a large amount of case law over the years. The importance of this stage should not be underestimated, either in terms of its importance to the parties or in the obligations imposed on both sides and their lawyers.

Disclosure is, however, also an expensive stage for the parties in commercial cases. There tend to be a vast number of potentially disclosable documents. It takes time to trace them all and to assess whether they are disclosable and, if so, whether they are privileged. It usually takes just as long to read the opponent's list and to inspect his documents. The solicitor should therefore discuss the costs implications with the client. If the case is weak, it may be better to try and settle before disclosure, rather than waste thousands of pounds in legal costs only to discover what was suspected earlier, ie that the client's cause is a lost one.

10.2.2 Control

Each party must disclose the documents in its control. It is important to realise just how wide this phrase is. It covers not only physical possession or custody of documents but the power to obtain control. Ownership of the document is not required, nor is any legal right or interest in the document. Thus a party must disclose any document which it holds as agent or employee for the true owner, if he issued it in such a capacity. The scope of disclosure in each action must therefore be looked at carefully on its own facts. For example, a director of a company may hold documents in both his personal capacity and also that of shareholder and director. If sued as director, then only the documents which he holds as such would be covered by the disclosure obligations of CPR 1998.

Common areas of difficulty include papers held by a parent company where only the subsidiary is a party to the action and vice versa. Case law suggests that the test is one of whether the parent company as a matter of fact controls the subsidiary rather than merely owning it. It was held in *Lonrho Ltd v Shell Petroleum Ltd (No 2)* [1980] 1 WLR 627 that documents were not in the control of the parent company, since it had no presently enforceable right to obtain the subsidiary's documents without the latter's consent (the parent could only insist on obtaining them by sacking the board of the subsidiary and replacing it with a new one).

Solicitors are agents of their clients and so may hold disclosable documents to their clients' power (eg title documents to clients' property, correspondence between the clients and third parties). On the other hand, some documents which the solicitor (or other professional agent, eg an accountant) has created for their own purposes (eg attendance notes, working drafts etc) will not be in the control of their client, since they belong to the agent.

Lastly, it should be noted that there is no obligation on a party to obtain documents which are not within a party's control but which he might be able to get hold of. The solicitor should make this point clear to the client and remind him not to obtain any papers from a third party without the solicitor's prior approval, in case by so doing they become disclosable.

10.2.3   Limits

It is important not to lose sight of the fact that one of the purposes of disclosure is to save time and costs. One way of saving costs is to limit the extent of disclosure, particularly in complex cases where there are copious documents. The solicitor should at the outset consider what form of disclosure is best suited to the particular case. If appropriate, they should try to agree with the other side a list of the issues in the case and, if possible, a limit on the extent of disclosure. Failing agreement, an application can be made to the court under r 31.5 of CPR 1998 for an order which limits the scope of disclosure either generally or, in the first instance, limits disclosure to documents relating to a particular issue (if that issue is likely to be decisive). The party must satisfy the court that further disclosure is either not necessary at all, or not necessary at that stage.

Where appropriate, the parties should also try to agree the method of listing documents (eg to allow generic listing of large numbers of documents of the same type such as invoices).

The Jackson Report had identified disclosure as one of the litigation processes in which costs could easily get out of control (for an example see the *Digicel* case discussed at **10.5** below). It was felt that costs could be saved if the scope of disclosure were, at least in some cases, to be reduced. For that reason changes were made to Part 31 of the CPR 1998 as part of the Jackson reforms in April 2013. Rule 31.5 was expanded and now reads as follows:

(1)   In all claims to which rule 31.5(2) does not apply –

    (a)   an order to give disclosure is an order to give standard disclosure unless the court directs otherwise;

    (b)   the court may dispense with or limit standard disclosure; and

    (c)   the parties may agree in writing to dispense with or to limit standard disclosure.

(2)   Unless the court otherwise orders, paragraphs (3) to (8) apply to all multi-track claims, other than those which include a claim for personal injuries.

(3)   Not less than 14 days before the first case management conference each party must file and serve a report verified by a statement of truth, which –

    (a)   describes briefly what documents exist or may exist that are or may be relevant to the matters in issue in the case;

    (b)   describes where and with whom those documents are or may be located;

    (c)   in the case of electronic documents, describes how those documents are stored;

    (d)   estimates the broad range of costs that could be involved in giving standard disclosure in the case, including the costs of searching for and disclosing any electronically stored documents; and

    (e)   states which of the directions under paragraphs (7) or (8) are to be sought.

(4)   In cases where the Electronic Documents Questionnaire has been exchanged, the Questionnaire should be filed with the report required by paragraph (3).

(5)   Not less than seven days before the first case management conference, and on any other occasion as the court may direct, the parties must, at a meeting or by telephone, discuss and seek to agree a proposal in relation to disclosure that meets the overriding objective.

(6)   If –

    (a)   the parties agree proposals for the scope of disclosure; and

    (b)   the court considers that the proposals are appropriate in all the circumstances,

the court may approve them without a hearing and give directions in the terms proposed.

(7)   At the first or any subsequent case management conference, the court will decide, having regard to the overriding objective and the need to limit disclosure to that which is necessary to deal with the case justly, which of the following orders to make in relation to disclosure –

    (a)   an order dispensing with disclosure;

    (b)   an order that a party disclose the documents on which it relies, and at the same time request any specific disclosure it requires from any other party;

(c)   an order that directs, where practicable, the disclosure to be given by each party on an issue by issue basis;

(d)   an order that each party disclose any documents which it is reasonable to suppose may contain information which enables that party to advance its own case or to damage that of any other party, or which leads to an enquiry which has either of those consequences;

(e)   an order that a party give standard disclosure;

(f)   any other order in relation to disclosure that the court considers appropriate.

(8)   The court may at any point give directions as to how disclosure is to be given, and in particular –

(a)   what searches are to be undertaken, of where, for what, in respect of which time periods and by whom and the extent of any search for electronically stored documents;

(b)   whether lists of documents are required;

(c)   how and when the disclosure statement is to be given;

(d)   in what format documents are to be disclosed (and whether any identification is required);

(e)   what is required in relation to documents that once existed but no longer exist; and

(f)   whether disclosure shall take place in stages.

(9)   To the extent that the documents to be disclosed are electronic, the provisions of Practice Direction 31B – Disclosure of Electronic Documents will apply in addition to paragraphs (3) to (8).

These provisions apply to all multi-track cases apart from those including a claim for personal injury. The changes are intended to focus the parties' attention on disclosure, and on the potential costs involved in the process, at an earlier stage. The potential costs will also have been considered in those cases where a costs budget is required (see **2.12** above). At least 14 days before the first CMC the parties must file and serve a disclosure report in Form N263, verified by a statement of truth. Where an Electronic Documents Questionnaire has been exchanged (see **10.5.2** below), as will often be the case in commercial cases, the Questionnaire should be filed with the report. The parties should then, at least seven days before the CMC, seek to agree a proposal in relation to disclosure that meets the overriding objective.

The court will then decide, at the CMC, which of the orders for disclosure set out in the 'menu' of options in r 31.5(7) is appropriate for the case. This means that standard disclosure may not be the 'default' order for disclosure that it has been in the past, but of course there are potentials risks for both sides if a more 'limited' order for disclosure is made. Can a case be dealt with 'justly' if the traditional disclosure obligations are reduced?

In the Business and Property Courts the new pilot on disclosure will run for two years from 1 January 2019 (see **10.10.3** below).

10.2.4 Multi-party

Where there is more than one claimant or defendant, or indeed where additional parties have been joined under Part 20, the parties will be entitled to obtain disclosure against each other only to the extent that there are issues in the action to be determined as between them. Thus disclosure will always apply between claimant and defendant and defendant and third party, but not necessarily between co-defendants, nor between a claimant and a third party.

Multi-party cases can also cause problems as to whether privilege has been waived or not (see **10.6.8**).

10.3 ADVISING THE CLIENT

10.3.1 Nature of advice

The importance of disclosure is that it reveals the existence of all disclosable non-privileged documents so that, in due course, the other side can read them. A party must reveal documents even though they may damage his case. Clients find it very difficult to understand why they have to make available information which their opponent does not know about and which will furthermore assist their opponent. This is particularly true of foreign clients from civil law jurisdictions, who will not be familiar with this 'cards on the table' approach.

A solicitor, as an officer of the court, is under a personal duty not only to ensure that their client appreciates the nature and extent of the duty to give disclosure, but also, in so far as possible, that they comply with that duty. Thus, a solicitor must make sure that their client understands what must be done in practical terms, and the solicitor should warn the client about disclosure at a sufficiently early stage of the case, so that the client will not destroy the documents. The timing of this advice will depend on the facts of each case, but it should never be any later than commencement of proceedings. The advice should contain an outline of the disclosure obligations, accompanied by practical advice, reminding the client of the issues in the case and what sort of documents to look out for. The client should also be reminded that disclosure is a continuing process (up to and including trial itself) and thus he should be told that no new documents should be created without prior consultation with his solicitor.

Failure by a solicitor immediately to disclose a document of which they become aware during the course of a case which should have been, but was not, disclosed, could amount to misleading the court – see para 1.4 of the SRA Code of Conduct 2019. If a client refused to allow disclosure, the solicitor should withdraw from the case.

Disclosure is a massive invasion of a party's privacy. Every 'document' (including tapes and material stored on computer) which deals with the subject matter of the dispute, including minutes of meetings at which the matter was discussed, has to be revealed unless it is privileged. A solicitor may have to advise on the relevance of particular documents, and may even have to go through the client's papers to check that full disclosure has been made.

An unscrupulous client may have already disposed of damaging documents before taking legal advice. This will not help him. He also has to disclose documents which have been in his control and explain what happened to those documents. If the court discovers that important documents have disappeared, it is likely to draw adverse inferences against the person responsible.

Solicitors need to have proper procedures for ensuring that their clients are fully aware of the obligations which arise on disclosure. Many firms of solicitors have standard letters on disclosure obligations which they will send to their clients at the start of the matter.

10.3.2 Practical tips

Depending upon the size and importance of the particular case, it will be necessary to meet the client to discuss how to locate and carry out the examination of all potentially disclosable documents. In order to comply with their obligations to the court, the solicitor will need to be briefed on the nature of the client's business so that they have a good idea of how the client's business is run and thus what sort of documents are likely to have been created in the normal course of business.

An appropriate timetable should be agreed, as well as the size and make-up of the team allocated to the disclosure process. The more complex the issues, the more highly qualified the legal team will need to be. The documents must first be identified and then reviewed by an appropriate person within the team to determine which, if any, documents are privileged. The list must be carefully drafted or the job will quickly become out of hand in a large action where thousands of documents are involved. It is important to realise that in the larger, document-heavy cases, disclosure can take a legal team several months to complete.

10.4 CONFIDENTIALITY

Any information a party obtains during disclosure is confidential. He can make use of the information for the purposes of the current action but he cannot use it for any other purpose without the court's permission. The case of *Miller v Scorey* [1996] 1 WLR 1122 illustrates the importance of this point.

The claimant commenced litigation against X in 1993. During disclosure he discovered information which suggested that he also had a claim against Y. He could have asked the court for permission to use this information to join Y as a defendant in the claim against X. He did not.

In 1995, the claimant commenced fresh proceedings against Y relying on the information he had obtained in the 1993 proceedings. He did not reveal that he was relying on information obtained by disclosure in the earlier proceedings so, by definition, he still had not obtained the permission of the court to use this information.

In 1996, the limitation period expired. Y applied to strike out the action against him relying on the claimant's contempt of court in using information obtained as a result of disclosure in the earlier litigation. Only then did the claimant ask for leave to use the information. The court refused leave and struck out the claimant's action against Y.

10.5 ELECTRONIC DISCLOSURE (E-DISCLOSURE)

For some time now the vast majority of documents held by commercial organisations have been in electronic form. The rules relating to disclosure of documents apply to electronic documents in just the same way as they apply to traditional paper documents.

The definition of 'document' in CPR 1998, r 31.4 covers anything in which information of any description is recorded. Paragraph 2A.1 of PD 31A explains how this applies to electronic documents:

> **2A.1**
>
> Rule 31.4 contains a broad definition of a document. This extends to electronic documents, including e-mail and other electronic communications, word processed documents and databases. In addition to documents that are readily accessible from computer systems and other electronic devices and media, the definition covers those documents that are stored on servers and back-up systems and electronic documents that have been 'deleted'. It also extends to additional information stored and associated with electronic documents known as metadata.

The sheer volume of electronic documents held by most commercial organisations gives rise to its own specific problems in relation to the disclosure process. Some of these problems came to light in the case of *Digicel v Cable and Wireless* [2008] EWHC 2522 (Ch).

10.5.1 The decision in *Digicel*

The background to this case was the liberalisation of the telecommunications markets in a number of Caribbean countries. The claimants alleged that the defendant companies had deliberately delayed interconnection with their network. The case was extremely complex, to the extent that the amended particulars of claim ran to more than 320 pages and the amended defence extended to more than 830 pages! The case came before the court on the issue of whether or not the defendants had complied with their disclosure obligations. On 6 February 2008 each party had been ordered to give standard disclosure by list by 27 June 2008. The defendants served a draft list of documents on 30 June 2008 and a final and signed list of documents on 17 July 2008. Both lists were basically the same. The defendants stated in the lists that, as regards electronic documents, there was no central electronic archive or repository for the defendants' electronic documents, and there was no single approach between the defendants as to the management and storage of electronic documents. The defendants had carried out electronic searches in the Caribbean jurisdictions by using 10 keywords. They had also carried out an electronic search in London using the same keywords together with four additional ones. The defendants stated in their list that no search had been made for documents stored on back-up tapes before the current proceedings began. The list stated that back-up tape restoration would have been disproportionate due to the significant time and costs involved.

On receipt of the defendants' draft list, the claimants' solicitors wrote to the defendants' solicitors criticising the small number of keywords used in the search and also criticising the failure to search for back-up tapes. On 31 July 2008 the claimants issued an application for specific disclosure in relation to the back-up tapes and the use of keywords in the search.

In resisting the application for specific disclosure, the defendants gave details of the search they had carried out for electronic documents. As is often the case in large-scale e-disclosure, the solicitors had instructed an information management and litigation support solutions provider specialising in large-scale electronic disclosure and data recovery. Initially 1,140,000 documents had been provided to the defendants' solicitors which, by various editing processes, were then reduced to 625,000 documents. LDM, the support solutions provider, placed these documents on a database and reduced them further to 197,000 potentially relevant electronic documents. These documents were returned to the defendants' solicitors and placed on their database for manual review. This review reduced the number of documents to be disclosed to 5,212, comprising some 29,983 pages filling 83 lever-arch files.

The disclosure exercise took 6,700 hours of lawyers' time, costing some £2 million in fees. In addition there were disbursements of some £175,000.

Thus the defendants had clearly spent an extremely large sum of money in attempting to comply with their disclosure obligations. Despite that, the court granted the application for specific disclosure. Mr Justice Morgan drew particular attention to the requirements of PD 31, para 2A. In particular he criticised the failure to comply with paras 2A.2 and 2A.3, which stated as follows:

> **2A.2**
>
> The parties should, prior to the first Case Management Conference, discuss any issues that may arise regarding searches for and the preservation of electronic documents. This may involve the parties providing information about the categories of electronic documents within their control, the computer systems, electronic devices and media on which any relevant documents may be held, the storage systems maintained by the parties and their document retention policies. In the case of difficulty or disagreement, the matter should be referred to a judge for directions at the earliest practical date, if possible at the first Case Management Conference.
>
> **2A.3**
>
> The parties should co-operate at an early stage as to the format in which electronic copy documents are to be provided on inspection. In the case of difficulty or disagreement, the matter should be referred to a Judge for directions at the earliest practical date, if possible at the first Case Management Conference.

The judge also emphasised the importance of the solicitors to the parties in making the initial determination of what is a reasonable search for documents by their clients. If the solicitors decide to advise on this and undertake disclosure without discussing the various issues with the other side, they must realise that this may well expose their clients to the risk of an application for specific disclosure. The attitude of the courts therefore is that parties are expected to negotiate the extent of the searches to be carried out prior to the disclosure deadline as opposed to simply dealing with it once disclosure has taken place. If parties are unable to come to agreement as to the extent of disclosure and the extent of searches for documents then they should refer the issue to the court to determine. This is something which ideally would be dealt with at the case management conference.

10.5.2 Dealing with e-disclosure in the light of the decision in *Digicel*

On 1 October 2010, a new Practice Direction, PD 31B, was introduced to regulate the approach to be taken by practitioners when considering e-disclosure. In a sense, this is a natural development of the decision in *Digicel* and the existing requirements of para 2A of PD 31.

The purpose of PD 31B is 'to encourage and assist the parties to reach agreement in relation to the disclosure of electronic documents in a proportionate and cost effective manner' (para 2). Paragraph 6 states that the parties and their legal representatives should bear in mind the following general principles:

(a)   Electronic documents should be managed efficiently in order to minimise the cost incurred.

(b)   Technology shall be used to ensure that document management activities are undertaken efficiently and effectively.

(c)   Disclosure should be given in a manner which gives effect to the overriding objective.

(d)   Electronic documents should generally be made available in a form which allows the party receiving the documents the same ability to access, search, review and display the documents as the party giving disclosure.

(e)   Disclosure of electronic documents which are of no relevance to the proceedings may place an excessive burden in time and cost on the party to whom disclosure is given.

In para 7, PD 31B re-emphasises the importance of notifying clients, as soon as litigation is contemplated, of the need to preserve disclosable documents, including those which would otherwise be deleted in accordance with a document retention policy or otherwise deleted in the ordinary course of business.

The Practice Direction then goes on to set out the requirements for discussions which must take place between the parties before the first CMC in relation to the use of technology and disclosure. To assist in this, PD 31B encourages the use and exchange of the Electronic Documents Questionnaire to provide information to the other party in relation to the scope, extent and most suitable format for disclosure of electronic documents in the proceedings. The answers to the Electronic Documents Questionnaire must be verified by a statement of truth.

Before the first CMC the parties must inform the court of the matters agreed in relation to the disclosure of electronic documents and the matters on which they disagree. If agreement has not been reached and it appears that such agreement is unlikely, the court will give written directions in relation to disclosure or order a separate hearing in relation to disclosure. The court can order the parties to complete and exchange all or any part of the Electronic Documents Questionnaire.

Paragraph 16 of PD 31B states that the person signing the Electronic Documents Questionnaire should attend the first CMC and any subsequent hearing when disclosure is likely to be considered.

The Practice Direction also gives detailed guidance on what may constitute a 'reasonable search' as required by r 31.7.

Practice Direction 31B and the Electronic Documents Questionnaire are reproduced at **Appendix 16** to this book.

10.6   PRIVILEGE

It is important to remember that there is no privilege from disclosure of documents, only from their inspection. Thus, although disclosure does require a party to reveal that he has privileged documents, it does not require him to identify those documents specifically, or to show them to his opponent.

Under r 31.19(3):

> A person who wishes to claim that he has a right or a duty to withhold inspection of a document, or part of a document, must state in writing:
> (a)   that he has such a right or duty; and
> (b)   the grounds on which he claims that right or duty.

The statement will usually be made in the list of documents.

In practice, most solicitors' firms will have a standard form of wording (which they will adapt as necessary for each case) which will appear in the list. This wording will cover each class of documents and state in general terms each ground of privilege claimed, but will not give any further details about the documents, ie it will not reveal the date, the maker, or anything about the contents. The form of wording will vary from case to case.

Privileged documents are those which are subject to legal professional privilege, those which might lead to the party being prosecuted (self-incrimination) and those which can be excluded on the ground of public interest. 'Without prejudice' documents are also privileged from being adduced as evidence in court.

Without prejudice correspondence between claimant and defendant will not normally be privileged from inspection since the parties have written to each other. (There would be little point in either claimant or defendant making a claim for privilege from inspection by the other of a communication which one sent to the other.) However, privilege may be claimed (and the documents thus listed in Part 2 rather than Part 1 of the list) where there is more than one claimant or defendant and not all the parties to the litigation have seen the correspondence. Thus, for example, for a letter written by C to D2, privilege can be claimed by C to prevent the document being shown to D1.

Details of much of the law relating to privilege are contained in the Legal Practice Guide, **Civil Litigation**. This chapter therefore aims to highlight only certain more complicated areas which were outside the scope of the basic civil litigation course.

The application of the rules of privilege is not an easy task. It may well require several hours of consideration, and even separate advice from counsel, in relation to any one document.

The fact that a document is confidential or obtained from a confidential source or prepared only for internal use (eg in the case of a corporate party) does not prevent it from being disclosed to, or inspected by, the other side. The only ground for resisting inspection is a claim that the document is privileged.

10.6.1 Legal professional privilege

'Legal professional privilege' includes both what may be termed 'legal advice' privilege (solicitor/client) and also 'litigation' privilege (solicitor/third party or client/third party). This section will consider each type of legal professional privilege in turn and will discuss some of the common areas of difficulty encountered in practice.

10.6.1.1 Legal advice privilege

Legal advice privilege applies only to communications between the client and members of legal professional bodies, such as solicitors and barristers. This includes legally qualified in-house lawyers acting in their capacity as such (and not as executives). It does not, however, extend to include, say, a compliance officer, even if that person regularly gives advice of a legal nature, unless they also have formal legal qualifications. (Note also, as an important point of detail, that the ECJ has held (in *AM & S Europe v Commission of the European Communities* [1983] QB 878) that this privilege may not protect communications with in-house lawyers where the company in question is being investigated for a suspected breach of (now) Articles 101 or 102 of the Treaty on the Functioning of the European Union.)

A solicitor also needs to make their client aware that any internal correspondence (including correspondence with insurers, reports prepared for insurers, board minutes, inter-company memoranda, reports on accidents at work, etc) will not be privileged even though it is highly confidential and potentially damaging. The client should not create any such documents once litigation is pending without first taking legal advice.

Alternatively, it may be possible for the client to ensure that such documents do attract privilege by instructing that any documents discussing the action or the background to it should only be created by, or at the request of, the in-house lawyer or the solicitor. Documents should be marked as so created on their front cover for ease of identification. Close liaison between client and solicitor at all times will be crucial to the success of a claim for privilege. Failure to ensure this could have disastrous consequences for the client if such documents are created relying on privilege but later have to be disclosed.

The House of Lords reviewed the scope of legal advice privilege in *Three Rivers District Council v Governor and Company of the Bank of England* [2004] UKHL 48. This decision came in the long-running litigation which followed the collapse of the Bank of Credit and Commerce International ('BCCI') in 1991, following which the Government set up the Bingham Inquiry to investigate the Bank of England's supervision of BCCI.

The Bank of England appointed Freshfields as its solicitors to deal with the Inquiry. Three senior officials at the Bank, known as the Bingham Inquiry Unit ('the BIU'), dealt with the matter.

In October 1992 the Inquiry published its findings. In 1993, 6,231 creditors of BCCI, together with the liquidator, commenced proceedings against the Bank of England alleging misfeasance.

The application in those proceedings, which ultimately led to the House of Lords judgment, was issued by the claimants in August 2003. It sought further disclosure of documents relating to the Inquiry. In particular, the claimants were seeking documents passing between the BIU and Freshfields. The Bank of England objected to having to show such documents to the claimants on the ground that they were covered by legal advice privilege. (Litigation privilege was not relevant because the Bingham Inquiry was not an adversarial process.)

When the matter came before the Court of Appeal in March 2004, that Court adopted a narrow construction of what constitutes legal advice, excluding what it called advice on 'presentational matters' and restricting legal advice privilege to advice as to legal rights and obligations.

The Bank appealed to the House of Lords and was successful in overturning the Court of Appeal's decision. The House of Lords stated that the advice given by Freshfields to the BIU on 'presentational matters' was covered by advice privilege, as would be any communication between solicitor and client as to what should be done in the relevant legal context.

The House of Lords declined, however, to give a ruling on another issue arising in the case, namely, who exactly the 'client' is for the purposes of advice privilege. In an earlier ruling in the same case, the Court of Appeal had stated that the 'client' was the BIU rather than all the Bank's employees.

The House of Lords had dismissed a petition for permission to appeal against that particular decision and therefore felt it inappropriate to return to the issue.

Where legal advice privilege does apply to communications between the solicitor and client, internally circulated documents or parts of documents revealing such communications are also privileged, whatever the purpose, other than fraud, for which such documents are brought into existence (*Bank of Nova Scotia v Hellenic Mutual War Risks Association (Bermuda), The Good Luck* [1992] 1 AC 233).

In *Property Alliance Group Ltd v The Royal Bank of Scotland Plc* [2015] EWHC 3187 (Ch), Snowden J held that documents prepared by solicitors acting for The Royal Bank of Scotland in relation to the fall-out from the Libor scandal were protected by legal advice privilege. The claimant had asked that the bank should be forced to allow the inspection of documents prepared by their solicitors for a special committee dealing with the matter. However, Snowden J stated (at 45):

There is a clear public interest in regulatory investigations being conducted efficiently and in accordance with law. The public interest will be advanced if the regulators can deal with experienced lawyers who can accurately advise their clients how to respond and co-operate. Such lawyers must be able to give their client candid factual briefings as well as legal advice, secure in the knowledge that any such communications and any record of their discussions and the decisions taken will not subsequently be disclosed without the client's consent.

10.6.1.2   Litigation privilege

There are two types of litigation privilege:

(a)   communications passing between the solicitor and a third party; and

(b)   communications passing between the party personally and a third party.

The first is usually quite straightforward. Where a solicitor is instructed in a case and writes to a witness, or takes a statement from a witness, such documents are clearly within the scope of litigation privilege.

The situation is a little more complex in relation to correspondence with, and reports obtained from, experts, but such complications arise only if you decide to use that particular piece of expert evidence at court. Expert evidence is considered further at **10.11**.

The second type of litigation privilege presents far more problems, and has been the subject of numerous court decisions. Here, the documents are privileged only if the dominant purpose for which they were produced was to obtain legal advice or evidence in respect of existing or contemplated litigation.

Where there may be more than one purpose for creating a document (eg a desire to avoid a similar future defect in manufacturing process and for use in possible litigation), the courts will apply strictly the test of the dominant purpose. This means that the more important purpose, in the mind of the client, *at the time of creating the document* must be the litigation. This can be a difficult test to apply after the event. This is particularly so when considering a damaging document which the client is very keen to keep out of the litigation. In relation to a document which pre-dated the issue of the claim form, it can also be hard to decide whether litigation was contemplated before the document was produced. If not, then no privilege can attach.

Damage reports or internal investigations carried out by the client are a common minefield for the solicitor, since such documents were often created before a claim form was issued, often for more than one purpose and often not by a legal adviser or in-house lawyer. Similarly, communications between the client and its insurers cause frequent problems both in deciding on the dominant purpose of the communication and whether litigation was contemplated at the time of its creation. It was held, in *Guinness Peat Properties Ltd v Fitzroy Robinson Partnership* [1987] 2 All ER 716, that regard should also be had, when applying the dominant purpose test, to the purpose of the person for whom the document was produced. In this case, the document was held to be privileged since the dominant purpose of the insurers (for whom the insured had produced the document) was to obtain legal advice. The position would have been quite different if it had been to enable them to assess the amount of the insurance claim.

In *Axa Seguros v Allianz Insurance & Others* [2011] EWHC 268 (Comm), the court had to decide whether reports produced by civil engineers following damage caused by a hurricane to a Mexican highway were privileged under the dominant purpose test. The court held that the reports had been produced for the dual purpose of assessing whether the highway had been constructed to internationally accepted standards and also to determine to what extent any damage had been caused by the hurricane. The dominant purpose test was not satisfied and therefore the reports were not privileged.

10.6.2   Public interest immunity

The law defining this privilege is set out in the leading cases in this area, namely, *Conway v Rimmer* [1968] AC 910 and *Burmah Oil Co Ltd v Governor and Company of the Bank of England* [1980] AC 1090. This head of privilege applies where it can be said that the disclosure of a document would be injurious to the public interest, so that withholding the document is necessary for the proper functioning of the public service; or, in other words, where the public interest in protecting the document from disclosure is more important than the public interest in the administration of justice. The interests of the administration of justice in this context are principally that a litigant has access to all the documents necessary to proceed with his case. The test does not turn upon whether or not the documents are 'State papers' (since the privilege can attach to much wider categories of documents), nor indeed whether their disclosure might prompt criticism of a government department. Confidentiality is not itself a ground of privilege, but may be a significant factor in the court's decision as to where the balance lies between the competing public interests.

The case of *Conway v Rimmer* made it clear that it is for the *court* to determine where the competing public interest lies, and the 'executive's' claim to privilege is not conclusive. The court may inspect the documents in order to decide where the public interest lies. It is also now clear from the important later House of Lords decision in *Air Canada v Secretary of State for Trade (No 2)* [1983] 2 AC 394 that there are two stages in challenging a claim to public interest immunity. It must first be shown that the documents are *likely* to be necessary to the case, ie that they would 'lend substantial support' to the case. If this can be shown, the court will inspect the documents, and if persuaded at this second stage that the documents *are* necessary, the court will order disclosure. This decision raises all sorts of problems for litigants, since they are not allowed to go on 'fishing expeditions', but they will not know whether documents may help their case unless they can see them.

Classic examples of documents deserving a high degree of protection, and for which privilege could therefore be claimed, include Cabinet papers and documents pertinent to the vital interests of the State.

The privilege does not depend upon an objection being made by the party (although making the claim where applicable has been held akin to a duty on the party) and the court may of its own motion raise the issue of public interest immunity in respect of any documents. If a party is in any doubt as to whether the privilege should be claimed, he should refer the matter to the court and can do so without notice to any other party.

10.6.3   Self-incrimination

This head of privilege enables a party to refuse to produce documents or to answer any questions where he can show a real risk of exposing himself or his spouse to criminal proceedings within the UK. The risk must be 'a real and reasonable risk'. The party cannot claim privilege where it can be shown that he is already at risk and the disclosure of the document(s) would not add to that risk.

This is a highly contentious area of the law, since the party is effectively admitting that he may be a crook but asking for the court's protection. There have been a number of recommendations that the rule be abolished or at least that its scope be reduced.

This topic has already been covered in some detail in **Chapter 8** in relation to freezing injunctions (see **8.7**). The rule applies in the same way to the disclosure process.

10.6.4   Common interest

This is a further example of legal professional privilege and applies to protect any document created by parties who have a common interest in a potential case or dispute, although subsequently not all such persons become parties to the litigation. The dominant purpose behind the exchange of information between the parties must be to inform each other of the facts, or the issue, or the advice received, or for the dominant purpose of receiving legal advice (see *Buttes Gas and Oil Co v Hammer and Occidental Petroleum Co* [1981] QB 223). The parties must have a genuine common interest in the litigation. It is not necessary for them both to be represented by the same lawyer, but their interests must be sufficiently close that they could (should they have chosen to) have used the same solicitor or lawyer (see *Bank of Nova Scotia v Hellenic Mutual War Risks Association (Bermuda), The Good Luck* [1992] 1 AC 233).

> **EXAMPLE**
>
> The floor at the second level of a new building, which is still in the construction stage, caves in for no obvious reason. Any correspondence sent between the solicitors for the architect and for the flooring contractor discussing the cause, the damage and the likely liability is privileged under this head. The companies are not yet co-defendants but fear that they may be sued at some stage in respect of this damage, for example by the original contractor.

Communications between co-claimants and co-defendants stand on the same footing as communications with non-professional agents and are only privileged in the same circumstances (see litigation privilege at **10.6.1.2**). So, in the above example, once both the architect and flooring contractor had been sued by the original contractor, they would become co-defendants to the action and the rules in **10.6.1** would apply rather than the common interest privilege rules set out in this section.

10.6.5 Witness statements (of fact and experts)

Service of a witness statement under an order of the court does not, of itself, waive privilege in connected documents (*Balkanbank v Taher* [1994] 4 All ER 239). There is no waiver unless and until the statement is deployed in court.

It is, however, unwise to serve the statement of a witness if that witness is not going to be called to give evidence. Service of a witness statement has certain consequences:

(a)   It can be used by the opponent in aid of disclosure. If it reveals the existence of other relevant, non-privileged documents, the opponent will seek disclosure of those documents. (Of course, the solicitor who served the statement would know that these documents should have been revealed on disclosure and should have advised their client to that effect.)

(b)   It can be used by the opponent to provide material for cross-examining other witnesses.

(c)   The opponent may put the witness statement in as hearsay evidence (CPR 1998, r 32.5(5)).

10.6.6 Connected documents

As indicated in the previous section, any non-privileged document referred to in the witness statement which is relevant to the case should, in any event, have been revealed on disclosure.

If, however, the witness statement refers to privileged documents, this is not a waiver of privilege and the opponent will not be entitled to inspect those privileged documents.

10.6.7 Copy documents

The various tests for the separate heads of privilege outlined above should be applied to each copy of a document as if it were an entirely separate document. The question which the solicitor must ask themselves is whether a particular document attracts privilege and not whether the original document did.

In practice, problems of legal professional privilege occur most frequently with copy documents. There has been a great deal of case law on this area and the position is still not clear-cut. If a problem occurs, the case will need to be studied in detail.

A pre-existing document not entitled to privilege does not become privileged merely because it is handed to a solicitor for the purposes of litigation (*Ventouris v Mountain, The Italia Express* [1991] 3 All ER 472).

The current view is that if a copy of a privileged document is taken *for a privileged purpose*, that copy will be privileged. If the copy is not taken for a privileged purpose, that copy must be made available for inspection. Equally, you cannot have a privileged copy of an unprivileged document (*Lubrizol v Esso Petroleum Co (No 4)* [1993] FSR 64). There may be an exception where the very selection of those copies by the party or its lawyers might reveal a trend of legal advice or thinking, provided the selection is made from documents held by a third party. Where, however, copies are made of certain of the client's own unprivileged documents, then these copies will not attract privilege (*Sumitomo Corporation v Credit Lyonnais Rouse Ltd* (2001) LTL, 20 July; *Lyell v Kennedy* (1884) 27 Ch D 1).

EXAMPLE

If the solicitors of Company A (claimant) take selected copies of unprivileged documents from a third party (a potential witness in the case), Company A may be able to rely on the argument that to disclose such documents to the defendant (Company B) would be to give away the line of advice given by its legal advisers. Company A must ensure that it at no time comes into control of the original documents as it would then have to disclose these under the normal disclosure rules. This can be avoided by ensuring that the review and selection of the documents to be copied takes place away from its offices. The third party must be well briefed as well so that no documents are sent to Company A in error.

This is a fairly common scenario in practice where parties are trying to gather evidence in support of their cases from various sources. It remains, however, an extremely uncertain area of the law and the client should be advised of the risks before any such copies are taken. It may be safer simply to review the documents elsewhere and to take notes from them. A decision can then be taken later on as to whether or not to obtain copies to use as evidence in the case.

10.6.8   Duration and waiver

The basic rule in relation to the duration of privilege is that a document, once privileged, is always privileged unless and until that privilege is waived. The privilege is that of the client and not the solicitor, so the solicitor must take great care not to waive it as the client's agent without express instructions from the client.

Accordingly, if a document was privileged in earlier, quite separate proceedings, the privilege will remain, even though it was prepared for those separate proceedings and at a time when the current action was not even in the contemplation of the parties. Equally, once privilege has been waived, it is lost for ever and cannot later be claimed for the same document. For example, if privilege is waived for an interim hearing, then it cannot be reclaimed for the purposes of trial later.

Extreme care must be taken when waiving privilege. It is not usually possible to waive privilege of only part of a document. Thus disclosure of part will amount to disclosure of the whole, despite a contrary intention, unless the document can be viewed as two quite distinct documents, each of which is complete and has nothing to do with the other part. (If the position were different, it would be possible for one party to mislead another by revealing part only of a document.)

The case of *Bank of Nova Scotia v Hellenic Mutual War Risks Association (Bermuda), The Good Luck* [1992] 1 AC 233 goes even further and suggests that waiver of privilege over one document may amount to waiver of privilege of all documents relating to the same subject matter or the same transaction. Equally, discussion of a privileged document whether orally or in writing (eg by reference in another document) may amount to waiver of privilege.

It is also unclear whether disclosure of documents to regulatory authorities of privileged material amounts to waiver. It may be possible to rely on public interest immunity if the client is compelled to produce the document. However, this should not be assumed and the potential consequences should be considered carefully before the document is produced.

10.6.9 Challenge to claim of privilege

Problems can arise where a claim to privilege is contested. If it is thought that a party is making a false claim to privilege, an application can be made to the court under r 31.19(5) for the court to decide whether a claim to privilege should be upheld. The court may then require the party claiming privilege to produce the document to the court so that the court may rule on the issue of whether or not the document is privileged. Where a party claims the privilege against self-incrimination, the solution in *AT & T Istel Ltd v Tully* [1993] AC 45 may be available (see **8.7**).

10.7 INSPECTION

10.7.1 Practical tips

On inspection, each party now looks at the documents in his opponent's list which are not privileged. Each solicitor can visit the opponent's solicitor's office and read the documents there and then, or may ask the opponent to send them photocopies of the documents.

It is more convenient to ask for photocopies which the solicitor can read at leisure in their own office. There is a danger in this, however. It is possible to 'blank out' from a photocopy incriminating remarks which have been written on the original. Inspection of the original will reveal if anything has been 'blanked' out. If possible, a solicitor should always inspect the originals. This can be a short inspection. The solicitor can make a note of the documents they want to read more carefully and ask for copies to take back to the office.

When inspecting a document, a solicitor looks for information which helps or hinders the client's case. They also look for other evidence which has not so far been revealed. Thus, a document may cross-refer to some other document which has not yet been revealed during disclosure. This can, if necessary, be cured by an application to the court for specific disclosure.

Sometimes, only part of a document is privileged from inspection. The entire document should be included in Part I of the list of documents. On inspection, the privileged parts of the document can be blanked out. Revealing the non-privileged parts of the document does not amount to a waiver of privilege in the rest of the document (*Bank of Nova Scotia v Hellenic Mutual War Risks Association (Bermuda), The Good Luck* [1992] 1 AC 233).

Similarly, if parts of a relevant document are irrelevant, those parts can be blanked out (*GE Capital Corporate Finance Group v Bankers Trust Co* [1995] 1 WLR 172). In this way, it may be possible for a party to protect confidential matters which it does not wish to disclose and which have nothing to do with the action.

10.7.2 Non-party inspection

In *Davies v Eli Lilley & Co* [1987] 1 All ER 801, the claimants wanted to show papers which they had obtained on inspection to a journalist who was not a party to the case. The journalist could not be said to be an expert but he knew a great deal about the issues because he had covered similar litigation in the USA. The claimants thought that he could give them valuable advice. The court was persuaded to allow this in the interests of justice once it was satisfied that there would be no breach by the journalist of the rules of confidentiality which arise on disclosure. This was, however, an exceptional case and is unlikely to be repeated often.

10.8 ATTACKING THE OTHER SIDE'S DISCLOSURE

10.8.1 Use of disclosure as a tactical weapon

In the past, some large companies exploited the rules relating to discovery (as it was then known) to put intolerable pressure on their litigation opponents. They would request production of vast numbers of documents, or swamp their opponent with vast numbers of documents to provoke the opponent to end the litigation to avoid the costs involved. Part of the purpose of the reforms introduced by CPR 1998 was to prevent such abuses.

On the other hand, litigants may abuse the disclosure rules in an attempt to conceal embarrassing evidence. The CPR 1998 still enable pressure (in terms of both time and cost) to be brought to bear on the other side by pushing for further disclosure or successfully challenging the completeness of their list. If this is followed up by an 'unless' order, which the other side cannot comply with, then their case may well be struck out or judgment entered against them.

It is important to plan ahead in any case, and anticipating the likely steps to be taken by the other side is part of this strategy. Wherever possible, the solicitor should try to anticipate the other side's moves so that they can obstruct or prevent them (if appropriate), or at least react quickly, in a calculated fashion, rather than as a panicked response.

10.8.2 Incomplete disclosure

After exchange of lists, a solicitor must look closely at their opponent's list to see if it is complete. The solicitor should discuss with their client whether there are any documents which should be in the list but are not.

The better acquainted the solicitor is with all the rules, the better they can use them to their client's ends and the more pressure that can be brought to bear on the other side during the disclosure process. Successful applications require a good deal of lateral thinking by the solicitor, together with an in-depth knowledge of the nature of the business of both the client and the other party, and thus of the type of documents which are likely to have been created.

If there are gaps in the list, the matter should first be raised informally with the other side. If this does not work, it is always possible to seek an order for specific disclosure.

As a last resort, if the opponent still fails to make proper disclosure, a solicitor should seek an 'unless order'. If the opponent still fails to comply, his claim or defence may be struck out and the case will be over.

If this is unsuccessful, it will then be for the party who suspects that there has been incomplete disclosure to raise the matter when cross-examining his opponent's witnesses at the trial.

A solicitor should also check for obvious gaps in their client's own list before serving it. If the omission will be spotted anyway, it is preferable that the client's own solicitor spots it rather than the opponent.

Disclosure is a continuing obligation. Even after lists have been exchanged, the solicitor must tell the other party if any further relevant documents come into their client's possession.

10.9 INADVERTENT DISCLOSURE

If a privileged document is disclosed, this may amount to a waiver of privilege. Similarly, privilege may be waived by allowing inspection of a privileged document. (See *Calcraft v Guest* [1898] 1 QB 759.)

If the error is spotted before inspection takes place, the party at fault should write to the other party explaining the error and why the document is privileged. He will then be entitled to claim privilege and to refuse to allow inspection of the document.

Life becomes more complicated if the other party has been able to see the document. This may arise because of a mistake on inspection, but nowadays it is more likely to arise because the privileged documents are delivered to the wrong address by courier or because a fax or e-mail is wrongly addressed.

Under r 31.20:

> Where a party inadvertently allows a privileged document to be inspected, the party who has inspected the document may use it or its contents only with the permission of the court.

The case of *Guinness Peat Properties Ltd v Fitzroy Robinson Partnership* [1987] 2 All ER 716 establishes that an injunction can be granted preventing a party who has received privileged information from making any use of that information if he obtained that information dishonestly or as a result of an obvious mistake.

EXAMPLE 1

In litigation between A and B, the case has come to trial. The case has been adjourned for lunch. A's barrister has left their papers in court during the luncheon adjournment. A clerk in the firm of solicitors acting for B steals A's barrister's papers and copies them during the luncheon adjournment. A can apply for an injunction preventing B from making use of the information contained in the stolen papers. The court will almost certainly grant the injunction.

EXAMPLE 2

In litigation between A and B, A's solicitors mistakenly send a letter addressed to their client to B's solicitors. A can apply for an injunction to prevent B from making use of the inadvertently disclosed privileged material.

The *Guinness Peat* case generated a significant amount of case law which established that where the inadvertent disclosure of privileged material was an obvious mistake, in that a reasonable solicitor would have realised that it was a mistake, the court would grant an injunction restraining the recipient of that information from making any use of it. This culminated in the case of *Ablitt v Mills & Reeve (A Firm)* (1995) *The Times*, 18 October.

In that case, the solicitors for the claimant inadvertently delivered several files of privileged documents to the defendants' solicitors. The defendants' solicitors, acting in compliance with the existing *Law Society's Guide to Professional Conduct*, informed their clients of this development. Following the *Law Society's Guide*, they advised their clients that the documents should be returned to the claimant's solicitors unread but that the clients had the right to require their solicitors to read the papers before doing so. They advised their clients of the risk that, if they did read the documents, the court would subsequently grant an injunction preventing the defendants from making any use of the privileged material the solicitors had read, together with orders for costs.

The clients told their solicitors to read the documents. The solicitors did so and then returned the documents to the claimant's solicitors. The claimant applied for an injunction preventing the defendants from making use of the privileged material which had been inadvertently disclosed. The court granted the injunction. It criticised the defendants' solicitors for following the Law Society guidance and asking their clients whether the clients wanted the solicitors to read the documents. The court's injunction effectively disqualified the defendants' solicitors from acting for the defendants in the case in question.

As a result of this case, The Law Society altered its advice to solicitors in such cases. Usually, a solicitor is under a duty to disclose to a client all information material to that client's matter (SRA Code of Conduct 2019, para 6.4). However, an exception to this duty is set out in para 6.4(d) – where 'the information is contained in a privileged document that you have knowledge of only because it has been mistakenly disclosed'.

As a result, if a solicitor receives privileged material and it is obvious that this is a result of a mistake, the solicitor should not read the material but should return it unread. Nothing need be said to the client.

On the other hand, if it is not obvious that the disclosing party has made a mistake, there is no obligation on the receiving party to ask if the disclosure was intended. He can read the documents and make full use of them (*Breeze v John Stacey & Sons Ltd* (1999) *The Times*, 8 July and *Al Fayed v Commissioner of Police for the Metropolis* (2002) *The Times*, 17 June).

One of the most common examples of inadvertent disclosure arises where privileged material (eg a communication to a client) is inadvertently emailed to a person who should not see that material (eg the other party or his solicitor). Most firms have standard wording at the end of their emails stating that the email and any attachment is intended for and confidential to the addressee and asking any unintended recipient to delete it.

10.10 LARGE-SCALE DISCLOSURE

10.10.1 Management and strategy

Disclosure is a large and very important part of the action, in terms of time, cost and strategy. It is therefore essential that it is carefully planned at the outset of the dispute.

Decisions will need to be taken with the client as to the likely size of disclosure, location of the documents, and the size and level of legal team assigned to the task, together with any assistance required from the client. The more time spent at the outset in the planning process, the less time that will be wasted later. Costly mistakes can be avoided by careful thinking at the outset rather than plunging in with the wrong approach or an inadequate system which later requires a complete overhaul or a fresh start.

10.10.2 Computerisation and IT

In large-scale litigation which is 'paper-intensive' and which is expected to go to trial, it will be appropriate at an early stage in the case to consider whether to invest in a document retrieval system. Such systems enable the legal advisers to manage a large volume of documents and to review them, process them and locate them quickly at any time, including during trial itself. This ease of access to any relevant document is a great tactical advantage.

Such systems have developed significantly in recent years, and many firms now have a standard software programme for inputting documents and creating a list of documents from that information. A database system should be used which can then be manipulated as the parties desire throughout the life of the action. Once the information has been inputted (usually by a team of paralegals supervised by qualified solicitors), it can be searched and reordered as often as desired.

Although these systems represent a considerable investment of both time and cost, they will prove very good value in the long run, and can produce huge savings in costs provided the case does not terminate early on. This results from the solicitor's ability to produce cheap copy documents (through use of electronic images rather than photocopies) and invaluable time-saving (by the ability to word search and thus locate documents at the touch of a button). These systems are expensive at an early stage of the case and this must be discussed with the client. The solicitor must explain that if the case does settle early, the client will not get the full benefit from the system and will not necessarily recoup the cost of setting it up either.

As with any IT system, it must be used intelligently or it can be dangerous. Documents must still be carefully reviewed, and the whole inputting process must of course be very carefully and consistently carried out by all members of the team.

10.10.3 Proposals for reform

In May 2016 the then Chancellor of the High Court, Sir Terence Etherton (now Master of the Rolls), established a Disclosure Working Group in response to the widespread concerns expressed by court users and the profession regarding the perceived excessive costs, scale and complexity of disclosure. The group, which comprised a wide range of lawyers, experts, judges, representatives of professional associations and users of the courts in the Rolls Building in London (now the Business and Property Courts), was tasked to identify the problems and propose a practical solution.

On 1 November 2017 the group produced a paper which contained its unanimous view that 'a wholesale cultural change is required and that this can only be achieved by the widespread promulgation of a completely new rule and guidelines on disclosure which will apply for the majority of cases proceeding in the Business and Property Courts'.

The group produced a series of proposals which are now being piloted across the Business and Property Courts of England and Wales (both in London at the Rolls Building and outside London at the various centres) for a three-year period from 1 January 2019. The details of these radical changes to the current rules are contained in PD 51U, which is reproduced at **Appendix 21**. Some of the key changes being introduced are as follows:

(i) The principles upon which disclosure is based are clearly stated in the Practice Direction.

(ii) What has been termed 'standard disclosure' disappears in its current form; its replacement will not be ordered in every case and will not be regarded as the default form of disclosure.

(iii) The duties of the parties, and of their lawyers, in relation to disclosure are expressly set out. These include a duty to cooperate with each other and assist the court over disclosure. They also include a duty to disclose known adverse documents, irrespective of whether an order to do so is made.

(iv) Save where the parties agree to dispense with this (and subject to several other exceptions), 'Initial Disclosure' of key/limited documents which are relied on by the disclosing party and are necessary for other parties to understand the case they have to meet will be given with statements of case. A search should not be required for Initial Disclosure, although one may be undertaken.

(v) For some cases, Initial Disclosure may obviate the need for any further disclosure (in whole or in part). It is not intended to be an onerous process and there are a number of exceptions where the provision of Initial Disclosure can be dispensed with entirely.

(vi) After close of statements of case, and before the Case Management Conference, the parties are required to discuss and jointly complete a joint Disclosure Review Document ('DRD') (which replaces the existing Electronic Disclosure Questionnaire) to:

  (i) List the main issues in the case for the purposes of disclosure (and the matters of common ground);

  (ii) Exchange proposals for 'Extended Disclosure' (and if so on what Disclosure Model for which issue(s)); and

  (iii) Share information about how documents are stored and how they might (if required) be searched and reviewed (including with the assistance of technology, and if so which).

(vii) The DRD is intended to provide a mandatory framework for parties and their advisers to co-operate and engage prior to the first Case Management Conference with a view to agreeing a proportionate and efficient approach to disclosure.

(viii) At the Case Management Conference, the court should consider by reference to the DRD, which of five 'Extended Disclosure' models (Model A to E) is to apply to which issue (or to all issues). The models range from an order for no disclosure in relation to a particular issue, through to the widest form of disclosure, requiring the production of documents which may lead to a train of enquiry.

(ix)   The court should be proactive in directing which is the appropriate Model and should not accept without question the Model proposed by the parties.

(x)   The fundamental yardstick for the parties and the court, throughout, should be what is appropriate in order fairly to resolve the issues in the case. The well-recognised test of reasonableness and proportionality will be applied by reference to defined criteria in the Practice Direction, which are relevant to disclosure. This test builds upon the overriding objective.

(xi)   In order to inform the court's decision on Extended Disclosure, the parties are obliged to co-operate and engage before the Case Management Conference so that the court can be informed: (a) of any joint view as to the Disclosure Model that should apply; and (b) of the estimated work and cost of using any Disclosure Model that is proposed by one or more of the parties.

(xii)   Form H Cost Budgets in relation to disclosure can be completed after an order for disclosure has been made rather than before, by which time the parties should have a much better sense of what the actual costs are likely to be. Parties will, however, be required to give estimates of the likely costs of disclosure when filing the completed DRD in order that the question of proportionality may be considered at the CMC before an order for disclosure is made.

Other provisions include:

(i)   In an appropriate case the court should be prepared to order that the question of which party bears the cost of disclosure is to be given separate consideration at a later stage;

(ii)   There are express sanctions for non-compliance;

(iii)   Other more detailed provisions of CPR 31 will remain unchanged (e.g. pre-action disclosure, subsequent use of disclosed documents, orders for disclosure against persons not a party, and others).

PART II – OTHER EVIDENCE

10.11   EXPERT EVIDENCE

Although experts' reports are privileged, the rules requiring exchange of expert evidence (see Legal Practice Guide, **Civil Litigation**) mean that the expert evidence which will be used at the trial must eventually be revealed to the other party. If the report is only partly favourable, but the expert will be giving evidence at the trial, the whole report must be revealed and not just the favourable parts. This rule cannot be avoided by the device of sending a favourable report accompanied by a letter setting out the possible weaknesses in the client's case. The letter is part of the report and if the report is revealed the letter must be as well.

Under r 35.10, an expert's report 'must state the substance of all material instructions, whether written or oral, on the basis of which the report was written'. These instructions are not privileged from inspection, although, by r 35.10(4), the court will not usually allow inspection of the instructions by the other party. One problem that may arise from this is that solicitors may be reluctant, when instructing experts, to indicate any possible weaknesses in the claimant's case. As a result, solicitors' instructions to experts may be less helpful than they could be.

A party who instructs an expert therefore has to decide, on receiving the expert's report, whether or not he will call that expert to give evidence at the trial. If so, the full report will have to be disclosed in due course. If the expert is not to be called as a witness, however, because their report is unfavourable, then their report is a privileged document and the other party will not be entitled to inspect it.

In the case of *Jackson v Marley Davenport Ltd* [2004] EWCA Civ 1225, the Court of Appeal confirmed that an earlier report made by an expert in preparation of a final report to be exchanged was privileged and therefore not available for inspection. Longmore LJ stated:

> There can be no doubt that, if an expert makes a report for the purpose of a party's legal advisers being able to give legal advice to their client, or for discussion in a conference of a party's legal advisers, such a report is the subject matter of litigation privilege at the time it is made. It has come into existence for

the purposes of litigation. It is common for drafts of expert reports to be circulated among a party's advisers before a final report is prepared for exchange with the other side. Such initial reports are privileged.

However, what is the position where a party has obtained an expert's report for use in the proceedings but then decides that he wishes to change expert?

In *Hajigeorgiou v Vasiliou* [2005] EWCA Civ 236, the defendants had a valuation carried out by Mr A before the CMC and named him at that hearing as having done so. A consent order was made permitting each party one valuer (unnamed). Subsequently the defendants repented of their reliance on Mr A and instead proposed to rely on Mr B. The claimant contended that the defendants should be refused permission to change expert, or at least that a condition should be imposed requiring the disclosure (and inspection) of Mr A's report. The Court held that because the court order simply allowed each party one valuer, and did not name Mr A, the defendant required no permission from the court to change to Mr B, and so the possibility of adding to any such permission a condition of disclosure of Mr A's report did not arise. The Court then went on to consider whether it would have had the power to impose such a condition. Dyson LJ (as he then was) stated at [29]:

> Expert shopping is undesirable and, wherever possible, the court will use its powers to prevent it. It needs to be emphasised that, if a party needs the permission of the court to rely on expert witness A in place of expert witness B, the court has the power to give permission on condition that A's report is disclosed to the other party or parties, and that such condition will usually be imposed. In imposing such a condition, the court is not abrogating or emasculating legal professional privilege; it is merely saying that, if a party seeks the court's permission to rely on a substitute expert, it will be required to waive privilege in the first expert's report as a condition of being permitted to do so.

Following on from this, in *Edwards-Tubb v JD Wetherspoon Plc* [2011] EWCA Civ 136 the Court of Appeal held that courts had the power to order a party to allow inspection of an expert's report obtained prior to the issue of proceedings (during the course of compliance with the personal injury pre-action protocol) as a condition of granting permission to use a different expert at trial.

The expert's function is not limited to providing a report and giving evidence. When another party's expert report is received, the solicitor will discuss that report with the expert they have instructed. The expert will give advice on the flaws in the other report, its effect, and the questions which need to be asked in cross-examination to show the weaknesses in the report. Such discussions may be interpreted as being part of the instructions to the expert. This might mean that they would have to be disclosed to the court under r 35.10 of CPR 1998. As a result, a solicitor may instruct two teams of experts. The first (expert advisers) will become part of the case management team. They will not be used at the trial, and therefore records of any discussions with them will not have to be revealed to the court. When they have completed their function, a second team of experts (expert witnesses) will be instructed. Their instructions will be disclosed to the court.

It is always worth considering trying to save costs at the trial by arranging a without prejudice meeting of both parties' experts under r 35.12 to narrow the area of disagreement between them.

The Guidance for the Instruction of Experts in Civil Claims (2014) applies to any steps taken for the purpose of civil proceedings by experts or those who instruct them. The introduction to the guidance sets out its objectives:

> 1.   The purpose of this guidance is to assist litigants, those instructing experts and experts to understand best practice in complying with Part 35 of the Civil Procedure Rules (CPR) and court orders. Experts and those who instruct them should ensure they are familiar with CPR 35 and the Practice Direction (PD35). This guidance replaces the Protocol for the instruction of experts in civil claims (2005, amended 2009).
>
> 2.   Those instructing experts, and the experts, must also have regard to the objectives underpinning the Pre-Action Protocols to:–

a.   encourage the exchange of early and full information about the expert issues involved in the prospective claim;

b.   enable the parties to avoid or reduce the scope of the litigation by agreeing the whole or part of an expert issue before proceedings are started; and

c.   support the efficient management of proceedings where litigation cannot be avoided.

3.   Additionally, experts and those instructing them should be aware that some cases will be governed by the specific pre-action protocols and some may be 'specialist proceedings' (CPR 49) where specific rules may apply.

The Guidance runs to 91 paragraphs and is essential reading for experts and those who instruct them.

10.11.1   Expert immunity

Until recently, experts who gave evidence in court had immunity from being sued for professional negligence by the party instructing them. The reasoning behind this was to ensure that experts, whose primary duty is to the court, were not reluctant to provide evidence which might be contrary to the interests of their instructing party.

Similar arguments had been used in the past to justify immunity from suit for advocates, but that immunity had been swept away by *Arthur J S Hall v Simons* [2002] 1 AC 615, HL.

In *Jones v Kaney* [2011] UKSC 13 the Supreme Court decided that the time had come to treat experts in the same way and abolish their immunity. Lord Philips stated (at para 56):

> An expert will be well aware of his duty to the court and that if he frankly accepts that he has changed his view it will be apparent that he is performing that duty. I do not see why he should be concerned that this will result in his being sued for breach of duty. It is paradoxical to postulate that in order to persuade an expert to perform the duty that he has undertaken to his client it is necessary to give him immunity from liability for breach of that duty.

10.11.2   Human rights

The case of *Daniels v Walker (Practice Note)* [2000] 1 WLR 1382, provided an interesting insight into how the courts will treat arguments under the Human Rights Act 1998 in relation to the provisions of CPR 1998. The case concerned the use of a single joint expert. The defendant disagreed with the joint expert's report and wanted to instruct another expert. One of the defendant's arguments was that failure to allow the defendant to do this would amount to a breach of Article 6 of the European Convention on Human Rights.

Lord Woolf gave this argument short shrift and said:

> Article 6 could not possibly have any application to the issues on the present appeal. The provisions of the CPR made it clear that the obligation on the court was to deal with cases justly.

It would seem, therefore, that attempts to challenge the validity of CPR 1998 on human rights grounds will be met with the riposte that their overriding objective – to deal with cases justly – ensures compliance with the provisions of the European Convention on Human Rights.

10.12   EXCHANGE OF WITNESS STATEMENTS

The requirement that the parties exchange the evidence they intend to call at the trial is another exception to the rules on privilege. As with expert evidence, the parties only have to exchange statements of witnesses who are going to give oral evidence at the trial. If a solicitor has a statement from a witness who does not support the client's case, that statement remains privileged and need not be exchanged.

Again, as with expert evidence, the full statement must be exchanged. A solicitor must not edit out damaging comments in the course of an otherwise favourable statement. They cannot omit something with a view to catching the other party by surprise at the trial. By r 32.10 of CPR 1998, a party will need the permission of the court to call evidence which has not previously been exchanged. The court is unlikely to grant leave if the omission was deliberate. In cases of accidental omission, leave to use the evidence might be granted, but the court would almost certainly grant the other side an adjournment to enable him to consider the new material. It will usually order the party in default to pay the costs wasted by their breach of CPR 1998.

Full details of the rules on exchange of witness statements are set out in the Legal Practice Guide, *Civil Litigation*.

Exchange of witness statements provides the best opportunity to review the case with the client. The parties now know as much about the case as they are going to know (subject to the possible use of requests for further information). It is now possible to make a sensible assessment of the likely outcome of the trial. There will be some cases where it is obvious that the conflict of evidence is so great that the result will depend on the impression that the judge forms of the witnesses. In most cases, however, if the client is litigating as a matter of business rather than as a matter of principle, it will be clear by now whether the case should be settled and, if so, on what terms.

If the matter does come to trial, the exchanged statements will usually stand as the evidence-in-chief of the witness under r 32.5(2) so that the witnesses have to attend only for cross-examination and re-examination.

10.13 FURTHER INFORMATION

In some cases, the exchange of witness statements will still leave the result of the case in doubt. In such cases, one or both of the parties may want to request further information under Part 18 of CPR 1998 in an attempt to clarify their position. Such requests will be granted, however, only if they are likely to help achieve the overriding objective to deal with cases justly (see **Chapter 1**).

10.14 NOTICES TO ADMIT

10.14.1 Notices to admit facts

Notices to admit facts should be used wherever possible to save time and costs at the trial. Service of a notice to admit facts pressurises the other party to admit facts he knows can be proved against him, because if he does not admit those facts, he will have to pay the costs of proving those facts irrespective of the result of the case.

10.14.2 Notices to admit documents

Under r 32.19:

> A party shall be deemed to admit the authenticity of a document disclosed to him under Part 31 (Disclosure and Inspection of Documents) unless he serves notice that he wishes the document to be proved at trial.

Such notices are likely to be rare.

10.15 DETENTION, PRESERVATION AND INSPECTION OF PROPERTY

The court can order that property which is the subject matter of the action shall be detained, preserved, inspected, sampled or experimented on. If a party needs such an order, he will usually seek it at a very early stage of the case, or even before commencing proceedings.

10.16 BANKERS' BOOKS

Sometimes a party needs information about the financial circumstances of his opponent (eg for enforcement or in support of a freezing injunction). The opponent's bank will have that information, but it owes its customer a duty of confidentiality and therefore cannot provide the information unless ordered to do so by a court. Under s 7 of the Bankers' Books Evidence Act 1879 the court can permit a party to inspect and copy bank records for the purposes of the action. The order may be sought without notice to the other party. The bank should be given three days' notice before it has to comply with the order so that it can challenge it if it sees fit.

The application is supported by evidence stating:

(a)   the nature of the proceedings;

(b)   why inspection is required (and that the entries are admissible evidence);

(c)   the period for which inspection is required.

A party cannot use this Act to inspect privileged material.

10.17 SUMMARY

Commercial litigation often involves large amounts of 'documentary' evidence (bearing in mind that material stored on computer is treated in the same way as any paper document). As a result, it is important for clients and lawyers to understand the rules on disclosure and inspection, together with the rules on privilege and what happens if privileged material is inadvertently disclosed.

APPEALS

LEARNING OUTCOMES

After reading this chapter you will understand:

- the rules relating to the conduct of appeals in Part 52 of CPR 1998 and the destination of appeals
- the procedure relating to appeals and the time limits for making an appeal.

11.1 INTRODUCTION

The system of appeals in the civil justice system in England and Wales was considered by Lord Woolf in his final *Access to Justice* report (HMSO, July 1996) where he defined the purpose of appeals in these terms:

> Appeals serve two purposes: the private purpose, which is to do justice in particular cases by correcting wrong decisions, and the public purpose, which is to ensure public confidence in the administration of justice by making such corrections and to clarify and develop the law and to set precedents.

Lord Woolf made various recommendations about appeals, but in the same year the Lord Chancellor commissioned a full review of civil appellate procedure under Sir Jeffrey Bowman. The 'Bowman Report' was published in September 1997 and was a more detailed version of Lord Woolf's recommendations (Lord Woolf had been a member of the review team).

The review team summarised the purpose of appeals in this way:

> There is a private and public purpose of appeals in civil cases. The private purpose is to correct an error, unfairness or wrong exercise of discretion which has led to an unjust result. The public purpose is to ensure public confidence in the administration of justice and, in appropriate cases, to:
>
> > Clarify and develop the law, practice and procedure; and
> > Help maintain the standards of first instance courts and tribunals.

The Bowman Report made 146 detailed recommendations, many of which were implemented by ss 54–59 of the Access to Justice Act 1999 and Part 52 of CPR 1998, which came into force on 2 May 2000. Guidelines as to the interpretation of the new rules were laid down by the Court of Appeal in *Tanfern Ltd v Cameron-MacDonald* [2000] 1 WLR 1311. In October 2012, the original PD 52 was replaced by PDs 52A–52E. In October 2016 the whole of Part 52 itself was updated.

11.2 PART 52

Part 52 of the CPR 1998 and the accompanying Practice Directions provide a comprehensive framework for the civil appeals system as it relates to the County Court, High Court and Court of Appeal. A crucial aspect of the system is the requirement for permission to appeal – there is generally no automatic right to appeal. By r 52.3:

(1) An appellant or respondent requires permission to appeal—

    (a) where the appeal is from a decision of a judge in the County Court or the High Court, or to the Court of Appeal from a decision of a judge in the family court, except where the appeal is against—

        (i) a committal order;

        (ii) a refusal to grant habeas corpus; or

        (iii) a secure accommodation order made under section 25 of the Children Act 1989; or

    (b) as provided by Practice Directions 52A to 52E.

    (Other enactments may provide that permission is required for particular appeals.)

(2) An application for permission to appeal may be made—

    (a) to the lower court at the hearing at which the decision to be appealed was made; or

    (b) to the appeal court in an appeal notice.

    (Rule 52.12 sets out the time limits for filing an appellant's notice at the appeal court. Rule 52.13 sets out the time limits for filing a respondent's notice at the appeal court. Any application for permission to appeal to the appeal court must be made in the appeal notice (see rules 52.12(1) and 52.13(3)).)

(3) Where the lower court refuses an application for permission to appeal—

    (a) a further application for permission may be made to the appeal court; and

    (b) the order refusing permission must specify—

        (i) the court to which any further application for permission should be made; and

        (ii) the level of judge who should hear the application.

The way in which applications for permission to appeal to the County Court and High Court are determined is set out in r 52.4:

(1) Where an application for permission to appeal is made to an appeal court other than the Court of Appeal, the appeal court will determine the application on paper without an oral hearing, except as provided for under paragraph (2).

(2) Subject to paragraph (3) and except where a rule or practice direction provides otherwise, where the appeal court, without a hearing, refuses permission to appeal, the person seeking permission may request the decision to be reconsidered at an oral hearing.

(3) Where in the appeal court a judge of the High Court, a Designated Civil Judge or a Specialist Circuit Judge refuses permission to appeal without an oral hearing and considers that the application is totally without merit, the judge may make an order that the person seeking permission may not request the decision to be reconsidered at an oral hearing.

(4) For the purposes of paragraph (3), 'Specialist Circuit Judge' means any Circuit Judge in the County Court nominated to hear cases in the Circuit Commercial, Chancery or Technology and Construction Court lists.

(5) Rule 3.3(5) (party able to apply to set aside, etc., a decision made of court's own initiative) does not apply to an order made under paragraph (3) that the person seeking permission may not request the decision to be reconsidered at an oral hearing.

(6) A request under paragraph (2) must be filed within 7 days after service of the notice that permission has been refused.

For appeals to the Court of Appeal, the provisions are set out in r 52.5:

(1) Where an application for permission to appeal is made to the Court of Appeal, the Court of Appeal will determine the application on paper without an oral hearing, except as provided for under paragraph (2).

(2) The judge considering the application on paper may direct that the application be determined at an oral hearing, and must so direct if the judge is of the opinion that the application cannot be fairly determined on paper without an oral hearing.

(3)   An oral hearing directed under paragraph (2) must be listed—

(a)   no later than 14 days from the date of the direction under that paragraph; and

(b)   before the judge who made that direction,

unless the court directs otherwise.

(4)   The Court of Appeal may, in any direction under paragraph (2)—

(a)   identify any issue or issues on which the party seeking permission should specifically focus its submissions at the oral hearing in order to assist the court to determine the application; and

(b)   direct the respondent to serve and file written submissions and to attend the oral hearing.

A request for permission to appeal should therefore generally be made orally to the court at the conclusion of the hearing at which the decision to be appealed against is made. If the request is unsuccessful, or no request is made, then the party can apply for permission from the appeal court itself. A request for permission from the appeal court should be included in the appeal notice (see **11.5**).

The appeal court will usually deal with a request for permission on paper, without a hearing. If the request is refused, the appellant may request an oral hearing. If the request is refused at the oral hearing, that is the end of the matter – there is no further appeal from this final refusal of permission to appeal by the appeal court.

For first appeals, permission to appeal will be given only where the court considers that the appeal would have a real prospect of success or there is some other compelling reason why the appeal should be heard. In *Tanfern Ltd v Cameron-MacDonald* [2000] 1 WLR 1311, Brooke LJ stated that 'real prospect of success' has the same meaning as the test applied in applications for summary judgment. There has to be a realistic, as opposed to a fanciful, prospect of success.

The other ground for granting permission to appeal – there is some other compelling reason why the appeal should be heard – could apply, for example, if there is an important question of law or general policy at stake which requires consideration by the Court of Appeal. This might justify a 'leapfrog appeal' (see **11.3.1**).

11.3   DESTINATION OF APPEALS

Paragraph 3.5 of PD 52A sets out to which court or judge an appeal is to be made. This may be summarised as follows:

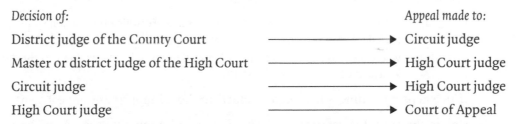

Decision of:	Appeal made to:
District judge of the County Court	Circuit judge
Master or district judge of the High Court	High Court judge
Circuit judge	High Court judge
High Court judge	Court of Appeal

The appeal therefore will normally lie to the 'next court up'. However, this is subject to certain qualifications designed to restrict the possibility of multiple appeals (as to which see **11.3.1**).

11.3.1   'Leapfrog appeals'

Where an appeal is to be heard by a circuit judge or High Court judge, r 52.23 gives the court power to order the appeal to be transferred to the Court of Appeal if it would raise an important point of principle or practice, or there is some other compelling reason for the Court of Appeal to hear it.

In *Clark (Inspector of Taxes) v Perks* [2000] 4 All ER 1, the Court of Appeal suggested that the lower court's power to transfer an appeal to the Court of Appeal should be used sparingly. If the lower court is in doubt as to what to do, it can refer the case to the Master of the Rolls for consideration, as he has an identical power to transfer under s 57 of the Access to Justice Act 1999. However, s 57 does not permit the 'leapfrogging' of an application for permission to appeal, as opposed to an appeal in respect of which permission has been granted; see *In the Matter of Claims Direct Test Cases* [2002] EWCA Civ 428.

11.4   APPEALS FROM THE APPELLATE COURT

Generally, the decision of the appellate court will be the final decision in a case. Second appeals to the Court of Appeal will be very much the exception. By r 52.7:

(1)   Permission is required from the Court of Appeal for any appeal to that court from a decision of the County Court, the family court or the High Court which was itself made on appeal, or a decision of the Upper Tribunal which was made on appeal from a decision of the First-tier Tribunal on a point of law where the Upper Tribunal has refused permission to appeal to the Court of Appeal.

(2)   The Court of Appeal will not give permission unless it considers that—

(a)   the appeal would—

(i)   have a real prospect of success; and

(ii)   raise an important point of principle or practice; or

(b)   there is some other compelling reason for the Court of Appeal to hear it.

This rule effectively reproduces s 55 of the Access to Justice Act 1999. The reasoning behind this restriction on the rights of parties to go beyond a first appeal had been set out in the Bowman Report. Judges of the quality of Lords Justices of Appeal were a scarce and valuable resource, and it was important that they were used effectively and only on work which was appropriate to them.

One reason behind this provision was undoubtedly to deter those litigants who refuse to accept a court's decision and want to appeal as far as they can, or could, go. It should be noted, however, that the prohibition on appeals from the appellate court without permission from the Court of Appeal applies equally to a party who was successful at first instance but then lost the appeal.

11.5   PROCEDURE

If permission to appeal is obtained from the lower court, the appellant must file the appropriate notice in Form N161 (a copy appears at **Appendix 17** to this book) at the appeal court. The time for doing so is within either:

(a)   such period as may be directed by the lower court (which may be longer or shorter than the period referred to in sub-paragraph (b)); or

(b)   where the lower court made no such direction, 21 days after the date of the decision that the appellant wishes to appeal. (r 52.12)

If an extension of time is needed, the appellant should apply to the appeal court.

Unless the appeal court orders otherwise, the notice must be served on the respondent as soon as practicable, but in any event not later than seven days after it is filed.

If permission to appeal was refused by the lower court, or no application for permission was made, an application for permission from the appellate court must be made in section 4 of Form N161.

The grounds of appeal should be set out in section 6 of Form N161. These should set out clearly why the appellant says:

(a)   that the decision of the lower court is wrong; or

(b) that the decision of the lower court is unjust because of a serious procedural or other irregularity,

as these are the grounds upon which the appeal court can allow the appeal (r 52.21(3)).

Detailed provisions about the documents to be lodged with the court prior to the hearing of the appeal can be found in Section VI of PD 52B for appeals in the County Court and High Court, and in Section VII of PD 52C for appeals to the Court of Appeal.

11.5.1 Respondent's notice (r 52.13)

If the respondent simply wishes the appellate court to uphold the judgment of the lower court, there is no obligation to file a respondent's notice.

However, if the respondent wants to ask the appeal court to uphold the order of the lower court for reasons different from or additional to those originally given by the lower court (as will often be the case), he must file a respondent's notice in Form N162. The respondent must also do so if he himself wishes to seek permission to appeal from the appeal court (a cross-appeal).

The time limit for the respondent to file the notice is, in essence, 14 days after it has become clear that the appeal will proceed. It is therefore 14 days after:

(a) the date the respondent is served with the appellant's notice where—

    (i) permission to appeal was given by the lower court; or

    (ii) permission is not required;

(b) the date the respondent is served with notification that the appeal court has given the appellant permission to appeal; or

(c) the date the respondent is served with notification that the application for permission to appeal and the appeal itself are to be heard together.

The respondent's notice must be served on the appellant as soon as practicable but in any event within seven days of being filed.

11.5.2 Hearing of the appeal

The general rule is that every appeal will be limited to a review of the decision of the lower court, rather than a complete rehearing (CPR 1998, r 52.21).

Unless it orders otherwise, the appeal court will not hear oral evidence or evidence which was not before the lower court. An example of a situation where the court did decide to allow the appellant to adduce new evidence was *Gillingham v Gillingham* [2001] 1 All ER 52, where a letter containing crucial evidence was allowed to be used although it had not been available at the original hearing.

The appeal court will allow an appeal only if it concludes that the decision of the lower court was wrong or unjust because of a serious procedural or other irregularity in the proceedings in the lower court.

11.6 SUMMARY

There is no automatic right of appeal in civil cases – permission to appeal is always required.

Permission can be obtained either from the court which made the decision to be appealed, or from the court which will hear the appeal.

The procedure and time limits for appeals are set out in CPR 1998, Part 52.

CHAPTER 12

SETTLEMENT AND ALTERNATIVES TO LITIGATION

LEARNING OUTCOMES

After reading this chapter you will understand:

- how to use Part 36 of CPR 1998
- the role of ADR in commercial dispute resolution.

12.1 INTRODUCTION

The vast majority of commercial disputes are resolved not by a judge at trial but by the parties reaching a settlement in one form or another. Many disputes are settled without court proceedings being issued; and even where they are issued, most cases will settle before trial. The traditional way of settling disputes has been by direct negotiation between the parties' solicitors. Increasingly, however, disputes are now settled by use of one of the methods of alternative dispute resolution (ADR), most commonly mediation.

In this chapter we shall consider the ways in which parties may settle, together with the use of the Civil Procedure Rules to aid settlement, before going on to consider in the next two chapters two particular alternatives to litigation, namely, arbitration and mediation.

12.2 NEGOTIATED SETTLEMENTS

12.2.1 Disputes settled before the issue of proceedings

Many cases settle in this way. The Civil Procedure Rules themselves, particularly through the Practice Direction on Pre-action Conduct and the pre-action protocols, are designed to encourage settlement of cases without the need for proceedings to be issued. Sanctions, normally in the form of costs, can be inflicted on a party who is deemed by the court to have behaved unreasonably in refusing to settle a case.

Where a dispute is settled without the need for proceedings, it is imperative that the terms of settlement are clearly recorded in writing. Any such agreement should also make it clear whether or not the terms of settlement include the payment of costs and/or interest. If one party does agree to pay the other party's costs then either a figure can be agreed as a term of the settlement, or, provided the liability for costs is clearly set out in the agreement, the party entitled to the costs can apply to the court under Part 8 of CPR 1998 for the court to assess those costs. If a party fails to comply with the terms of a settlement (for example by not paying an agreed figure for compensation) then the other party could simply issue proceedings and, if the defaulting party attempts to defend those proceedings, make an application for summary judgment under Part 24 of CPR 1998 on the basis that the defaulting party has no defence with a real prospect of success. This should be fairly straightforward, provided the terms of agreement are clearly expressed.

12.2.2 Settlement after the issue of proceedings

Where a case is settled after the issue of proceedings then the usual way to record that settlement is either by way of a consent order or a *Tomlin* order, whereby the proceedings are stayed on the agreed terms. Again, any agreement reached on the issue of costs and/or interest should be set out as part of the order. See LPC Guide, *Civil Litigation* at **13.3.2**.

12.3   THE USE OF PART 36

A good understanding of Part 36 of CPR 1998 and how to use it effectively in litigation is a key skill for any dispute resolution lawyer. Where proceedings are issued, at some stage in virtually every case it is to be expected that one or other of the parties may make a Part 36 offer. Whilst under r 44.3 of CPR 1998 the court can take into account any admissible offer to settle proceedings in deciding the issue of costs, the advantage of making an offer under Part 36 is that the cost consequences are, to a certain extent, more certain.

12.3.1 Costs orders and the impact of Part 36

Traditionally, a solicitor would advise a client at the start of the case that at the end of the case the loser will usually be ordered to pay the winner's reasonable costs – albeit that they would not necessarily be the same as the costs payable by the client to the solicitor under the terms of the retainer. This is embodied in r 44.2(2)(a) of CPR 1998. However, in complex cases where there are several issues to decide, it may be more difficult to ascertain exactly who is the 'winner' in relation to each of the issues before the court.

An example of this came in the case of *Multiplex Constructions (UK) Ltd v Cleveland Bridge UK Ltd* [2008] EWHC 2280 (TCC) (arising out of the construction of Wembley Stadium), to be of general application. The *Multiplex* case was a complex construction dispute involving many issues between the parties. Both parties succeeded and failed on some issues. The end result was that the defendant had to pay the claimant £6.154 million.

The court then had to determine what was the appropriate order for costs. After reviewing the authorities, Mr Justice Jackson derived the following eight principles:

(i)   In commercial litigation where each party has claims and asserts that a balance is owing in its own favour, the party which ends up receiving payment should generally be characterised as the overall winner of the entire action.

(ii)   In considering how to exercise its discretion the court should take as its starting point the general rule that the successful party is entitled to an order for costs.

(iii)   The judge must then consider what departures are required from that starting point, having regard to all the circumstances of the case.

(iv)   Where the circumstances of the case require an issue-based costs order, that is what the judge should make. However, the judge should hesitate before doing so, because of the practical difficulties which this causes and because of the steer given by rule 44.2(7).

(v)   In many cases the judge can and should reflect the relative success of the parties on different issues by making a proportionate costs order.

(vi)   In considering the circumstances of the case the judge will have regard not only to part 36 offers made but also to each party's approach to negotiations (insofar as admissible) and general conduct of the litigation.

(vii)   If (a) one party makes an order offer under part 36 or an admissible offer within rule 44.2(4)(c) which is nearly but not quite sufficient, and (b) the other party rejects that offer outright without any attempt to negotiate, then it might be appropriate to penalise the second party in costs.

(viii)   In assessing a proportionate costs order the judge should consider what costs are referable to each issue and what costs are common to several issues. It will often be reasonable for the overall winner to recover not only the costs specific to the issues which he has won but also the common costs.

In the *Multiplex* case itself, the application of these principles to the facts of the case resulted in the defendant being ordered to pay 20% of the claimant's costs.

As part of the Jackson reforms introduced in April 2013, CPR 1998, r 36.14 was amended to increase the sanctions imposed on a defendant who fails to accept a claimant's Part 36 offer and where judgment thereafter against the defendant is at least as advantageous to the claimant as the proposals contained in that Part 36 offer. In this situation, in addition to the costs and interest sanctions which were already in place, the defendant will normally have to pay an additional amount of 10% of the damages awarded in the case of damages up to £500,000, and 5% of the damages above that figure, up to a maximum additional amount of £75,000. The new sanction only applies to Part 36 offers made on or after 1 April 2013.

This new provision is clearly intended to encourage defendants to think carefully before rejecting a reasonable Part 36 offer from the claimant.

12.4   ALTERNATIVES TO LITIGATION

As briefly considered in **Chapter 1**, there is a whole range of ADR options available today, and it is the professional duty of a solicitor to be able to advise a client appropriately on that range of options. Failure to do so may amount to a breach of Principle 7 of the SRA Code of Conduct 2019 – to act in the best interests of your client.

A convenient method of categorising the various ADR options is as determinative methods (ie those which result in a binding decision) and non-determinative methods (ie evaluative processes which result in a voluntary settlement agreement). Determinative ADR processes include the following:

(a)   *Arbitration*. This is the most important of the determinative processes and has been in existence for many years. It is considered in detail in **Chapter 13**.

(b)   *Expert determination*. In this process the parties agree to appoint an expert who will make a binding decision. Obviously this is an appropriate process only if the parties are prepared to agree to accept the expert's decision. It is perhaps most appropriate in cases where, for example, a valuation is required or a decision is needed on a specific technical point.

(c)   *Med-Arb*. This is a two-stage process whereby initially the parties agree to go to mediation, but if that fails to result in a settlement, an arbitration will follow. That of course will produce a binding result.

(d)   *Final offer arbitration*. In this form of ADR, the parties agree to appoint a neutral third party to whom they submit their offers of settlement. That third party then chooses one of the settlement offers and the parties are bound by that.

(e)   *Statutory adjudication*. This procedure is available under the Housing Grants, Construction and Regeneration Act 1996 to resolve commercial construction disputes and is intended to be quicker and cheaper than arbitration. Parties can have a binding decision within around 35 days. The adjudicator determines disputes that arise in the course of a construction project so that it is not delayed by a lengthy disagreement and/or litigation or arbitration. The parties may retain the right to litigate the dispute on completion of the project if they so choose. Subject to this, the adjudicator's decision is binding. However, it can be enforced only by issuing proceedings and applying for a summary judgment (*Macob Civil Engineering Limited v Morrison Construction Limited* (1999) 3 EGLR 7, QBD). Such proceedings should be issued in the TCC.

Non-determinative forms of ADR give the parties more control over the outcome. They include:

(a)   *Negotiation between the parties.* We have already considered this at **12.2** above.

(b)   *Mediation.* This is basically an assisted negotiation between the parties facilitated by a neutral third party. Mediation is considered in detail in **Chapter 14**.

(c)   *Conciliation.* This is a more proactive version of mediation, with the third party actively encouraging the parties to settle the dispute by making suggestions regarding the parties' settlement options.

(d)   *Mini-trial.* This normally comprises a tribunal of three people: a neutral chair and a senior representative from each party. Each side makes a presentation to the tribunal which then retires to discuss the dispute. Unless the parties request it, the chair does not make a binding determination.

(e)   *Expert appraisal.* Unlike expert determination, this is a process whereby the expert is asked for their opinion but it is not binding on the parties.

(f)   *Early neutral evaluation.* This is a procedure available in the Commercial Court and the TCC whereby a judge will offer their view of the merits of each party's case. If settlement is not reached then the judge will have no further involvement in the action.

12.5   CHOOSING ADR

A solicitor should discuss with the client the possible uses of ADR whenever a dispute arises in a commercial matter. If the client is willing (or has already agreed) to use ADR, it should be used unless it is obviously inappropriate, for example because an injunction is required or the other party cannot be trusted to comply with an award or to cooperate in the process. In *Dunnett v Railtrack plc* [2002] 2 All ER 850 the Court of Appeal refused to make a costs order against an unsuccessful appellant because the respondent had refused to consider the use of arbitration or mediation to settle the dispute, despite the court, when granting permission to appeal, making a strong suggestion to that effect. There is no point, however, in proceeding with ADR if it looks like failing. In such cases, at the first sign of non-cooperation or lack of trust (eg where the opponent will not help in the selection of the neutral), litigation or arbitration should be used. In *Hurst v Leeming* [2003] 1 Lloyd's Rep 379, the court held that a barrister was justified in refusing to proceed to mediation in a professional negligence case where the attitude and character of the claimant made it very unlikely that mediation would succeed. This does not necessarily mean abandoning ADR. It may be appropriate to continue with ADR in conjunction with litigation, using the latter as a spur to cooperation with the former.

In *Halsey v Milton Keynes General NHS Trust* [2004] EWCA Civ 576 the Court of Appeal laid down guidelines as to the factors which may be relevant to the question of whether a party has unreasonably refused ADR, which may lead the court to depart from the general rule on costs in r 44.3 (that the unsuccessful party will be ordered to pay the costs of the successful party). The Court stated that these factors include, but are not limited to, the following:

(a)   the nature of the dispute;

(b)   the merits of the case;

(c)   the extent to which other settlement methods have been attempted;

(d)   whether the costs of the ADR would be disproportionately high;

(e)   whether any delay in setting up and attending the ADR would have been prejudicial;

(f)   whether the ADR had a reasonable prospect of success.

Lord Justice Dyson, who gave the judgment in *Halsey*, then went on to expand on those guidelines as follows:

17.   (a) **The nature of the dispute.** Even the most ardent supporters of ADR acknowledge that the subject-matter of some disputes renders them intrinsically unsuitable for ADR. The Commercial Court Working Party on ADR stated in 1999:

> 'The Working Party believes that there are many cases within the range of Commercial Court work which do not lend themselves to ADR procedures. The most obvious kind is where the parties wish the court to determine issues of law or construction which may be essential to the future trading relations of the parties, as under an on-going long term contract, or where the issues are generally important for those participating in a particular trade or market. There may also be issues which involve allegations of fraud or other commercially disreputable conduct against an individual or group which most probably could not be successfully mediated.'

Other examples falling within this category are cases where a party wants the court to resolve a point of law which arises from time to time, and it is considered that a binding precedent would be useful; or cases where injunctive or other relief is essential to protect the position of a party. But in our view, most cases are not by their very nature unsuitable for ADR.

18.   (b) **The merits of the case.** The fact that a party reasonably believes that he has a strong case is relevant to the question whether he has acted reasonably in refusing ADR. If the position were otherwise, there would be considerable scope for a claimant to use the threat of costs sanctions to extract a settlement from the defendant even where the claim is without merit. Courts should be particularly astute to this danger. Large organisations, especially public bodies, are vulnerable to pressure from claimants who, having weak cases, invite mediation as a tactical ploy. They calculate that such a defendant may at least make a nuisance-value offer to buy off the cost of a mediation and the risk of being penalised in costs for refusing a mediation even if ultimately successful.

19.   Some cases are clear-cut. A good example is where a party would have succeeded in an application for summary judgment pursuant to CPR 24.2, but for some reason he did not make such an application. Other cases are more border-line. In truly border-line cases, the fact that a party refused to agree to ADR because he thought that he would win should be given little or no weight by the court when considering whether the refusal to agree to ADR was reasonable. Border-line cases are likely to be suitable for ADR unless there are significant countervailing factors which tip the scales the other way. In Hurst, Lightman J said:

> 'The fact that a party believes that he has a watertight case again is no justification for refusing mediation. That is the frame of mind of so many litigants.'

In our judgment, this statement should be qualified. The fact that a party unreasonably believes that his case is watertight is no justification for refusing mediation. But the fact that a party reasonably believes that he has a watertight case may well be sufficient justification for a refusal to mediate.

20.   (c) **Other settlement methods have been attempted.** The fact that settlement offers have already been made, but rejected, is a relevant factor. It may show that one party is making efforts to settle, and that the other party has unrealistic views of the merits of the case. But it is also right to point out that mediation often succeeds where previous attempts to settle have failed. Although the fact that settlement offers have already been made is potentially relevant to the question whether a refusal to mediate is unreasonable, on analysis it is in truth no more than an aspect of factor (f).

21.   (d) **The costs of mediation would be disproportionately high.** This is a factor of particular importance where, on a realistic assessment, the sums at stake in the litigation are comparatively small. A mediation can sometimes be at least as expensive as a day in court. The parties will often have legal representation before the mediator, and the mediator's fees will usually be borne equally by the parties regardless of the outcome (although the costs of a mediation may be the subject of a costs order by the court after a trial). Since the prospects of a successful mediation cannot be predicted with confidence (see further para 27 below), the possibility of the ultimately successful party being required to incur the costs of an abortive mediation is a relevant factor that may be taken into account in deciding whether the successful party acted unreasonably in refusing to agree to ADR.

22.   **(e) Delay.** If mediation is suggested late in the day, acceptance of it may have the effect of delaying the trial of the action. This is a factor which it may be relevant to take into account in deciding whether a refusal to agree to ADR was unreasonable.

23.   **(f) Whether the mediation had a reasonable prospect of success.** In *Hurst*, Lightman J said that he considered that the 'critical factor' in that case was whether 'objectively viewed' a mediation had any real prospect of success. He continued (p 381):

> 'If mediation can have no real prospect of success, a party may, with impunity, refuse to proceed to mediation on this ground. But refusal is a high risk course to take, for if the Court finds that there was a real prospect, the party refusing to proceed to mediation may, as I have said, be severely penalized. Further, the hurdle in the way of a party refusing to proceed to mediation on this ground is high, for in making this objective assessment of the prospects of mediation, the starting point must surely be the fact that the mediation process itself can and often does bring about a more sensible and more conciliatory attitude on the part of the parties than might otherwise be expected to prevail before the mediation, and may produce a recognition of the strengths and weaknesses by each party of his own case and of that of his opponent, and a willingness to accept the give and take essential to a successful mediation. What appears to be incapable of mediation before the mediation process begins often proves capable of satisfactory resolution later.'

24.   Consistently with the view expressed in this passage, Lightman J said that on the facts of that case he was persuaded that 'quite exceptionally' the successful party was justified in taking the view that mediation was not appropriate because it had no realistic prospects of success.

25.   In our view, the question whether the mediation had a reasonable prospect of success will often be relevant to the reasonableness of A's refusal to accept B's invitation to agree to it. But it is not necessarily determinative of the fundamental question, which is whether the successful party acted unreasonably in refusing to agree to mediation. This can be illustrated by a consideration of two cases. In a situation where B has adopted a position of intransigence, A may reasonably take the view that a mediation has no reasonable prospect of success because B is most unlikely to accept a reasonable compromise. That would be a proper basis for concluding that a mediation would have no reasonable prospect of success, and that for this reason A's refusal to mediate was reasonable.

26.   On the other hand, if A has been unreasonably obdurate, the court might well decide, on that account, that a mediation would have had no reasonable prospect of success. But obviously this would not be a proper reason for concluding that A's refusal to mediate was reasonable. A successful party cannot rely on his own unreasonableness in such circumstances. We do not, therefore, accept that, as suggested by Lightman J, it is appropriate for the court to confine itself to a consideration of whether, viewed objectively, a mediation would have had a reasonable prospect of success. That is an unduly narrow approach: it focuses on the nature of the dispute, and leaves out of account the parties' willingness to compromise and the reasonableness of their attitudes.

27.   Nor should it be overlooked that the potential success of a mediation may not only depend on the willingness of the parties to compromise. Some disputes are inherently more intractable than others. Some mediators are more skilled than others. It may therefore, sometimes be difficult for the court to decide whether the mediation would have had a reasonable prospect of success.

28.   The burden should not be on the refusing party to satisfy the court that mediation had no reasonable prospect of success. As we have already stated, the fundamental question is whether it has been shown by the unsuccessful party that the successful party unreasonably refused to agree to mediation. The question whether there was a reasonable prospect that a mediation would have been successful is but one of a number of potentially relevant factors which may need to be considered in determining the answer to that fundamental question. Since the burden of proving an unreasonable refusal is on the unsuccessful party, we see no reason why the burden of proof should lie on the successful party to show that mediation did not have any reasonable prospect of success. In most cases it would not be possible for the successful party to prove that a mediation had no reasonable prospect of success. In our judgment, it would not be right to stigmatise as unreasonable a refusal by the successful party to agree to a mediation unless he showed that a mediation had no reasonable prospect of success. That would be to tip

the scales too heavily against the right of a successful party to refuse a mediation and insist on an adjudication of the dispute by the court. It seems to us that a fairer balance is struck if the burden is placed on the unsuccessful party to show that there was a reasonable prospect that mediation would have been successful. This is not an unduly onerous burden to discharge: he does not have to prove that a mediation would in fact have succeeded. It is significantly easier for the unsuccessful party to prove that there was a reasonable prospect that a mediation would have succeeded than for the successful party to prove the contrary.

The Court of Appeal reaffirmed these principles in *Burchell v Bullard* [2005] EWCA Civ 358. Ward LJ stated:

The court [in *Halsey*] has given its stamp of approval to mediation and it is now the legal profession which must become fully aware of and acknowledge its value. The profession can no longer with impunity shrug aside reasonable requests to mediate. The parties cannot ignore a proper request to mediate simply because it was made before the claim was issued.

This final point is reinforced by para 8 of the Practice Direction on Pre-action Conduct which states that whilst ADR is not compulsory, the parties should consider whether some form of ADR procedure might enable them to settle the matter without starting proceedings.

However, in *Daniels v The Commissioner of Police for the Metropolis* [2005] EWCA Civ 1312, the Court of Appeal made it clear that it was entirely reasonable for a defendant, especially a public body such as the police, to refuse to use ADR in circumstances where it wished to contest what it considered to be an unfounded claim. The successful defendants were entitled to their costs.

What is the position where one party simply fails to respond to a proposal to use ADR? This point has recently come before the court in *PGF II SA v OMFS Company 1 Ltd* [2013] EWCA Civ 1288. The case concerned a claim for the alleged breach of a tenant's repairing covenants in a commercial lease. The claimant's claim was originally for more than £1.9 million. The defendant denied liability entirely. At or shortly before the commencement of proceedings the claimant made a Part 36 offer of £1.125 million.

Several months later, on 11 April 2011, there was an exchange of e-mail correspondence. The claimant made a second Part 36 offer of £1.25 million plus interest. In a separate letter the claimant invited the defendant to take part in mediation, proposing various dates. The letter concluded by seeking the defendant's agreement to mediate and/or an explanation of any refusal. On the same day the defendant sent the claimant a Part 36 offer of £700,000 inclusive of interest. So the gap between the parties was now £550,000.

Neither Part 36 offer was accepted. The claimant's invitation to mediate received no response from the defendant of any kind. On 19 July the claimant sent a further invitation to the defendant to mediate: 'Please confirm whether your client is willing to attend a mediation and, if so, provide us with dates of availability. If you are not prepared to attend a mediation, please could you let us know why.' A chasing letter was sent on 1 August. There was still no response.

On 20 December the claimant made a further Part 36 offer of £1.05 million plus interest, narrowing the gap to £350,000 plus interest.

The trial was to start on 11 January 2012. In its skeleton argument, exchanged on 10 January, the defendant took up for the first time the point that the air conditioning system in respect of which about £250,000 was claimed for dilapidations, did not form part of the demise. The defendant gave notice of its intention to seek leave to amend its defence to that effect the next day.

The claimant responded the same day by accepting the defendant's Part 36 offer, thereby settling the proceedings save as to costs. The ordinary consequence of the acceptance would have been a split costs order whereby the defendant would pay the claimant's costs up to 2

May 2011 and the claimant would pay the defendant's costs from that date until 10 January (CPR 1998, r 36.10(4) and (5)). At the hearing the next day the claimant argued that the usual costs order should not be made for two reasons: (i) the late amendment; and (ii) the unreasonable refusal to mediate (on the basis that the lack of any response equated to a refusal). The late amendment point failed, but the mediation point succeeded to the extent that the judge deprived the defendant of its costs from 2 May, although he did not agree with the claimant's request that the defendant pay its costs from that date. So in effect the court ordered each side to pay its own costs from 2 May 2011. The amount involved was about £250,000 for each side.

The defendant appealed and the claimant cross-appealed. Both appeals were dismissed. The defendant's arguments below had been based on three grounds:

(1)   It denied that its silence amounted to a refusal.

(2)   It denied that any deemed refusal was unreasonable.

(3)   It submitted that, since the expenditure of £250,000 odd by each side during the relevant period was attributable to the claimant's failure to accept a reasonable Part 36 offer until the day before trial, no departure from the Part 36 costs consequences should be ordered.

In his judgment in the Court of Appeal, Briggs LJ reviewed the law established in *Halsey* and the interaction of Part 36 and ADR. He referred to the focus in the Jackson Report on proportionality and its relevance to the use of ADR (at [26] and [27]):

> 26.   Secondly, the intense focus in Jackson LJ's report into civil litigation costs upon achieving proportionality between the cost of litigation and the value of that which is at stake led, as I have described, to his clear endorsement of ADR as a process which is still insufficiently understood and still under-used.

> 27.   Thirdly, the constraints which now affect the provision of state resources for the conduct of civil litigation (and which appear likely to do so for the foreseeable future) call for an ever-increasing focus upon means of ensuring that court time, both for trial and for case management, is proportionately directed towards those disputes which really need it, with an ever-increasing responsibility thrown upon the parties to civil litigation to engage in ADR, wherever that offers a reasonable prospect of producing a just settlement at proportionate cost. Just as it risks a waste of the court's resources to have to try a case which could have been justly settled, earlier and at a fraction of the cost by ADR, so it is a waste of its resources to have to manage the parties towards ADR by robust encouragement, where they could and should have engaged with each other in considering its suitability, without the need for the court's active intervention.

Briggs LJ agreed with the trial judge that silence amounted to a refusal and that the refusal was unreasonable. He was not persuaded by the defendant's counsel's argument that 'this was a hard-nosed commercial dispute about money between parties with no continuing relationship, and therefore not susceptible to the ability of a mediator to devise solutions beyond the capacity of the court to order'. He had some sympathy with the defendant's submission that the trial judge had not exercised his discretion properly in departing from the usual costs order under Part 36 in the way he did. He said, however, that whilst he would have exercised his discretion slightly differently (in that he would not have deprived the defendant of all of its costs), the way in which the trial judge had exercised his discretion was within the range of proper responses and therefore he would not interfere with the decision.

At the conclusion of his judgment (at [56]), Briggs LJ made some general remarks about ADR which are of significant importance:

> Finally, as is recognised by the weight placed on the judge's decision in the passage in the ADR Handbook to which I have referred, this case sends out an important message to civil litigants, requiring them to engage with a serious invitation to participate in ADR, even if they have reasons which might justify a refusal, or the undertaking of some other form of ADR, or ADR at some other time in the litigation. To allow the present appeal would, as it seems to me, blunt that message. The

court's task in encouraging the more proportionate conduct of civil litigation is so important in current economic circumstances that it is appropriate to emphasise that message by a sanction which, even if a little more vigorous than I would have preferred, nonetheless operates *pour encourager les autres*.

The clear message from this case is that the Jackson reforms have emphasised the crucial role of ADR in our system of litigation and that parties ignore it at their peril.

12.6 THE FUTURE OF ADR

Alternative dispute resolution is becoming increasingly popular. The clear message from cases such as *Halsey* and *Burchell* is that an unreasonable refusal to use mediation, or some other suitable method of ADR, is likely to lead to costs penalties. The use of 'ADR orders' by the courts to encourage this process is likely to increase. There is also a current draft EU directive on civil and commercial matters which seeks to establish a consistent regime over mediation quality and standards in Europe, based on the assumption that ADR is here to stay. However, forcing the parties to the negotiating table may be counterproductive, particularly during the early stages of a dispute when feelings often run high. Also, assessing whether a party has acted with a lack of good faith may be difficult unless the parties or the mediator are required to divulge privileged or confidential information. It is also possible that obliging parties to engage in ADR could be challenged as a contravention of the right to a fair trial under Article 6(1) of the European Convention on Human Rights. This was pointed out by the Court of Appeal in *Halsey v Milton Keynes General NHS Trust* (see **12.5**).

The Civil Justice Council (CJC) ADR Working Group considered the future of ADR during 2016–18 and produced its final report in November 2018. It made a number of recommendations, several of which are intended to increase public awareness of the availability of ADR, including greater encouragement of the use of ADR by government and the courts. One recommendation was that the *Halsey* guidelines for the imposition of costs sanctions should be reviewed and should narrow the circumstances in which a refusal to mediate is regarded as reasonable. It did not, however, recommend that the use of some form of ADR should be compulsory in civil proceedings.

However, following on from this, in July 2021 the CJC published another report on the legality and desirability of compulsory ADR. On legality, it concluded that parties can lawfully be compelled to take part in ADR. On desirability, it identified conditions in which compulsion to participate in ADR could be a desirable and effective development. It concluded its executive summary as follows:

8. In our view, appropriate forms of compulsory ADR, where a return to the normal adjudicative process is always available, are capable of overcoming the objections voiced in the case law and elsewhere and could be introduced.

9. The rules of civil procedure in England and Wales have already developed to involve compulsory participation in ADR at a number of points. These compulsory processes are both successful and accepted.

10. Provided certain factors are borne in mind in designing the scheme, a procedural rule which requires parties to attempt ADR at a certain point or points, and/or empowers the court to make an order to that effect, is, in our opinion, compatible with Article 6 of the European Convention on Human Rights. The factors requiring consideration whenever compulsion is being considered will include:
    - the cost and time burden on the parties;
    - whether the process is particularly suitable in certain specialist areas of civil justice;
    - the importance of confidence in the ADR provider (and the role of regulation where the provider is private);
    - whether the parties engaged in the ADR need access to legal advice and whether they have it;
    - the stage(s) of proceedings at which ADR may be required; and

- whether the terms of the obligation to participate are sufficiently clear to the parties to encourage compliance and permit enforcement.

11. It is appropriate to permit sanctions for breach of a rule or order requiring participation in ADR. If ADR is no longer 'alternative' or external to civil justice, then parties can surely be compelled to participate in ADR as readily as they can be compelled to disclose documents or explain their cases. The sanction for failure to participate may be to prevent the claim or defence continuing, either by making the commencement of proceedings conditional on entering ADR, or empowering the court to strike out a claim/defence if a party fails to comply with a compulsory ADR order at a later stage in the proceedings. Any strike-out could be set aside if there was a valid reason for non-compliance.

12. This is consistent with the use of initial prompts towards settlement in an online procedure and the active role of a case officer or judge in seeking to facilitate settlement.

13. We do not make detailed proposals for reform in this paper, but make three specific observations on the form compulsory ADR might take:

    - First, where participation in a suitable and effective form of ADR occasions no expense of time or money by the parties, making it compulsory will not usually be controversial.

    - Second, we foresee that greater use of compulsory judge-led ADR processes will prove acceptable, given they are free and appear effective in the contexts in which they are already compulsory.

    - Third, compulsory mediation may be considered, provided it is sufficiently regulated and made available where appropriate in short, affordable formats.

At the moment, there are no definite proposals to amend the rules to bring these proposals into effect. The idea of compulsory ADR remains controversial within the legal profession.

12.7 FURTHER READING

S Blake, J Browne and S Sime, *The Jackson ADR Handbook* (2016).

ARBITRATION

LEARNING OUTCOMES

After reading this chapter you will understand:

- the context of commercial arbitration
- the importance of the arbitration agreement
- how to appoint the arbitrator
- how to commence the arbitration
- the usual procedural matters in an arbitration
- how to prepare for the arbitration hearing
- how to challenge any award made at the arbitration hearing
- how to enforce an arbitration award
- how to stay litigation brought despite there being a valid arbitration agreement.

13.1 INTRODUCTION

The term 'arbitration' has a number of meanings. In county courts, it is often used to refer to the informal small claims track. However, in the context of CDR, it is the formal procedure whereby one or more independent parties arbitrate a dispute. Traditionally, arbitration has been prevalent, as a means of dispute resolution, in the shipping and construction industries. Nevertheless, a lawyer may be involved in the arbitration of a wide range of disputes, from landlord and tenant, oil industry, commodities or financial markets disputes to general commercial disputes. Arbitration is considered in this broad commercial context in this chapter.

As discussed in **Chapter 1**, a dispute may be arbitrated because the original contract between the parties provides for the arbitration of any dispute. Otherwise the parties may agree to arbitrate once the dispute has arisen.

Businesspersons frequently refer their disputes to arbitration as it enables them to have those disputes resolved in private, by a person or group of people they have chosen who are experienced in the trade or business in question. Arbitration avoids a public hearing in open court by a judge who may have no special expertise about the matters in dispute, and who will, therefore, have to choose between the conflicting views of each side's expert witnesses.

Another major attraction is the international recognition and support that arbitration has achieved. Treaties such as the United Nations Convention on the Recognition and Enforcement of Foreign Arbitral Awards 1958 ('the New York Convention') ensure widespread acceptance that agreements to refer disputes to arbitration should be upheld by the courts and awards enforced, regardless of the jurisdiction in which they were made. The growth in cross-border commerce has made this increasingly important. The New York Convention has been adopted by some 145 countries. The basic premise of the Convention is to provide for a minimum international standard by which the courts of all its signatory States have to recognise and enforce awards made in another signatory State, without subjecting such an award to procedures that are more onerous than those applied to the enforcement of domestic awards.

As a result, it can be easier in practice to enforce an arbitration award in a different jurisdiction than it is to enforce a court judgment.

Arbitration also enables the parties to decide the procedure the arbitrator will follow and what their powers will be, because this is primarily governed by the terms of their agreement to arbitrate.

Arbitration agreements may be ad hoc agreements tailor-made to a particular dispute or contract. However, many other contracts contain arbitration agreements which incorporate the standard arbitration rules of an established arbitral body. Solicitors involved in arbitration will regularly come across the arbitration rules of bodies such as (among others):

(a)   Chartered Institute of Arbitrators;

(b)   London Maritime Arbitrators' Association;

(c)   Federation of Oils, Seeds and Fats Association (FOSFA);

(d)   Grain and Feed Trade Association (GAFTA);

(e)   International Chamber of Commerce (ICC);

(f)   Royal Institution of Chartered Surveyors;

(g)   Institute of Civil Engineers;

(h)   United Nations' Commission on International Trade Law (UNCITRAL);

(i)   London Court of International Arbitration;

(j)   London Bar Arbitration Scheme;

(k)   Joint Contracts Tribunal (JCT).

Some of these are trade associations or professional bodies. For example, the Royal Institution of Chartered Surveyors and the Institute of Civil Engineers provide arbitration services for construction and engineering disputes. Others are international arbitral organisations specialising in international commercial arbitration, for example ICC, based in Paris, and UNCITRAL. Often, in the case of international transactions, the parties may choose to arbitrate in a country with no connection with the dispute. This is because some countries, such as France and Switzerland, have established solid reputations in conducting arbitrations. In fact, in such countries, arbitration is an industry in itself. The rules of such international arbitral bodies are outside the scope of this book.

This book deals with arbitrations conducted in England and Wales under the Arbitration Act 1996 (AA 1996). The guiding principles behind the statute are set out in s 1:

(a)   the object of arbitration is to obtain the fair resolution of disputes by an impartial tribunal without unnecessary delay or expense;

(b)   the parties should be free to agree how their disputes are resolved, subject only to such safeguards as are necessary in the public interest;

(c)   ... the court should not intervene except as provided by [the Act].

Arbitration in England and Wales has a high reputation throughout the commercial world, both domestically and internationally. As a result, many disputes are dealt with by arbitration in this country even though neither party has any connection with this country and the contract was neither made nor performed in this country (and may not be governed by the laws of this country). Thus arbitration in England and Wales may be selected as the appropriate process for resolution of a £10,000 trade dispute between English tradesmen, as well as of a multi-million pound claim brought by a Saudi Arabian oil dealer against a Malaysian oil refiner. The latter claim may have no connection with England at all, other than the fact that England was chosen as the place of arbitration.

Generally speaking, an arbitrator has the same powers as any court. Nevertheless, in some circumstances the arbitrator will require the court's assistance. For instance, an arbitrator does not have the power to make orders such as injunctions which carry the sanction of imprisonment for non-compliance. In such cases, the parties and/or the arbitrator can seek the aid of the court under ss 42–44 of the AA 1996, so that the court can exercise its wider powers before referring the matter back to the arbitrator.

Another example is that sometimes the parties to a dispute which is being resolved by arbitration will find that the dispute turns on a point of law. Although the arbitrator may decide the point of law for themselves, this may lead to an appeal to the court on that point of law (see **13.8.3**), so it may be preferable to refer the matter to the court under s 45 for a decision on the legal point. Where court involvement is necessary, the matter will normally be dealt with in the Commercial Court. The procedure is set out in CPR 1998, Part 62 and its Practice Direction.

13.2 THE ARBITRATION AGREEMENT

13.2.1 The terms of the agreement

In *Premium Nafta Products Ltd and Others v Fili Shipping Company Ltd and Others* [2007] UKHL 40, the House of Lords reviewed the case law relating to the interpretation of arbitration clauses. The arbitration clause in the case was as follows:

41.   (a)   This charter shall be construed and the relations between the parties determined in accordance with the laws of England.

(b)   Any dispute arising under this charter shall be decided by the English courts to whose jurisdiction the parties hereby agree.

(c)   Notwithstanding the foregoing, but without prejudice to any party's right to arrest or maintain the arrest of any maritime property, either party may, by giving written notice of election to the other party, elect to have any such dispute referred ... to arbitration in London, one arbitrator to be nominated by Owners and the other by Charterers, and in case the arbitrators shall not agree to the decision of an umpire, whose decision shall be final and binding upon both parties. Arbitration shall take place in London in accordance with the London Maritime Association of Arbitrators, in accordance with the provisions of the Arbitration Act 1950, or any statutory modification or re-enactment thereof for the time being in force.

The House of Lords stated that it was time to draw a line under earlier authorities on the distinction between 'disputes arising under' and 'disputes arising out of' an agreement. The House said that its approach to the construction of the arbitration clause was governed by the principle of separability in s 7 of the AA 1996, which states:

> Unless otherwise agreed by the parties, an arbitration agreement which forms or was intended to form part of another agreement (whether or not in writing) shall not be regarded as invalid, non-existent or ineffective because that other agreement is invalid, or did not come into existence or has become ineffective, and it shall for that purpose be treated as a distinct agreement.

The House of Lords held that the construction of an arbitration clause had to start from the assumption that the parties, as rational businesspersons, were likely to have intended any dispute arising out of the relationship into which they had entered, or purported to have entered, to be decided by the same tribunal.

Therefore even if the main contract was invalid or could be rescinded, the arbitration agreement remained valid.

In this particular case, the appellants' argument was that the main agreement had been entered into as a result of bribery. However, that did not show that there was any bribery in relation to the arbitration agreement which remained valid. The arbitration agreement could only be invalidated on a ground which related directly to it.

A clause used by the Chartered Institute of Arbitrators for parties who wish to have future disputes referred to arbitration says:

> Any dispute arising out of or in connection with this contract shall be referred to and finally resolved by arbitration under the Rules of the Chartered Institute of Arbitrators, which Rules are deemed to be incorporated by reference to this clause.

This appears comprehensive enough to cover any dispute which might arise, whether it be about the existence, creation, performance or termination of the contract, or about related pre-contractual matters.

In *Enka Insaat Ve Sanayi AS v OOO Insurance Company Chubb* [2020] UKSC 38, the Supreme Court had to consider how the governing law of an arbitration agreement is to be determined when the law applicable to the contract containing it differs from the 'seat' of the arbitration. The case concerned a power plant in Russia which was severely damaged by fire. The contract contained an arbitration clause under which the seat of the arbitration was London but did not specifically state which law would apply to the arbitration. However, the law applicable to the parties' substantive contractual obligations was Russian law. The court, by a 3:2 majority, held that in this situation the arbitration agreement was governed by the law with which it was most closely connected and that would generally be the law of the seat of the arbitration – so English law in this case.

13.2.2   Incorporating the Arbitration Act 1996

The AA 1996 applies only to arbitration agreements which are in writing (s 5). However, s 5 gives a wide meaning to the term 'agreement in writing'. It covers anything which has been 'recorded by any means' (eg a tape recording) and includes:

(a)   exchanges of letters or other communications;

(b)   agreements evidenced in writing (either by the parties or by a third party acting with the authority of the parties); and

(c)   oral agreements to written terms.

By s 5(5), if the parties make written submissions during an arbitration or in court proceedings, and one party alleges that there is a non-written arbitration agreement and the other party does not deny this, those written submissions will create an arbitration agreement to which the AA 1996 can apply.

If there is an arbitration agreement, certain provisions of the AA 1996 are mandatory and will apply irrespective of any attempt by the parties to exclude the Act. These provisions are listed in Sch 1 to the AA 1996. The relevant mandatory provisions of the AA 1996 will be dealt with as and when they are relevant to later parts of this chapter.

A schedule of the main provisions of the AA 1996, showing which are mandatory and which are not, appears at the end of this chapter.

As far as the rest of the AA 1996 is concerned, the parties may, if they wish, make such arrangements as they see fit. The AA 1996 will apply only if the agreement does not cover a particular point which is dealt with in the Act.

13.2.3 Incorporating an arbitration clause

Even if an agreement does not contain an arbitration clause, it is possible to incorporate an arbitration clause from another document into the agreement by referring to the arbitration clause in such a way as to make it part of the agreement (s 6(2)). For example, in a construction contract, a builder and a land owner might agree in writing to refer all disputes to arbitration. The builder may then enter into a sub-contract with a plumber who will do part of the work required under the main contract. That sub-contract may not itself contain an arbitration clause, but a clause which said 'The provisions of the main contract [the contract between the builder and the land owner] shall apply to this contract unless agreed to the contrary' would be sufficient to incorporate the arbitration clause in the main contract into the sub-contract.

By s 7 of the AA 1996, even if the main contract were to be invalid, the arbitration clause would still be effective as far as the sub-contract is concerned.

13.3 APPOINTING THE ARBITRATOR

The arbitration agreement may name the arbitrator. This is rare. It is more usual for the agreement to state how the arbitrator will be appointed.

Section 15(1) provides: 'The parties are free to agree on the number of arbitrators to form the tribunal and whether there is to be a chairperson or umpire.'

13.3.1 Sole arbitrators

By s 15(3), '[i]f there is no agreement as to the number of arbitrators, the tribunal shall consist of a sole arbitrator'.

Section 16(1) makes it clear that the parties can agree their own procedure for appointing a sole arbitrator. If they have not agreed a procedure then, by s 16(3), either party can make a written request to the other to make a joint appointment within 28 days of the request.

If the agreed procedure or the s 16(3) procedure does not work, either party may apply to the court under s 18. The court's powers are listed in s 18(3). It will usually appoint an arbitrator, although it may simply give directions to the parties on how to proceed in making the appointment.

EXAMPLE

A and B have an arbitration agreement which provides that the parties shall agree on the identity of a sole arbitrator. When a dispute arises, A writes to B suggesting X as arbitrator. B objects to X as arbitrator. A asks B to suggest an alternative arbitrator. B does not respond. A can apply to the court under s 18. B will have an opportunity to make representations to the court, but if he fails to do so, the court is likely to appoint X as the sole arbitrator.

Very often, the party who initiates the arbitration will submit a list of, for example, three candidates and then the parties will try to agree on one of the candidates.

13.3.2 Three arbitrators

The arbitration agreement may specify three arbitrators. As usual, the parties are free to agree on the procedure for appointing the arbitrators. If they do not do so then, under s 16(5), each party will appoint an arbitrator within 14 days of one party requesting the other to make an appointment. The two arbitrators will then appoint a third arbitrator to act as chairperson of the tribunal.

EXAMPLE

A and B have an arbitration agreement which provides that there should be three arbitrators. When a dispute arises, A writes to B nominating X as an arbitrator and asking B to nominate an arbitrator. B nominates Y. X and Y meet and agree to ask Z to act as their chairperson.

13.3.2.1 One party does not make an appointment

If, in the above example, B had failed to nominate an arbitrator, A would be entitled to rely on the provisions of s 17 of the AA 1996 and give written notice to B that he proposed to appoint X as sole arbitrator. B would then have seven days to appoint his arbitrator. If he still failed to make an appointment, A would be entitled to confirm X as sole arbitrator. B's only remedy thereafter would be to apply to the court under s 18 and ask the court to revoke X's appointment and to appoint new arbitrators or give directions as to the appointment of arbitrators. On the facts as outlined here, it is unlikely that B's application to the court would be successful.

13.3.2.2 The arbitrators cannot agree on a chairperson

If, in the above example, X and Y had been unable to agree on the identity of the third arbitrator then, unless the arbitration agreement provided otherwise (because the parties are always free to agree on some alternative procedure for dealing with problems in the appointment of an arbitrator, no matter how many arbitrators there may be), either A or B would be entitled to apply to the court under s 18 and ask the court to solve the problem.

13.3.3 Two arbitrators

A tribunal consisting of just two arbitrators creates the obvious risk that the arbitrators will not be able to agree on a solution to the dispute. It is therefore rare to have an arbitration agreement which provides for two arbitrators. The AA 1996 discourages an arrangement for two arbitrators, because s 15(2) says that any agreement which provides for an even number of arbitrators 'shall be understood as requiring the appointment of an additional arbitrator as chairperson of the tribunal'. However, the number of arbitrators is a matter for the parties to the agreement, and if they do want to have an even number of arbitrators, they can do so by expressly stating in their agreement that there shall not be a chairperson. By s 22 of the AA 1996, the parties are free to agree on how the tribunal shall exercise its powers. In the absence of any agreement, s 22 provides that decisions shall be made by a majority vote. If there is no majority and no chairperson (or umpire – see **13.3.4**), the parties will have to apply to the court for directions under s 18.

Where there are to be two arbitrators, the parties can agree on the procedure for appointing the arbitrators. In the absence of any agreement, by s 16(4) each party will appoint its own arbitrator within 14 days of a request from one party to the other to appoint an arbitrator. If one party does not make an appointment, s 17 will apply (see **13.3.2.1**).

13.3.4 Chairperson distinguished from umpire

Where there are three arbitrators, the AA 1996 assumes that one of them will be a chairperson. The parties are free to agree on the chairperson's functions. If they do not deal with this matter in their agreement then, under s 20, all decisions will be made by a majority vote (including the chairperson's vote). If, for example, there are four arbitrators and there is no majority decision, the chairperson has a casting vote.

Although it is more common to have a chairperson, s 15(1) gives the parties freedom to choose an umpire instead. A chairperson is a member of the arbitration tribunal from the outset. An umpire becomes involved later on. Thus the parties might agree to have two arbitrators and that, if the two nominated arbitrators cannot reach agreement on any matter, they shall then appoint an umpire who will resolve the contentious issue for the arbitrators.

It is, of course, for the parties to agree on the procedure for appointing any umpire, but if they have not done so, s 16(6) will apply. Each party will appoint its arbitrator in the usual way (see **13.3.3** for how this is done and how any problems with the appointment are resolved). The two arbitrators will then be free to appoint an umpire at any time. In the absence of any agreement to the contrary, s 16(6) provides that the arbitrators should appoint an umpire as soon as they are unable to agree on any matter. The AA 1996 also requires the two arbitrators to appoint an umpire before the final hearing of the case unless the parties have agreed to the contrary.

Under s 21 of the AA 1996, it is for the parties to agree on the functions of any umpire. In the absence of any agreement, the umpire will attend the proceedings and receive copies of all the papers. They will not, however, take any active part in the arbitration unless and until the arbitrators are unable to agree on a matter. If this happens, the original arbitrators will cease to act and the umpire will take over the case as if they were the sole arbitrator.

13.3.5 Appointing authorities

The parties to an arbitration agreement may agree to ask a third party (eg the President of The Law Society) to appoint an arbitrator for them. This practice has become less common since some appointing authorities started to charge substantial fees for making an appointment.

If the appointing authority fails to make an appointment, the parties can apply to the court under s 18 and ask the court to appoint an arbitrator.

13.3.6 Inability or refusal to act

If a nominated arbitrator is unable or unwilling to take up the post of arbitrator, the parties are free to agree on a procedure for appointing a replacement. If they cannot do so, they may apply to the court under s 18 and ask the court to appoint a replacement or to make directions as to how to resolve the problem.

13.4 COMMENCEMENT OF THE ARBITRATION

13.4.1 How to begin

The arbitration agreement will usually tell the parties how to begin the arbitration. A common procedure is for the applicant to send a written request to arbitrate to the respondent, setting out:

(a) the names and addresses of the parties;

(b) a brief statement of the nature and circumstances of the dispute and the relief being sought; and

(c) who the claimant thinks the arbitrators should be and/or how they should be appointed (if the claimant has to appoint an arbitrator, the request would contain the name and address of the nominated arbitrator).

The request will often be accompanied by a copy of the arbitration agreement.

For the purposes of the Limitation Acts and any time limits in the arbitration agreement itself (see **13.10**), it is necessary to determine when arbitration proceedings have commenced. The parties can reach whatever agreement they see fit on this point. If they have not reached any agreement, s 14 of the AA 1996 will help.

Under s 14, if the arbitration agreement identifies who the arbitrator shall be, the arbitration commences when one party gives written notice to the other requiring him to submit the dispute to arbitration. If, as is more usual, the parties are to appoint the arbitrator or arbitrators when a dispute arises, the arbitration will commence when one party serves the other with written notice requiring it to appoint or agree to the appointment of an arbitrator. Such notice should deal with the following points:

(a)   reference to the arbitration clause in the contract;

(b)   the dispute that has arisen;

(c)   requirement for the party to agree with the appointment of an arbitrator – often the notice will give a list of several proposed arbitrators.

Finally, if the arbitrator is to be appointed by a third party, the arbitration commences as soon as one party asks the appointing authority to make an appointment.

Note: The rest of this chapter assumes that there will be a sole arbitrator. References to the arbitrator include references to a panel of arbitrators.

13.4.2   The arbitrator's duties on being appointed

The arbitrator will be appointed shortly after the commencement of the arbitration. The claimant will send the arbitrator a copy of the arbitration agreement so that the arbitrator can decide not only that they are competent and have the time to do the job, but also that the agreement gives them power to act and that they have been validly appointed. By s 30 of AA 1996, unless otherwise agreed, it is for the arbitrator to decide whether or not there is a valid arbitration agreement, whether the tribunal is properly constituted and what matters have been submitted for arbitration.

At this stage, the arbitrator should disclose any circumstances which might lead any of the parties to doubt the arbitrator's impartiality. The Chartered Institute of Arbitrators has drawn up guidelines of good practice for arbitrators which suggest that the nominated arbitrator should reveal:

(a)   past or present business relationships with any party or important witness;

(b)   substantial social relationships with any party or important witness;

(c)   prior knowledge of the dispute;

(d)   commitments which may affect their availability.

The business or social relationships which the arbitrator should reveal include those of their family, firm and business partners.

13.4.3   Objections to the arbitrator's jurisdiction

Sections 31 and 32 of the AA 1996 deal with challenges to the arbitrator's jurisdiction. Both sections are mandatory (ie the parties cannot exclude them in their arbitration agreement). Section 31 deals with making an objection to the arbitrator; s 32 with making an objection to the court.

Under s 31, a party who wishes to object to the arbitrator's jurisdiction should do so no later than the first step he takes in dealing with the merits of the application after the arbitrator has been appointed.

> **EXAMPLE**
>
> A has commenced arbitration proceedings against B. B has reason to believe that the arbitrator appointed by A is not a suitable arbitrator. B can raise an objection immediately or on sending in his defence to A's claim. If, however, he sends in a defence without objecting to the appointment of the arbitrator, he is deemed to have waived his right to object, although under s 31(3) the arbitrator does have a discretion to accept a late objection if he considers that the delay is justified (eg B was not aware of circumstances affecting the arbitrator's suitability when the proceedings began).

Similarly, if any party during the course of the arbitration considers that the arbitrator is exceeding their powers, that party should object immediately or may be taken to have waived the right to do so.

Where an objection is made to the arbitrator's jurisdiction, the arbitrator may deal with the point there and then, or, with the consent of the parties, defer ruling on the jurisdiction point until the arbitrator comes to deal with the merits of the substantive application.

Under s 32, a party to an arbitration may apply to the court to challenge the arbitrator's jurisdiction. A party may do this only with the consent of the other parties or with the consent of the arbitrator. If the application is made with the consent of the arbitrator, the court will consider the application only if:

(a) a decision will save substantial costs;

(b) there has been no delay in making the application; and

(c) there is good reason for the matter to be considered by the court.

Bearing in mind the general principle in s 1 of the AA 1996 that the court should not intervene in an arbitration, successful applications under s 32 are likely to be rare.

By s 73 of the AA 1996, a party who continues to take part in an arbitration after the party knew or should have known that there were grounds for objecting to the jurisdiction cannot subsequently apply to the court under s 32. The parties cannot contract out of s 73.

13.5 THE PRELIMINARY MEETING

Although there are no rigid procedural rules in arbitration, it is common, once the arbitrator has accepted office, for the arbitrator to arrange a preliminary meeting with the parties. This meeting is the equivalent of the case management conference in a civil case.

13.5.1 Procedure

Under s 34, it is for the arbitrator to decide all procedural and evidential matters, subject to the rights of the parties to agree their own procedure. The arbitrator decides, after consulting the parties, the timetable for resolving the dispute and the procedure to be followed. The issues which may be discussed include those set out in **13.5.1.1** to **13.5.1.7** below. The list is by no means exhaustive. Not all the points will arise in every case. The fact that the parties are able to participate in these matters is one of the great advantages of arbitration.

13.5.1.1 Statements of case

Are written statements of case necessary? If so, when should they be supplied? Can they be amended later? Is a reply needed? Is there a counterclaim? The arbitrator will arrange a timetable for this.

13.5.1.2 Documents

Is disclosure appropriate? If so, what form should it take and what should the timetable be? What documents will be admissible at the hearing of the reference, and how and when should they be presented to the arbitrator? How many copies will be needed at the hearing of the reference?

13.5.1.3 Experts

Is expert evidence needed at all, or will the parties leave the matter to the arbitrator's skill and judgement? If expert evidence is needed, will the arbitrator appoint their own expert, or will the parties call their own experts? If the parties intend to call experts, how many will there be and when (if at all) should there be mutual disclosure of reports? Is oral evidence necessary, or can the matter be disposed of solely on the basis of written reports?

13.5.1.4   Evidence

Should the arbitrator apply strict rules of evidence or not? Will the evidence be oral or documentary? Should it be disclosed in advance? Will the witnesses be sworn? Should there be written requests for further information? Are any orders needed for the preservation of evidence?

13.5.1.5   Points of law

Should points of law be referred to the High Court under s 45 of the AA 1996 (see **13.5.2**), or should the arbitrator be left to take their own legal advice or to reach their own decision in the light of submissions made by the parties' own lawyers?

13.5.1.6   Preservation of property

Under s 38(4), unless agreed to the contrary, the arbitrator can give directions regarding any property involved in the proceedings relating to the inspection, photographing, preservation, custody or detention of that property by the arbitrator, an expert or a party, or to authorise experiments and/or the taking of samples.

13.5.1.7   The hearing

Whose responsibility is it to make the arrangements for the hearing? When and where will it take place? What language should be used at the hearing (one or both of the parties may be from outside the UK) and will translations of documents be required? Will there be oral evidence or submissions, or will the arbitrator just read the documents?

13.5.2   Preliminary points of law

Under s 45 of the AA 1996, a party may apply (on giving notice to the other parties) to the court for a ruling on any question of law arising during the proceedings which substantially affects the rights of one or more of the parties. The application can be made only with the consent of all other parties or with the consent of the arbitrator. If it is made with only the arbitrator's consent, the court will make a ruling only if it is likely to result in a substantial saving in costs and there has been no delay in making the application.

The parties have the right to agree to exclude the court's jurisdiction under s 45. Where one or both of the parties are not based in the UK, they may have agreed to arbitration in England only if there was no risk of being involved in court proceedings in England as well. In such cases, agreements excluding s 45 are likely to be common. Further, it should be noted that, by s 45(1), an agreement that the arbitrator need not give reasons for their decision (see **13.7.3** and **13.8.3**) is deemed to be an agreement to exclude the court's jurisdiction under s 45.

13.5.3   The arbitrator's fee

One additional matter which has to be considered at or before the preliminary meeting (usually when the arbitrator accepts the appointment) is the question of the arbitrator's fee. The arbitrator will indicate how much they will charge for their services (or the basis on which their fees will be calculated) and how much has to be paid in advance (if any). The arbitrator's agreement to act is conditional on reaching satisfactory agreement about his fee.

13.6   PREPARATIONS FOR THE HEARING

13.6.1   The arbitrator's duties

Both in the preparation for the hearing and during the hearing itself the arbitrator must comply with s 33(1) of the AA 1996. This states:

The tribunal shall—

(a)   act fairly and impartially as between the parties, giving each party a reasonable opportunity of putting his case and dealing with that of his opponent, and

(b) adopt procedures suitable to the circumstances of the particular case, avoiding unnecessary delay or expense, so as to provide a fair means for the resolution of the matters falling to be determined.

Section 33(2) goes on to provide:

The tribunal shall comply with that general duty in conducting the arbitral proceedings, in its decisions on matters of procedure and evidence and in the exercise of all other powers conferred on it.

At the risk of labouring the obvious, neither the parties nor the arbitrator can contract out of s 33.

13.6.2 The parties' duties

Both in preparing for the hearing and during the hearing itself the parties must comply with s 40 of the AA 1996. This provides:

(1) The parties shall do all things necessary for the proper and expeditious conduct of the arbitral proceedings.

(2) This includes—

(a) complying without delay with any determination of the tribunal as to procedural or evidential matters, or with any order or directions of the tribunal, and

(b) where appropriate, taking without delay any necessary steps to obtain a decision of the court on a preliminary question of jurisdiction or law ...

(See **13.4.3** and **13.5.2**.)

Again, the parties cannot contract out of s 40, even with the arbitrator's consent.

13.6.3 Correspondence

Although the preliminary meeting deals with the preparations for the hearing, further problems may arise as time passes by. The arbitrator can call further meetings, or they may deal with the problems by correspondence.

Whatever is written to the arbitrator must be copied to the other side. All communications by the arbitrator are sent to both parties.

13.6.4 Want of prosecution

A party who expects to lose the case may try to postpone the inevitable by failing to cooperate with the arbitrator (eg by failing to reply to correspondence or to attend meetings). If the party in default is the claimant then the arbitrator can dismiss the claim for want of prosecution under s 41(3) of the AA 1996, unless the arbitration agreement states to the contrary (as the parties are free to agree on the arbitrator's powers if a party fails to comply with their s 40 duties (see **13.6.2**)). The arbitrator can do this if there has been inordinate and inexcusable delay which creates a substantial risk that it will not be possible to reach a fair decision or which 'has caused or is likely to cause' the respondent serious prejudice. The arbitrator should not exercise their powers under this section where the limitation period has not yet expired, unless there are exceptional circumstances (see *James Lazenby & Co v McNicholas Construction Co Ltd* [1995] 1 WLR 615).

13.6.5 Proceeding without notice

If it is the respondent who is not cooperating, the arbitrator may rely on s 41(4) of the AA 1996, if either the respondent:

(a) is not present at a hearing of which he had been notified; or

(b) fails to provide written evidence or submissions after being given proper notice,

and he has not provided a good explanation for his default. This section provides that the arbitrator can deal with the matter on the basis of the arguments and/or evidence provided by the claimant.

13.6.6   Peremptory orders

Under s 41(5) of the AA 1996, if any party fails to comply with the arbitrator's directions, the arbitrator can make a peremptory order giving the party in default a specified period of time to comply with the order. Such an order can perhaps be viewed as the equivalent of an 'unless' order under the CPR 1998 (see LPC Guide, **Civil Litigation** at **9.3.4**). If the party does not comply with the order then, under s 41(7), the arbitrator can either:

(a)   prevent the party in default from relying on any material which was covered by the order; or

(b)   draw any appropriate adverse inference; or

(c)   proceed to make an award on the basis of the existing evidence; or

(d)   impose costs penalties.

EXAMPLE

During the course of an arbitration of a dispute between A and B, the arbitrator orders both parties to exchange the expert reports they propose to rely on at the hearing. A sends B a copy of his expert's report. B fails to provide A with a copy of B's expert evidence. The arbitrator can order B to provide copies of his expert evidence within 14 days. If B still fails to provide copies of his expert evidence, the arbitrator may: (i) direct that B shall not be entitled to use that evidence at the hearing; (ii) infer that the evidence B had was unreliable; (iii) decide the case on the basis of A's expert evidence and any expert evidence the arbitrator may himself have obtained; and (iv) order B to pay the costs wasted by his failure to comply with the arbitrator's order.

Alternatively, the arbitrator (or one of the parties acting with the consent of the arbitrator) may apply to the court for an order under s 42 requiring a party to comply with a peremptory order made by the arbitrator. This might be appropriate where, for example, one party has documents which are crucial to the other party's case and he will not hand over the papers to the other party. The advantage of applying to the court is that the court can attach a penal notice to its order so that non-compliance may be punished as a contempt of court.

The power to apply to the court under s 42 can be excluded by the arbitration agreement. It is important to remember that the basic principle is still that the parties are free to agree on what should happen if one party fails to carry out his obligations and that the provisions of ss 41 and 42 apply only in the absence of any agreement to the contrary.

13.6.7   Help from the High Court

In addition to its powers under s 42 of the AA 1996, the court has power under s 44 to make orders relating to:

(a)   taking evidence from witnesses;

(b)   preserving evidence;

(c)   inspecting, photographing, preserving, taking samples or experimenting on any property or goods involved in the proceedings and for the custody or detention of such property. To do this, it can authorise any person to enter the premises of any party;

(d)   selling goods which are involved in the proceedings;

(e)   interim injunctions; and

(f)   appointing a receiver.

The arbitration agreement may exclude all or part of the court's powers under s 44. The court will, in any event, make an order only if the arbitrator has no power to make the order or their order would not be effective.

> **EXAMPLE**
>
> In the course of an arbitration between A and B it becomes apparent that B is about to dispose of his property in such a way as to make it very difficult to enforce any award which may be made against him at the end of the arbitration. The arbitrator has no power under the arbitration agreement to require B to desist from doing this (or even if he has such power, it is obvious that B will ignore any direction given by the arbitrator). A may apply to the court under s 44 for a freezing injunction (see **Chapter 8**) (with the usual penal notice attached).

Normally, a party can apply to the court under s 44 only if he has the consent of the arbitrator or the other parties. Nevertheless, by s 44(3), in cases of urgency, a party can apply to the court for orders to preserve evidence or assets without first obtaining the arbitrator's consent. The Court of Appeal considered the interpretation of s 44(3) in the case of *Cetelem SA v Roust Holdings Ltd* [2005] EWCA Civ 618, where it upheld the granting of a freezing injunction preventing the defendant from dealing with its shares.

Applications to the court are governed by Part 62 of CPR 1998 and the associated Practice Direction. They will normally be dealt with by the Commercial Court.

13.6.8 Security for costs

Under s 38(3), unless the parties have agreed otherwise, the arbitrator may require an applicant to provide security for the respondent's costs before proceeding any further with the arbitration. However, unless agreed to the contrary, an arbitrator cannot require security for costs solely because the applicant is based outside the UK. One of the objectives of the AA 1996 is to encourage foreign businessmen to use the English arbitration system, and it is important that they should not be deterred by a fear that they might have to put money up front if they were to arbitrate in this country.

The usual ground for ordering security for costs would be because of doubts about the applicant's financial ability to meet any award of costs.

If the applicant fails to provide the required security, the arbitrator can make a peremptory order. If the applicant still fails to comply then, under s 41(6), unless agreed to the contrary, the arbitrator can dismiss the claim.

13.6.9 Provisional awards

By s 39 of the AA 1996, the arbitrator does have power to make a provisional order for the payment of money or disposal of property between the parties or for an interim payment of costs. However, by s 39(4), the arbitrator has this power only if it is expressly conferred by the arbitration agreement.

13.6.10 Without prejudice offers

There will be occasions when the respondent wants to settle and to put pressure on the applicant to do so. The respondent could send the equivalent of a Part 36 offer, ie a letter in which an offer is made 'without prejudice save as to costs'.

13.7 THE HEARING AND THE AWARD

The parties and the arbitrator will settle the arrangements for hearing the reference at the preliminary meeting.

13.7.1   The hearing

By s 46, the arbitrator will decide the dispute under the law the parties have chosen. Section 47 gives the arbitrator power, unless the parties agree otherwise, to make different awards on different issues at different times.

> **EXAMPLE**
>
> During the course of the arbitration, the arbitrator may first hear evidence on whether there has been a breach of contract. If she rules that there has been no breach of contract, that will effectively be the end of the matter. If she decides that there has been a breach of contract, she may then proceed to hear evidence about the amount of harm caused by the breach so that she can decide what compensation to award.

The parties can, of course, agree what powers the arbitrator shall have. In the absence of any agreement to the contrary, the arbitrator may make a declaration, may order payments of money, and has the same powers as a court to order a party to do something or to stop doing it. The arbitrator may also order specific performance of a contract (except one relating to land) and order the rectification, setting aside or cancellation of any document (s 48).

13.7.2   Removal of arbitrator

13.7.2.1   The powers of the parties

The parties may agree what they like regarding their powers to revoke the arbitrator's appointment. In the absence of any agreement to the contrary, s 23 gives the parties power to revoke the arbitrator's appointment if all parties agree in writing.

13.7.2.2   The powers of the court

If the parties cannot agree on the revocation of the arbitrator's powers, either party may apply to the court for an order removing the arbitrator from office on certain grounds. Section 24, which gives this power, cannot be suspended by the agreement of the parties.

The grounds for removing an arbitrator under s 24 are either:

(a)   that there are justifiable doubts about their impartiality;

(b)   that they lack the qualifications required by the arbitration agreement;

(c)   that there are justifiable doubts about their physical or mental ability to conduct the proceedings; or

(d)   that they have failed to conduct the proceedings properly or with reasonable speed, and this will cause substantial injustice.

As far as impartiality is concerned, the test to be applied is that applied to all persons acting in a judicial capacity, ie whether having regard to the relevant circumstances, there was a real danger of bias, in the sense that the arbitrator might unfairly regard or have regarded with favour or disfavour the case of one party. A direct pecuniary interest in the outcome will be assumed to amount to bias and lead to automatic disqualification (*R v Gough* [1993] AC 646).

If an arbitrator ceases to act for any of the above reasons or because they resign or die, the parties can agree on how the arbitrator should be replaced. If they cannot agree, they should follow the usual procedures for appointing an arbitrator under s 16 or apply to the court under s 18 (see **13.3**).

13.7.3   The award

Although the parties are, of course, free to agree what they like about the form and content of the arbitration award, under s 52, unless agreed to the contrary, the award should be in writing and signed by the arbitrator, and should give reasons for the award. By s 55, unless agreed to the contrary, the arbitrator will serve copies of the award on the parties.

13.7.4 Costs

Under s 61, unless agreed to the contrary, the arbitrator can order one party to pay the costs of the arbitration. Section 61(2) says that, unless agreed to the contrary, the general principle will be that costs should follow the event (ie the loser pays the costs). 'Costs' in this context includes the arbitrator's fees (s 59).

Any provision in an arbitration agreement that one party shall pay the costs of the arbitration in any event is void, unless the agreement was made after the dispute arose (s 60).

13.7.5 The arbitrator's fee

Section 56 of the AA 1996 (which cannot be excluded by the parties) gives the arbitrator power to refuse to deliver an award to the parties until the arbitrator's fees and expenses have been paid. Very often, of course, the arbitrator will have required some or all of their fees to be paid before commencing the arbitration. However, in so far as any of their fees and expenses are still outstanding at the time of the award, they will refuse to publish the award until they have been paid. Effectively, this means that the winner will have to pay the fees to the arbitrator in order to get the award and will then seek to recover those fees from the losing party (see **13.9**).

Sections 28 and 56 of the AA 1996 give the court power to resolve any dispute about the amount of the arbitrator's fees.

13.7.6 Interest

Under s 49 of the AA 1996, the parties can agree on the arbitrator's powers to award interest. Unless agreed to the contrary, the arbitrator has power to make such award of interest as they think fit. This includes the power to award compound interest rather than simple interest, which is a power which is not usually available to a court.

13.7.7 Settlement

If the parties do settle their dispute during the arbitration then, by s 51, unless agreed to the contrary, the arbitrator will record the settlement in the form of an agreed award. This will have the same status as an award made after a disputed hearing. All the normal rules relating to the award, costs, and arbitrator's fees and expenses (see **13.7.3–13.7.6**) apply to an agreed award.

13.8 CHALLENGING THE AWARD

Most arbitration agreements stipulate what is to happen if one or more of the parties are dissatisfied with the arbitrator's decision. It is important to remember that what follows in this section of this chapter applies only once the parties have exhausted their remedies under the arbitration agreement.

13.8.1 Issues of jurisdiction

Section 67 of the AA 1996 (which cannot be excluded by agreement) gives a party the right to apply to the court to challenge an award on the grounds of lack of jurisdiction. The courts have so far considered applications on the basis that:

(a)   the arbitration agreement was not binding on the applicant;

(b)   the arbitration clause was void for ambiguity and uncertainty; and

(c)   the arbitrator did not have the jurisdiction to deal with issues covered by their award.

13.8.2 Issues of fact

Subject to the provisions of the arbitration agreement, the arbitrator's decision is final on questions of fact. There is no right of appeal to the courts on a question of fact.

It is, however, possible to challenge the arbitrator's award on the basis of a serious irregularity under s 68 of the AA 1996 (which cannot be excluded by the parties). Section 68 defines a serious irregularity as any of the following:

(a)   failure to comply with the general duties imposed on the arbitrator by s 33 (see **13.6.1**);

(b)   exceeding the arbitrator's powers or the powers of anyone else involved in the arbitration (although this would normally fall under s 67 (see **13.8.1**));

(c)   failure to follow agreed procedures;

(d)   failure to deal with all the issues;

(e)   any arbitral or other institution or person vested by the parties with powers in relation to the proceedings or the award exceeding its powers;

(f)   uncertainty or ambiguity as to the effect of the award;

(g)   the award was obtained by fraud or the award (or the way in which it was obtained) is contrary to public policy;

(h)   the award fails to comply with the required formalities;

(i)   an admitted irregularity in the conduct of the proceedings.

The meaning of some of these terms is not immediately obvious (eg obtaining an award in a manner which is contrary to public policy) and will have to be clarified by the courts as and when the opportunity arises. It is also unclear why, for example, the court should be asked to interfere with an award simply because of a formal defect (especially as the arbitrator has power under s 57 to correct errors in the award).

If an application under s 68 succeeds, the court will normally refer the matter back to the arbitrator; but if it considers this to be inappropriate, it can set aside all or part of the award.

In *Lesotho Highlands Development Authority v Impregilo SpA and Others* [2005] UKHL 43, HL, the applicant challenged the arbitrator's award on ground (b) above. The House of Lords (Lord Steyn giving the leading judgment) stated that s 68 should be narrowly construed: 'Section 68(2)(b) does not permit a challenge on the ground that the tribunal arrived at a wrong conclusion as a matter of law or fact. It is not apt to cover a mere error of law' (AA 1996, s 69 – see **13.8.3** below – had been excluded by the arbitration agreement). The decision has been welcomed as upholding an important principle behind the Act, namely, that the courts should be reluctant to intervene in arbitrations. Parties who choose to resolve disputes by arbitration do so because they prefer that method of dispute resolution to court proceedings. The more the English courts are willing to intervene, the less attractive England becomes as a venue for international commercial arbitration.

In relation to this point, in April 2013 the Commercial Court introduced a new procedure for summary dismissal of challenges to arbitral awards under s 68. The threshold for bringing a successful challenge as set out above is very high, but it was felt that this did not always deter parties from bringing challenges purely in order to delay enforcement of the award. Now, para O8.8 of the Commercial Court Guide allows the court to exercise its powers under CPR 1998 to dismiss an application under s 68 of the Act without a hearing, if the court considers that the challenge has no real prospect of success. The respondent to the challenge can also request the court to deal with the application on paper, without an oral hearing. If the court does dismiss the application in this way, the applicant has the right to apply to the court to request a hearing of the application. However, the applicant is at risk of being liable for costs on the indemnity basis if it loses at the hearing.

13.8.3   Issues of law

Under s 69 of the AA 1996, unless otherwise agreed, a party may appeal to the court on any question of law arising out of the award. Where one or both of the parties to the arbitration are based outside the UK, they are likely to prefer finality to the prospect of being involved in litigation in the English courts, so agreements excluding s 69 will be common.

An agreement that the arbitrator need not give reasons for their decision is treated as an agreement to exclude s 69 (s 69(1)).

An appeal can be made only if the court grants permission (or if all parties consent, which is unlikely). The court will grant permission only if a decision will substantially affect the rights of one or more parties and it is 'just and proper' for the court to decide the issue. Even then, the court will intervene only if the arbitrator's decision is obviously wrong or 'the question is one of general public importance and the decision of the tribunal is at least open to serious doubt'.

Applications for permission to appeal against an award on a point of law will usually be determined by the court reading the parties' submissions and there will usually be no formal hearing.

If the court does decide to allow the appeal, it will normally refer the matter back to the arbitrator; but if this is inappropriate, it may vary or set aside the award.

13.8.4   Supplementary provisions

There are certain matters which are common to ss 67, 68 and 69.

By s 70(3), any application or appeal must be made within 28 days of the end of the arbitral process. This might be 28 days from the date of the award, but if the arbitration agreement stipulates that other appeal procedures must be followed before applying to the court, the 28 days will run from the date when the parties were informed of the result of those other procedures.

By s 70(4), the court may require the arbitrator to give reasons or additional reasons for their award.

The court may order the applicant/appellant to provide security for costs and may require the amount of the award to be paid into court pending the court's decision. The applicant/appellant will not be able to proceed until he has complied with these requirements.

By s 71(3), if an award is referred back to the arbitrator, the arbitrator must make a fresh decision within three months (or such other period stipulated by the court).

The provisions of s 73, whereby a party may lose the right to object if he is guilty of unreasonable delay (see **13.4.3**), apply to ss 67 and 68, but not to appeals on a point of law under s 69.

Sections 70, 71 and 73 are all mandatory provisions and cannot be excluded by agreement of the parties.

13.8.5   Further appeals

An appeal from a decision of the court to the Court of Appeal under any of the provisions of the AA 1996 (not just those dealt with in this section of this chapter) can be made only with the permission of the court of first instance (which will usually be the Commercial Court). If the courts continue to follow their previous practices under the earlier legislation, such permission will rarely be granted.

In *Henry Boot Construction (UK) Ltd v Malmaison Hotel (Manchester) Ltd* [2000] 3 WLR 1824, a majority in the Court of Appeal (the matter was obiter) took the view that s 55 of the Access to Justice Act 1999 and r 52.13 of CPR 1998 (see **Chapter 11**) had no effect in relation to an appeal to the Court of Appeal under s 69(8) of the AA 1996. Once a party has obtained permission from the court of first instance to appeal, he is not subsequently required to seek permission from the Court of Appeal.

13.9   ENFORCING THE AWARD

Arbitration is the only alternative to litigation which produces a result which can be enforced without commencing litigation.

The normal way of enforcing the award is under s 66 of the AA 1996 (which cannot be excluded by the parties). This enables the winning party to apply to the High Court for leave to enforce the award as if it were a court judgment.

The procedure is set out in the Commercial Court Guide and is beyond the scope of this book.

If leave is granted, the order must be served on the debtor who has 14 days to apply to have it set aside (eg because the award is tainted by misconduct or is wrong in law). (The order must inform the debtor of this right.) If no such application is made or it fails, the applicant can use all the usual methods of enforcement.

13.10   TIME LIMITS

By s 13 of the AA 1996 (which cannot be excluded by the parties), the Limitation Acts apply to arbitrations in the same way as they apply to other disputes. Most arbitration agreements, however, require the parties to commence the arbitration in a much shorter period than the usual limitation period. Once the time limit in the arbitration agreement has expired, it is normally too late to refer the matter to arbitration, but the arbitration agreement is still effective to prevent either party taking the dispute to the courts, so the aggrieved party will be without a remedy.

Section 12 of the AA 1996 (which cannot be excluded by the agreement of the parties) enables the High Court to grant an extension of time for referring a dispute to arbitration. The parties must first have used any provisions of the arbitration agreement (eg applying to the arbitrator for an extension of time) before applying to the court. The section allows the court only to extend the time for commencing the arbitration.

The grounds for granting an extension are set out in s 12(3). The extension will be granted in only two cases. The first is where 'the circumstances are such as were outside the reasonable contemplation of the parties when they agreed [the time limit]'. The Court of Appeal considered the correct interpretation of this in *Harbour & General Works Ltd v Environment Agency* [2000] 1 WLR 950. The claimant had narrowly missed the time limit because of an administrative oversight. The extension was refused on the basis that this was far from so uncommon as to be treated as beyond the parties' contemplation. The Court of Appeal commented that an extension should only be considered where, had the parties known of the circumstances at the time of the agreement, they would at least have contemplated that the time bar might not apply. The second ground under s 12(3) is that 'the conduct of one party makes it unjust to hold the other party to the strict terms' of the time limit.

EXAMPLE

A and B have an arbitration agreement whereby all disputes must be referred to arbitration within six months of the dispute arising. A dispute does arise and A wants to refer the matter to arbitration. B persuades A that this is unnecessary because they will be able to negotiate an amicable settlement. The negotiations appear to be proceeding amicably and a settlement is about to be reached. The day after the six-month time limit for referring the dispute to arbitration elapses, B withdraws from the negotiations. The implication is that B was not negotiating in good faith and was simply lulling A into a sense of false security, playing for time until the time limit had expired. This would probably persuade the court to extend the time limit, provided A does not delay in applying to the court.

An arbitration agreement may contain other time limits (eg time limits for serving documents). It is possible (after exhausting all procedures specified in the arbitration agreement) to apply to the court under s 79 for an order extending such time limits. The court will extend the time limit only if 'a substantial injustice would otherwise be done'.

The parties can agree to exclude s 79 in their arbitration agreement. It is likely that such agreements will be common.

13.11 STAYING LITIGATION

Sometimes one of the parties to an arbitration agreement issues court proceedings instead of referring the dispute to arbitration. The defendant must, of course, acknowledge service of the claim form or the claimant will enter a default judgment against him. Having done so, the defendant can then apply to the court under s 9 of the AA 1996 for an order staying the court proceedings and referring the matter to arbitration. By s 9(3):

> An application may not be made by a person before taking the appropriate procedural step (if any) to acknowledge the legal proceedings against him or after he has taken any step in those proceedings to answer the substantive claim.

A 'step in [the] proceedings to answer the substantive claim' would usually be the service of a defence. In *Bilta v Nazir and Others* [2010] EWHC 1086 (Ch), the court held that seeking an extension of time to serve the defence and obtaining a consent order confirming the agreement to extend time did not amount to such a step. The court held that the defendant was entitled to have more time to consider the case to be put against it and to decide what position to adopt as regards court proceedings or arbitration.

The court also held that Part 11 of the CPR 1998 did not apply to such applications, which were governed by r 62.8. Unlike Part 11, this does not impose a time limit of 14 days (28 days in the Commercial Court and Circuit Commercial Courts) from filing the acknowledgement of service within which the application must be made.

By s 9(4), the court will grant a stay unless it is satisfied that 'the arbitration agreement is null and void, inoperative, or incapable of being performed'. It will be very rare for these conditions to be satisfied, so the normal course of action will be for the court to grant a stay. In doing so, the fact that the court has powers which the arbitrator does not have (eg to grant summary judgment) is irrelevant. It is also irrelevant that the dispute is about a point of law or, even, that the claimant does not think that there is a dispute and is alleging that the attempt to refer the matter to arbitration by the defendant is simply a ploy to delay payment of compensation. There was a dispute where a claim was made, which the other party refused to admit or did not pay, whether or not there was any answer to the claim in fact or in law. (See the decision of the Court of Appeal in *Halki Shipping Corporation v Sopex Oils Ltd, The Halki* [1998] 1 WLR 726.)

The fact that the defendant wishes to refer the matter to arbitration only so that he can defeat the claimant's action, by relying on a clause in the arbitration agreement which says that it is too late for the matter to be referred to arbitration, is not a ground for refusing to stay the litigation. Such matters should be dealt with by an application to the court under s 12 (see **13.10**).

13.12 SERVICE OF DOCUMENTS

The parties can reach their own agreement on how documents should be served during the course of the arbitration. Otherwise, s 76 states that a properly addressed, pre-paid envelope delivered by post to the addressee's last known place of residence or business address, or to the registered or principal office of a corporation, is effective service. If this is not reasonably practical (eg the other party's address is not known), the court can make directions as to service (eg the document shall be sent to the address of the other party's accountant) or may dispense with service.

13.13   JUDGE-ARBITRATORS

Under s 93 of the AA 1996, a judge can accept appointment as a sole arbitrator or as an umpire if the Lord Chief Justice is satisfied that they can be freed from their other duties. Schedule 2 to the AA 1996 makes certain modifications to the normal rules where the arbitration is being conducted by a judge.

Applications to the court where the arbitrator is a judge will be made to the Court of Appeal.

Where the arbitrator is a judge, they can grant permission to enforce the award under s 66 (see **13.9**) without the need for a separate application for permission.

The other provisions of Sch 2 are technical in nature and do not need to be considered in a book of this nature.

13.14   EXPERT DETERMINATION

Expert determination is closely related to but different from arbitration. Again, the parties to a dispute seek to have it resolved by a person they have chosen rather than by the court. There are, however, significant differences between arbitration and expert determination.

An arbitrator's award is enforceable in the courts. An expert's award is not, save that the successful party can bring a breach of contract action against a party who does not comply with the expert's decision. He also will apply under Part 24 for summary judgment if there is a contract whereby the parties have agreed to accept the expert's decision. As a result, the court has much less formal control over the actions of an expert than over an arbitrator. (However, if the court considers that the expert has been guilty of misconduct, it is unlikely to grant judgment to the party seeking to enforce the expert's award.)

As an expert is not performing a judicial function, they can be sued in negligence if they make a mistake, although, since they will not usually be obliged to give reasons for their decision, they may be difficult to challenge. An arbitrator has immunity under s 29 of the AA 1996 for anything done as arbitrator, unless it was done in bad faith.

If the parties use expert determination, they will not be able to make use of the AA 1996. The agreement appointing the expert may have to be carefully drafted. There should be provision for the expert to be appointed by an appointing authority if the parties cannot agree on whom to appoint. The court has no power to appoint the expert.

13.15   SUMMARY

Many commercial contracts contain arbitration clauses under which disputes between the parties will be resolved by way of arbitration rather than court proceedings.

Arbitration is a formal dispute resolution process under the control of an independent arbitrator or panel of arbitrators rather than a judge.

The parties involved are often free to decide the procedure they wish to follow, although many professional and commercial bodies have standard arbitration rules.

Arbitrations in England and Wales are regulated by the Arbitration Act 1996.

Decisions of arbitrators are enforceable through the courts.

13.16   THE ARBITRATION ACT 1996 AT A GLANCE

SECTION NUMBER	SUBJECT	IS IT MANDATORY?
s 1	Guiding principles	N/A
s 5	Agreements to be in writing – widely defined	N/A
s 9	Staying legal proceedings	Yes
s 12	Power of court to grant extensions of time for the commencement of arbitration proceedings	Yes
s 13	Limitation Act applies to arbitration proceedings	Yes
s 14	Commencement of arbitration proceedings – written notice	No
ss 15 and 16	Appointment of arbitrators	No
s 24	Power of court to remove arbitrator	Yes
s 33	Arbitrators' duties	Yes
s 34	Power of arbitrators over procedural and evidential matters	No
s 38	General powers of arbitrators including power to award security for costs	No
s 40	General duty of parties	Yes
s 41	Powers of arbitrators where party in default – power to make peremptory orders	No
s 42	Enforcement of peremptory orders through the courts	No
s 45	Power of arbitrators to make different awards on different issues at different times	No
s 47	Ability of arbitrators to make different awards on different issues at different times	No
s 56	Ability of arbitrators to withhold award in the event of non-payment	Yes
s 60	Prohibition on agreement to pay costs in any event	Yes
s 61	Arbitrators' ability to award costs	No
s 66	Enforcement of the award	Yes
ss 67 and 68	Right to challenge the award – substantive jurisdiction and serious irregularity	Yes
s 69	Appeal on question of law	No
s 79	Power of court to extend time limits relating to arbitration proceedings	No
Sch 1	Mandatory provisions of Part 1	N/A

MEDIATION

> **LEARNING OUTCOMES**
>
> After reading this chapter you will understand:
>
> - how to prepare for a mediation
> - how the mediation is conducted.

As we have already seen at **12.4**, mediation is a form of non-determinative ADR, and is without doubt the most popular. One of its attractions for parties involved in a dispute is the fact that any agreement reached at the mediation must be consensual – it cannot be imposed by the mediator. The Centre for Effective Dispute Resolution (CEDR) defines mediation as

> a flexible process conducted confidentially in which a neutral person (the mediator) actively assists parties in working towards a negotiated agreement of a dispute or difference, with the parties in ultimate control of the decision to settle and the terms of resolution.

14.1 WHEN TO MEDIATE?

Mediation is a key tool in dispute resolution, and in many cases its use should be part of your overall strategy to resolve the dispute on the best possible terms for the client. As we have already seen, there are professional obligations to discuss some form of ADR with the client and also a requirement under CPR 1998 (r 1.4). Mediation can take place at any time during the course of the dispute resolution process – before any court proceedings are issued or during those court proceedings. It can even take place after judgment, for example when an appeal is pending. It should not be considered as an 'either or' option – litigate or mediate – but as an important method of trying to achieve your client's objectives. Whether, when and how you should use mediation to do this will often be a key part of your dispute resolution strategy.

14.2 SETTING UP THE MEDIATION PROCESS

Once the parties have agreed to mediate, what needs to be done to begin that process? In a contractual dispute, there may well be a term in the contract (similar to an arbitration clause) which deals with the mediation process to be followed. If not, the parties will have to reach agreement as to how the mediation is to be conducted and, of course, who is going to act as the mediator.

The parties can either select a mediator themselves or request an ADR organisation, such as CEDR or the ADR Group, to appoint a mediator on their behalf. The parties will also have to make arrangements relating to the venue for the mediation.

Although one of the main advantages of mediation is that it is generally far less expensive than proceeding to trial, there will of course be costs involved in the mediation process. The parties will have to agree who is to be responsible for the mediator's costs and the costs of the venue where the mediation is to take place. Usually, these will be shared between the parties, and the parties will also usually agree to pay their own legal costs of the mediation in the event of a successful outcome. If the mediation fails, however, it is quite likely that the costs incurred by a party in relation to the mediation will form part of the overall costs of the case, which will usually be paid by the unsuccessful party subject to assessment by the court.

14.3   PREPARING FOR THE MEDIATION

As with advocacy at any court hearing, thorough preparation is the key to ensuring that you are able to achieve the best outcome for your client at the mediation. You will need to have a clear understanding of the strengths and weaknesses of your client's case, and the risks associated with proceeding to trial should the mediation prove unsuccessful. You will need to decide who is going to attend the mediation on behalf of the client (ensuring that whoever does attend has authority to settle the case) and also decide which members of the legal team should be there. For example, if you have already instructed counsel in the case, should counsel be present at the mediation or should it simply be conducted by the solicitors involved? If experts have been instructed, will it help if those experts are also present?

Prior to the mediation taking place, the parties should always try to agree a bundle of relevant documents which will be used during the mediation. Further, it will usually be the case that each party, or the parties jointly, prepares a case summary setting out the case as they see it for submission to the mediator in advance of the mediation. Before attending the mediation itself, you should clearly explain to the client the way in which the mediation is going to be conducted and also the consequences of failing to reach agreement at the mediation.

14.4   THE MEDIATION

The way in which the mediation is conducted may well have been set out in the mediation agreement, but it is essential that the procedure is flexible and suits the needs of the parties. Whilst there is no fixed format for the conduct of a mediation, it is common for the mediator to invite each party to make an opening statement. Following the opening statements, it is usual for each party to retire to separate rooms and for the mediator then to engage in private sessions with each party to discuss their positions, concerns, needs and wants. The mediator is not simply a messenger, however; as an active participant in the mediation they will encourage each party to consider various options based on the information the mediator has gleaned from them during the private sessions.

If the parties are able to reach a settlement then it is essential – and indeed this is usually a term of the mediation agreement – that such settlement be recorded in writing and be signed by all parties at the mediation. The agreement must be drafted carefully, which may take some time, but that is a small price to pay for certainty. If the agreement is not completed at the mediation then there is always a risk that the parties may change their minds overnight. If proceedings have already been started, the parties will subsequently have to lodge a consent order with the court setting out the basis on which the action has been settled.

If no agreement is reached at the mediation then this does not necessarily mean that the mediation has been fruitless; the parties may now have a better understanding of where the other stands on the issues in the case, and many cases do settle after what, on the face of it, appears to be an unsuccessful mediation.

As mediations are conducted on a 'without prejudice' basis, the general rule is that nothing discussed or revealed at the mediation may be revealed to the court should the proceedings continue.

CHAPTER 15

ENFORCEMENT AND INSOLVENCY

LEARNING OUTCOMES

After reading this chapter you will understand:

- how to enforce a judgment
- the use of insolvency proceedings as an alternative to litigation
- the advantages and disadvantages of using insolvency proceedings.

15.1 INTRODUCTION

As we saw in **Chapter 1**, financial considerations are a central issue in CDR. There is absolutely no point in taking proceedings against a party if at the end of the day you will not be able successfully to enforce any agreement reached or judgment obtained. The ability to enforce any judgment or agreement, and the prospects of success in doing so, must be a consideration throughout.

15.2 ENFORCEMENT – A REMINDER OF THE BASICS

Enforcement against a judgment debtor is dealt with in detail in the Legal Practice Guide, **Civil Litigation**. This chapter reconsiders briefly these main points and then looks at some methods of enforcement which are usually more relevant to commercial litigation than to other types of litigation.

15.2.1 Locating the assets

A solicitor must consider enforcement at the beginning of the case, not at the end. There is no point in suing a person who cannot meet any judgment which may be obtained against him. Before issuing proceedings, a solicitor must be satisfied that the defendant has assets which will meet any judgment obtained against him, and that those assets can be traced. Many apparently affluent debtors turn out to be men of straw when their creditors finally catch up with them.

Sometimes the client already has the necessary information about the proposed defendant (eg because enquiries were made about his finances before entering into the original contract), but it will often be necessary to use enquiry agents to make further enquiries about his financial status. An oral examination under CPR 1998, Part 71 can be used as a means of establishing a judgment debtor's finances, but only at the end of the case, once judgment has been obtained. It is too late then to find out whether the judgment debtor was worth suing.

In appropriate cases, a claimant can use a freezing injunction to preserve the defendant's assets pending judgment. If he obtains such an injunction, he can also obtain an order for disclosure of the defendant's assets, whereby at a very early stage of the proceedings, the defendant has to produce evidence about his assets (usually limited to those within the jurisdiction). In appropriate cases, he can be cross-examined about that evidence (see **8.6.2**).

15.2.2   The standard methods of enforcement

15.2.2.1   Taking control of goods (CPR 1998, Part 83)

This is seizure and sale of the debtor's goods. In the High Court, this is carried out by a High Court Enforcement Officer, and in the County Court by an enforcement officer. This can be a quick and effective method of enforcement as often the mere threat of a seizure of goods is enough to produce payment from the debtor. Further details concerning the procedure can be found in the Legal Practice Guide, *Civil Litigation*.

15.2.2.2   Third party debt orders (CPR 1998, Part 72)

Third party debt orders allow the judgment creditor to intercept money owed to his judgment debtor by a third party and have the money paid to the judgment creditor in total or partial satisfaction of the judgment debt. These proceedings are often used where the judgment debtor has a bank or building society account, so that the money in that account can be paid to the judgment creditor.

The judgment creditor applies without notice, with supporting evidence, for an order to show cause. This order, called an interim third party debt order, freezes the money owed to the judgment debtor, pending an on notice hearing. The judgment creditor then serves the order on the third party. If the third party is a deposit-taking institution (eg a bank, building society or finance house) the judgment creditor should serve the third party at its head office. It is also good practice to serve a copy on the branch where the judgment debtor has his account. The judgment creditor will then serve the order on the judgment debtor.

There will then be an on notice hearing at which the court will decide whether to order the third party to pay the money to the judgment creditor. At that hearing, the court will also consider whether the order would prejudice other creditors of the judgment debtor. If the third party does not appear or does not dispute the debt, the court will usually make the interim order final, ie a final order which will be enforced against the third party. If the third party denies the debt, the court will have to investigate his claim before deciding whether to order him to pay the judgment creditor or to refuse to make the order final.

15.2.2.3   Charging orders on land (CPR 1998, Part 73)

A charging order gives the judgment creditor a charge over the judgment debtor's land. If the land is jointly owned then (if the co-owner is not a party to the debt) only the judgment debtor's beneficial interest in the land can be charged.

The judgment creditor applies without notice for an interim charging order, giving full details of any other creditors known to him. The interim charging order temporarily charges the judgment debtor's land and fixes a hearing date when the judgment creditor will apply for the order to be made final. The judgment creditor then serves the order on the judgment debtor. The court may also direct him to serve the order on one or more of the judgment debtor's other creditors and any other interested person (eg the judgment debtor's spouse or any other person living in the property). These people will be able to argue at the hearing that the order should not be made final.

In the meantime, the judgment creditor will register the interim order at HM Land Registry or the Land Charges Registry, as appropriate, to prevent any dealings with the land pending the hearing. Where the land is registered land, the order is protected by a notice at HM Land Registry. In the case of unregistered land, the order is registered at the Land Charges Registry as an order affecting land. If the land is jointly-owned land and one of the owners is not a debtor, then a caution may be lodged if it is registered land. However, where the land is unregistered land, it may not be protected by registering a Land Charge (see Sch 3, para 12 to the Trusts of Land and Appointment of Trustees Act 1996, which inserts s 6(1A) into the Land Charges Act 1972). There may be little point in practice, therefore, in obtaining a charging order over a debtor's beneficial interest in jointly-owned unregistered land, when it cannot be protected by registration.

The judgment creditor should also give notice of the order to anyone else who has a charge over the land.

The court has a discretion whether to make the charging order final, although the burden of proof is on the judgment debtor and the others opposing the order. It will not make the order final if there is a reasonable chance that the debt will be paid in the near future or if the debt is relatively small compared to the value of the property to be charged. Nor will it make the order if it would give the applicant an unfair advantage over the other creditors. If the judgment debtor has been made bankrupt or wound up, the order will normally be refused (*Roberts Petroleum Ltd v Bernard Kenny Ltd* [1983] 2 AC 192). If the court does not make the order final, it will discharge the order.

Sometimes the judgment debtor will be involved in divorce proceedings when the judgment creditor applies for the charging order. If the judgment debtor's spouse is seeking a transfer of property order under s 24 of the Matrimonial Causes Act 1973, the application for a charging order should be transferred to the Family Division, so that that court can deal with both matters at the same time. Even so, that court is unlikely to transfer the property to the judgment debtor's spouse if this would defeat the claims of the creditors. The most the court is likely to do is to protect the spouse's right to occupy the house by placing restrictions on the circumstances in which it can be sold (*First National Securities Ltd v Hegerty* [1984] 3 WLR 769; *Harman v Glencross* [1986] 2 WLR 637).

If the court makes the order final, the judgment creditor will register it in the same way as he registered the interim order. This ensures that when the judgment debtor sells the land, the judgment creditor is paid from the proceeds of sale. In the meantime the charge merely provides the judgment creditor with security. However, it may be some time before the judgment debtor decides to sell the land and the judgment creditor is paid from the proceeds of sale. If, therefore, the judgment creditor wishes to force the judgment debtor to sell the land, to realise the monies, he may apply for an order for sale. This is done by commencing new proceedings using the Part 8 procedure. It is in the court's discretion whether it makes an order for sale, and it is unlikely to do so if the amount of the debt secured by the charge is small.

15.3 INSOLVENCY PROCEEDINGS

Insolvency proceedings can be used as a means of enforcement because, once a judgment creditor has attempted to enforce a judgment and that judgment remains unsatisfied, that is evidence that the judgment debtor is unable to pay his debts (Insolvency Act 1986, ss 123(1) and 268(1)).

However, a judgment creditor who finds that he has to use insolvency proceedings after he has used litigation unsuccessfully, is probably a judgment creditor who made inadequate enquiries before commencing the litigation. He now finds himself in the position of having sued a person who was not worth suing, and the litigation was probably a waste of his time and money. The time to decide on whether or not to commence insolvency proceedings is before litigation, not afterwards.

In the case of an undisputed debt of £750 or more owed by a company, a creditor can serve a statutory demand on a debtor. For individual debtors the figure is £5,000. If the debtor does not pay the debt within three weeks, this is also evidence of inability to pay debts and entitles the creditor to issue insolvency proceedings.

In the case of undisputed debts of £750/£5,000 or more, therefore, a creditor has a choice. He can serve a statutory demand and follow it up by insolvency proceedings. Alternatively, he can send a letter before action and follow it up with court proceedings, an application for summary judgment if the debtor attempts to defend the proceedings, and then take the usual steps to enforce that judgment if payment is still not forthcoming.

15.3.1 The advantages of the insolvency route

Many debtors are not particularly worried about the prospect of being sued. Court proceedings take time and cost the creditor money. Although the creditor may get an order for costs, this will not cover all his legal costs, so he will never recover the full amount of the debt because he will have to use part of it to pay his unrecovered costs. The debtor will also have to pay interest on the debt from the time proceedings were issued, but he may regard this as an acceptable price to pay for being able to avoid paying the debt for a few more months. There may also be scope for negotiating a reduction in the debt during the proceedings.

Most importantly, most litigation is not very public. It is unlikely to become public knowledge that the debtor is being sued, and anyone who does learn of this may not be unduly worried by the knowledge, given that most businesses are involved in litigation at some time or other.

On the other hand, insolvency proceedings are public knowledge. Winding-up petitions are advertised, and credit reference agencies take note of such advertisements and pass the information on to their customers. This will affect the debtor's ability to obtain credit in future and this will damage their business, possibly irreparably.

For many debtors, therefore, the threat of insolvency proceedings is far more potent than the threat of litigation and is far more likely to result in immediate payment. It is, perhaps, also fair to say that some creditors take a certain pride in threatening insolvency proceedings.

15.3.2 The disadvantages of insolvency proceedings

A statutory demand is fine if it produces payment. The problem arises if the debtor still does not pay. The creditor then has to decide whether to take the matter further by issuing insolvency proceedings. It will appear odd if he does not carry through the threat, but if he does issue a winding-up petition, he will have to advertise it. This will result in all the other creditors joining in to pursue their claims, and it may then become impossible for the creditor who initiated the proceedings to recover all of his debt. Indeed, if he is an unsecured creditor and is not a preferential creditor, he may end up with little or nothing.

15.3.3 The statutory demand procedure – corporate debtors

The procedures for serving a statutory demand against a corporate debtor and an individual debtor (see **15.3.4**) are very similar, but it is important to take care to apply the appropriate Rules in each case and not to assume that they are the same. The procedures for challenging the statutory demand are very different.

An example of a statutory demand against a corporate debtor can be found in **Appendix 18** to this book.

15.3.3.1 Use and abuse

The statutory demand is intended to give a clear warning to a debtor company that unless it pays the debt in the next three weeks, it is at risk of being compulsorily wound up. The procedure is only available for undisputed debts of at least £750. It is an abuse of process to serve a statutory demand when the creditor knows that the debt is disputed. It is, however, legitimate to use a statutory demand where there is an undisputed debt of at least £750, even though the exact amount of the debt is in dispute.

15.3.3.2 Prescribed form

The Insolvency Rules 2016 set out the form that a statutory demand must take. It must name the parties and specify the amount of the debt. It must also give full details of when the debt was incurred and the consideration for the debt.

15.3.3.3 Service

Section 123(1)(a) simply says that the statutory demand should be served by leaving it at the debtor company's registered office. It does not say who should leave it there.

Many solicitors regard the safest course of action as being to serve the demand personally, although *Re a Company (No 008790 of 1990)* [1992] BCC 11 decided that the demand had been properly served if the demand was left at the registered office by any person, including the postman. The crucial point is, perhaps, that it is all too easy for the company to deny ever receiving a statutory demand sent by ordinary post. At the very least, the demand should be served by recorded delivery so that someone has to sign to acknowledge receipt.

15.3.3.4 Time period

The statutory demand allows the debtor three weeks to pay the debt. This excludes the day of service. If a statutory demand is served on 1 March, time does not start to run until 2 March. The three-week period then elapses on 22 March, but the creditor cannot issue a petition until the day after time has expired (ie 23 March). Obviously, if payment was received on 23 March the creditor would not actually issue a petition, but it would be a brave debtor who deliberately delayed payment until then. If the creditor legitimately issues a petition before payment is received, the debtor will usually have to reimburse the creditor for the costs of doing so.

15.3.3.5 Disputed statutory demand

In personal insolvency cases, the debtor can apply to set aside the statutory demand (see **15.3.4**). There is no formal procedure for setting aside a statutory demand served on a company. However, given the devastating effect which a winding-up petition can have on a company's business reputation, and the right of a company to protect its legitimate business interests, the courts will grant an injunction to restrain the presentation of an unjustified winding-up petition.

The grounds for seeking an injunction to restrain a winding-up petition will usually be that the debt is disputed and that the statutory demand was therefore an abuse of process. Injunctions have also been granted, however, on the basis that the statutory demand was not properly served, or that it contained errors which made it misleading. Procedural or drafting errors will result in an injunction only if the debtor can show that it has been prejudiced by the errors.

If an injunction restraining the petition is granted, the creditor will almost certainly be ordered to pay the debtor's costs.

15.3.4 The statutory demand procedure – individual insolvency

The rules on the use and abuse of statutory demands are the same for both individual and corporate insolvency (see **15.3.3**).

15.3.4.1 Prescribed forms

There are three types of statutory demand forms prescribed in r 10 of the Insolvency Rules 2016. There is one form for judgment debts, one for immediate debts and one for future debts. However, provided the debtor has not been misled and he can identify the issues in the claim, the fact that the creditor has used the wrong form will not invalidate the statutory demand (see *Re a Debtor (No 1 of 1987)* [1989] 1 WLR 271).

15.3.4.2 Service

Although r 10.3 of the Insolvency Rules 2016 treats personal service as being the usual method of serving a statutory demand (because this is the easiest way to rebut claims that the debtor never received the demand), it recognises that it is much easier for an individual debtor to evade service of a statutory demand. It therefore simply requires the creditor to do all that is reasonable to bring the statutory demand to the debtor's attention. This might include postal service (preferably by recorded delivery), or even substituted service on someone who, or by some means which, is likely to bring the statutory demand to the debtor's attention. Evidence of service other than personal service will be relevant in any application to set aside the statutory demand or any other challenge to later bankruptcy proceedings.

Rule 10.3 allows the creditor to rely upon any acknowledgement by the debtor that he has received the demand. Any method of service will be effective if it provokes a response (no matter how crude) from the debtor which shows that he has, in fact, received the demand.

15.3.4.3 Time period

The period for compliance with the demand is exactly the same (and is calculated in the same way) as for corporate insolvency. However, s 270 of the Insolvency Act 1986 allows the creditor to present a petition in less than three weeks if he can prove that there is a serious risk that the value of the debtor's assets is about to diminish significantly (eg he is trying to move his property out of the country).

15.3.4.4 Setting aside the statutory demand

On service of the statutory demand, the debtor has 18 days in which to apply to set aside the statutory demand. He will apply to the court which would have jurisdiction to hear the bankruptcy petition. There is a prescribed form of application and supporting affidavit. The debtor must use these. A letter to the court will not suffice (see *Ariyo v Sovereign Leasing plc* (1997) *The Times*, 4 August).

If the application to set aside the statutory demand is clearly doomed to fail, the court can dismiss it summarily without a full hearing. If there is to be a full hearing, all parties must be given at least seven days' notice of that hearing. The application will succeed if the court is satisfied that there are substantial grounds for disputing the debt, or if the debtor has a good right to a counterclaim or set-off, or if the creditor has adequate security for his debt or if the demand ought to be set aside on other grounds.

Matters of form are rarely good grounds for setting aside a statutory demand. Normally, the debtor will have to satisfy the court that it is unjust for the creditor to rely on the demand as proof of the debtor's inability to pay his debts by, for example, showing that he has paid the undisputed part of the debt, or that the undisputed part of the debt is less than £5,000.

15.3.5 The subsequent procedure

15.3.5.1 Corporate debtors

If the statutory demand is not challenged successfully, the next stage is to issue a winding-up petition against the company. The facts in the petition must be verified by a statement of truth. A hearing date will be fixed by the court. This will probably be in some six to eight weeks' time.

The petition must then be served on the company. Following service, the petition must be advertised in the *London Gazette* at least seven days after service has taken place and at least seven days before the hearing of the petition. Advertisement of the petition is a key stage in the process. This is because it alerts other creditors to the situation and can result, for example, in the company's bank freezing the company's account. There may also be difficulties in relation to any settlement which is subsequently reached between the creditor and debtor company.

At least five days before the date of the hearing, the petitioning creditor must file a Certificate of Compliance on all statutory matters (for example service and advertisement). At the hearing itself, although the court has the discretion to dismiss or adjourn the petition, provided the debt is still outstanding and the procedural requirements have been complied with, the petitioning creditor is usually entitled as of right to a winding-up order. Once this happens the Official Receiver will be notified.

15.3.5.2 Individual debtors

Again, assuming that the statutory demand is not challenged successfully, the next stage is to issue a bankruptcy petition against the individual. Again the court will fix a hearing date, but one significant difference between bankruptcy and the winding-up procedure is that there is no requirement for the bankruptcy petition to be advertised. If a bankruptcy order is made at the hearing then the Official Receiver will become the trustee in bankruptcy of the debtor.

15.3.6 Effect of insolvency proceedings on other proceedings

Once a winding-up or bankruptcy petition has been presented, the court has power to stay any other proceedings against the debtor pending the outcome of the insolvency proceedings (Insolvency Act 1986, ss 126 and 285). The court will be likely to grant a stay since any such proceedings will be a waste of time and money if the petition is successful.

The reason for this is that, if a winding-up or bankruptcy order is made, any enforcement proceedings commenced after the presentation of the petition are void, unless the court orders otherwise, and any enforcement proceedings which are incomplete will be set aside (Insolvency Act 1986, ss 128, 183, 184 and 346).

15.3.7 Settlement of insolvency proceedings

If a creditor and debtor reach a settlement of their claim after service of a statutory demand and before the presentation of a petition, the settlement should be entirely safe for both parties. It simply means that the statutory demand has achieved its intended result, and there is no real risk of the settlement being set aside as a preference, since a payment made by the debtor to ward off insolvency proceedings is a payment made for good consideration.

Settlements made after the presentation of the petition are rather more unreliable. The settlement may still be valid as between creditor and debtor if it is made for good consideration (eg, payment is made in return for withdrawal of the petition); but the presentation of an insolvency petition is a public act (especially once a winding-up petition has been advertised), and the debtor may find that even though he has settled the claim by the petitioning creditor, some other creditor may apply to be substituted as a new petitioning creditor so that the debtor is still faced with the imminent threat of insolvency.

15.3.8 Maximising the assets

If the case does go all the way and the debtor company is wound up, creditors should remember the rules on wrongful and fraudulent trading which can result in directors of a company being required to make personal contributions to the company's assets to help meet its debts. Those directors may also face disqualification proceedings, and the threat of such proceedings may persuade directors to make voluntary contributions without any need for wrongful or fraudulent trading proceedings.

Creditors should also remember the rules on preferences which relate to both corporate and individual insolvency proceedings, and which can result in the setting aside of transactions, especially with 'connected persons', leading to the recovery of assets previously disposed of by the debtor.

These topics are covered in more detail in the Legal Practice Guide, **Business Law and Practice**.

15.3.9   Voluntary procedures

This chapter has dealt with compulsory insolvency. Readers should remember that there is a wide range of voluntary procedures whereby a debtor can enter into a composition with his or its creditors. These are dealt with in the Legal Practice Guide, **Business Law and Practice**.

15.4   SUMMARY

Enforcement should be considered before commencing proceedings, and if the proposed defendant is not worth suing, the client should write off the debt or consider whether insolvency proceedings would be appropriate. Insolvency proceedings are not appropriate if the debt is disputed.

If judgment is obtained against the defendant, it can be enforced against his goods by execution, against his bank account (or other debts owed to the judgment debtor) by third party debt proceedings and against his land by a charging order. Charging orders can also be made against other properties listed in the Charging Orders Act 1979.

Insolvency proceedings are an alternative to litigation followed by enforcement of a judgment. Ironically, insolvency proceedings (or the threat of them) are likely to be more effective against a solvent debtor than an insolvent debtor.

15.5   FURTHER READING

J O'Hare and K Browne, *Civil Litigation* (20th edn, 2021).

PART II

FOREIGN ELEMENT

FOREIGN ELEMENT: COMMENCING PROCEEDINGS

LEARNING OUTCOMES

After reading this chapter you will understand:

- how the Brussels Regulation governs the conduct of civil proceedings within the EU
- the rules relating to taking proceedings against a party outside the EU
- the circumstances in which proceedings commenced in England and Wales may be stayed
- the advantages and disadvantages of litigation abroad.

16.1 INTRODUCTION

When first instructed in relation to a potential piece of litigation, the solicitor will have to consider, as one of the preliminary steps, where the action should be conducted or, if an action has already commenced, whether proceedings have been issued in the correct country. These preliminary considerations are essential, particularly where one of the parties, or the subject matter of the action, is foreign or located abroad.

There are different complex sets of rules which apply to determine jurisdiction and which depend on whether the foreign country involved (whether because of the nationality/domicile of one of the parties or the subject matter of the action) is an EU State, part of the UK or somewhere else in the world.

In a contractual dispute, it is essential for the solicitor to check whether the contract contains an arbitration or jurisdiction clause which then may take precedence over the applicable rules (see **16.2.2** and **16.2.10**).

The Brussels Convention on Jurisdiction and the Enforcement of Judgments in Civil and Commercial Matters (Brussels, 1968) ('the Brussels Convention') dealt with the issue of jurisdiction as between Member States of the EU. In a slightly amended form, it became part of English law by virtue of the Civil Jurisdiction and Judgments Act 1982 (CJJA 1982). The CJJA 1982 also regulates jurisdiction as between the various parts of the UK.

On 1 March 2002, the Brussels Convention was largely replaced by Council Regulation 44/2001 ('the Brussels Regulation'). The Brussels Regulation largely followed the existing provisions of the Brussels Convention, but did make some changes in order to clarify and simplify various aspects of jurisdiction.

Following a lengthy period of consultation, the Brussels Regulation has now been updated by Council Regulation 1215/2012. The Brussels Regulation (recast) will apply to proceedings instituted within EU countries on or after 10 January 2015. Whilst much of the previous Regulation remains unchanged, there have been some important amendments to the previous Regulation which are referred to below.

The non-EU Western European countries of Iceland, Norway and Switzerland come under the Lugano Convention. The Lugano Convention on Jurisdiction and the Enforcement of Judgments in Civil and Commercial Matters (Lugano, 1988) was replaced by the 2007 Lugano Convention, the effects of which are much the same as the Brussels Regulation. The operative provisions of Lugano 2007 and the Brussels Regulation follow the same numbering.

The Channel Islands and the Isle of Man are not part of the UK or the EU. They are subject to the common law rules on jurisdiction which the English courts apply to the rest of the world.

This chapter deals first with the rules in Chapter II of the Brussels Regulation which decide which State's courts have jurisdiction in litigation involving parties based in different Member States of the EU. The CJJA 1982, however, also had to deal with the fact that, although the UK is a Member State of the EU, it has three internal jurisdictions (England and Wales, Scotland, and Northern Ireland). The CJJA 1982 had to deal with the problem of litigants based in different jurisdictions within the UK. In the main, it adopted the rules of the Brussels Convention, but it did depart from this Convention in three cases, which are dealt with at **16.3**.

In reading this chapter, it will become apparent that there are some cases where a party will be able to commence proceedings in more than one State, and **16.7–16.9** deal with the complex issue of 'forum shopping' (ie deciding in which country it is best to commence proceedings).

16.2   THE EUROPEAN UNION

The effect of Brexit

As far as legal proceedings are concerned, Article 67(1) of the EU–UK Withdrawal Agreement states that the current EU rules on international jurisdiction will continue to apply to proceedings instituted before the end of the transition period on 31 December 2020. Similarly, the EU rules on the recognition and enforcement of judgments (see **Chapter 17**) will continue to apply to the recognition and enforcement of judgments given in legal proceedings instituted before the end of the transition period.

But from 1 January 2021 the Brussels Regulation (recast) will no longer apply to the UK. What will take its place?

The UK has submitted its application to re-accede to the Lugano Convention. Although supported by Iceland, Norway and Switzerland, this still requires the consent of the EU which has not yet been forthcoming.

Pending that, there is a potential issue in relation to requiring the permission of the court to serve proceedings out of the jurisdiction, particularly in cases where the contract between the parties contains a jurisdiction clause in favour of England and Wales (see **16.2.10** below).

In some cases a party may be able to rely on the 2005 Hague Choice of Court Convention which applies to exclusive choice of court agreements entered into after 1 October 2015. This would enable a party to issue proceedings in this country against a defendant domiciled in another contracting country (which includes all EU states, Mexico, Montenegro and

Singapore) and serve them abroad without requiring permission to do so. This is now covered by CPR 1998, r 6.33(2B)(a).

In cases where the Hague Convention does not apply, r 6.33(2B)(b) now allows service out of the jurisdiction without permission where 'a contract contains a term to the effect that the court shall have jurisdiction to determine the claim'.

This provision will be relevant where the defendant resides in a non-Hague Convention country or where the jurisdiction clause is not exclusive, which is a requirement of the Hague Convention. If a party wants any dispute arising out of a contract to be determined in the English and Welsh courts, it is therefore crucial to include such a jurisdiction clause if at all possible.

The remaining parts of this section (**16.2**) remain valid for proceedings that were commenced before 1 January 2021 and may become relevant again as and when the UK is able to re-accede to the Lugano Convention.

16.2.1 Civil and commercial matters

It is important to note that the Brussels Regulation (recast) (hereinafter 'the Brussels Regulation') applies only to civil and commercial matters. As a result, for example, revenue, customs and administrative matters, questions of status or legal capacity and bankruptcy are excluded from the Brussels Regulation, and each Member State can apply its own rules in deciding whether or not to accept jurisdiction.

Moreover, the Brussels Regulation does not apply to arbitration (including disputes as to whether there is an arbitration agreement: Case C-190/89 *Marc Rich & Co AG v Societa Italiana Impianti PA, The Atlantic Emperor* [1992] 1 Lloyd's Rep 342). A client who enters into an agreement whereby all disputes will be resolved by arbitration in England has by-passed the Brussels Regulation. Arbitration in England has a very high reputation throughout the commercial world. Foreign businesspersons may well be prepared to accept English arbitration instead of litigation in their own country.

Guidance as to how the Courts of Member States should consider arbitration clauses is provided in recital 12 to the Brussels Regulation. This states:

> This Regulation shall not apply to arbitration. Nothing in this Regulation should prevent the courts of a Member State, when seised of an action in a matter in respect of which the parties have entered into an arbitration agreement, from referring the parties to arbitration, from staying or dismissing the proceedings, or from examining whether the arbitration agreement is null and void, inoperative or incapable of being performed, in accordance with their national law.
>
> A ruling given by a Court of a Member State as to whether an arbitration agreement is null and void, inoperative or incapable of being performed should not be subject to the rules of recognition and enforcement laid down in this Regulation, regardless of whether the court decided on this as a principal issue or as an incidental question.

16.2.2 The basic rule

The defendant must be sued in his local courts (Article 4 of the Brussels Regulation). If he is an individual, his local courts are in the place where he is domiciled. Section 41 of the CJJA 1982 defines domicile as a place with which a person has a substantial connection, bearing in mind the nature and circumstances of his residence. Three months' residence will prima facie establish domicile.

If the defendant is a corporate body, it should be sued where it 'has its seat', ie its registered office or other official address, or the place where it is centrally managed or controlled (Article 63).

In both cases, the defendant's domicile is ascertained on the basis of the facts as they existed when the proceedings were issued (see *Canada Trust Co v Stolzenberg (No 2)* [1998] 1 WLR 547).

An English claimant who wants to sue a French defendant will therefore have to sue in France (assuming the defendant is domiciled there), unless he can find an exception to the basic rule which allows him to sue in England.

Notwithstanding the basic rule, it is possible to seek interim relief such as an injunction in the courts of any Member State of the EU in aid of proceedings being taken elsewhere in the EU, if it is just and convenient to do so (see **8.10.2**).

16.2.3   Defendant companies

By Article 7(5) of the Brussels Regulation, if a company domiciled in one EU State has a branch, agency or other establishment in another EU State, and the dispute arises out of the activities of that branch, agency or other establishment, the company can be sued in the courts of the State where that branch, agency or other establishment is located. So, for example, if a French company has an office in England and that office fails to pay a debt owed to an English client, that company can be sued in England.

This applies only if the foreign company has set up a branch, agency or other establishment in England. If it has merely instructed an independent trader to represent its interests in this country, then the basic rule under the Brussels Regulation applies and it must be sued in its local courts.

16.2.4   Co-defendants

If one of the defendants is domiciled in England, he can be sued here and other defendants can be joined as parties even though they are domiciled elsewhere in the EU (Article 8(1)).

Similarly, if proceedings are properly brought against a defendant in England, that defendant can issue Part 20 proceedings joining parties over whom the English courts would not otherwise have jurisdiction. Note, however, that this only applies where the court has jurisdiction over the primary defendant under the basic rule. If the court is exercising jurisdiction under one of the other alternatives to the basic rule (eg, contract and tort cases – see **16.2.5** and **16.2.6**), other co-defendants cannot be joined under the provision (Case C-51/97 *Reunion Européene v Spliethoffs Bevrachtingskantoor* [1998] ECR I-6511).

16.2.5   Contract cases

In matters relating to a contract, Article 7(1) of the Brussels Regulation confers jurisdiction in contract cases on the courts of the State for the place of performance of the obligation in question.

Unless otherwise agreed (eg by some provision in the contract), the place of performance of the obligation in question shall be:

(a)   in the case of sale of goods, the place in the Member State where the goods were delivered or should have been delivered;

(b)   in the case of the provision of services, the place in the Member State where, under the contract, the services were provided or should have been provided.

EXAMPLE 1

A French businessperson employs an English company to build a factory for her in France and there is a dispute about the construction of the building. The French businessperson can sue in France because that was the place where the factory was to be built.

> **EXAMPLE 2**
>
> A German company supplies an English company with machinery. The English company alleges that it was not fit for its particular purpose. The courts where the goods were delivered will have jurisdiction: the disputed term is the obligation to supply goods fit for their purpose and this obligation is performed at the time of delivery (*Viskase Ltd v Paul Kiefal GmbH* [1999] 1 WLR 1305).
>
> What if the English company had not paid for the machinery? Assuming that payment was to be made to a bank in Germany, the German company could take proceedings for non-payment of any balance due in Germany (and see **Example 3** below).

> **EXAMPLE 3**
>
> An English company wishes to sue an Italian company for non-payment of shipbroking fees. If, under the contract, payment was to take place in England, proceedings can take place here (*Atlas Shipping Agency (UK) Ltd and United Shipping Services Ltd v Suisse Atlantique Société d'Armement Maritime SA, Labuk Bay Shipping Inc and Ulugan Bay Shipping Inc, The Gulf Grain and El Amaan* [1995] 2 Lloyd's Rep 188).

Where more than one obligation is in dispute, the courts for the place where the principal obligation was to be performed have jurisdiction (Case 266/85 *Shenavai v Kreischer* [1987] 3 CMLR 782). Occasionally, the terms in dispute will rank equally. In such a case, only the defendant's local court will be able to hear the entire claim. A court elsewhere will only be able to deal with that part of the dispute which relates to the term to be performed within its jurisdiction (Case C-420/97 *Leathertex Divisione Sintetici SpA v Bodetex BVBA* [1999] 2 All ER (Comm) 769).

16.2.6 Tort cases

Article 7(2) of the Brussels Regulation confers jurisdiction in tort cases on the courts of the State where the harmful event occurred or may occur. This includes the place where the harm caused by the tort occurred (Case 211/76 *Handelskwekerij GJ Bier BV v Mines de Potasse D'Alsace SA* [1978] QB 708). Thus, if a French manufacturer makes a piece of machinery negligently and sells it to an English customer who is harmed by the defect in England, the customer can sue either in France (where the tort was committed) or in England (where the damage occurred). A court can hear a case under this rule even though only part of the harm was caused within its jurisdiction (*Shevill v Presse Alliance SA* [1992] 1 All ER 409). On appeal, however, the *Shevill* case introduced a new dimension for cases where harm has occurred in more than one State (Case C-68/93 [1995] 2 AC 18). The European Court of Justice (ECJ) ruled that the courts for the State where the defendant was domiciled or 'had its seat' (see **16.2.2**) could deal with the harm caused in all Member States of the EU, whereas the court for the State where the harm occurred could only award remedies for the harm which occurred in that State.

Ironically, the claimant in *Shevill* continued with her action in the place where the harm occurred (England) rather than in the place where the defendant was based, presumably because it was a defamation action and the law and level of damages in England were more favourable to her than under French law.

Article 7(3) was given a further refinement by the Court of Appeal in *Marinari v Lloyds Bank* [1996] QB 217. Although the claimant had suffered financial loss in this country, the physical damage had occurred in another EU State. The Court of Appeal held that 'the place where the harm occurred' meant the place where the physical harm had occurred, so that the English courts did not have jurisdiction to hear the case.

The court for the State where the claimant commences proceedings decides whether the defendant's conduct is a tort or has caused a harmful event under the laws of that State.

In cases of negligent misstatement and (presumably) all other misrepresentation cases, jurisdiction is conferred on the courts for the State where the misrepresentation was made, not where it was received (see *Domicrest Ltd v Swiss Bank Corporation* [1999] QB 548).

16.2.7   Insurance contracts

Insurance contracts are governed by Articles 10–16 of the Brussels Regulation. The insured can always sue the insurer in the courts for the State where the insured is based, although he may use the insurer's local court if he prefers. If the insurer is suing the insured, he must do so in the insured's local courts.

Liability insurers and insurers of immovable property can be sued in the courts for the State where the harm giving rise to the claim occurred.

An insurance contract cannot exclude the above rules. When the insured makes a claim, however, the parties may agree to confer jurisdiction on the courts of some other State.

The provisions in Articles 10–16 do not apply to reinsurance (see the House of Lords decision in *Agnew v Lansforsakringsbolagens AB* [2000] 1 All ER 737).

16.2.8   Consumer contracts

Articles 17–19 of the Brussels Regulation lay down similar rules for consumer contracts to those which apply to insurance contracts. Thus, the consumer can usually 'play at home' (although there are special rules for transport contracts) and the jurisdiction rules can only be altered by agreement after a dispute has arisen.

The Brussels Regulation defines a consumer as a person entering into a contract 'for a purpose which can be regarded as being outside his trade or profession'.

A consumer contract is defined as either:

(a)   a sale of goods on instalment credit terms, or

(b)   a loan repayable by instalments or any other form of credit made to finance the sale of goods [eg hire purchase], or

(c)   a contract concluded with a person who pursues commercial or professional activities in the Member State of the consumer's domicile or, by any means, directs such activities to that Member State or to several states including that Member State, and the contract falls within the scope of such activities.

Paragraph (c) will include selling over the Internet.

16.2.9   Exclusive jurisdiction (Article 24)

Most of the 'exceptions' to the basic rule that the defendant is sued in his local courts are, in fact, *alternatives* to the basic rule. There is nothing to stop a claimant in a breach of contract case from suing the defendant in the State where the defendant is domiciled rather than in the State where the contract was to be performed if that is more convenient. The rules on insurance and consumer contracts are true exceptions to the basic rule, but do make limited provision for the parties to agree to refer the dispute to some other State's courts. There are, however, five cases where the Brussels Regulation confers jurisdiction exclusively on the courts of one State and the parties cannot alter the rules by agreement and do not have the option of suing in the defendant's local courts.

16.2.9.1   Land

In 'proceedings relating to rights in rem in or tenancies of immovable property', the Brussels Regulation confers exclusive jurisdiction on the courts for the State where the property is situated. So if someone domiciled in England owns property in France, and there is a dispute about, for example, rights of way, repairs, or payments of rent, any court proceedings must be taken in France, whether the owner is the claimant or the defendant.

This rule can cause considerable inconvenience. There is a minor exception for short leases where both parties have the same domicile, but more importantly, there is case law which avoids some of the problems this rule can cause.

Equitable interests

In *Webb v Webb* [1992] 1 All ER 17, a father had purchased a holiday flat in France in his son's name. He subsequently issued proceedings in England claiming ownership of the flat. The English courts accepted jurisdiction even though the property in question was in France. They did so because the father was seeking a declaration of trust (ie that the son was holding the property on trust for him) and they said that this was not covered by (now) Article 24. This decision was subsequently confirmed by the ECJ ([1994] 3 WLR 801). Indeed, the English court suggested that any claim for any equitable remedy (eg specific performance) would take the case outside (now) Article 18 and leave the claimant free to sue in the defendant's local court if he so chose.

16.2.9.2 Companies

Proceedings relating to the validity of the constitution of a company, association or other legal person or its dissolution must be taken in the State where the company has its seat (see **16.2.2**).

16.2.9.3 Intellectual property

Proceedings relating to the registration or validity of patents, trade marks, designs and other registered intellectual property rights must be taken in the State where the registration was applied for or has taken place. The exclusive jurisdiction rule only applies to disputes about the registration or validity of these intellectual property rights. If the dispute is about whether they have been infringed, the normal rules in **16.2.2**, **16.2.5** and **16.2.6** apply.

16.2.9.4 Entries in public registers

Proceedings which have as their object the validity of entries in public registers must be taken in the courts of the State in which the register is kept.

16.2.9.5 Enforcement

Any disputes arising out of the enforcement of a judgment must be heard in the State where the judgment is being enforced.

16.2.10 Jurisdiction agreements (Article 25)

The parties to a contract or a dispute may enter into a jurisdiction agreement conferring jurisdiction on the courts of whichever State they choose. They can thus exclude the other terms of the Brussels Regulation. The agreement must be in writing or evidenced in writing, or be capable of being inferred from an international trade or commercial activity of which the parties were or should have been aware.

One of the most significant changes made by the Brussels Regulation (recast) to the previous Regulation concerns jurisdiction agreements. Under the previous Regulation, one or more of the parties had to be domiciled in a Member State. Under the new provision, the parties may be domiciled anywhere. The new provision is set out below:

Article 25

1. If the parties, regardless of their domicile, have agreed that a court or the courts of a Member State are to have jurisdiction to settle any disputes which have arisen or which may arise in connection with a particular legal relationship, that court or those courts shall have jurisdiction, unless the agreement is null and void as to its substantive validity under the law of that Member State. Such jurisdiction shall be exclusive unless the parties have agreed otherwise. The agreement conferring jurisdiction shall be either:

(a)   in writing or evidenced in writing;

(b)   in a form which accords with practices which the parties have established between themselves; or

(c)   in international trade or commerce, in a form which accords with a usage of which the parties are or ought to have been aware and which in such trade or commerce is widely known to, and regularly observed by, parties to contracts of the type involved in the particular trade or commerce concerned.

2.   Any communication by electronic means which provides a durable record of the agreement shall be equivalent to 'writing'.

3.   The court or courts of a Member State on which a trust instrument has conferred jurisdiction shall have exclusive jurisdiction in any proceedings brought against a settlor, trustee or beneficiary, if relations between those persons or their rights or obligations under the trust are involved.

4.   Agreements or provisions of a trust instrument conferring jurisdiction shall have no legal force if they are contrary to Articles 15, 19 or 23, or if the courts whose jurisdiction they purport to exclude have exclusive jurisdiction by virtue of Article 24.

5.   An agreement conferring jurisdiction which forms part of a contract shall be treated as an agreement independent of the other terms of the contract.

       The validity of the agreement conferring jurisdiction cannot be contested solely on the ground that the contract is not valid.

If the contract deals with jurisdiction, it should also state which country's law is to apply to the contract – a choice of law clause. If there is no choice of law clause, English courts will apply the rules of the Rome Convention (see **16.10**).

A jurisdiction agreement cannot be used to exclude the rules on insurance and consumer contracts or the exclusive jurisdiction rules (see **16.2.7–16.2.9**).

16.2.11   Submission to the jurisdiction (Article 26)

If the defendant voluntarily submits to the jurisdiction of a foreign court then, irrespective of the terms of the Brussels Regulation, that court will usually be entitled to deal with the case. Thus, if a French person is sued in the English courts and acknowledges service of the claim form and continues to take part in the proceedings, the English court can hear the case and the defendant cannot later argue that the court did not have jurisdiction.

A defendant who has been sued here and who considers that the English courts do not have jurisdiction will have to acknowledge service of the claim form. If he does not, the claimant will enter a default judgment. Once he has acknowledged service, he should apply under Part 11 of CPR 1998 for a declaration that the court does not have jurisdiction. If he does not make that application within 14 days of filing the acknowledgement of service (28 days in the Commercial Court and Circuit Commercial Courts), he will be treated as having accepted that the English courts have jurisdiction to try the claim. The application under Part 11 automatically extends the time for filing a defence until the court rules on the jurisdiction issue. If the court decides to accept jurisdiction, it will then give directions for the time for filing a defence.

It is not possible to submit to the jurisdiction if the exclusive jurisdiction rules apply (see **16.2.9**).

16.3   THE UNITED KINGDOM

If there is a dispute between, for example, a claimant based in Scotland and a defendant based in England, the rules on whether the Scottish or English courts have jurisdiction are broadly the same as the rules which apply under the Brussels Regulation (see **16.2**). The full rules governing such disputes are set out in Sch 4 to the CJJA 1982, which for ease of reference is described in this chapter as the 'UK Convention'. There are three main differences between the Brussels Regulation and the rules governing disputes where one party is based in one part of the UK and the other party is based in another part of the UK.

16.3.1 Intellectual property rights

Intellectual property rights are not 'civil and commercial matters' for the purposes of the UK Convention. As a result, there is no exclusive jurisdiction rule for disputes concerning the registration or validity of such rights within the UK. Disputes within the UK about such matters are subject to the common law rules which apply to the rest of the world.

16.3.2 Insurance contracts

There are no special rules in the UK Convention for insurance contracts.

16.3.3 Jurisdiction agreements

The UK Convention does not require jurisdiction agreements to be written or evidenced in writing. It recognises oral agreements.

16.4 THE REST OF THE WORLD

16.4.1 Suing in England

16.4.1.1 Individual defendants

The English courts can hear any proceedings if the claim form was served on the defendant while he was present in England and Wales (no matter how briefly).

16.4.1.2 Corporate defendants

If a foreign company has an established place of business within the jurisdiction, proceedings can be served on it there under s 1139 of the Companies Act 2006 in order to give the English court jurisdiction. The claim form must be addressed to the person whose name has been delivered to the Registrar of Companies as a person resident in Britain who is authorised to accept service on the company's behalf.

16.4.1.3 Permission to serve out of the jurisdiction

If it is not possible to effect service within the jurisdiction, the claimant needs permission under r 6.36 of CPR 1998 to serve the claim form out of the jurisdiction. He must show that the matter falls within para 3.1 of PD 6B. There are some 20 jurisdictional categories or 'gateways' set out there. The objective is to enable the court to exercise jurisdiction over defendants in the rest of the world where the subject matter of the dispute has a sufficiently close connection with this country. The more important grounds include the following:

(a) The claim is in respect of a contract made within the jurisdiction or which is governed by English law.

(b) The claim is made in respect of a breach of contract committed within the jurisdiction.

(c) The claim is made in tort where the damage was sustained within the jurisdiction or the damage sustained resulted from an act committed within the jurisdiction.

In *FS Cairo v Brownlie* [2021] UKSC 45, the Supreme Court, in upholding the earlier decision of the Court of Appeal, confirmed that this ground included cases where, although the original incident was a car accident in Egypt, the claimant had sustained damage within the jurisdiction (England and Wales) as she continued to suffer after returning home.

(d) The claim is made against a person (the 'defendant') on whom the claim form has been or will be served, and there is between the claimant and defendant a real issue to be tried and the claimant wishes to serve the claim form on another person who is a necessary or proper party to that claim.

Even if para 3.1 applies, the claimant will not be given permission unless he also establishes that the claim has a reasonable prospect of success and that England is the most convenient place for the case to be tried (*Seaconsar (Far East) Ltd v Bank Markazi Jomhouri Islami Iran* [1993] 4 All ER 456 and *Spiliada Maritime Corp v Cansulex Ltd, The Spiliada* [1987] AC 460).

The claimant applies for permission without notice with supporting evidence. The evidence should deal with the matters referred to above. It must also give details of anything that casts doubt on the application.

Permission is granted for only one country at a time.

16.4.1.4 Service of documents subsequent to the claim form

Where the particulars of claim are not served with the claim form, there is no need to apply to the court for permission to serve them out of the jurisdiction (r 6.38(2)).

Subject to this exception, r 6.38(1) provides that where permission has been required to serve the claim form out of the jurisdiction, permission is also needed to serve any other document in the proceedings if it is to be served outside the jurisdiction. In most cases, such permission will not be required since the defendant is obliged by r 6.23(2) to give an address for service within the United Kingdom. (This will usually be that of the defendant's solicitor.) If that address is in Scotland or Northern Ireland, permission is not required – r 6.38(3).

16.4.1.5 Part 20 claims

Where a defendant issues a Part 20 third party claim form and the third party is outside the EU, permission to serve out will need to be obtained.

Where, however, the Part 20 claim is a counterclaim, such permission will not be required. Rule 6.36 is concerned only with the service of claim forms and a counterclaim is made by the defendant in his statement of case; no Part 20 claim form is issued. This is in line with pre-CPR authorities which make clear that by suing in England, a foreign claimant submits to the jurisdiction in relation to any counterclaim (*Derby & Co v Larsson* [1976] 1 WLR 202).

16.4.2 Being sued abroad

Apart from the Hague Convention, Brussels Regulation and Brussels and Lugano Conventions, England is not a party to any other Convention on jurisdiction. The question of whether an English defendant can be sued in a foreign country depends on that country's jurisdiction rules.

16.5 SERVICE

16.5.1 Regulation and Convention countries

If proceedings were instituted before 1 January 2021 and the English courts have jurisdiction under the Brussels Regulation, Brussels Convention or Lugano Convention, the claimant does not need permission to serve out of the jurisdiction.

If proceedings were instituted on or after 1 January 2021 then if the claim falls within the provisions of r 6.33(2B)(a) (Hague Convention cases) or r 6.33(2B)(b) (contract contains a jurisdiction clause in favour of England and Wales), the claimant does not need permission to serve out of the jurisdiction.

The claim form must be accompanied by practice form N510, setting out the grounds under r 6.33 on which the claimant relies.

The claim form must be served within six months after the date of issue (as compared with four months where it is served within the jurisdiction). The fact that the law of the State where the claim form is served allows a longer period is irrelevant (*Abdullah Ali Almunajem Sons Co v Recourse Shipping Co Ltd* [1994] 1 Lloyd's Rep 584).

The defendant has 21 days from the date of service of the particulars of claim to acknowledge service or file a defence. If he chooses to acknowledge, he must file his defence within 35 days of service of the particulars of claim.

16.5.1.1 Methods of service

Service must be by a method permitted by the laws of the country where it is effected.

Within the EU, there is nothing to prevent the claimant from posting the claim form to the defendant, provided that service by post is permitted in the State where it is to occur. The State may have rules about how postal service must be effected which will need to be followed.

Alternatively, where service is to be effected in a State which is a signatory to the Hague Convention, the claimant may request the court to arrange service by a central authority. This method is not available for service in Scotland, Northern Ireland or the Republic of Ireland.

16.5.1.2 Default judgments

Once the claim form has been served, the defendant should acknowledge service and serve a defence. If he fails to do either of these two things, the claimant is, of course, entitled to enter a default judgment. Unlike the procedure where both parties are based in England (see the Legal Practice Guide, *Civil Litigation*), the claimant has to make a formal application under Part 23. He applies without notice with supporting evidence explaining:

(a) why the English court has jurisdiction;

(b) how the claim form was served; and

(c) that no other court has exclusive jurisdiction.

This enables the court to satisfy itself that it does have jurisdiction to grant judgment.

16.5.2 Non-Convention countries

16.5.2.1 The Commonwealth, the Channel Islands, and the Isle of Man

Direct service on the defendant should be arranged in the Channel Islands, the Isle of Man or any independent Commonwealth country. Service must be effected under the rules of the territory in question.

16.5.2.2 Parties to other civil procedure Conventions

There are other States with which England has entered into other Conventions on the service of proceedings. These go beyond the scope of this book.

16.5.2.3 Other States

As far as other States are concerned, service is usually effected through the government of the State in question or the British Consul.

16.5.2.4 Default judgments

If the defendant does not acknowledge service of the claim form or serve a defence, the claimant is entitled to a default judgment. He does not have to make a special application to the court because the court has already satisfied itself that it does have jurisdiction (see **16.4.1**). The claimant can therefore enter default judgment in the usual way (see the Legal Practice Guide, *Civil Litigation*).

16.6 STAYING ENGLISH PROCEEDINGS

If a claimant sues a foreign defendant in England, the defendant may seek a stay of proceedings so that the matter can be litigated in another country. The grounds for seeking such a stay will depend upon whether the parties are both based in the EU.

16.6.1   The parties are based in different EU States

The court will first look to see whether there is a binding jurisdiction agreement or whether the defendant has done something whereby he is deemed to have submitted to the jurisdiction. In relation to jurisdiction agreements, Article 31(2) states:

> ... where a court of a Member State on which an agreement as referred to in Article 25 confers exclusive jurisdiction is seised, any court of another Member State shall stay the proceedings until such time as the Court seised on the basis of the agreement declares that it has no jurisdiction under the agreement.

This provision is designed to enhance the effectiveness of jurisdiction agreements. This is further supported by recital 22 to the Regulation which states:

> However, in order to enhance the effectiveness of exclusive choice-of-court agreements and to avoid abusive litigation tactics, it is necessary to provide for an exception to the general *lis pendens* rule in order to deal satisfactorily with a particular situation in which concurrent proceedings may arise. This is the situation where a court not designated in an exclusive choice-of-court agreement has been seised of proceedings and the designated court is seised subsequently of proceedings involving the same cause of action and between the same parties. In such a case, the court first seised should be required to stay its proceedings as soon as the designated court has been seised and until such time as the latter court declares that it has no jurisdiction under the exclusive choice-of-court agreement. This is to ensure that, in such a situation, the designated court has priority to decide on the validity of the agreement and on the extent to which the agreement applies to the dispute pending before it. The designated court should be able to proceed irrespective of whether the non-designated court has already decided on the stay of proceedings.

Assuming that this is not the case and that the English court does have jurisdiction under the Brussels Regulation, then the defendant cannot stop the English proceedings even if he can show that it would be more convenient for the litigation to be conducted in some other EU State. He can stop the English proceedings only if he can show that proceedings have already been commenced elsewhere in the EU – that the court of another Member State is already 'seised' of the matter.

If proceedings involving the *same* parties and the *same* cause of action have already been commenced in some other EU State, the English courts cannot hear the case (Brussels Regulation, Article 29).

If the proceedings elsewhere in the EU do not involve the *same* cause of action but involve a *related* cause of action, the English court has a discretion to decide whether or not to accept jurisdiction (Brussels Regulation, Article 30). In exercising this discretion, the English court has to consider whether there is any risk that its judgment will conflict with the judgment of the other EU court dealing with the related issue. If there is any such danger, the English courts should decline jurisdiction (see *Virgin Aviation Services Ltd v CAD Aviation Services* (1990) *The Times, 2 February*).

By Article 32 of the Brussels Regulation, a court shall be deemed to be seised:

(a)   at the time when the document instituting the proceedings or an equivalent document is lodged with the court, provided that the claimant has not subsequently failed to take the steps he was required to take to have service effected on the defendant; or

(b)   if the document has to be served before being lodged with the court, at the time when it is received by the authority responsible for service, provided that the claimant has not subsequently failed to take the steps he was required to take to have the document lodged with the court.

So in England and Wales the courts are first seised of proceedings when the claim form is issued, provided that service is then effected on the defendant in accordance with CPR 1998.

Winning the 'jurisdiction race' can be of great tactical importance, and there have been cases in recent years where although the English courts clearly had jurisdiction under the Brussels

Regulation, a foreign defendant has used the device of applying in another court which had jurisdiction under the Brussels Regulation for a 'declaration of non-liability'. By serving notice of this application before the English claimant could serve his claim form, the defendant was able to ensure that the case was heard in a State which suited his convenience rather than the convenience of the English claimant. The English courts were traditionally reluctant to grant declarations of non-liability, but the Court of Appeal has since indicated that there is no reason why one should not be granted in appropriate circumstances (*Messier-Dowty Ltd & X-MD Ltd v Sabena SA, GIE Airbus Industrie & British Aerospace Airbus Ltd* [2000] 1 All ER (Comm) 833).

An example of the effect of these provisions and the ways parties may use them for tactical purposes is the case of *J P Morgan Ltd v Primacom* [2005] EWHC 508. The claimant acted as agent for a number of banks that had provided a loan facility to the defendant, a German group of companies. The defendant failed to make interest payments on time and accountants were appointed to prepare a report on its financial position.

The defendant then issued proceedings in Germany claiming that, by virtue of certain provisions in German law, no interest was due under the loan agreement because it was contrary to German public policy (its argument was that the interest rate charged was double the market rate). It issued these proceedings in Germany despite the fact that the agreement between the parties was governed by English law and contained an exclusive English jurisdiction clause.

The claimant then commenced three sets of proceedings against the defendant in the Commercial Court – the first for an injunction preventing the defendant from disposing of a Dutch subsidiary company without its consent (an interim injunction was granted), the second for disclosure of the accountants' report, and the third for a declaration that the loan agreement was binding and enforceable and that the defendant was in default.

The defendant applied, under Part 11 of CPR 1998, for a stay of all three sets of proceedings on the basis that the German courts were 'first seised', relying on (now) Article 29 or alternatively (now) Article 30 of the Brussels Regulation.

The judge held that the third set of proceedings involved the same parties and the same cause of action, and that therefore he was bound, under (now) Article 29, to stay those proceedings until the German courts decided whether or not they had jurisdiction.

However, in relation to the first and second sets of proceedings, the judge found that although they clearly involved the same parties, they only involved a related cause of action and that therefore he had a discretion under (now) Article 30 as to whether to stay the English proceedings. He decided that all the relevant discretionary factors were against a stay and therefore allowed those English proceedings to continue.

16.6.2 The parties are based in different parts of the UK

A defendant may object to the jurisdiction of the English courts on the ground, for example, that it would be more convenient for the action to be tried by the courts of Northern Ireland (*Cumming v Scottish Daily Record and Sunday Mail* [1995] EMLR 538) (see **16.6.3**).

The defendant can also object to proceedings in one part of the UK on the grounds that proceedings have already been commenced in another part of the UK (see **16.6.1**).

16.6.3 One of the parties is based outside the EU

If one of the parties is based outside the EU, that party can object to the jurisdiction of the English courts on the ground that the English courts are not the most appropriate ones for resolving the dispute. He has to prove that it is possible for the claimant to issue proceedings in another State. The defendant may also try to argue that the ground relied upon by the claimant under para 3.1 of PD 6B (see **16.4.1.3** above) is not present or that the claimant does not have a claim with a reasonable prospect of success. The claimant then has to prove that the

English courts are the most convenient place to deal with the litigation bearing in mind the convenience of the parties and the witnesses and the interests of justice (*Spiliada Maritime Corp v Cansulex Ltd, The Spiliada* [1987] AC 460).

The technical term for this objection is *forum non conveniens*. In multi-party litigation, if part of the proceedings have been commenced outside the EU, that party can raise the issue of *forum non conveniens* even though all the other parties are based in the EU (*Re Harrods (Buenos Aires) Ltd* [1992] Ch 72).

In *Connelly v RTZ Corporation* [1997] 3 WLR 373, the claimant commenced proceedings in England against defendants based in Namibia. The defendants objected to the jurisdiction on the grounds that the incident occurred in Namibia and all the witnesses lived in Namibia. The claimant argued that he could not afford to bring proceedings in Namibia because he would not qualify for legal aid there, and that the only way in which he could afford to bring proceedings anywhere in the world was to bring them in England where he could get legal aid. The House of Lords decided that the English courts were the most convenient place to deal with the case (presumably on the basis that it was more convenient to have an inconvenient trial than no trial at all).

16.6.4   Interim relief

By Article 35 of the Brussels Regulation, application may be made to the courts of a Member State for such provisional, including protective, measures as may be available under the law of that State, even if the courts of another Member State have jurisdiction as to the substance of the matter.

It is therefore possible for the English courts to grant a party an interim injunction even if, for example, the French courts have jurisdiction and are already seised of the matter.

16.7   WHERE TO SUE (OR BE SUED)

An English client will usually prefer to resolve his disputes in England, and his solicitor must study the jurisdiction rules carefully to achieve this result wherever appropriate. There are, however, four potential drawbacks to English proceedings against a foreign defendant:

(a)   If the contract is governed by foreign law, the parties will have to call expert evidence regarding the law in question. This can be very expensive.

(b)   If the defendant's property is outside the jurisdiction, there can be a delay in enforcing judgment (see **Chapter 17**).

(c)   If the harm caused by the defendant's tort has occurred in more than one State within the EU, it may be preferable to sue in the defendant's 'home State' (see **16.2.6**).

(d)   Where the dispute concerns a contract, it is also possible (under the principle in *Leathertex Divisione Sintetici SpA v Bodetex BVBA* – see **16.2.5**) that only the defendant's home court will be able to deal with the entire dispute.

16.8   THE PERILS OF FOREIGN LITIGATION

There will be cases where it is not possible to avoid litigation in a foreign country, or where it is desirable to take proceedings abroad. A solicitor will instruct foreign lawyers as agents, but they will still have to bear certain dangers in mind.

16.8.1   Limitation periods

Foreign limitation periods may be much shorter than the English equivalents.

16.8.2   Causes of action

Some countries may not recognise a cause of action which is part of English law. Others may allow claims which would not be actionable here.

16.8.3   Remedies

Remedies may differ, especially at the interim stage. For example, not all countries have an equivalent to our search orders, while other countries exercise much tighter control over the defendant's property pending trial than we do under the freezing injunction and give creditors greater rights to an early judgment.

16.8.4   Time

The time it takes for an action to come to trial can vary widely from State to State. There is a significant difference between, for example, the pace of German and Italian litigation.

16.8.5   Costs

In most countries costs follow the event, but this is not always the case, and even where costs are awarded to the winner, they may be based on the value of the claim rather than the amount of work involved. Contingency fee systems are common.

16.8.6   Judicial expertise

In some countries, the judges will have considerable commercial expertise, being local businesspersons themselves. Alternatively, the judges may be aided by lay assessors.

16.8.7   Miscellaneous

There may also be different rules on, for example, whether a claim carries interest or on the enforcement of judgments.

16.9   COMMON LAW VERSUS CIVIL LAW

Common law systems, like those used in the USA and most Commonwealth countries, will have many features with which an English lawyer will be familiar, although there may well be differences in, for example, contingency fees, the level of costs and the amount of pre-trial disclosure.

Civil law systems are very different. For a start, there will be no (or very limited) disclosure of documents. The main difference, however, lies in the role of the judge. We are used to the case building to a formal climax (the trial) at which the parties have a major say in what evidence the judge is to hear. That is not what happens in most of the rest of Europe.

Under the civil code systems, if the parties choose to litigate then, generally, they place themselves in the hands of a judge who has to decide where the truth lies. The judge investigates the case. They interview the parties. They then decide what witnesses they would like to hear and question those witnesses. In some countries, the parties' lawyers are then entitled to ask their own questions of the witness. In other countries, the lawyers are not allowed to speak to the witnesses at all.

The judge also decides whether expert evidence is needed, and if it is, they usually choose who that expert will be. It can be extremely difficult to challenge the views of such an expert.

As a result, litigation elsewhere in Europe places much greater emphasis on detailed statements of case and written evidence than an English lawyer is accustomed to. On the other hand, the rules on admissibility of evidence tend to be less complex and cross-examination of witnesses is relatively rare.

The CPR 1998 have reduced, to some extent, the differences between English and European litigation, as English judges take more and more responsibility for managing the case, appointing experts and deciding what evidence they wish to hear.

16.10   ROME I – REGULATION 593/2008

Whereas the Brussels Regulation (recast) applies to jurisdiction issues, Rome I, which applies to the Member States of the EU, deals with the choice of laws in the context of contractual obligations.

Following Brexit, Rome I continued to apply to contracts concluded before 1 January 2021. For contracts concluded after that date, Rome I has been converted into UK law as retained EU law so the provisions set out below continue to operate in UK domestic law. The same applies to Rome II – see **16.11**.

16.10.1   The basic position under Rome I

Article 1(2) specifies the matters to which the Regulation does not apply, for example wills and probate, and matters governed by company law.

Article 3(1) allows the parties to choose the law of the contract, either expressly or impliedly. If they have done so, then that is the applicable law that governs the contract.

If no such choice has been made then the rules in Article 4 apply. Typically, in a sale of goods contract, this means that the law of the country where the seller has his habitual residence will apply, unless the buyer is a consumer, who cannot be denied the use of laws which cannot be derogated from in his own jurisdiction.

16.10.2   Other exceptions to the seller's law applying

Article 4(1)(c) deals with a right in 'immovable property'. The presumption here is that the contract is governed by the law of the country where the immovable property is situated. This does not apply to contracts for repair or construction of immovable property.

Article 5(1) provides that, in a contract for the carriage of goods (not *sale* of goods), it is the country where the carrier has its place of business if that is also the country of loading or discharging the goods, or if it is also the country where the consignor has its principal place of business.

Article 4(4) provides that the court may decide that the contract is more closely connected with another country and apply that country's laws.

16.10.3   Local 'mandatory rules'

There are limitations on the use of the applicable law. If any provisions of the applicable law conflict with local laws of the jurisdiction where the dispute is heard, relating to the contract, those conflicting provisions of the applicable law cannot validly be used. These local law provisions are the 'mandatory rules' which are referred to in Article 9 of the Regulation. These are 'rules' which cannot be derogated from (eg, in the case of the UK, the Financial Services and Markets Act 2000). Article 9 provides that the choice of foreign law by the parties will not prejudice the application of the mandatory rules of the home country to the contract. So, even if the applicable law was held to be, say, Austrian law, the Financial Services and Markets Act 2000 could also apply to a relevant dispute heard by a court in England and Wales, and would override any inconsistent provisions in Austrian law.

16.10.4   Exceptions for consumer and employment contracts

Articles 6 and 8 are intended to give protection to the weaker party to a contract.

Article 6 deals with certain types of consumer contract. Where no choice has been made, such contracts are governed by the law of the consumer's habitual residence. Where a choice has been made, the chosen law operates subject to any rules for the protection of the consumer applicable in the consumer's country of habitual residence.

Article 8 deals with individual contracts of employment. Where there is no choice of law in the contract then the presumption is that contained in Article 8(2). This is basically that the law is that of the country where the work takes place, or where the business is situated if the work takes place in a different country. However, a contractual choice of law cannot operate so as to deprive the employee of the protection of the mandatory rules which would apply under Article 8(2).

16.11 ROME II – REGULATION 864/2007

Non-contractual obligations are dealt with under what is generally referred to as 'Rome II'. In brief this states that the applicable law for the resolution of non-contractual disputes (ie torts) is determined on the basis of where the damage occurs or is likely to occur, regardless of the country or countries in which the act giving rise to the damage occurs.

16.12 SUMMARY

The law relating to jurisdiction is quite complicated. The key issue is to appreciate when proceedings can be served out of the jurisdiction without permission of the court (CPR 1998, r 6.33) and when that permission is required (r 6.36). As we have seen, the position is different for proceedings instituted before 1 January 2021 and proceedings instituted after that date.

The current position therefore is that permission will not be required if the case is covered by the Hague Convention (exclusive choice of court agreement conferring jurisdiction on UK courts) or, if not, the contract contains a jurisdiction clause conferring jurisdiction on UK courts (r 6.33(2B)). These cases will all relate to contractual disputes.

In other types of dispute, permission of the court will be required to serve the defendant out of the jurisdiction – but remember that if it is possible to serve the defendant within the jurisdiction (even if the defendant is domiciled abroad) no such permission is required. It is open to a defendant to challenge the jurisdiction of UK courts on the basis that a court in a different country would be a more convenient court to hear the case.

A table setting out the main elements of these provisions is set out below. This is followed by a flowchart on EU jurisdiction.

	European Union	**Rest of the World**
What is the basic rule for asserting jurisdiction?	D to be sued in his local courts: domicile for individual. Seat for company.	England and Wales courts claim to jurisdiction on whether process was served on D within the jurisdiction. Courts in other jurisdictions will have their own rules.
Are there exceptions to the basic rule?	Yes: see **16.2.1–16.2.11**	Yes: the claimant may be able to apply for permission to serve the proceedings outside England and Wales under r 6.36.
How is service effected abroad?	Permission to serve out of the jurisdiction is not required. Claim form must be accompanied by form N510. The claim form may be served by any method allowed by the country where it served.	If service is effected within England and Wales the 'ordinary' rules as to service apply. If service is effected outside the jurisdiction, the claimant must first have permission under r 6.36. Service must be effected in a way that is approved by the country where the proceedings are served.

	European Union	Rest of the World
On what basis is it possible to challenge jurisdiction?	The challenge of 'forum non conveniens' is not available. (NB There are conflicting authorities about whether it can be argued when both parties are in different parts of the UK.) D can challenge the proceedings on the basis that the Regulation rules are not satisfied. The procedure to be followed is that in Part 11. This requires D to acknowledge and dispute jurisdiction within 14 days (28 days in Commercial Court and Circuit Commercial Courts) of filing the acknowledgement of service. If that challenge fails, D may have the option of appealing to a higher court of that State or to the European Court of Justice. If the proceedings were commenced after proceedings were started elsewhere in the EU, then the later proceedings: (a) will not be accepted if they involve the same parties and relate to the same causes of action; (b) may not be proceeded with at the court's discretion if the cause of action is similar and involves some or all of the same parties. If there is a danger of conflicting judgments being made by two different courts within the EU, the court that was seised second will usually decline to accept the proceedings. Again, the procedure in Part 11 should be followed.	D can challenge on the basis of *forum non conveniens*, using the procedure in Part 11, and on the basis that the claim does not have a reasonable prospect of success. D can also challenge the ground relied on to obtain permission to serve out (again under Part 11). The basis on which you could challenge the jurisdiction of the courts of another country is, of course, a matter for the law of that country.

EU Jurisdiction Flowchart

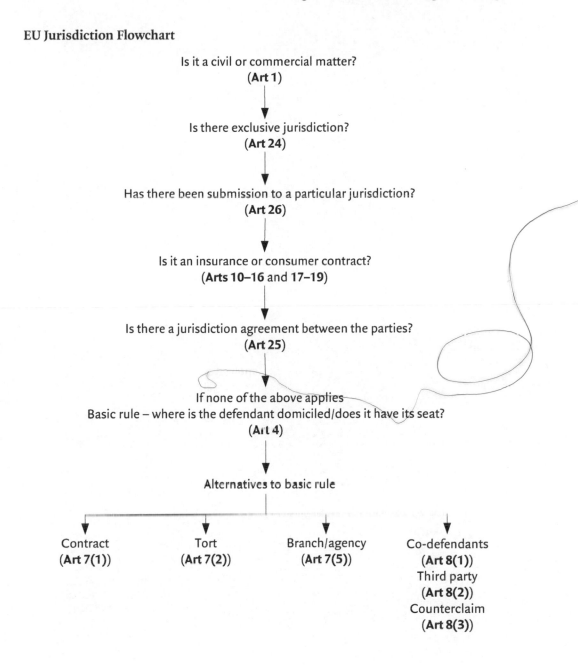

Is it a civil or commercial matter?
(Art 1)

Is there exclusive jurisdiction?
(Art 24)

Has there been submission to a particular jurisdiction?
(Art 26)

Is it an insurance or consumer contract?
(Arts 10–16 and **17–19)**

Is there a jurisdiction agreement between the parties?
(Art 25)

If none of the above applies
Basic rule – where is the defendant domiciled/does it have its seat?
(Art 4)

Alternatives to basic rule

Contract	Tort	Branch/agency	Co-defendants
(Art 7(1))	**(Art 7(2))**	**(Art 7(5))**	**(Art 8(1))**
			Third party
			(Art 8(2))
			Counterclaim
			(Art 8(3))

FOREIGN ELEMENT: ENFORCEMENT PROCEEDINGS

LEARNING OUTCOMES

After reading this chapter you will understand:

- the methods of enforcing a judgment obtained in England and Wales outside the jurisdiction
- the methods of enforcing a judgment obtained outside the jurisdiction within England and Wales.

17.1 INTRODUCTION

The methods of enforcing English judgments abroad and foreign judgments in England depend on the arrangements (if any) which have been made with the foreign country in question either by Treaty or Convention. There are four different systems:

(a) The Brussels Regulation (recast) (hereinafter 'the Brussels Regulation') deals with enforcement of judgments within the EU and the UK. It establishes a system of registration of foreign judgments. Once those judgments are registered, they can be enforced in the same manner as a judgment of the courts for the place of registration. The Lugano Convention (see **16.1**) sets up a similar system for the enforcement of judgments of courts of the former European Free Trade Association (EFTA) States.

This will continue to apply in relation to judgments obtained in proceedings instituted before 1 January 2021. For proceedings instituted after that date, the Brussels Regulation will no longer apply and in effect is superseded by the provisions of the Hague Convention in relation to judgments obtained in cases covered by that Convention – ie contractual disputes where there was an exclusive jurisdiction clause in the contract.

(b) Registration systems were also set up under the Administration of Justice Act 1920 (AJA 1920) and the Foreign Judgments (Reciprocal Enforcement) Act 1933 (FJ(RE)A 1933). They cover most Commonwealth and former Commonwealth States, and some European States like Malta. There are only minor differences between the two Acts and the 1968 Convention (see **17.4** and **17.5** for details of recognition and registration of judgments under the 1933 and 1920 Acts respectively).

Countries covered by the AJA 1920 include Barbados, the Falkland Islands, Hong Kong, Jamaica, Malaysia, most of the Australian states, New Zealand, Singapore and Zimbabwe. Examples of other countries to which the provisions of FJ(RE)A 1933 apply include Israel, one Australian state (namely the Australian Capital Territory), Canada, the Isle of Man, Guernsey, Jersey, India and Pakistan.

(c)   There are many countries not covered by the above systems. The USA is probably the most important example. Enforcement of judgments of the courts of these countries is covered by the common law.

(d)   It is important to realise that many foreign courts are very reluctant to enforce default judgments. If most of the defendant's assets are located abroad, it would be wise to ascertain if the courts of the country where the assets are located will recognise and enforce default judgments. If there is likely to be a problem about this then, even though the claimant may be entitled to a default judgment, the claimant should set the matter down for trial after the defendant has failed to acknowledge service of the claim form or to serve a defence (giving the defendant notice of this), and prove the case by calling evidence at the trial (*Berliner Bank v Karageorgis* [1996] 1 Lloyd's Rep 426).

17.2   THE EUROPEAN UNION

For the effect of Brexit, see **16.2**.

17.2.1   Recognition

Article 36 of the Brussels Regulation requires all Member States to recognise and enforce the judgments of other Member States.

This is a significant change from the previous position. Article 36(1) in effect abolishes what was formerly known as 'exequatur'– an intermediate step that, until the recast Regulation, needed to be taken before a judgment issued by a court or tribunal in one Member State could be enforced in a court or tribunal of another Member State. This means that the party wishing to enforce the judgment will be able to apply directly to the competent enforcement authorities in the Member State in which enforcement is sought without first having to go through the intermediate step of *exequatur* – that is without having to obtain a declaration of enforceability.

Detailed provisions in relation to enforcement in another Member State are set out in Articles 39–44.

17.2.2   Registering the judgment of another EU State

17.2.2.1   Leave to register

The rules governing registration and enforcement of judgments of Member States (with the exception of Denmark) are set out in CPR 1998, Part 74. These provisions have made changes to the previous position under the Brussels Convention in an attempt to make enforcement of foreign judgments quicker and more straightforward.

The application for registration is made to the Queen's Bench Division of the High Court.

The application may be made without notice being served on any other party. The application must produce a copy of the judgment and a certificate using a standard form which is set out in Annex V to the Brussels Regulation. This certificate gives details of the court, parties and nature of the judgment. In addition, by r 74.4 of CPR 1998, the application must be supported by written evidence:

(a)   stating whether the judgment provides for payment of a sum or sums of money;

(b)   stating whether interest is recoverable on the judgment or any part of it in accordance with the law of the State in which the judgment was given, and if so:

> (i)   the rate of interest,
>
> (ii)   the date from which interest is recoverable, and
>
> (iii) the date on which interest ceases to accrue;
>
> and

(c)   exhibiting, where the judgment or document is not in English, a translation of it into English certified in accordance with Article 57 of the Brussels Regulation.

If leave to register is granted, the order will state a time for appealing against the granting of leave. It will also state that the judgment will not be enforced until that time limit has expired.

Notice of registration then has to be served on the debtor (leave to serve out of the jurisdiction is not required). The notice gives details of the judgment and the order for registration; the creditor's address for service; and the debtor's rights of appeal.

17.2.2.2   Appeal

If the debtor wishes to appeal against the order for registration, he has one month to do so. In the meantime, the creditor cannot take any enforcement steps, although he can seek orders preserving the property of the debtor so that it remains available for enforcement (eg a freezing injunction).

The appeal is made by an application notice supported by written evidence. Although the application to register is made to a Master, any appeal is to a judge. The same applies to an appeal by the creditor against a refusal to register. If an appeal against the registration is lodged then the judgment cannot be enforced until that appeal has been disposed of.

This period of delay in enforcing the judgment in order to give the debtor time to appeal is a matter which should be taken into account when deciding where to commence proceedings (assuming there is a choice). It may be more appropriate to commence proceedings in the State where the defendant's assets are, so that when judgment is obtained, the creditor can proceed directly to enforce the judgment without any further delay. However, if the original judgment carries interest and full details of the interest are given when it is registered, the debt can be enforced with interest.

17.2.3   Enforcing a UK judgment in the EU

The first step towards enforcing a UK judgment in the EU is to obtain a certified copy of the judgment, applying without notice with supporting evidence to the court which granted the judgment. The evidence (in the form of a witness statement or affidavit) must:

(a)   give particulars of the proceedings in which the judgment was obtained;

(b)   contain evidence of service of the claim form by which the proceedings were begun where judgment was given in default of appearance by the defendant; and

(c)   where appropriate, include any document showing that for these proceedings the applicant is an assisted person or an LSC-funded client, as defined in CPR 1998, r 43.2(1)(h) and (i).

The court will issue a certificate dealing with all these matters, together with a copy of the claim form, etc used to commence proceedings. The creditor's solicitors will appoint foreign agents if they do not themselves have a branch in the State in question, and will send the certificate to the agents so that they can follow the appropriate local procedure. The creditor's solicitors will probably need to supply a translation of the judgment.

17.2.4   European Enforcement Orders

New provisions relating to European Enforcement Orders (EEOs) were added to Part 74 in October 2005 as section V. Regulation (EC) No 805/2004 (which created EEOs) applies to 'judgments, court settlements and authentic instruments on uncontested claims' (Article 3).

Uncontested claims include default judgments, admissions and settlements. The purpose of the Regulation, and section V of Part 74, is to simplify the procedure for enforcing this type of judgment in other EU countries. In England and Wales the result is that the registration of such a judgment will follow the same rules as registration of a judgment from another part of the UK – see **17.3.2** below.

17.3   THE UNITED KINGDOM

17.3.1   Recognition

The rules on recognition of judgments obtained in Scotland and Northern Ireland are the same as in the EU (see **17.2.1**).

17.3.2   Registration in England

The applicant obtains a certificate relating to the judgment and a certified copy. He must lodge this in the Royal Courts of Justice within six months. If the judgment is a money judgment, it is then enforceable here as if it were an English judgment.

If the judgment is a non-money judgment, the creditor must apply for leave to enforce it in England (CPR 1998, r 74.16). He applies without notice, but the court can require him to issue a Part 8 claim form. The application is supported by a certified copy of the judgment. If the courts grant an order for registration of the judgment, notice of registration must be served on the respondent as with EU judgments and the respondent can apply to have the registration set aside.

17.3.3   Enforcing an English judgment in Scotland and Northern Ireland

17.3.3.1   Money judgments

Where a money judgment has been obtained, the creditor applies for a certificate regarding the judgment, and files written evidence which states:

(a)   the amount due under the judgment plus details of any interest;

(b)   that the time for appealing has expired and no stay of execution has been granted;

(c)   the addresses of the parties.

If a certificate is granted, it must be registered in the appropriate court within six months so that it can be enforced as if it were a judgment of that court.

17.3.3.2   Other judgments

Where the judgment is other than for money, the applicant applies without notice for a certified copy of the judgment with the certificate and supporting evidence described above.

17.4   REGISTRATION UNDER THE FOREIGN JUDGMENTS (RECIPROCAL ENFORCEMENT) ACT 1933

For the purposes of the FJ(RE)A 1933 and AJA 1920 (see **17.5**), the court will have jurisdiction if the defendant either:

(a)   is resident here; or

(b)   has its principal place of business here; or

(c)   agrees to submit to the jurisdiction; or

(d)   voluntarily takes part in the proceedings.

17.4.1   Recognition

Under the FJ(RE)A 1933, registration of a foreign judgment must be set aside if:

(a)   the debtor was given insufficient notice of the original proceedings;

(b)   the original court lacked jurisdiction;

(c)   the judgment was obtained by fraud;

(d)   the judgment is not covered by the Act or was registered in breach of the Act;

(e)   the applicant is not entitled to enforce the judgment;

(f)   enforcement would be contrary to public policy;

(g)   the debtor did not submit to the jurisdiction of the original court.

There is also a discretion to set aside the registration if there is another final and conclusive judgment between the parties on the same issue.

17.4.2   Registration

The FJ(RE)A 1933 only applies to judgments for a sum of money which are final and conclusive. If, therefore, the judgment is still liable to be set aside, it cannot be registered here.

There is a six-year time limit on registering judgments under this Act.

As with the CJJA 1982, the application is made without notice with supporting written evidence, but the court may require a Part 8 claim form. The written evidence must, in its heading, set out the name of the Act, the court which granted the judgment and the date of the judgment. It must state:

(a)   the amount outstanding under the judgment;

(b)   the names, trades and addresses of the parties;

(c)   that the witness believes the creditor is entitled to enforce the judgment;

(d)   that the judgment is not covered by s 5 of the Protection of Trading Interests Act 1980 (see **17.6.1**);

(e)   that the judgment is still enforceable;

(f)   that there are no grounds for setting aside the registration;

(g)   the details of any interest recoverable;

(h)   any parts of the judgment which are not being registered (eg because they are not for the payment of money).

The evidence must be accompanied by the judgment and, if the judgment is not in English, also by a certified translation of the judgment. As the application of the FJ(RE)A 1933 to any State is governed by an Order in Council relating to that State, it may be necessary to consult the relevant Order in Council to see whether any other evidence is required.

The applicant may be required to give security for costs.

The rest of the procedure is the same as under the CJJA 1982. Interest on the judgment is recoverable.

17.4.3   Enforcement abroad

The procedure for enforcement abroad is broadly the same as under the CJJA 1982, but the court will also issue a further certificate stating:

(a)   the method used to serve the claim form;

(b)   objections the debtor made to the jurisdiction (if any);

(c)   what statements of case were served;

(d)   when the time for appealing expires;

(e)   whether notice of appeal has been given;

(f)   the rate of interest on the judgment.

17.5 ADMINISTRATION OF JUSTICE ACT 1920

17.5.1 Recognition

Under the AJA 1920, the judgment will not be recognised if:

(a)   recognition would be contrary to public policy;

(b)   proceedings were not properly served on the debtor;

(c)   the original court lacked jurisdiction;

(d)   the debtor was not in business or ordinarily resident in the State where the judgment was obtained and he did not submit to the jurisdiction;

(e)   the judgment was obtained by fraud; or

(f)   the defendant is appealing against the judgment.

17.5.2 Registration

The judgment must be for a sum of money. The application for leave to register is made in the usual way. It must be made within 12 months of the judgment, unless the court grants an extension of time. As under the FJ(RE)A 1933, the creditor may be required to issue a Part 8 claim form. The written evidence must deal with items (a) to (d) in the list for the FJ(RE)A 1933 set out at **17.4.1**. It must also state that there are no grounds for refusing registration. Again, security for costs may be required. The procedure for registration is the same as under the other two Acts but interest is not recoverable.

17.5.3 Enforcement abroad

To enforce a judgment abroad, the evidence in support of the application for a certified copy of the judgment merely has to give details of the judgment, the territory where the debtor resides, and the names, trades and addresses of both parties. Apart from that, the procedure is broadly the same as under the CJJA 1982.

17.6 COMMON LAW

If the judgment is one to which the above procedures do not apply (either because of the nature of the judgment or because it was made in a State which is not covered by them), its enforcement here is a matter for the common law.

17.6.1 Recognition

The judgment will not be recognised at common law if:

(a)   the proceedings were contrary to natural justice (eg the defendant was not given a fair chance to be heard);

(b)   it was obtained by fraud;

(c)   recognition would be contrary to public policy;

(d)   the foreign court lacked jurisdiction;

(e)   the judgment is covered by s 5 of the Protection of Trading Interests Act 1980 (which is primarily aimed at US anti-trust legislation).

17.6.2 Enforcement here

It is always open to a foreign judgment creditor to commence fresh proceedings in England if he has a cause of action here. More usually, however, he will treat the foreign judgment as a contract containing an implied promise to pay the judgment debt. He will issue proceedings alleging breach of that contract and apply for summary judgment under Part 24 of CPR 1998. (The court may award interest on the judgment.) This method is available to him only if the foreign judgment is a final judgment for the payment of a fixed sum of money. If there is an appeal in the foreign court, proceedings in this country to enforce the judgment may be stayed.

17.6.3 Enforcement there

Enforcement abroad is a matter for the law and courts of the country where the creditor is seeking to enforce an English judgment.

17.7 SUMMARY

The procedure for enforcing an English judgment in a foreign country or a foreign judgment in England depends on the place where enforcement is to take place. If the creditor wishes to enforce the judgment in another EU State or another part of the UK, he must comply with the rules laid down in CPR 1998, Part 74 (see **17.2** and, if the judgment is to be enforced elsewhere in the UK, **17.3**). If the creditor wishes to enforce the judgment in a Commonwealth or former Commonwealth State, he will probably have to use the procedures laid down under either the FJ(RE)A 1933 or the AJA 1920 (see **17.4** and **17.5**). If there is no Act of Parliament governing enforcement in the foreign State, the common law or the law of the State where the judgment is to be enforced will apply (see **17.6**).

APPENDICES

Appendix 1

Outline chart of typical case management sequence for cases in the Commercial Court

The references in the second column are to CPR 1998, Part 58 and to paragraph numbers in the Commercial Court Guide.

1	**Claim form** issued, served and filed (r 58.5 and paras B2–B7)
2	[**Applications** made, where necessary] (PD 58, *para* 3 and paras F1–F5 and F15)
3	[**Early case management conference,** if appropriate] (PD 58, *para* 10 and para D3.6)
4	**Acknowledgement of service** filed (r 58.6 and para B9)
5	[**Particulars of claim** served and filed, if they did not accompany the claim form and were not contained in the claim form] (r 58.5 and paras C1–C2)
6	**Defence** served and filed (r 58.10 and paras C1, C3)
7	**Reply** (if any) served and filed (r 58.10 and paras C1, C4)
8	**Case memorandum** prepared (PD 58, *para* 10 and para D5)
9	**List of Common Ground and Issues** prepared (PD 58, *para* 10 and para D6)
10	**Case management bundle** prepared (PD 58, *para* 10 and para D7)
11	**Professional estimate of trial length** prepared (para D17)
12	**Case management information sheet** lodged and served (PD 58, *para* 10 and para D8.5 and Appendix 2)
13	[**Designated judge** identified in appropriate cases] (para D4)
14	**Case management conference** (para D8) a. **pre-trial timetable** set (Appendix 4) [b. **ADR directions** made, if appropriate and if not already made [paras G1.5–1.8 and Appendix 3) c. **trial date fixed** (or, exceptionally, provisional range of dates for trial specified)
15	[**ADR directions** followed, where made] (Section G)

16	Pre-trial timetable followed: **Disclosure, inspection, witness statements, expert reports** (Sections E, H and Appendix 8)
17	[**Applications** made, where necessary] (Section F)
18	**Progress monitoring information sheet** lodged and served (paras D12.2–D12.3 and Appendix 2)
19	**Progress monitoring date** (para D12.1)
20	[**Reconvened case management conference**, if appropriate] (para D13)
21	**Confirmed estimate of trial length** prepared (para D17.4)
22	**Pre-trial checklist** lodged and served (para D14 and Appendix 2)
23	**Fixed trial date confirmed** (or where applicable, trial date fixed within provisional range of dates for trial) (para D16)
24	**Meeting of experts** (paras H2.19–H2.27 and Appendix 8)
25	[**Pre-trial review**, if ordered, with consideration of trial timetable] (para D18)
26	**Trial bundles** prepared and provided to the court (para J4 and Appendix 7)
27	Written trial **skeleton arguments** exchanged, and provided to the court (para J6; see also paras J5 and J6 for **trial timetable, reading list, authorities, chronology, indices and dramatis personae**)
28	**Trial** commences

Appendix 2

Case Management Information Sheet

The information supplied should be printed in bold characters

Party filing information sheet:

Name of solicitors:

Name(s) of advocates for trial:

[Note: This Sheet should normally be completed with the involvement of the advocate(s) instructed for trial. If the claimant is a litigant in person this fact should be noted at the foot of the sheet and proposals made as to which party is to have responsibility for the preparation and upkeep of the case management bundle.]

Preliminary:

(1) Is the case suitable for the Shorter Trials Scheme or the Flexible Trials Scheme in the interest of reducing the length and cost of trial?

(2) Please state whether the Case Management Conference (CMC) requires a High Court Judge or whether it is suitable for hearing by a Deputy High Court Judge.

(3) If costs budgeting and costs management is applicable, do you consider that this CMC is an appropriate time to deal with those questions? Is this agreed between the parties?

Issues:

(4) Are amendments to or is information about any statement of case required? If yes, please give brief details of what is required.

(5) Can you make any additional admissions? If yes, please give brief details of the additional admissions.

(6) Are any of the issues in the case suitable for trial as preliminary issues?

Disclosure:

(7) Have reports been produced on disclosure of documents? If not, is it considered that they are unnecessary or disproportionate? Is this agreed?

(8) What form of disclosure is appropriate, and for what issues? Is this agreed?

(9) By what date can you give this form of disclosure?

(10) If a form of disclosure requiring a search is sought or agreed, do you contend that the search should be limited and if so in what way and why? Is this agreed?

(11) What (if any) use of IT is proposed to assist with disclosure? Has this been discussed between the parties?

(12) What timing and method is appropriate for inspection of documents? Is this agreed?

Evidence:

(13) (a) On the evidence of how many witnesses of fact do you intend to rely at trial (subject to the directions of the Court)? Please give their names, or explain why this is not being done.

    (b) By what date can you serve signed witness statements?

    (c) How many of these witnesses of fact do you intend to call to give oral evidence at trial (subject to the directions of the Court)? Please give their names, or explain why this is not being done.

    (d) Will interpreters be required for any witness? What arrangements may be necessary for the translation of witness statements?

    (e)   Do you wish any witness to give oral evidence by video link? Please give his or her name, or explain why this is not being done. Please state the country and city from which the witness will be asked to give evidence by video link.

    (f)   Are directions to be sought for permission for any of the witness statements to be more than 30 pages in length? If so, this will need to be justified by letter or skeleton argument.

(14) (a)   On what issues may expert evidence be required?

      (b)   What is the estimated cost of the proposed expert evidence?

      (c)   Is this a case in which the use of a single joint expert might be suitable (see rule 35.7)?

      (d)   On the evidence of how many expert witnesses do you intend to rely at trial (subject to the directions of the Court)? Please give their names, or explain why this is not being done. Please identify each expert's field of expertise.

      (e)   By what date can you serve signed expert reports? Is this a case for sequential exchange of expert reports?

      (f)   When will the experts be available for a meeting or meetings of experts? Is this a case for the experts to meet before reports?

      (g)   How many of these expert witnesses do you intend to call to give oral evidence at trial (subject to the directions of the Court)? Please give their names, or explain why this is not being done.

      (h)   Will interpreters be required for any expert witness? What arrangements may be necessary for the translation of reports?

      (i)   Do you wish any expert witness to give oral evidence by video link? Please give his or her name, or explain why this is not being done. Please state the country and city from which the witness will be asked to give evidence by video link.

      (j)   Might this be a case for any expert evidence to be taken concurrently at trial?

Trial:

(15) What are the advocates' present provisional estimates of (i) the minimum and maximum lengths of the trial (ii) the pre-reading time likely to be required for the Judge?

(16) What is the earliest date by which you believe you can be ready for trial?

(17) Is this a case in which a pre-trial review is likely to be useful?

(18) What use of IT is proposed at trial? Has this been discussed between the parties?

Resolution without trial:

(19) Is there any way in which the Court can assist the parties to resolve their dispute or particular issues in it without the need for a trial or a full trial?

(20) (a)   Might some form of Alternative Dispute Resolution procedure assist to resolve or narrow the dispute or particular issues in it?

      (b)   Has the question at (a) been considered between the client and legal representatives (including the advocate(s) retained)?

      (c)   Has the question at (a) been explored with the other parties in the case?

      (d)   Do you request that the case is adjourned while the parties try to settle the case by Alternative Dispute Resolution or other means?

      (e)   Would an ADR order in the form of Appendix 3 to the Commercial Court Guide be appropriate?

      (f)   Are any other special directions needed to allow for Alternative Dispute Resolution?

(21) Has Early Neutral Evaluation been considered?

Other matters:

(22) What other applications will you wish to make at the CMC?

(23) Does provision need to be made in the pre-trial timetable for any application or procedural step not otherwise dealt with above? If yes, please specify the application or procedural step.

(24) Are there, or are there likely in due course to be, any related proceedings (e.g. a Part 20 claim)? Please give brief details.

(25) Please indicate whether it is considered that the case is unsuitable for trial by a Deputy High Court Judge rather than a High Court Judge. If the case is considered to be unsuitable for trial by a Deputy High Court Judge please give reasons for this view.

(26) Please indicate whether it is considered that the case should be allocated to a designated Judge. If so please give reasons for this view and write to the Judge in Charge of the Commercial Court in accordance with D4.2.

[Signature of solicitors]

Note: This information sheet must be filed with the Commercial Court Listing Office at least 7 days before the Case Management Conference (with a copy to all other parties): see D8.5 of the Commercial Court Guide.

Appendix 3

Standard Pre-Trial Timetable

1. [Form of disclosure, divided by issues] is to be made by [*], with inspection [*] days after notice. [Detail different forms of disclosure for different groups of issues where appropriate].

2. Signed statements of witnesses of fact, and hearsay notices where required by rule 33.2, are to be exchanged not later than [*].

3. Unless otherwise ordered, witness statements are to stand as the evidence in chief of the witness at trial.

4. Signed reports of experts
    (i)   are to be confined to one expert for each party from each of the following fields of expertise: [*];
    (ii)   are to be confined to the following issues: [*];
    (iii) are to be exchanged [sequentially/simultaneously];
    (iv)   are to be exchanged not later than [date or dates for each report in each field of expertise].

5. Meeting of experts
    (i)   The experts are to meet [before and] after reports by [*] [and by *];
    (ii)   The joint memorandum of the experts is to be completed by [*];
    (iii) Any short supplemental expert reports are to be exchanged [sequentially/ simultaneously] by not later than [date or dates for each supplemental report].

6. [If the experts' reports cannot be agreed, the parties are to be at liberty to call expert witnesses at the trial, limited to those experts whose reports have been exchanged pursuant to 4. above.]

    [Or: The parties are to be at liberty to apply to call as expert witnesses at the trial those experts whose reports they have exchanged pursuant to 4. above, such application to be made not earlier than [*] and not later than [*].]

7. [The trial reading list for the Judge is to:
    (a)   identify the issues that the Court will be asked to decide with the assistance of expert evidence;
    (b)   in respect of each such issue, briefly state each party's case;
    (c)   in respect of each such issue, identify the pages of the expert evidence that need to be read.]

8. The proposed use of IT at trial is as follows: []

9. Preparation of trial bundles in electronic or hard copy form (or part electronic, part hard copy) to be completed in accordance with Appendix 7 to the Commercial Court Guide by not later than [*].

10. The estimated length of the trial is [*]. This includes [*] pre-trial reading time.

11. Within [*] days the parties are to attend on the Commercial Court Listing Office to fix the date for trial which shall be not before [*].

12. The progress monitoring date is [*]. Each party is to provide a completed progress monitoring information sheet to the Commercial Court Listing Office at least 3 days before the progress monitoring date (with a copy to all other parties).

13. Each party is to provide a completed pre-trial checklist not later than 3 weeks before the date fixed for trial.

14. [There is to be a pre-trial review not earlier than [*] and not later than [*]].
15. Save as varied by this order or further order, the practice and procedures set out in the Admiralty & Commercial Courts Guide are to be followed.
16. Costs in the case.
17. Liberty to restore the Case Management Conference.

Appendix 4

Progress Monitoring Information Sheet

[SHORT TITLE OF CASE and FOLIO NUMBER]

Fixed trial date/provisional range of dates for trial specified in the pre-trial timetable:

Party filing information sheet:

Name of solicitors:

Name(s) of advocates for trial:

[Note: this information sheet should normally be completed with the involvement of the advocate(s) instructed for trial]

(1) Have you complied with the pre-trial timetable in all respects?

(2) If you have not complied, in what respects have you not complied?

(3) Will you be ready for a trial commencing on the fixed date (or, where applicable, within the provisional range of dates) specified in the pre-trial timetable?

(4) If you will not be ready, why will you not be ready?

[Signature of solicitors]

Note: This information sheet must be filed with the Listing Office at least 3 days before the progress monitoring date (with a copy to all other parties): see D12.2 of the Commercial Court Guide.

Appendix 5

Pre-Trial Checklist

The information supplied should be printed in bold characters

[SHORT TITLE OF CASE and FOLIO NUMBER]

a. Trial date:

b. Party filing checklist:

c. Name of solicitors:

d. Name(s) of advocates for trial:

[**Note:** this checklist should normally be completed with the involvement of the advocate(s) instructed for trial.]

1. Have you completed preparation of trial bundles in accordance with Appendix 7 to the Commercial Court Guide?

2. If not, when will the preparation of the trial bundles be completed?

3. Which witnesses of fact do you intend to call?

4. (a) Which expert witness(es) do you intend to call (if directions for expert evidence have been given)?

   (b) Have the experts narrowed the areas of disputed expert opinion as far as possible?

   (c) If directions for expert evidence to be taken concurrently have not been made, will they be sought from the Judge at trial?

   (d) If this is or may be a case for expert evidence to be taken concurrently has there been a discussion between advocates as to the most suitable procedure: see H2.34 in the Commercial Court Guide?

5. Will an interpreter be required for any witness and if so, have any necessary directions already been given?

6. Have directions been given for any witness to give evidence by video link? If so, have all necessary arrangements been made?

7. What are the advocates' confirmed estimates of (i) the minimum and maximum lengths of the trial (ii) the pre-reading time likely to be required for the Judge? (A confirmed estimate of length signed by the advocates should be attached)?

8. What is your estimate of costs already incurred and to be incurred at trial?

[Signature of solicitors]

Appendix 6

List of documents: standard disclosure

List of documents: standard disclosure

Notes:

- The rules relating to standard disclosure are contained in Part 31 of the Civil Procedure Rules and Section E of the Commercial Court Guide.

- Documents to be included under standard disclosure are contained in Rule 31.6

- A document has or will have been in your control if you have or have had possession, or a right of possession, of it **or** a right to inspect or take copies of it.

In the High Court of Justice	
Queen's Bench Division **Commercial Court** **Royal Courts of Justice**	
Claim No.	
Claimant(s) (including ref)	
Defendant(s) (including ref)	
Date	
Party returning this form	

Disclosure Statement of (Claimant)(Defendant)

1. (I/We), (name(s)) state that (I/we) have carried out a reasonable search to locate all the documents which

(I am *or*) _____ *here name the party* is)

required to disclose under (the order made by the court *or* the agreement in writing made between the parties on) *(insert date)* _____

2. The extent of the search that (I/we) made to locate documents that

(I am *or*) _____ *here name the party* is)

required to disclose was as follows:

3. (I/We) limited the search in the following respects:-

☐ I did not search for documents:-

   ☐ pre-dating [   ]

   ☐ located elsewhere than

                                                                  [   ]

   ☐ in categories other than

                                                                    [   ]

   ☐ for electronic documents

☐ I carried out a search for electronic documents contained on or created by the following:
(list what was searched and extent of search)

[   ]

☐ I did not search for the following:-

   ☐ documents created before [   ]

   documents contained on or created by the ☐ Claimant   ☐ Defendant

☐ PCs	☐ portable data storage media
☐ databases	☐ servers
☐ back-up tapes	☐ off-site storage
☐ mobile phones	☐ laptops
☐ notebooks	☐ handheld devices
☐ PDA devices	

   documents contained on or created by the ☐ Claimant   ☐ Defendant

☐ mail files	☐ document files
☐ calendar files	☐ web-based applications
☐ spreadsheet files	☐ graphic and presentation files

   documents other than by reference to the following keyword(s)/concepts
(delete if your search was not confined to specific keywords or concepts)

[   ]

4. The facts considered in arriving at the decision that it was reasonable to limit the search in the respects identified above were as follows
(the facts must be set out in detail: see paragraph E3.6 of the Commercial Court Guide):

5. (I/We) certify that (I/we) understand the duty of disclosure and to the best of (my/our) knowledge

(I have *or* [   ] *here name the party* has)

carried out that duty. (I/We) further certify that the list above is a complete list of all documents which are or

have been in (my *or* [   ] *here name the*

party's) control which (I am *or here name the party* is) obliged under (the said order *or* the said agreement in writing) to disclose.

6. (I *or* [   ] *here name the party*)

understand(s) that (I *or* [   ] *here name*

the party) must inform the court and the other parties immediately if any further documents required to be

disclosed by Rule 31.6 comes into (my *or* [   ]

here name the party's) control at any time before the conclusion of the case.

7. ((I *or* [   ] *here name the party*)

(have/has) not permitted inspection of documents within the category or class of documents (as set out below) required to be disclosed under Rule 31(6)(b) or (c) on the grounds that to do so would be disproportionate to the issues in the case.

Signed [   ]   **Date** [   ]

Name(s) [   ]

Position or office held [   ]

Please state why you are the appropriate person(s) to make the disclosure statement.

List and number here, in a convenient order, the documents (or bundles of documents if of the same nature, e.g. invoices) in your/the claimant's/the defendant's control, which you/the claimant/the defendant do/does not object to being inspected. Give a short description of each document or bundle so that it can be identified, and say if it is kept elsewhere i.e. with a bank or solicitor

A. (I)(The claimant)(The defendant) (have/has) control of the documents numbered and listed here. (I)(the claimant)(the defendant) (do not)(does not) object to you inspecting them/producing copies.

List and number here, as above, the documents in the claimant's/the defendant's control which the claimant/the defendant objects to being inspected. (Rule 31.19)

B. (I)(The claimant)(The defendant) (have)(has) control of the documents numbered and listed here, but (I)(the claimant)(the defendant) (object)(objects) to you inspecting them:

Say what the claimant's/the defendant's objections are

(I)(The claimant)(The defendant) (object)(objects) to you inspecting these documents because:

List and number here, the documents the claimant/the defendant once had in his/her/its control, but which the claimant/the defendant no longer has. For each document listed, say when it was last in the claimant's/the defendant's control and where it is now.

C. (I)(The claimant)(The defendant) (have)(had) the documents numbered and listed below, but they are no longer in (my)(the claimant's)(the defendant's) control.

Appendix 7

Specimen skeleton argument

IN THE HIGH COURT OF JUSTICE   2020 Folio 296

QUEEN'S BENCH DIVISION

COMMERCIAL COURT

Between   Williamson Superstores plc   Claimant

and

Haggerty Transport plc   Defendant

DEFENDANT'S SKELETON ARGUMENT FOR TRIAL

COUNSEL FOR THE PARTIES

Claimant's counsel   Joanna Smith instructed by Ballards

Defendant's counsel   Glenda Jones instructed by Tuckers

DRAMATIS PERSONAE

FOR THE CLAIMANT

(1)   James Williamson, managing director of the Claimant company.

(2)   Colin Carvell, head of production at the Claimant's dairy.

(3)   Ryan Beckham, van loader employed by the Claimant.

(4–12)   Other van loaders employed by the Claimant. [In practice each van loader would be identified by name.]

(13)   Kim Draper, branch manager of the Claimant's Houghton branch.

(14–37) Other branch managers employed by the Claimant. [In practice each branch manager would be identified by name.]

(38)   Victor Cunningham, depot manager of Price and Green, waste disposal consultants.

(39)   Graham Brace, chief accountant for the Claimant.

(40)   Joe Bloggs, a member of the general public and a customer of the Claimant.

(41–50) Other members of the public who are customers of the Claimant. [In practice each customer would be identified by name.]

FOR THE DEFENDANT

(1)   Denise Haggerty, managing director of the Defendant company.

(2)   David Hampton, van driver, employed by the Defendant.

(3–26)   Other van drivers employed by the Defendant. [In practice each van driver would be identified by name.]

(27)   Courtney Lara, maintenance supervisor, employed by the Defendant.

(28)   Ray Pallister, a consultant in food hygiene, and the Defendant's expert witness.

NATURE OF THE DISPUTE BETWEEN THE PARTIES

Under a contract dated 15 October 2008, the Defendant company agreed to transport the Claimant's produce from the Claimant's manufacturing depots to the Claimant's retail outlets. This contract was last renewed on 16 October 2017 for a period of three years.

On 13 April 2020, the Defendant company delivered 25 van loads of dairy produce from the Claimant's dairy to 25 retail outlets of the Claimant company. On arrival the produce was found to be unfit for human consumption. The Claimant alleges that the produce became unfit during transit because of some defect in the Defendant's van's refrigeration units or some other default by the Defendant or the Defendant's employees. As a result, the Claimant has repudiated its contract with the Defendant and is seeking damages for the value of the damaged produce, the costs of disposing of it, and loss of profit caused by the damage done by the incident to the Claimant's trading reputation.

The Defendant denies that it was responsible for the damage to the produce. As a result the Defendant will argue that the Claimant was not entitled to repudiate the contract and has raised a counterclaim for damages for loss of profit under the contract, including the amount payable for the delivery on 13 April 2020.

CHRONOLOGY OF EVENTS

On or about 30 March 2020, the Claimant gave instructions to the Defendant to deliver 25 consignments of dairy produce.

The delivery took place on 13 April 2020. The produce was found to be unfit for human consumption on delivery.

The Claimant purported to repudiate its contract with the Defendant on 14 April 2020.

ISSUES ARISING AT THE TRIAL

(1) Was it the fault of the Defendant that the produce was delivered in a state in which it was unfit for human consumption?

(2) If so, was the Claimant entitled to repudiate the contract?

(3) If the Claimant was entitled to repudiate the contract, what damages is the Claimant entitled to?

(4) If the Claimant was not entitled to repudiate the contract, either because the Defendant was not at fault or as a matter of law, what damages is the Defendant entitled to under its counterclaim?

DEFENDANT'S SUBMISSIONS

(1) It was not the fault of the Defendant that the produce was delivered in a state which was unfit for human consumption. The damage was caused either directly or indirectly in the manufacturing process.

The Defendant will rely on evidence from its van drivers that the vans used to deliver the produce were in good working order on the day in question and that the refrigeration units were set to the correct temperatures for transporting dairy produce.

The Defendant will rely on evidence from its maintenance supervisor, Courtney Lara, that the vans were properly maintained and had not been tampered with.

The Defendant will rely on the expert evidence of Ray Pallister that it would not be possible for the produce to deteriorate to the extent that it was not fit for human consumption during the time in which the produce was in transit unless the produce was already defective at the time when it was loaded onto the Defendant's vans. The Defendant will also rely on the absence of expert evidence from the Claimant on this point.

(2)   If the Defendant was at fault, the Defendant will argue that the Claimant was not, in law, entitled to repudiate the contract for this breach of contract.

The Defendant will rely on the following authorities in support of this contention.

[List cases relied on.]

(3)   If the Claimant was entitled to repudiate the contract, the Defendant will argue that the Claimant is not entitled to damages for loss of trading reputation.

The Defendant will rely on points arising out of cross examination of Joe Bloggs and the other sample witnesses who are alleged to be customers of the Claimant.

The Defendant will rely on the following authorities in support of this contention.

[List cases relied on.]

ORDER SOUGHT

The Defendant will be seeking an order for judgment in its favour on both the Claimant's claim and the Defendant's counterclaim, for damages to be assessed and costs to be formally assessed if not agreed.

Appendix 8

Expert Evidence – Requirements of General Application

1. It is the duty of an expert to help the Court on the matters within the expert's expertise: rule 35.3(1). This duty is paramount and overrides any obligation to the person from whom the expert has received instructions or by whom she or he is paid: rule 35.3(2).

2. Expert evidence presented to the Court should be, and should be seen to be, the independent product of the expert uninfluenced by the pressures of litigation.

3. An expert witness should provide independent assistance to the Court by way of objective unbiased opinion in relation to matters within her or his expertise. An expert witness should never assume the role of an advocate.

4. An expert witness should not omit to consider material facts which could detract from her or his concluded opinion.

5. An expert witness should make it clear when a particular question or issue falls outside her or his expertise.

6. If an expert's opinion is not properly researched because she or he considers that insufficient data is available, this must be stated in her or his report with an indication that the opinion is no more than a provisional one.

7. In a case where an expert witness who has prepared a report is unable to confirm that the report contains the truth, the whole truth and nothing but the truth without some qualification, that qualification must be stated in the report.

8. If, after exchange of reports, an expert witness changes her or his view on a material matter having read another expert's report or for any other reason, such change of view should be communicated in writing (through the party's legal representatives) to the other side without delay, and when appropriate to the Court.

9. All expert evidence – written or oral – should be as concise as possible.

10. An expert witness should be ready to take initiative to narrow the areas of disputed expert opinion as far as possible, including by initiating further dialogue between experts.

Please see also section H of the Commercial Court Guide.

Appendix 9

Summary of alternative procedure for claims under Part 8

The Part 8 procedure is usually used in cases where there is no substantial dispute of fact, for example in cases where the only issue is the construction of a document or a statute.

1. Claimant issues Part 8 claim form and serves the claim form and supporting written evidence[1]

NB: there are no particulars of claim.

2. Defendant acknowledges service and files written evidence in support[1]

Within 14 days of service of the claim form.

The defendant must notify the court if he does not intend to file any evidence.

NB: there is no defence and no possibility of the claimant entering judgment in default.

3. Claimant's written evidence in reply[1]

Within 14 days of receipt of defendant's written evidence (if any evidence in reply is required).

The parties may extend this time limit to a maximum of 28 days by written agreement. The agreement must be filed at court. Any longer extension requires an application to the court.

NB: no allocation questionnaires are filed.

4. The court gives directions or fixes a hearing date

The court may have given case management directions when the claim was issued, but will often consider its file for the purpose of deciding how the case should be dealt with after the expiry of the defendant's deadline for filing evidence.

If necessary the court can hold a case management conference, but in many cases no oral directions hearing is required. Instead, the court may be able to make a **final order in writing** or to **direct a hearing before a judge** (to resolve the substantive issues). The judge can require oral evidence to be given, but will more commonly rely on the parties' written evidence.

---

[1] The evidence is in the form of witness statement(s) or affidavit(s).

Appendix 10

Pre-action Protocol for Construction and Engineering Disputes 2nd edition

1 Introduction

1.1 This Pre-Action Protocol applies to all construction and engineering disputes (including professional negligence claims against architects, engineers and quantity surveyors).

2 Exceptions

2.1 A Claimant shall not be required to comply with this Protocol before commencing proceedings to the extent that the proposed proceedings (i) are for the enforcement of the decision of an adjudicator to whom a dispute has been referred pursuant to section 108 of the Housing Grants, Construction and Regeneration Act 1996 ("the 1996 Act"), (ii) include a claim for interim injunctive relief, (iii) will be the subject of a claim for summary judgment pursuant to Part 24 of the Civil Procedure Rules, or (iv) relate to the same or substantially the same issues as have been the subject of recent adjudication under the 1996 Act, or some other formal alternative dispute resolution procedure.

2.2 A Claimant shall not be required to comply with this Protocol before commencing proceedings if all the parties to the proposed proceedings expressly so agree in writing.

3 Objectives

3.1 The objectives of this Protocol are:

    3.1.1 to exchange sufficient information about the proposed proceedings broadly to allow the parties to understand each other's position and make informed decisions about settlement and how to proceed;

    3.1.2 to make appropriate attempts to resolve the matter without starting proceedings and, in particular, to consider the use of an appropriate form of ADR in order to do so.

4 Compliance

4.1 If proceedings are commenced, the Court will be able to treat the standards set in this Protocol as the normal reasonable and proportionate approach to pre-action conduct. It is likely to be only in exceptional circumstances, such as a flagrant or very significant disregard for the terms of this Protocol, that the Court will impose cost consequences on a party for non-compliance with this Protocol.

5 Proportionality

5.1 The overriding objective (CPR rule 1.1) applies to the pre-action period. The Protocol must not be used as a tactical device to secure advantage for one party or to generate unnecessary costs. In many cases, including those of modest value, the letter of claim and the response can be simple and the costs of both sides should be kept to a modest level. In all cases, the costs incurred at the Protocol stage should be proportionate to the complexity of the case and the amount of money which is at stake. The Protocol is not intended to impose a requirement on the parties to marshal and disclose all the supporting details and evidence that may ultimately be required if the case proceeds to litigation.

6   Overview of the Protocol

General aim

6.1   The general aim of this Protocol is to ensure that before Court proceedings commence:

6.1.1   the Claimant and the Defendant have provided sufficient information for each party to know the outline nature of the other's case;

6.1.2   each party has had an opportunity to consider the outline of the other's case, and to accept or reject all or any part of the outline case made against him at the earliest possible stage;

6.1.3   there is more pre-action contact between the parties;

6.1.4   better and earlier exchange of information occurs;

6.1.5   there is better pre-action investigation by the parties;

6.1.6   the parties have usually met formally on at least one occasion; and

6.1.7   the parties are in a position where they may be able to settle cases early, fairly and inexpensively without recourse to litigation; and

6.1.8   proceedings will be conducted efficiently if litigation does become necessary.

7   The Letter of Claim

7.1   Prior to commencing proceedings, the Claimant or his solicitor shall send to each proposed Defendant (if appropriate to his registered address) a copy of a letter of claim which shall contain the following information:

7.1.1   the Claimant's full name and address;

7.1.2   the full name and address of each proposed Defendant;

7.1.3   a brief summary of the claim or claims including (a) a list of principal contractual or statutory provisions relied on (b) a summary of the relief claimed including, where applicable, the monetary value of any claim or claims with a proportionate level of breakdown. The extent of the brief summary should be proportionate to the claim. Generally, it is not expected or required that expert reports should be provided but, in cases where they are succinct and central to the claim, they can form a helpful way of explaining the Claimant's position;

7.1.4   the names of any experts already instructed by the Claimant on whose evidence he intends to rely identifying the issues to which that evidence will be directed; and

7.1.5   the Claimant's confirmation as to whether or not it wishes the Protocol Referee Procedure to apply as provided at paragraph 11 below.

8   The Defendant's Response

The Defendant's acknowledgment

8.1   Within 14 calendar days of receipt of the letter of claim, the Defendant should acknowledge its receipt in writing and may give the name and address of his insurer (if any) and shall also confirm whether or not it wishes the Protocol Referee Procedure as provided at paragraph 11 below to apply. If there has been no acknowledgment by or on behalf of the Defendant within 14 days, the Claimant will be entitled to commence proceedings without further compliance with this Protocol.

Objections to the Court's jurisdiction or the named Defendant

8.2 If the Defendant intends to take any objection to all or any part of the Claimant's claim on the grounds that (i) the Court lacks jurisdiction, (ii) the matter should be referred to arbitration, or (iii) the Defendant named in the letter of claim is the wrong Defendant, that objection should be raised by the Defendant within 28 days after receipt of the Letter of Claim. The letter of objection shall specify the parts of the claim to which the objection relates, setting out the grounds relied on, and, where appropriate, shall identify the correct Defendant (if known). Any failure to take such objection shall not prejudice the Defendant's rights to do so in any subsequent proceedings, but the Court may take such failure into account when considering the question of costs.

8.3 Where such notice of objection is given, the Defendant is not required to send a letter of response in accordance with paragraph 8.5 in relation to the claim or those parts of it to which the objection relates (as the case may be).

8.4 If at any stage before the Claimant commences proceedings, the Defendant withdraws his objection, then paragraph 8.5 and the remaining part of this Protocol will apply to the claim or those parts of it to which the objection related as if the letter of claim had been received on the date on which notice of withdrawal of the objection had been given.

The Defendant's Response

8.5 Within 28 days from the date of receipt of the letter of claim, the Defendant shall send a letter of response to the Claimant which shall contain the following information:

8.5.1 A brief and proportionate summary of the Defendant's response to the claim or claims and, if the Defendant intends to make a Counterclaim, a brief summary of the Counterclaim containing the matters set out in paragraph 7.1.3 above;

8.5.2 the names of any experts already instructed on whose evidence it is intended to rely, identifying the issues to which that evidence will be directed;

8.5.3 the names of any third parties the Defendant intends to/is considering submitting to a Pre-action Protocol process.

8.6 If no response is received by the Claimant within the period of 28 days, the Claimant shall be entitled to commence proceedings without further compliance with this Protocol.

Claimant's Response to Counterclaim

8.7 The Claimant shall provide a Response to any Counterclaim within 21 days of the Defendant's Letter of Response. The Response shall contain a brief and proportionate summary of the Claimant's Response to the Counterclaim.

9 Pre-Action Meeting

9.1 Within 21 days after receipt by the Claimant of the Defendant's letter of response, or (if the Claimant intends to respond to the Counterclaim) after receipt by the Defendant of the Claimant's letter of response to the Counterclaim, the parties should normally meet.

9.2 It is not intended by this Protocol to prescribe in detail the manner in which the meeting should be conducted. However, the Court will normally expect that those attending will include:

9.2.1 where the party is an individual, that individual, and where the party is a corporate body, a representative of that body who has authority to settle or recommend settlement of the dispute;

9.2.2 a legal representative of each party (if one has been instructed);

9.2.3 where the involvement of insurers has been disclosed, a representative of the insurer (who may be its legal representative); and

9.2.4 where a claim is made or defended on behalf of some other party (such as, for example, a claim made by a main contractor pursuant to a contractual obligation to pass on subcontractor claims), the party on whose behalf the claim is made or defended and/or his legal representatives.

9.3 Generally, the aim of the meeting is for the parties to agree what are the main issues in the case, to identify the root cause of disagreement, and to consider (i) whether, and if so how, the case might be resolved without recourse to litigation, and (ii) if litigation is unavoidable, what steps should be taken to ensure that it is conducted in accordance with the overriding objective as defined in rule 1.1 of the Civil Procedure Rules. Alternatively, the meeting can itself take the form of an ADR process such as mediation.

9.4 If the parties are unable to agree on a means of resolving the dispute other than by litigation they should seek to agree:

9.4.1 if there is any area where expert evidence is likely to be required, how expert evidence is to be dealt with including whether a joint expert might be appointed, and if so, who that should be; and (so far as is practicable);

9.4.2 the extent of disclosure of documents with a view to saving costs and to the use of the e-disclosure protocol; and

9.4.3 the conduct of the litigation with the aim of minimising cost and delay.

9.5 Any party who attended any pre-action meeting shall be at liberty and may be required to disclose to the Court:

9.5.1 that the meeting took place, when and who attended;

9.5.2 the identity of any party who refused to attend, and the grounds for such refusal;

9.5.3 if the meeting did not take place, why not;

9.5.4 any agreements concluded between the parties; and

9.5.5 the fact of whether alternative means of resolving the dispute were considered or agreed.

9.6 Except as provided in paragraph 9.5, everything said at a pre-action meeting shall be treated as "without prejudice".

10   Other Matters

10.1 The parties may agree longer periods of time for compliance with any of the steps described above save that no extension in respect of any step shall exceed 28 days in the aggregate.

10.2 The Protocol process will be concluded at the completion of the pre-action meeting or, if no meeting takes place, 14 days after the expiry of the period in which the meeting should otherwise have taken place.

11   Protocol Referee Procedure

11.1 For the purposes of assisting the parties in participating in and complying with the Protocol, the parties may agree to engage in the current version of the Protocol Referee Procedure.

11.2 The Protocol Referee Procedure shall be published from time to time jointly by TeCSA and TECBAR on their respective websites.

12   Limitation of Action

12.1 If by reason of complying with any part of this protocol a Claimant's claim may be time-barred under any provision of the Limitation Act 1980, or any other legislation which imposes a time limit for bringing an action, the Claimant may commence proceedings without complying with this Protocol. In such circumstances, a Claimant who commences proceedings without complying with all, or any part, of this Protocol must apply to the Court on notice for directions as to the timetable and form of procedure to be adopted, at the same time as he requests the Court to issue proceedings. The Court will consider whether to order a stay of the whole or part of the proceedings pending compliance with this Protocol.

Appendix 11

Example of Scott Schedule

IN THE HIGH COURT OF JUSTICE 2020 s No

THE TECHNOLOGY AND CONSTRUCTION COURT

JOHN SMITH Claimant

– and –

BOTCHIT BUILDERS Defendants
LIMITED

CLAIMANT'S SCOTT SCHEDULE
DELIVERED PURSUANT TO THE ORDER OF
HIS HONOUR JUDGE DATED 2020

---

1 Item No	2 Claimant's description of each item of disrepair	3 Claimant's costs	4 Defendant's comments	5 Defendant's costs	6 For TCC judge
1	Inadequate bonding of the fibreboard to the steel angle generally along the perimeter of the roof	£800.00	Allegation denied. The fibreboard was adequately bonded to the steel angle	£250.00	
2	Inadequate anchoring of felt at top of perimeter upstand resulting in stripping of felt along the perimeter	£350.00	Allegation denied. The Defendants admit only that there would probably have been a small amount of what is known as 'birds mouthing' of the felt on the upstand which should have been dealt with by routine maintenance	£50.00	
3	Inadequately formed felt around rainwater sumps resulting in a raised rim around the sump delaying drainage of water and causing ponding on the flat roof	£200.00	Allegation denied. The Defendants' workmanship in the vicinity of the rainwater sumps was of a good standard	£75.00	
4	etc		etc		

Delivered by the Claimant this day of 2020

Delivered by the Defendants this day of 2020

Appendix 12

Specimen order for an injunction

CLAIM No: 2000

IN THE HIGH COURT OF JUSTICE

Queen's Bench Division,

Before the honourable MR JUSTICE DASH

Between   Applicant

and

Respondent

PENAL NOTICE

If you the within named [   ] disobey this Order you may be held to be in contempt of court and liable to imprisonment or fined or your assets seized.

<u>**IMPORTANT:**</u>

<u>**NOTICE TO THE RESPONDENT**</u>

You should read the terms of the Order and Guidance Notes carefully. You are advised to consult a solicitor as soon as possible.

(1)   This Order [prohibits you from doing] [obliges you to do] the acts set out in this Order. You have a right to ask the Court to vary or discharge this Order.

(2)   If you disobey this Order you may be found guilty of Contempt of Court and may be sent to prison or fined. [In the case of a corporate respondent, it may be fined, its directors may be fined or its assets may be seized.][1]

The Order was made today [date] by Counsel for the Applicant to Mr Justice Dash [and was attended by Counsel for the Respondent]. The Judge heard the Application and read the Evidence listed in Schedule A and accepted the undertakings set out in Schedule B at the end of this Order as a result of the application.

IT IS ORDERED that:

THE INJUNCTION

(1)   Until after [date] [final judgment in this Action] the Respondent must/must not [Body of Injunction to go here]

---

[1] Include the words in square brackets in case of a corporate Respondent. This notice is not a substitute for the indorsement of a penal notice.

COSTS OF THE APPLICATION

(2)   [The Respondent shall pay the Applicant's costs of this Application.]/[The costs of this Application are reserved to be dealt with by the Judge who tries this Action.]/[The costs of this Application are to be costs in the case.]/[The costs of this Application are to be the Applicant's costs in the case.]

EFFECT OF THIS ORDER

(1)   A Respondent who is an individual who is ordered not to do something must not do it himself or in any other way. He must not do it through others acting on his behalf or on his instructions or with his encouragement.

(2)   A Respondent which is a corporation and which is ordered not to do something must not do it itself or by its directors, officers, employees or agents or in any other way.

GUIDANCE NOTES

VARIATION OR DISCHARGE OF THIS ORDER

The Respondent may apply to the Court at any time to vary or discharge this Order but if he wishes to do so he must first inform the Applicant's Legal Representatives.

INTERPRETATION OF THIS ORDER

(1)   In this Order, where there is more than one Respondent (unless otherwise stated), references to 'the Respondent' mean both or all of them;

(2)   an Order requiring 'the Respondent' to do or not to do anything applies to all Respondents.

COMMUNICATIONS WITH THE COURT

All communications to the Court about this Order should be sent to Room W11, Royal Courts of Justice, Strand, London WC2A 2LL quoting the case number. The office is open between 10 am and 4.30 pm Monday to Friday. The telephone number is 020 7936 6009.

SCHEDULE A

Evidence

The Applicant relied on the following witness statements:

[name]   [number of witness statements]   [date made]   [filed on behalf of]

(1)

(2)

SCHEDULE B

Undertaking given to the Court by the Applicant

If the Court later finds that this Order has caused loss to the Respondent, and decides that the Respondent should be compensated for that loss, the Applicant will comply with any Order the Court may make.

NAME AND ADDRESS OF APPLICANT'S LEGAL REPRESENTATIVES

The Applicant's Legal Representatives are:

[Name, address reference, fax and telephone numbers both in and out of office hours.]

Appendix 13

Specimen order for injunction before issue of a claim form

IN THE HIGH COURT OF JUSTICE
CHANCERY DIVISION,
STRAND,
LONDON WC2A 2LL

BEFORE THE HONOURABLE MR JUSTICE DAY

CLAIM No: 2000

DATED

IN AN ACTION INTENDED TO BE BETWEEN

Applicant

and

Respondent

PENAL NOTICE

If you the within named [   ] disobey this Order you may be held to be in contempt of court and liable to imprisonment or fined or your assets seized.

IMPORTANT:

NOTICE TO THE RESPONDENT

You should read the terms of the Order and Guidance Notes carefully. You are advised to consult a solicitor as soon as possible.

(1)   This Order [prohibits you from doing] [obliges you to do] the acts set out in this Order. You have a right to ask the Court to vary or discharge this Order.

(2)   If you disobey this Order you may be found guilty of Contempt of Court and may be sent to prison or fined. [In the case of a corporate Respondent, it may be fined, its directors may be sent to prison or fined or its assets may be seized.][1]

THE ORDER

An Application was made today [date] by Counsel for (who is to be the Claimant in an Action against) to the Judge who heard the Application supported by the Evidence listed in Schedule A and accepted the undertakings set out in Schedule B at the end of this Order as a result of the Application.

IT IS ORDERED that:

The Defendant must/must not [Body of Injunction to go here]

---

[1] Include the words in square brackets in case of a corporate Applicant. This notice is not a substitute for the indorsement of a penal notice.

EFFECT OF THIS ORDER

(1)   A Respondent who is an individual who is ordered not to do something must not do it himself or in any other way. He must not do it through others acting on his behalf or on his instructions or with his encouragement.

(2)   A Respondent which is a corporation and which is ordered not to do something must not do it itself or by its directors, officers, employees, or agents or in any other way.

GUIDANCE NOTES

VARIATION OR DISCHARGE OF THIS ORDER

The Respondent may apply to the Court at any time to vary or discharge this Order but if he wishes to do so he must first inform the Applicant's Legal Representatives.

INTERPRETATION OF THIS ORDER

(1)   In this Order, where there is more than one Respondent, references to 'the Respondent' mean both or all of them;

(2)   a requirement to serve on 'the Respondent' means on each of them. However, the order is effective against any Respondent on whom it is served;

(3)   an Order requiring 'the Respondent' to do or not to do anything applies to all Respondents.

COMMUNICATIONS WITH THE COURT

All communications to the Court about this Order should be sent to Room TM510, Royal Courts of Justice, Strand, London WC2A 2LL quoting the case number. The office is open between 10 am and 4.30 pm Monday to Friday. The telephone number is 020 7936 6827.

SCHEDULE A

Witness Statements

The Applicant relied on the following Witness Statements:

[name]   *[number of witness statements]*   *[date made]*   *[filed on behalf of]*

SCHEDULE B

Undertakings given to the Court by the Applicant

(1)   If the Court later finds that this Order has caused loss to the Respondent, and decides that the Respondent should be compensated for that loss, the Applicant will comply with any Order the Court may make.

(2)   As soon as practicable the Applicant will issue and serve on the Respondent a Claim Form [in the form of the draft produced to the Court] [serve on the Respondent the Claim Form] claiming appropriate relief together with this Order.

(3)   The Applicant will file a witness statement [substantially in the terms of the draft witness statement produced to the Court] (confirming the substance of what was said to the Court by the Applicant's Counsel/Solicitors).

[(4)   Where a return date has been given – as soon as practicable the Applicant will serve on the Respondent an application for the return date together with a copy of the witness statements and exhibits containing the evidence relied on by the Applicant.]

NAME AND ADDRESS OF APPLICANT'S LEGAL REPRESENTATIVES

The Applicant's Legal Representatives are:

[Name, address reference, fax and telephone numbers both in and out of office hours.]

Appendix 14

Specimen freezing injunction

FREEZING INJUNCTION	IN THE HIGH COURT OF JUSTICE
	[ ] DIVISION
Before The Honourable Mr Justice	[ ]

Claim No.

Dated

Applicant

Seal

Respondent

Name, address and reference of Respondent

PENAL NOTICE

IF YOU [   ]¹ DISOBEY THIS ORDER YOU MAY BE HELD TO BE IN CONTEMPT OF COURT AND MAY BE IMPRISONED, FINED OR HAVE YOUR ASSETS SEIZED.

ANY OTHER PERSON WHO KNOWS OF THIS ORDER AND DOES ANYTHING WHICH HELPS OR PERMITS THE RESPONDENT TO BREACH THE TERMS OF THIS ORDER MAY ALSO BE HELD TO BE IN CONTEMPT OF COURT AND MAY BE IMPRISONED, FINED OR HAVE THEIR ASSETS SEIZED.

1 Insert name of Respondent

THIS ORDER

1.   This is a Freezing Injunction made against [   ] ('the Respondent') on [   ] by Mr Justice [   ] on the application of [   ] ('the Applicant'). The Judge read the Affidavits listed in Schedule A and accepted the undertakings set out in Schedule B at the end of this Order.

2.   This order was made at a hearing without notice to the Respondent. The Respondent has a right to apply to the court to vary or discharge the order – see paragraph 13 below.

3.   There will be a further hearing in respect of this order on [   ] ('the return date').

4.   If there is more than one Respondent—

    (a)   unless otherwise stated, references in this order to 'the Respondent' mean both or all of them; and

    (b)   this order is effective against any Respondent on whom it is served or who is given notice of it.

FREEZING INJUNCTION

[For injunction limited to assets in England and Wales]

5.   Until the return date or further order of the court, the Respondent must not remove from England and Wales or in any way dispose of, deal with or diminish the value of any of his assets which are in England and Wales up to the value of £   .

[For worldwide injunction]

5.   Until the return date or further order of the court, the Respondent must not—

    (1)   remove from England and Wales any of his assets which are in England and Wales up to the value of £   ; or

    (2)   in any way dispose of, deal with or diminish the value of any of his assets whether they are in or outside England and Wales up to the same value.

[For either form of injunction]

6.   Paragraph 5 applies to all the Respondent's assets whether or not they are in his own name and whether they are solely or jointly owned. For the purpose of this order the Respondent's assets include any asset which he has the power, directly or indirectly, to dispose of or deal with as if it were his own. The Respondent is to be regarded as having such power if a third party holds or controls the asset in accordance with his direct or indirect instructions.

7.   This prohibition includes the following assets in particular—

    (a)   the property known as [title/address] or the net sale money after payment of any mortgages if it has been sold;

    (b)   the property and assets of the Respondent's business [known as [name]] [carried on at [address]] or the sale money if any of them have been sold; and

    (c)   any money standing to the credit of any bank account including the amount of any cheque drawn on such account which has not been cleared.

[For injunction limited to assets in England and Wales]

8.   If the total value free of charges or other securities ('unencumbered value') of the Respondent's assets in England and Wales exceeds £   , the Respondent may remove any of those assets from England and Wales or may dispose of or deal with them so long as the total unencumbered value of his assets still in England and Wales remains above £   .

[For worldwide injunction]

8.   (1)   If the total value free of charges or other securities ('unencumbered value') of the Respondent's assets in England and Wales exceeds £   , the Respondent may remove any of those assets from England and Wales or may dispose of or deal with

them so long as the total unencumbered value of the Respondent's assets still in England and Wales remains above £　　.

(2) If the total unencumbered value of the Respondent's assets in England and Wales does not exceed £　　, the Respondent must not remove any of those assets from England and Wales and must not dispose of or deal with any of them. If the Respondent has other assets outside England and Wales, he may dispose of or deal with those assets outside England and Wales so long as the total unencumbered value of all his assets whether in or outside England and Wales remains above £　　.

PROVISION OF INFORMATION

9.　(1) Unless paragraph (2) applies, the Respondent must [immediately] [within hours of service of this order] and to the best of his ability inform the Applicant's solicitors of all his assets [in England and Wales] [worldwide] [exceeding £　　in value] whether in his own name or not and whether solely or jointly owned, giving the value, location and details of all such assets.

(2) If the provision of any of this information is likely to incriminate the Respondent, he may be entitled to refuse to provide it, but is recommended to take legal advice before refusing to provide the information. Wrongful refusal to provide the information is contempt of court and may render the Respondent liable to be imprisoned, fined or have his assets seized.

10.　Within [　　] working days after being served with this order, the Respondent must swear and serve on the Applicant's solicitors an affidavit setting out the above information.

EXCEPTIONS TO THIS ORDER

11.　(1) This order does not prohibit the Respondent from spending £　　a week towards his ordinary living expenses and also £　　[or a reasonable sum] on legal advice and representation. [But before spending any money the Respondent must tell the Applicant's legal representatives where the money is to come from.]

[(2) This order does not prohibit the Respondent from dealing with or disposing of any of his assets in the ordinary and proper course of business.]

(3) The Respondent may agree with the Applicant's legal representatives that the above spending limits should be increased or that this order should be varied in any other respect, but any agreement must be in writing.

(4) The order will cease to have effect if the Respondent—

(a) provides security by paying the sum of £　　into court, to be held to the order of the court; or

(b) makes provision for security in that sum by another method agreed with the Applicant's legal representatives.

COSTS

12.　The costs of this application are reserved to the judge hearing the application on the return date.

VARIATION OR DISCHARGE OF THIS ORDER

13.　Anyone served with or notified of this order may apply to the court at any time to vary or discharge this order (or so much of it as affects that person), but they must first inform the Applicant's solicitors. If any evidence is to be relied upon in support of the application, the substance of it must be communicated in writing to the Applicant's solicitors in advance.

INTERPRETATION OF THIS ORDER

14.   A Respondent who is an individual who is ordered not to do something must not do it himself or in any other way. He must not do it through others acting on his behalf or on his instructions or with his encouragement.

15.   A Respondent which is not an individual which is ordered not to do something must not do it itself or by its directors, officers, partners, employees or agents or in any other way.

PARTIES OTHER THAN THE APPLICANT AND RESPONDENT

16.   Effect of this order

It is a contempt of court for any person notified of this order knowingly to assist in or permit a breach of this order. Any person doing so may be imprisoned, fined or have their assets seized.

17.   Set off by banks

This injunction does not prevent any bank from exercising any right of set off it may have in respect of any facility which it gave to the respondent before it was notified of this order.

18.   Withdrawals by the Respondent

No bank need enquire as to the application or proposed application of any money withdrawn by the Respondent if the withdrawal appears to be permitted by this order.

[For worldwide injunction]

19.   Persons outside England and Wales

(1)   Except as provided in paragraph (2) below, the terms of this order do not affect or concern anyone outside the jurisdiction of this court.

(2)   The terms of this order will affect the following persons in a country or state outside the jurisdiction of this court —

   (a)   the Respondent or his officer or agent appointed by power of attorney;

   (b)   any person who—

      (i)   is subject to the jurisdiction of this court;

      (ii)   has been given written notice of this order at his residence or place of business within the jurisdiction of this court; and

      (iii)   is able to prevent acts or omissions outside the jurisdiction of this court which constitute or assist in a breach of the terms of this order; and

   (c)   any other person, only to the extent that this order is declared enforceable by or is enforced by a court in that country or state.

[For worldwide injunction]

20.   Assets located outside England and Wales

Nothing in this order shall, in respect of assets located outside England and Wales, prevent any third party from complying with—

(1)   what it reasonably believes to be its obligations, contractual or otherwise, under the laws and obligations of the country or state in which those assets are situated or under the proper law of any contract between itself and the Respondent; and

(2)   any orders of the courts of that country or state, provided that reasonable notice of any application for such an order is given to the Applicant's solicitors.

COMMUNICATIONS WITH THE COURT

All communications to the court about this order should be sent to—

[Insert the address and telephone number of the appropriate Court Office]

If the order is made at the Royal Courts of Justice, communications should be addressed as follows—

Where the order is made in the Chancery Division

Chancery Associates, Ground Floor, The Rolls Building, 7 Rolls Buildings, Fetter Lane, London EC4A 1NL, quoting the case number. The telephone number is 020 7947 6733.

Where the order is made in the Queen's Bench Division

Room E07, Royal Courts of Justice, Strand, London WC2A 2LL quoting the case number. The telephone number is 0207 947 6010.

Where the order is made in the Commercial Court

7 Rolls Building, Fetter Lane, London, EC4A 1NL, quoting the case number. The telephone number is 0207 947 6826.

The offices are open between 10 am and 4.30 pm Monday to Friday.

SCHEDULE A

AFFIDAVITS

The Applicant relied on the following affidavits—

[name]   [number of affidavit]   [date sworn]   [filed on behalf of]

SCHEDULE B

UNDERTAKINGS GIVEN TO THE COURT BY THE APPLICANT

(1) If the court later finds that this order has caused loss to the Respondent, anddecides that the Respondent should be compensated for that loss, the Applicant will comply with any order the court may make.

[(2) The Applicant will—

(a) on or before [date] cause a written guarantee in the sum of £ to be issued from a bank with a place of business within England or Wales, in respect of any order the court may make pursuant to paragraph (1) above; and

(b) immediately upon issue of the guarantee, cause a copy of it to be served on the Respondent.]

(3) As soon as practicable the Applicant will issue and serve a claim form [in the form of the draft produced to the court] [claiming the appropriate relief].

(4) The Applicant will [swear and file an affidavit] [cause an affidavit to be sworn and filed] [substantially in the terms of the draft affidavit produced to the court] [confirming the substance of what was said to the court by the Applicant's counsel/solicitors].

(5) The Applicant will serve upon the Respondent [together with this order] [as soon as practicable]—

(i) copies of the affidavits and exhibits containing the evidence relied upon by the Applicant, and any other documents provided to the court on the making of the application;

(ii) the claim form; and

(iii) an application notice for continuation of the order.

[(6) Anyone notified of this order will be given a copy of it by the Applicant's legal representatives.]

(7) The Applicant will pay the reasonable costs of anyone other than the Respondent which have been incurred as a result of this order including the costs of finding out whether that person holds any of the Respondent's assets and if the court later finds that this order has caused such person loss, and decides that such person should be

compensated for that loss, the Applicant will comply with any order the court may make.

(8)   If this order ceases to have effect (for example, if the Respondent provides security or the Applicant does not provide a bank guarantee as provided for above) the Applicant will immediately take all reasonable steps to inform in writing anyone to whom he has given notice of this order, or who he has reasonable grounds for supposing may act upon this order, that it has ceased to have effect.

(9)   The Applicant will not without the permission of the court use any information obtained as a result of this order for the purpose of any civil or criminal proceedings, either in England and Wales or in any other jurisdiction, other than this claim.

(10)   The Applicant will not without the permission of the court seek to enforce this order in any country outside England and Wales [or seek an order of a similar nature including orders conferring a charge or other security against the Respondent or the Respondent's assets].

Appendix 15

Specimen search order

SEARCH ORDER

Before The Honourable Mr Justice

IN THE HIGH COURT OF JUSTICE
[   ] **DIVISION**
[   ]

Claim No.

Dated

Applicant

Seal

Respondent

Name, address and reference of Respondent

PENAL NOTICE

IF YOU [   ]¹ DISOBEY THIS ORDER YOU MAY BE HELD TO BE IN CONTEMPT OF COURT AND MAY BE IMPRISONED, FINED OR HAVE YOUR ASSETS SEIZED.

ANY OTHER PERSON WHO KNOWS OF THIS ORDER AND DOES ANYTHING WHICH HELPS OR PERMITS THE RESPONDENT TO BREACH THE TERMS OF THIS ORDER MAY ALSO BE HELD TO BE IN CONTEMPT OF COURT AND MAY BE IMPRISONED, FINED OR HAVE THEIR ASSETS SEIZED.

1 Insert name of Respondent

THIS ORDER

1.   This is a Search Order made against [   ] ('the Respondent') on [   ] by Mr Justice [   ] on the application of [   ] ('the Applicant'). The Judge read the Affidavits listed in Schedule F and accepted the undertakings set out in Schedules C, D and E at the end of this order.

2.   This order was made at a hearing without notice to the Respondent. The Respondent has a right to apply to the court to vary or discharge the order – see paragraph 27 below.

3.   There will be a further hearing in respect of this order on [   ] ('the return date').

4.   If there is more than one Respondent—

(a)   unless otherwise stated, references in this order to 'the Respondent' mean both or all of them; and

(b)   this order is effective against any Respondent on whom it is served or who is given notice of it.

5.   This order must be complied with by—

(a)   the Respondent;

(b)   any director, officer, partner or responsible employee of the Respondent; and

(c)   if the Respondent is an individual, any other person having responsible control of the premises to be searched.

THE SEARCH

6.   The Respondent must permit the following persons[8]—

(a)   [   ] ('the Supervising Solicitor');

(b)   [   ], a solicitor in the firm of [   ], the Applicant's solicitors; and

(c)   up to [   ] other persons[9] being [their identity or capacity] accompanying them,

(together 'the search party'), to enter the premises mentioned in Schedule A to this order and any other premises of the Respondent disclosed under paragraph 18 below and any vehicles under the Respondent's control on or around the premises ('the premises') so that they can search for, inspect, photograph or photocopy, and deliver into the safekeeping of the Applicant's solicitors all the documents and articles which are listed in Schedule B to this order ('the listed items').

7.   Having permitted the search party to enter the premises, the Respondent must allow the search party to remain on the premises until the search is complete. In the event that it becomes necessary for any of those persons to leave the premises before the search is complete, the Respondent must allow them to re-enter the premises immediately upon their seeking re-entry on the same or the following day in order to complete the search.

RESTRICTIONS ON SEARCH

8.   This order may not be carried out at the same time as a police search warrant.

9.   Before the Respondent allows anybody onto the premises to carry out this order, he is entitled to have the Supervising Solicitor explain to him what it means in everyday language.

10.   The Respondent is entitled to seek legal advice and to ask the court to vary or discharge this order. Whilst doing so, he may ask the Supervising Solicitor to delay starting the search for up to 2 hours or such other longer period as the Supervising Solicitor may permit. However, the Respondent must—

(a)   comply with the terms of paragraph 27 below;

(b)   not disturb or remove any listed items; and

(c)   permit the Supervising Solicitor to enter, but not start to search.

11. (1) Before permitting entry to the premises by any person other than the Supervising Solicitor, the Respondent may, for a short time (not to exceed two hours, unless the Supervising Solicitor agrees to a longer period)—

   (a) gather together any documents he believes may be incriminating or privileged; and

   (b) hand them to the Supervising Solicitor for him to assess whether they are incriminating or privileged as claimed.

   (2) If the Supervising Solicitor decides that the Respondent is entitled to withhold production of any of the documents on the ground that they are privileged or incriminating, he will exclude them from the search, record them in a list for inclusion in his report and return them to the Respondent.

   (3) If the Supervising Solicitor believes that the Respondent may be entitled to withhold production of the whole or any part of a document on the ground that it or part of it may be privileged or incriminating or if the Respondent claims to be entitled to withhold production on those grounds, the Supervising Solicitor will exclude it from the search and retain it in his possession pending further order of the court.

12. If the Respondent wishes to take legal advice and gather documents as permitted, he must first inform the Supervising Solicitor and keep him informed of the steps being taken.

13. No item may be removed from the premises until a list of the items to be removed has been prepared, and a copy of the list has been supplied to the Respondent, and he has been given a reasonable opportunity to check the list.

14. The premises must not be searched, and items must not be removed from them, except in the presence of the Respondent.

15. If the Supervising Solicitor is satisfied that full compliance with paragraphs 13 or 14 is not practicable, he may permit the search to proceed and items to be removed without fully complying with them.

DELIVERY UP OF ARTICLES/DOCUMENTS

16. The Respondent must immediately hand over to the Applicant's solicitors any of the listed items, which are in his possession or under his control, save for any computer or hard disk integral to any computer. Any items the subject of a dispute as to whether they are listed items must immediately be handed over to the Supervising Solicitor for safe keeping pending resolution of the dispute or further order of the court.

17. The Respondent must immediately give the search party effective access to the computers on the premises, with all necessary passwords, to enable the computers to be searched. If they contain any listed items the Respondent must cause the listed items to be displayed so that they can be read and copied.[11] The Respondent must provide the Applicant's Solicitors with copies of all listed items contained in the computers. All reasonable steps shall be taken by the Applicant and the Applicant's solicitors to ensure that no damage is done to any computer or data. The Applicant and his representatives may not themselves search the Respondent's computers unless they have sufficient expertise to do so without damaging the Respondent's system.

PROVISION OF INFORMATION

18. The Respondent must immediately inform the Applicant's Solicitors (in the presence of the Supervising Solicitor) so far as he is aware—

   (a) where all the listed items are;

   (b) the name and address of everyone who has supplied him, or offered to supply him, with listed items;

      (c)   the name and address of everyone to whom he has supplied, or offered to supply, listed items; and

      (d)   full details of the dates and quantities of every such supply and offer.

19.   Within [   ] working days after being served with this order the Respondent must swear and serve an affidavit setting out the above information.[12]

PROHIBITED ACTS

20.   Except for the purpose of obtaining legal advice, the Respondent must not directly or indirectly inform anyone of these proceedings or of the contents of this order, or warn anyone that proceedings have been or may be brought against him by the Applicant until 4.30 pm on the return date or further order of the court.

21.   Until 4.30 pm on the return date the Respondent must not destroy, tamper with, cancel or part with possession, power, custody or control of the listed items otherwise than in accordance with the terms of this order.

22.   [Insert any negative injunctions.]

23.   [Insert any further order.]

COSTS

24.   The costs of this application are reserved to the judge hearing the application on the return date.

RESTRICTIONS ON SERVICE

25.   This order may only be served between [ ] am/pm and [ ] am/pm [and on a weekday].[13]

26.   This order must be served by the Supervising Solicitor, and paragraph 6 of the order must be carried out in his presence and under his supervision.

VARIATION AND DISCHARGE OF THIS ORDER

27.   Anyone served with or notified of this order may apply to the court at any time to vary or discharge this order (or so much of it as affects that person), but they must first inform the Applicant's solicitors. If any evidence is to be relied upon in support of the application, the substance of it must be communicated in writing to the Applicant's solicitors in advance.

INTERPRETATION OF THIS ORDER

28.   Any requirement that something shall be done to or in the presence of the Respondent means—

      (a)   if there is more than one Respondent, to or in the presence of any one of them; and

      (b)   if a Respondent is not an individual, to or in the presence of a director, officer, partner or responsible employee.

29.   A Respondent who is an individual who is ordered not to do something must not do it himself or in any other way. He must not do it through others acting on his behalf or on his instructions or with his encouragement.

30.   A Respondent which is not an individual which is ordered not to do something must not do it itself or by its directors, officers, partners, employees or agents or in any other way.

COMMUNICATIONS WITH THE COURT

All communications to the court about this order should be sent to—

[Insert the address and telephone number of the appropriate Court Office]

If the order is made at the Royal Courts of Justice, communications should be addressed as follows—

Where the order is made in the Chancery Division

Chancery Associates, Ground Floor, The Rolls Building, 7 Rolls Buildings, Fetter Lane, London EC4A 1NL, quoting the case number. The telephone number is 020 7947 6733.

Where the order is made in the Queen's Bench Division

Room E07, Royal Courts of Justice, Strand, London WC2A 2LL quoting the case number. The telephone number is 0207 947 6010.

Where the order is made in the Commercial Court

7 Rolls Building, Fetter Lane, London, EC4A 1NL, quoting the case number. The telephone number is 0207 947 6826.

The offices are open between 10 am and 4.30 pm Monday to Friday.

SCHEDULE A

THE PREMISES

SCHEDULE B

THE LISTED ITEMS

SCHEDULE C

UNDERTAKINGS GIVEN TO THE COURT BY THE APPLICANT

(1)   If the court later finds that this order or carrying it out has caused loss to the Respondent, and decides that the Respondent should be compensated for that loss, the Applicant will comply with any order the court may make. Further if the carrying out of this order has been in breach of the terms of this order or otherwise in a manner inconsistent with the Applicant's solicitors' duties as officers of the court, the Applicant will comply with any order for damages the court may make.

[(2)   As soon as practicable the Applicant will issue a claim form [in the form of the draft produced to the court] [claiming the appropriate relief].]

(3)   The Applicant will [swear and file an affidavit] [cause an affidavit to be sworn and filed] [substantially in the terms of the draft affidavit produced to the court] [confirming the substance of what was said to the court by the Applicant's counsel/solicitors].

(4)   The Applicant will not, without the permission of the court, use any information or documents obtained as a result of carrying out this order nor inform anyone else of these proceedings except for the purposes of these proceedings (including adding further Respondents) or commencing civil proceedings in relation to the same or related subject matter to these proceedings until after the return date.

[(5)   The Applicant will maintain pending further order the sum of £ [   ] in an account controlled by the Applicant's solicitors.]

[(6)   The Applicant will insure the items removed from the premises.]

SCHEDULE D

UNDERTAKINGS GIVEN BY THE APPLICANT'S SOLICITORS

(1)   The Applicant's solicitors will provide to the Supervising Solicitor for service on the Respondent—

    (i)   a service copy of this order;

    (ii)   the claim form (with defendant's response pack) or, if not issued, the draft produced to the court;

    (iii)   an application for hearing on the return date;

    (iv)   copies of the affidavits [or draft affidavits] and exhibits capable of being copied containing the evidence relied upon by the applicant;

    (v)   a note of any allegation of fact made orally to the court where such allegation is not contained in the affidavits or draft affidavits read by the judge; and

(vi)   a copy of the skeleton argument produced to the court by the Applicant's [counsel/ solicitors].

(2)   The Applicants' solicitors will answer at once to the best of their ability any question whether a particular item is a listed item.

(3)   Subject as provided below the Applicant's solicitors will retain in their own safe keeping all items obtained as a result of this order until the court directs otherwise.

(4)   The Applicant's solicitors will return the originals of all documents obtained as a result of this order (except original documents which belong to the Applicant) as soon as possible and in any event within [two] working days of their removal.

SCHEDULE E

UNDERTAKINGS GIVEN BY THE SUPERVISING SOLICITOR

(1)   The Supervising Solicitor will use his best endeavours to serve this order upon the Respondent and at the same time to serve upon the Respondent the other documents required to be served and referred to in paragraph (1) of Schedule D.

(2)   The Supervising Solicitor will offer to explain to the person served with the order its meaning and effect fairly and in everyday language, and to inform him of his right to take legal advice (including an explanation that the Respondent may be entitled to avail himself of the privilege against self-incrimination and legal professional privilege) and to apply to vary or discharge this order as mentioned in paragraph 27 above.

(3)   The Supervising Solicitor will retain in the safe keeping of his firm all items retained by him as a result of this order until the court directs otherwise.

(4)   Unless and until the court otherwise orders, or unless otherwise necessary to comply with any duty to the court pursuant to this order, the Supervising Solicitor shall not disclose to any person any information relating to those items, and shall keep the existence of such items confidential.

(5)   Within [48] hours of completion of the search the Supervising Solicitor will make and provide to the Applicant's solicitors, the Respondent or his solicitors and to the judge who made this order (for the purposes of the court file) a written report on the carrying out of the order.

SCHEDULE F

AFFIDAVITS

The Applicant relied on the following affidavits—

[name]   [number of affidavit]   [date sworn]   [filed on behalf of]

NAME AND ADDRESS OF APPLICANT'S SOLICITORS

The Applicant's solicitors are—

[Name, address, reference, fax and telephone numbers both in and out of office hours.]

FOOTNOTES

…

8   Where the premises are likely to be occupied by an unaccompanied woman and the Supervising Solicitor is a man, at least one of the persons accompanying him should be a woman.

9   None of these persons should be people who could gain personally or commercially from anything they might read or see on the premises, unless their presence is essential.

10   If it is envisaged that the Respondent's computers are to be imaged (i.e. the hard drives are to be copied wholesale, thereby reproducing listed items and other items indiscriminately), special provision needs to be made and independent computer

specialists need to be appointed, who should be required to give undertakings to the court.

11   The period should ordinarily be longer than the period in paragraph (2) of Schedule D, if any of the information is likely to be included in listed items taken away of which the Respondent does not have copies.

12   Normally, the order should be served in the morning (not before 9.30 am) and on a weekday to enable the Respondent more readily to obtain legal advice.

Appendix 16

CPR 1998, PD 31B and Electronic Documents Questionnaire

Purpose, scope and interpretation

1   Rule 31.4 contains a broad definition of 'document'. This extends to Electronic Documents.

2   The purpose of this Practice Direction is to encourage and assist the parties to reach agreement in relation to the disclosure of Electronic Documents in a proportionate and cost-effective manner.

3   Unless the court orders otherwise, this Practice Direction only applies to proceedings that are (or are likely to be) allocated to the multi-track.

4   Unless the court orders otherwise, this Practice Direction only applies to proceedings started on or after 1st October 2010. Paragraph 2A.2 to 2A.5 of Practice Direction 31A in force immediately before that date continues to apply to proceedings started before that date.

5   In this Practice Direction –

(1)   'Data Sampling' means the process of checking data by identifying and checking representative individual documents;

(2)   'Disclosure Data' means data relating to disclosed documents, including for example the type of document, the date of the document, the names of the author or sender and the recipient, and the party disclosing the document;

(3)   'Electronic Document' means any document held in electronic form. It includes, for example, e-mail and other electronic communications such as text messages and voicemail, word-processed documents and databases, and documents stored on portable devices such as memory sticks and mobile phones. In addition to documents that are readily accessible from computer systems and other electronic devices and media, it includes documents that are stored on servers and back-up systems and documents that have been deleted. It also includes Metadata and other embedded data which is not typically visible on screen or a print out;

(4)   'Electronic Image' means an electronic representation of a paper document;

(5)   'Electronic Documents Questionnaire' means the questionnaire in the Schedule to this Practice Direction;

(6)   'Keyword Search' means a software-aided search for words across the text of an Electronic Document;

(7)   'Metadata' is data about data. In the case of an Electronic Document, Metadata is typically embedded information about the document which is not readily accessible once the Native Electronic Document has been converted into an Electronic Image or paper document. It may include (for example) the date and time of creation or modification of a word-processing file, or the author and the date and time of sending an e-mail. Metadata may be created automatically by a computer system or manually by a user;

(8)   'Native Electronic Document' or 'Native Format' means an Electronic Document stored in the original form in which it was created by a computer software program; and

(9)   'Optical Character Recognition (OCR)' means the computer-facilitated recognition of printed or written text characters in an Electronic Image in which the text-based contents cannot be searched electronically.

General principles

6   When considering disclosure of Electronic Documents, the parties and their legal representatives should bear in mind the following general principles –

(1)   Electronic Documents should be managed efficiently in order to minimise the cost incurred;

(2)   technology should be used in order to ensure that document management activities are undertaken efficiently and effectively;

(3)   disclosure should be given in a manner which gives effect to the overriding objective;

(4)   Electronic Documents should generally be made available for inspection in a form which allows the party receiving the documents the same ability to access, search, review and display the documents as the party giving disclosure; and

(5)   disclosure of Electronic Documents which are of no relevance to the proceedings may place an excessive burden in time and cost on the party to whom disclosure is given.

Preservation of documents

7   As soon as litigation is contemplated, the parties' legal representatives must notify their clients of the need to preserve disclosable documents. The documents to be preserved include Electronic Documents which would otherwise be deleted in accordance with a document retention policy or otherwise deleted in the ordinary course of business.

Discussions between the parties before the first Case Management Conference in relation to the use of technology and disclosure

8   The parties and their legal representatives must, before the first case management conference, discuss the use of technology in the management of Electronic Documents and the conduct of proceedings, in particular for the purpose of –

(1)   creating lists of documents to be disclosed;

(2)   giving disclosure by providing documents and information regarding documents in electronic format; and

(3)   presenting documents and other material to the court at the trial.

9   The parties and their legal representatives must also, before the first case management conference, discuss the disclosure of Electronic Documents. In some cases (for example heavy and complex cases) it may be appropriate to begin discussions before proceedings are commenced. The discussions should include (where appropriate) the following matters –

(1)   the categories of Electronic Documents within the parties' control, the computer systems, electronic devices and media on which any relevant documents may be held, storage systems and document retention policies;

(2)   the scope of the reasonable search for Electronic Documents required by rule 31.7;

(3)   the tools and techniques (if any) which should be considered to reduce the burden and cost of disclosure of Electronic Documents, including –

(a) limiting disclosure of documents or certain categories of documents to particular date ranges, to particular custodians of documents, or to particular types of documents;

(b) the use of agreed Keyword Searches;

(c) the use of agreed software tools;

(d) the methods to be used to identify duplicate documents;

(e) the use of Data Sampling;

(f) the methods to be used to identify privileged documents and other non-disclosable documents, to redact documents (where redaction is appropriate), and for dealing with privileged or other documents which have been inadvertently disclosed; and

(g) the use of a staged approach to the disclosure of Electronic Documents;

(4) the preservation of Electronic Documents, with a view to preventing loss of such documents before the trial;

(5) the exchange of data relating to Electronic Documents in an agreed electronic format using agreed fields;

(6) the formats in which Electronic Documents are to be provided on inspection and the methods to be used;

(7) the basis of charging for or sharing the cost of the provision of Electronic Documents, and whether any arrangements for charging or sharing of costs are final or are subject to re-allocation in accordance with any order for costs subsequently made; and

(8) whether it would be appropriate to use the services of a neutral electronic repository for storage of Electronic Documents.

The Electronic Documents Questionnaire

10   In some cases the parties may find it helpful to exchange the Electronic Documents Questionnaire in order to provide information to each other in relation to the scope, extent and most suitable format for disclosure of Electronic Documents in the proceedings.

11   The answers to the Electronic Documents Questionnaire must be verified by a statement of truth.

12   Answers to the Electronic Documents Questionnaire will only be available for inspection by non-parties if permission is given under rule 5.4C(2).

13   Rule 31.22 makes provision regulating the use of answers to the Electronic Documents Questionnaire.

Preparation for the first Case Management Conference

14   The documents submitted to the court in advance of the first case management conference should include a summary of the matters on which the parties agree in relation to the disclosure of Electronic Documents and a summary of the matters on which they disagree.

15   If the parties indicate that they have been unable to reach agreement in relation to the disclosure of Electronic Documents and that no agreement is likely, the court will give written directions in relation to disclosure or order a separate hearing in relation to disclosure. When doing so, the court will consider making an order that the parties must complete and exchange all or any part of the Electronic Documents Questionnaire within 14 days or such other period as the court may direct.

16   The person signing the Electronic Documents Questionnaire should attend the first case management conference, and any subsequent hearing at which disclosure is likely to be considered.

Where the parties are unable to reach an appropriate agreement in relation to the disclosure of Electronic Documents

17   If at any time it becomes apparent that the parties are unable to reach agreement in relation to the disclosure of Electronic Documents, the parties should seek directions from the court at the earliest practical date.

18   If the court considers that the parties' agreement in relation to the disclosure of Electronic Documents is inappropriate or insufficient, the court will give directions in relation to disclosure. When doing so, the court will consider making an order that the parties must complete and exchange all or any part of the Electronic Documents Questionnaire within 14 days or such other period as the court may direct.

19   If a party gives disclosure of Electronic Documents without first discussing with other parties how to plan and manage such disclosure, the court may require that party to carry out further searches for documents or to repeat other steps which that party has already carried out.

The reasonable search

20   The extent of the reasonable search required by rule 31.7 for the purposes of standard disclosure is affected by the existence of Electronic Documents. The extent of the search which must be made will depend on the circumstances of the case including, in particular, the factors referred to in rule 31.7(2). The parties should bear in mind that the overriding objective includes dealing with the case in ways which are proportionate.

21   The factors that may be relevant in deciding the reasonableness of a search for Electronic Documents include (but are not limited to) the following –

(1)   the number of documents involved;

(2)   the nature and complexity of the proceedings;

(3)   the ease and expense of retrieval of any particular document. This includes:

(a)   the accessibility of Electronic Documents including e-mail communications on computer systems, servers, back-up systems and other electronic devices or media that may contain such documents taking into account alterations or developments in hardware or software systems used by the disclosing party and/or available to enable access to such documents;

(b)   the location of relevant Electronic Documents, data, computer systems, servers, back-up systems and other electronic devices or media that may contain such documents;

(c)   the likelihood of locating relevant data;

(d)   the cost of recovering any Electronic Documents;

(e)   the cost of disclosing and providing inspection of any relevant Electronic Documents; and

(f)   the likelihood that Electronic Documents will be materially altered in the course of recovery, disclosure or inspection;

(4)   the availability of documents or contents of documents from other sources; and

(5)   the significance of any document which is likely to be located during the search.

22   Depending on the circumstances, it may be reasonable to search all of the parties' electronic storage systems, or to search only some part of those systems. For example, it may be reasonable to decide not to search for documents coming into existence before a

particular date, or to limit the search to documents in a particular place or places, or to documents falling into particular categories.

23   In some cases a staged approach may be appropriate, with disclosure initially being given of limited categories of documents. Those categories may subsequently be extended or limited depending on the results initially obtained.

24   The primary source of disclosure of Electronic Documents is normally reasonably accessible data. A party requesting under rule 31.12 specific disclosure of Electronic Documents which are not reasonably accessible must demonstrate that the relevance and materiality justify the cost and burden of retrieving and producing it.

Keyword and other automated searches

25   It may be reasonable to search for Electronic Documents by means of Keyword Searches or other automated methods of searching if a full review of each and every document would be unreasonable.

26   However, it will often be insufficient to use simple Keyword Searches or other automated methods of searching alone. The injudicious use of Keyword Searches and other automated search techniques –

(1)   may result in failure to find important documents which ought to be disclosed, and/or

(2)   may find excessive quantities of irrelevant documents, which if disclosed would place an excessive burden in time and cost on the party to whom disclosure is given.

27   The parties should consider supplementing Keyword Searches and other automated searches with additional techniques such as individually reviewing certain documents or categories of documents (for example important documents generated by key personnel) and taking such other steps as may be required in order to justify the selection to the court.

Disclosure of Metadata

28   Where copies of disclosed documents are provided in Native Format in accordance with paragraph 33 below, some Metadata will be disclosed with each document. A party requesting disclosure of additional Metadata or forensic image copies of disclosed documents (for example in relation to a dispute concerning authenticity) must demonstrate that the relevance and materiality of the requested Metadata justify the cost and burden of producing that Metadata.

29   Parties using document management or litigation support systems should be alert to the possibility that Metadata or other useful information relating to documents may not be stored with the documents.

Lists of Documents

30   If a party is giving disclosure of Electronic Documents, paragraph 3 of Practice Direction 31A is to be read subject to the following –

(1)   Form N265 may be amended to accommodate the sub-paragraphs which follow;

(2)   a list of documents may by agreement between the parties be an electronic file in .csv (comma-separated values) or other agreed format;

(3)   documents may be listed otherwise than in date order where a different order would be more convenient;

(4)   save where otherwise agreed or ordered, documents should be listed individually if a party already possesses data relating to the document (for example, type of

document and date of creation) which make this possible (so that as far as possible each document may be given a unique reference number);

(5)   a party should be consistent in the way in which documents are listed;

(6)   consistent column headings should be repeated on each page of the list on which documents are listed, where the software used for preparing the list enables this to be carried out automatically; and

(7)   the disclosure list number used in any supplemental list of documents should be unique and should run sequentially from the last number used in the previous list.

Provision of Disclosure Data in electronic form

31   Where a party provides another party with Disclosure Data in electronic form, the following provisions will apply unless the parties agree or the court directs otherwise –

(1)   Disclosure Data should be set out in a single, continuous table or spreadsheet, each separate column containing exclusively one of the following types of Disclosure Data –

(a)   disclosure list number (sequential)

(b)   date

(c)   document type

(d)   author/sender

(e)   recipient

(f)   disclosure list number of any parent or covering document;

(2)   other than for disclosure list numbers, blank entries are permissible and preferred if there is no relevant Disclosure Data (that is, the field should be left blank rather than state 'Undated');

(3)   dates should be set out in the alphanumeric form '01 Jan 2010'; and

(4)   Disclosure Data should be set out in a consistent manner.

Provision of electronic copies of disclosed documents

32   The parties should co-operate at an early stage about the format in which Electronic Documents are to be provided on inspection. In the case of difficulty or disagreement, the matter should be referred to the court for directions at the earliest practical date, if possible at the first case management conference.

33   Save where otherwise agreed or ordered, electronic copies of disclosed documents should be provided in their Native Format, in a manner which preserves Metadata relating to the date of creation of each document.

34   A party should provide any available searchable OCR versions of Electronic Documents with the original. A party may however choose not to provide OCR versions of documents which have been redacted. If OCR versions are provided, they are provided on an 'as is' basis, with no assurance to the other party that the OCR versions are complete or accurate.

35   (1)   Subject to sub-paragraph (2) below, if a party is providing in electronic form copies of disclosed documents and wishes to redact or otherwise make alterations to a document or documents, then –

(a)   the party redacting or altering the document must inform the other party in accordance with rule 31.19 that redacted or altered versions are being supplied; and

(b)   the party redacting or altering the document must ensure that the original unredacted and unaltered version is preserved, so that it remains available to be inspected if required.

(2)   Sub-paragraph (1) above does not apply where the only alteration made to the document is an alteration to the Metadata as a result of the ordinary process of copying and/or accessing the document. Sub-paragraph (1) does apply to the alteration or suppression of Metadata in other situations.

Specialised technology

36   If Electronic Documents are best accessed using technology which is not readily available to the party entitled to disclosure, and that party reasonably requires additional inspection facilities, the party making disclosure shall co-operate in making available to the other party such reasonable additional inspection facilities as may be appropriate in order to afford inspection in accordance with rule 31.3.

SCHEDULE

Electronic Documents Questionnaire

Part 1 – Your disclosure

Extent of a reasonable search

Date range and custodians

1.   What date range do you consider that your searches for Electronic Documents should cover ('the date range')?
2.   Identify the custodians or creators of your Electronic Documents whose repositories of documents you consider should be searched.

Communications

3.   Which forms of electronic communication were in use during the date range (so far as is relevant to these proceedings)?

A	B	C	D	E
Communication	In use during the date range? (yes/no)	Are you searching for relevant documents in this category? (yes/no)	Where and on what type of software/ equipment/ media is this communication stored?	(a) Are back-ups or archives of this communication available, and (b) if so, are you searching the back-ups or archives?
i) E-mail				
ii) Other (provide details for each type)				

Electronic Documents

4.   Apart from attachments to e-mails, which forms of Electronic Documents were created or stored by you during the date range?

A	B	C	D	E
Document Type	In use during the date range? (yes/no)	Are you searching for relevant documents in this category? (yes/no)	Where and on what type of software/ equipment/ media are these documents?	(a) Are back-ups or archives of these documents available, and (b) if so, are you searching the back-ups or archives?
i) Word (or equivalent - state which)				
ii) Excel (or equivalent - state which)				
iii) Electronic Images				
iv) Other (state which)				

Databases of Electronic Documents

5. In the following table identify database systems, including document management systems, used by you during the date range and which may contain disclosable Electronic Documents.

A	B	C	D	E
Name	Brief description	Nature of data held	Are you disclosing documents held in this database? (yes/no)	Proposals for provision of relevant documents to or access by other parties to this litigation
1.				
2. (etc)				

Method of search

Key words

6. Do you consider that Keyword Searches should be used as part of the process of determining which Electronic Documents you should disclose?

   If yes, provide details of –

   (1) the keywords used or to be used (by reference, if applicable, to individual custodians, creators, repositories, file types and/or date ranges); and

   (2) the extent to which the Keyword Searches have been or will be supplemented by a review of individual documents.

Other types of automated searches

7. Do you consider that automated searches or automated techniques other than Keyword Searches (for example, concept searches or clustering) should be used as part of the process of determining which Electronic Documents you should disclose? If yes, provide details of –

   (1) the process(es) used or to be used (by reference, if applicable, to individual custodians, creators, repositories, file types and/or date ranges);

(2)   the extent to which the processes have been or will be supplemented by a review of individual documents; and

(3)   how the methodology of automated searches will be made available for consideration by other parties.

8.   If the answer to Question 6 or 7 is yes, state whether attachments to (a) e-mails (b) compressed files (c) embedded files and (d) imaged text will respond to your Keyword Searches or other automated search.

9.   Are you using or intending to use computer software for other purposes in relation to disclosure? If so, provide details of the software, processes and methods to be used.

Potential problems with the extent of search and accessibility of Electronic Documents

10.   Do any of the sources and/or documents identified in this Electronic Documents Questionnaire raise questions about the reasonableness of the search which ought to be taken into account? If so, give details.

11.   Are any documents which may be disclosable encrypted, password-protected or for other reasons difficult to access, or do you have any reason to believe that they may be? If so, state which of the categories identified at Questions 3, 4 and 5 above are affected, and your proposals for making them accessible.

12.   Are you aware of any other points in relation to disclosure of your Electronic Documents which require discussion between the parties? If so, give details.

Preservation of Electronic Documents

13.   Do you have a document retention policy?

14.   Have you given an instruction to preserve Electronic Documents, and if so, when?

Inspection

15.   Subject to re-consideration after receiving the responses of other parties to this Electronic Documents Questionnaire, (a) in what format and (b) on what media do you intend to provide to other parties copies of disclosed documents which are or will be available in electronic form?

16.   Subject to re-consideration after receiving the responses of other parties to this Electronic Documents Questionnaire, do you intend to provide other parties with Disclosure Data electronically, and if so, (a) in what format and (b) on what media?

17.   Insofar as you have available or will have available searchable OCR versions of Electronic Documents, do you intend to provide the searchable OCR version to other parties? If not, why not?

Part 2 - The disclosure of other parties

The extent and content of their search

18.   Do you at this stage have any proposals about the date ranges which should be searched by other parties to the proceedings? If so, provide details.

19.   Do you at this stage have any proposals about the custodians or creators whose repositories of documents should be searched for disclosable documents by other parties to the proceedings? If so, provide details.

20.   Do you consider that the other party(ies) should disclose all available Metadata attaching to any documents? If yes, provide details of the documents or categories of documents.

Proposals for the method to be adopted for their searches

21. Do you at this stage have any proposals about the Keyword Searches, or other automated searches, which should be applied by other parties to their document sets? If so, provide details.

Inspection

22. Subject to re-consideration after receiving the responses of other parties to this Electronic Documents Questionnaire, (a) in what format and (b) on what media do you wish to receive copies of disclosed documents which are or will be available in electronic form?

23. Subject to re-consideration after receiving the responses of other parties to this Electronic Documents Questionnaire, do you wish to receive Disclosure Data electronically, and if so, (a) in what format and (b) on what media?

STATEMENT OF TRUTH

*[I believe][The [claimant][defendant] believes] that the facts stated in the answers to this Electronic Documents Questionnaire are true.

*I am duly authorised by the [claimant][defendant] to sign this statement.

Full name ....

Name of legal representative's firm ....

Signed ....

Position or office held (if signing on behalf of firm or company) ....

Date ....

*delete as appropriate

WARNING: Unless the court makes some other order, the answers given in this document may only be used for the purposes of the proceedings in which the document is produced unless it has been read to or by the court or referred to at a hearing which has been held in public or the Court gives permission or the party who has completed this questionnaire agrees.

Guidance Notes:

1. Technical expressions are defined in Practice Direction 31B.
2. The questions in the Electronic Documents Questionnaire are not intended to give rise to any implication about how disclosure should or should not be carried out. They are intended only to provide information to other parties and to the court.
3. Further facts and matters may come to parties' attention over the course of the proceedings which affect the answers to the Electronic Documents Questionnaire. Where detailed information is not yet available at the time the Electronic Documents Questionnaire is first answered, parties should give such information as they can, and supplement or amend their answers when further information is available. Answers should be updated by notifying other parties and the court without undue delay, and in any event before each case management conference at which disclosure is likely to be considered.
4. Some of the questions in the Electronic Documents Questionnaire require only a brief answer which may need to be elaborated after Electronic Documents Questionnaires have been exchanged. The purpose of such questions is to assist the parties in

identifying the points which may require elaboration in order for meaningful discussions to take place between them.

5.   Questions which refer to sources of Electronic Documents that are not considered to be relevant may be answered with a statement to that effect.

6.   Questions about 'your' documents and about software, hardware or systems used by 'you' are directed, in the case of solicitors, to the solicitor's lay client's documents or to documents prepared on the lay client's behalf.

Appendix 17

Notice of appeal

Appellant's notice

(All appeals except small claims track appeals and appeals to the Family Division of the High Court)

For Court use only	
Appeal Court Ref. No.	
Date filed	

Notes for guidance are available which will help you complete this form. Please read them carefully before you complete each section.

SEAL

Section 1	Details of the claim or case you are appealing against

Claim or Case no. [   ]

Fee Account no. (if applicable) [   ]

Help with Fees - Ref no. (if applicable) H W F - [   ] [   ] [   ] - [   ] [   ] [   ]

Name(s) of the ☐ Claimant(s) ☐ Applicant(s) ☐ Petitioner(s)

[   ]

Name(s) of the ☐ Defendant(s) ☐ Respondent(s)

[   ]

Details of the party appealing ('The Appellant')

Name

[   ]

Address (including postcode)

	Tel No.	
	Fax	
	E-mail	

Details of the Respondent to the appeal

Name

[   ]

Address (including postcode)

	Tel No.	
	Fax	
	E-mail	

Details of additional parties (if any) are attached ☐ Yes ☐ No

Section 2   Details of the appeal

From which court is the appeal being brought?

☐   The County Court at

☐   The Family Court at

☐   High Court

    ☐   Queen's Bench Division

    ☐   Chancery Division

    ☐   Family Division

☐   Other (please specify)

What is the name of the Judge whose decision you want to appeal?

What is the status of the Judge whose decision you want to appeal?

☐ District Judge or Deputy   ☐ Circuit Judge or Recorder   ☐ Tribunal Judge

☐ Master or Deputy   ☐ High Court Judge or Deputy   ☐ Justice(s) of the Peace

What is the date of the decision you wish to appeal against?

Is the decision you wish to appeal a previous appeal decision?   ☐ Yes   ☐ No

Section 3 Legal representation

Are you legally represented?   ☐ Yes   ☐ No

If Yes, is your legal representative (please tick as appropriate)

☐ a solicitor

☐ direct access counsel instructed to conduct litigation on your behalf

☐ direct access counsel instructed to represent you at hearings only

Name of your legal representative

The address (including postcode) of your legal representative

	Tel No.	
	Fax	
	E-mail	
	DX	
	Ref.	

Are you, the Appellant, in receipt of a
Civil Legal Aid Certificate?   ☐ Yes   ☐ No

Is the respondent legally represented?   ☐ Yes   ☐ No
                                                                         If 'Yes', please give details of the
                                                                         respondent's legal representative below

Name and address (including postcode) of the respondent's legal representative

	Tel No.	
	Fax	
	E-mail	
	DX	
	Ref.	

Section 4   Permission to appeal

Do you need permission to appeal?   ☐ Yes   ☐ No

Has permission to appeal been granted?

☐ **Yes** (Complete Box A)   ☐ **No** (Complete Box B)

Box A

Date of order granting permission

Name of Judge granting permission

Box B

I

the Appellant('s legal representative) seek permission to appeal.

If permission to appeal has been granted **in part** by the lower court, do you seek permission to appeal in respect of the grounds refused by the lower court?   ☐ Yes   ☐ No

Section 5   Other information required for the appeal

Please set out the order (or part of the order) you wish to appeal against

Have you lodged this notice with the court in time?   ☐ Yes   ☐ No
(There are different types of appeal -
see Guidance Notes N161A)   If **'No'** you must also complete
Part B of Section 9 and Section 10

Section 6   Grounds of appeal

Please state, in numbered paragraphs, **on a separate sheet** attached to this notice and entitled 'Grounds of Appeal' (also in the top right hand corner add your claim or case number and full name), why you are saying that the Judge who made the order you are appealing was wrong.

☐ I confirm that the grounds of appeal are attached to this notice.

Section 7   Arguments in support of grounds for appeal

☐ I confirm that the arguments (known as a 'Skeleton Argument') in support of the 'Grounds of Appeal' are set out **on a separate sheet** and attached to this notice.

OR   (in the case of appeals other than to the Court of Appeal)

☐ I confirm that the arguments (known as a 'Skeleton Argument') in support of the 'Grounds of Appeal' will follow within 14 days of filing this Appellant's Notice. A skeleton argument should only be filed if appropriate, in accordance with CPR Practice Direction 52B, paragraph 8.3.

Section 8   What are you asking the Appeal Court to do?

I am asking the appeal court to:-
(please tick the appropriate box)

☐ set aside the order which I am appealing

☐ vary the order which I am appealing and substitute the following order. Set out in the following space the order you are asking for:-

```


```

☐ order a new trial

Section 9   Other applications

Complete this section **only** if you are making any additional applications.

Part A

☐ I apply for a stay of execution. (You must set out in Section 10 your reasons for seeking a stay of execution and evidence in support of your application.)

Part B

☐ I apply for an extension of time for filing my appeal notice. (You must set out in Section 10 the reasons for the delay and what steps you have taken since the decision you are appealing.)

Part C

☐ I apply for an order that:

```


```

(You must set out in Section 10 your reasons and your evidence in support of your application.)

Section 10   Evidence in support

In support of my application(s) in Section 9, I wish to rely upon the following reasons and evidence:

Statement of Truth – This must be completed in support of the evidence in Section 10

I believe (The appellant believes) that the facts stated in this section are true.

Full name

Name of appellant's legal representative firm

signed

Appellant ('s legal representative)

position or office held

(if signing on behalf of firm or company)

Section 11   Supporting documents

To support your appeal you should file with this notice all relevant documents listed below. To show which documents you are filing, please tick the appropriate boxes.

If you do not have a document that you intend to use to support your appeal complete the box over the page.

In the County Court or High Court:

☐ three copies of the appellant's notice for the appeal court and three copies of the grounds of appeal;

☐ one additional copy of the appellant's notice and grounds of appeal for each of the respondents;

☐ one copy of the sealed (stamped by the court) order being appealed;

☐ a copy of any order giving or refusing permission to appeal; together with a copy of the judge's reasons for allowing or refusing permission to appeal; and

☐ a copy of the Civil Legal Aid Agency Certificate (if legally represented).

In the Court of Appeal:

☐ three copies of the appellant's notice and three copies of the grounds of appeal on a separate sheet attached to each appellant's notice;

☐ one additional copy of the appellant's notice and one copy of the grounds of appeal for each of the respondents;

☐ one copy of the sealed (stamped by the court) order or tribunal determination being appealed;

☐ a copy of any order giving or refusing permission to appeal together with a copy of the judge's reasons for allowing or refusing permission to appeal;

☐ one copy of any witness statement or affidavit in support of any application included in the appellant's notice;

☐ where the decision of the lower court was itself made on appeal, a copy of the first order, the reasons given by the judge who made it and the appellant's notice of appeal against that order;

☐ in a claim for judicial review or a statutory appeal a copy of the original decision which was the subject of the application to the lower court;

☐ one copy of the skeleton arguments in support of the appeal or application for permission to appeal;

☐ a copy of the approved transcript of judgment; and

☐ a copy of the Civil Legal Aid Certificate (if applicable)

Reasons why you have not supplied a document and date when you expect it to be available:-

Title of document and reason not supplied	Date when it will be supplied

Section 12   The notice of appeal must be signed here

Signed [   ] Appellant('s legal representative)

Appendix 18

Example of a statutory demand against a company

Rule 7.3
SD 1

Statutory Demand
under section 123(1)(a) of the Insolvency Act 1986 [*]
under section 222(1)(a) of the Insolvency Act 1986 [*]
*[*Delete whichever is not applicable*]

Warning

- This is an **important** document. This demand must be dealt with **within 21 days** after its service upon the company or a winding-up order could be made in respect of the company.

- Please read the demand and notes carefully.

Notes for Creditor

- The person making this demand must complete the whole of sections 1, 2 (including Part B if applicable) and 3 and the authentication (including the date) at the end.

- The details given in Section 1 must comply with rule 1.6 of the Insolvency (England and Wales) Rules 2016 (IR 2016).

- The Details of Debt (Section 2) must include all the relevant the matters listed in the margin notes at Section 2. These should be set out in the order given unless the person completing the demand considers that a different order would be more convenient for the recipient.

- The creditor must give details of an individual with whom the Company can communicate about the Demand in Section 3.

- The authentication must comply with rule 1.5 of the IR 2016. If signatory of the demand is a solicitor or other agent of the creditor the name of his/her firm should be given.

Section 1 - DEMAND

To

Name: Gates Launderettes Limited   (The Company)
[*If registered, insert its registered name; if unregistered, its name*]

Registered No. 234567
[*If incorporated in England and Wales under the Companies Act 2006 or a previous Companies Act, its registered number*]

Address: 73 Cider Street, Slough SL1 1PP

[*If registered, insert its registered office, if unregistered, the postal address of any principal place of business*]

[*Or, if the Debtor Company was incorporated outside the UK insert the following details*]*

Country or territory in which incorporated:

Registered No. (if any):

No. (if any) **under which registered under Part 34 of Companies Act 2006:**
*[*delete if not applicable*]

This demand is made under section 123(1)(a) of the Insolvency Act 1986 and is served on you by the creditor [*insert details of Creditor below*]

Name: Brewsters Limited
[*If a registered company, insert its registered name; if unregistered, its name; if an individual, his or her full name*]

Registered No. 765432
[*If a company incorporated in England and Wales under the Companies Act 2006 or a previous Companies Act, insert its registered number*]

Address: Unit 12 Brownside Industrial Estate, Reading RG2 6DS

[*If a registered company, insert its registered office; if unregistered, the postal address of any principal place of business; if an individual, his or her personal or professional address (as appropriate)*]

[*Or, if the Creditor is a company incorporated outside the UK insert the following details*]*
Country or territory in which incorporated:
Registered No. (if any):
No. (if any) **under which registered under Part 34 of Companies Act 2006:**
*[*delete if not applicable*]

The creditor claims that the Company owes the sum of £65,350.80, full details of which are set out in section 2 of this Demand.

Section 2

A. Details of Debt

These details must include the following information:

(a) the amount of the debt as at the date of this demand;

(b) the consideration for the debt (or if is there is no consideration the way in which it arose); the date on which the debt arose should also be included;

(c) if the demand is founded on a judgment or order of a court, details of the judgment or order;

(d) if the creditor is entitled to the debt by way of assignment, a statement to that effect and that the details of the relevant assignment(s) are given in Part B below (which must then also be filled in);

(e) if the sums demanded include (i) any charge by way of interest not previously notified to the company as included in its liability and/or (ii) any other charge accruing due from time to time, each such charge must be separately identified (if claimed) with the amount or rate of the charge and the grounds upon which payment is claimed: the amount claimed for such charges must be limited to that which has accrued due at the date of the demand.

> On 1 March 2020 the creditor agreed to sell to the debtor company machinery to the value of £63,450. The machinery was delivered to the debtor company on 14 March 2020 and payment in full was due on 21 March 2020. The debtor company has failed to make any payment to the creditor. The creditor also claims interest pursuant to the Late Payment of Commercial Debts (Interest) Act 1998 at the rate of 8.1% per annum (8% over the relevant reference rate) for the period 22 March 2020 to 3 August 2020 being 135 days and amounting to £1,900.80. The total debt due at the date of this demand is therefore £65,350.80.

Part B [For completion if the creditor is entitled to the debt by way of assignment]

	Name	Date(s) of Assignment
Original creditor		
Assignees		

SD1 - Statutory Demand under section 123(1)(a) or 222(1)(a) of the Insolvency Act 1986 (04.17)

Section 3

The Company must pay the above debt within 21 days of service of this demand on the Company after which the creditor may present a winding-up petition unless the Company offers security for the debt and the creditor agrees to accept security or the Company compounds the debt with the creditor's agreement.

The individual or individuals to whom any communication regarding this demand may be addressed is/are:

Name COLLAWS

Address 14 Ship
Street, Weyford
WE18 HQ

Electronic address

Telephone Number
01904 876550

Reference
BM/ABC/BREWSTER

How to comply with a statutory demand

If the Company wishes to avoid a winding-up petition being presented it must pay the debt shown on page 1, details of which are set out on page 2 of this notice, within the period of **21 days after** its service upon the Company. Alternatively, the Company can attempt to come to a settlement with the creditor. To do this an officer or representative of the Company should:

- inform the individual (or one of the individuals) named in Part A above immediately that it is willing and able to offer security for the debt to the creditor's satisfaction; or

- inform the individual (or one of the individuals) named in Part A immediately that it is willing and able to compound for the debt to the creditor's satisfaction.

If the Company disputes the demand in whole or in part it should contact the individual (or one of the individuals) named in Part A immediately.

REMEMBER!	**The Company has only 21 days after the date of service on it of this document before the creditor may present a winding-up petition.**
NOTE:	**The Company has the right to make an application to the court(*) for an injunction restraining the creditor from presenting a winding-up petition or from advertising it.**
Insert the name of the court (hearing centre) to which, according to present information, the company must make the application	(*) The court to which an application should be made is: Reading

Note: The demand must be dated, and authenticated either by the creditor, or a person authorised to make the demand on the creditor's behalf. A demand which is authenticated by a person other than the creditor must state that the person is authorised to make this demand on the creditor's behalf and state the person's relationship to the creditor.

> **Authentication**
>
> Signature of individual: *Collaws*
>
> Name: COLLAWS
>
> (Block Letters)
>
> Date: 3 August 2020
>
> Address: 14 Ship Street, Weyford WE1 8HQ
>
> Telephone number: 01904 876550   Ref: BM/ABC/BREWSTER
>
> [I, the above-signed, not being the creditor herein, state as follows:
>
> I am authorised to make this demand on the creditor's behalf.
>
> My position in/relationship to the creditor is Solicitor.
>
> [*if the creditor is a body corporate of which the signatory is the sole member*] I am the sole member of the creditor]]

SD1 - Statutory Demand under section 123(1)(a) or 222(1)(a) of the Insolvency Act 1986 (04.17)

Appendix 19

The Business and Property Courts – Advisory Note

This note is likely to be updated on a regular basis

Introduction

1. The Business and Property Courts ("B&PCs") were launched in July 2017 and became operational on 2nd October 2017. They have been created as a single umbrella for specialist civil jurisdictions across England and Wales. In London, these specialist civil jurisdictions operate together in the Rolls Building on Fetter Lane, forming the largest specialist centre for financial, business and property litigation in the world.

2. Business and Property Courts have also been established in the five main centres outside London where specialist business similar to that in the Rolls Building is undertaken, namely, Birmingham, Bristol, Cardiff, Leeds and Manchester. They will also be established in Newcastle and Liverpool shortly. The main centre for the Business and Property Courts in Wales is in Cardiff, but judges of the courts will sit in other venues in Wales when appropriate and practicable. Specialist County Court cases that fall within the ambit of the B&PCs will internally be marked "Business and Property Courts Work" (encompassing what was previously "Chancery Business" for specialist work of a Chancery nature and TCC work in the County Court (CPR PD 60 para 3.2; 3.4 and CPR 60.4(c))) (please see paragraph 4.3 of the draft practice direction which is awaiting publication but is attached in its current draft form). The Mercantile Court has been renamed the Circuit Commercial Court, and Mercantile Judges are now Circuit Commercial Judges.

3. The Business and Property Courts are divided into separate specialist courts or lists, some of which are further subdivided into sub-lists. These courts and lists are dealt with in more detail below.

4. Although the various specialist civil work has been brought together under one umbrella, the courts themselves will continue to operate in the same way as at present, applying the same practices and procedures under the Civil Procedure Rules and Insolvency Rules as before and retaining their own procedural Guides. The way in which cases are dealt with in each type of court will not change. Claims which have been proceeding in the Chancery Division before 2nd October remain under the control of the same Master (or Judge) as before until further order. The Practice Direction setting up the Business and Property Courts contains new provisions, particularly as regards issue and transfer of proceedings (see paragraphs 13 to 19).

5. The new arrangements will allow, over time, for greater flexibility in cross-deployment of judges with suitable expertise and experience to sit on appropriate business and property cases. It will also be simpler to issue claims in any of the B&PCs and to transfer claims between the Rolls Building and the other specialist centres.

Issuing Proceedings in the Business and Property Courts

6. Presently electronic filing and issue is only available in London. For the time being, claim forms should continue to be issued in the same way as before in the other Business and Property Courts centres.

7. The new types of case numbers (available on CE-File) will not, however, be provided in the other centres until electronic filing begins in those centres in 2018.

8. Court users will at present, when issuing proceedings electronically on CE-File, see the heading "Business and Property Courts of England and Wales" on the system. They will then be asked to say which court or list, and if applicable, which sub-list, they wish their case to be assigned to. This will depend on the principal subject matter of the dispute. For example, if the dispute involves land, even if the land is for commercial use, it should be assigned to the Property, Trusts and Probate List. Similarly, a dispute about pensions should be assigned to the Business List, sub-list Pensions, even if professional negligence is also involved. Where several issues arise, involving different courts, lists or sub-lists, the user must consider whether there are issues requiring the expertise of a specialist judge and if so must select the court, list or sub-list in which the relevant specialist judges sit.

9. Cases issued in centres outside London, after 2nd October 2017 and before electronic filing becomes available outside London, should identify the list or court in which the claimant wishes the case to proceed, as above. Users issuing in the centres outside London will have to indicate on the claim form or to listing staff in those centres the court, list or sub-list to which their claim should be allocated.

10. Users must choose one of the following:
    (1) Admiralty Court (QBD)
    (2) Business List (ChD) (with further choice of Financial Services and Regulatory or Pensions sub-lists available)
    (3) Commercial Court (QBD) (with the option to issue in the London Circuit Commercial Court instead in London, or a single option of issuing in the Circuit Commercial Court in other centres)
    (4) Competition List (ChD)
    (5) Financial List (ChD/QBD)
    (6) Insolvency and Companies List (ChD) (with further option of Insolvency or Companies sub-lists)
    (7) Intellectual Property List (ChD) (with further choice of Patents Court or IPEC)
    (8) Property, Trusts and Probate List (ChD)
    (9) Revenue List (ChD)
    (10) Technology and Construction Court (QBD)

11. Once CE-File has been extended to the other centres, the user will also be asked to identify on CE-File the hearing centre in which they wish to issue the proceedings. In the meantime, users issuing in the centres outside London will have to issue in the centre on the circuit with which the claim has significant links. Links, as specified in the Practice Direction, are established where:
    a. one or more of the parties has an address or registered office in the circuit (particularly if the party is non-represented);
    b. at least one of the witnesses expected to give oral evidence is located within the circuit;
    c. the dispute occurred in a location within the circuit;
    d. the dispute concerns land, goods or other assets located in the circuit; or
    e. the parties' legal representatives are based in the circuit.

12. Claims with significant links to a particular circuit must be issued in the District Registry located in the circuit. Although a claimant must base a decision on any information available about links to a particular circuit, there is no obligation to make extra inquiries to determine whether there may be other links outside the claimant's current knowledge.

13. Care should be taken to ensure that any proceedings are brought in the correct court and hearing centre. If users are uncertain as to the availability of a specialist judge in an

area they should contact the relevant Listing Office. It is important to note however that if a claim is issued in the wrong court, list or sub-list, or in the wrong hearing centre, this will not invalidate the issue of the claim. If there is such an error the court may remedy it by making an order under CPR rule 3.10(b).

The Constituent Courts and Lists

14.   In order to help users identify the correct court, list or sub-list in which to issue, a brief description of each one of the Business and Property Courts follows. The various examples of cases dealt with in each category are not exhaustive:

(1) Admiralty Court (QBD)

The Admiralty Court deals with shipping and maritime disputes. This list deals with cases such as:

*   collisions between ships
*   disputes over the transport of cargo
*   salvage of a ship, cargo or crew
*   disputes over goods supplied to a ship
*   disputes over mortgages and other security over ships
*   claims by passengers for injuries suffered
*   claims by ship crew for unpaid wages
*   claims by ship-owners to limit liability for loss or damage

The Admiralty Court deals with claims brought against the owner of a ship ('in personam' claims) and claims brought against the ship itself ('in rem' claims). The court can seize ('arrest') ships and cargos to prevent them being moved and can also sell them within England and Wales.

(2) Business List (ChD)

The scope of the Chancery Business List is broad. It includes a wide range business disputes, often with an international dimension. Frequently these concern a business structure (company, LLP, LP, partnership etc), claims against directors for breach of fiduciary duty, or disputes about contractual arrangements between investors such as share purchase agreements. They also include claims in tort, such as conspiracy or fraud, claims for professional negligence (e.g. against solicitors, accountants, surveyors, valuers), claims for breach of contract, specific performance, rectification and injunctive relief as well as other equitable remedies.

The Business List also includes pensions claims, and a sub-list exists to reflect that. The sub-list covers all claims where pensions are the subject matter of the dispute. Many pension schemes, particularly occupational pension schemes, are established under a trust. Not all pensions cases however are brought under the court's trusts jurisdiction. For example, trustees and/or employers may bring claims for professional negligence against former advisers, or action taken under statutory powers, for example by the Pensions Regulator, or statutory appeals, for example from the Pensions Ombudsman.

The Business List also includes a Financial Services and Regulatory sub-list, to cover financial claims where the Financial Conduct Authority is a party, claims under the Financial Services and Markets Act 2000, and claims involving regulators (other than the Pensions Regulator).

(3) Commercial Court (QBD)

(a) Commercial Court

The Commercial Court deals with complex cases arising out of business disputes, both national and international, encompassing all aspects of commercial disputes, in the fields of banking and finance, shipping, insurance and reinsurance and commodities. The Court also acts as a supervisory court for arbitration, dealing with the granting of freezing and other relief in aid of arbitration, challenges to arbitration awards and enforcement of awards.

This list deals with cases such as:

* disputes over contracts and business documents
* insurance and reinsurance
* sale of commodities
* import, export and transport ('carriage') of goods
* issues relating to international and commercial arbitration
* banking and financial services
* agency and management agreements
* sale and purchase of businesses and commercial share sale agreements
* oil, gas and energy disputes
* professional negligence in commercial circumstances

(b) Circuit Commercial Court (QBD) (formerly the Mercantile Court)

Formerly known as the Mercantile Court, it deals with business disputes of all kinds apart from those which, because of their size, value or complexity, will be heard by the Commercial Court. As well as large cases, it also decides smaller business disputes. There are no restrictions on the size of claims which can be brought to the Circuit Commercial Court. The Court also acts as a supervisory court for arbitration, dealing most often with the challenges to arbitration awards and enforcement of awards. Cases will ordinarily be heard if they are of a genuine business nature and appropriate for the court. This list deals with cases such as:

* disputes over contracts and business documents
* insurance and reinsurance
* sale of goods
* import, export and transport ('carriage') of goods
* professional negligence in commercial circumstances (eg solicitors and accountants)
* issues relating to arbitration awards
* restraint of trade
* banking and financial services
* agency and management agreements
* share sale agreements
* confidential information
* injunctions

(4) Competition List (ChD)

This list deals with claims brought under Article 101 and Article 102 of the Treaty on the Functioning of the European Union ("TFEU"), and also claims brought under the corresponding provisions of UK domestic law contained in Chapters I and II of Part 1 of the Competition Act 1998.

Article 101 (EU law claims) and Chapter I of Part 1 of the Competition Act 1998 (UK domestic law claims) prohibit agreements, concerted practices, or decisions by associations of undertakings whose object or effect is to prevent, restrict or distort competition.

Article 102 (EU law claims) and Chapter II of Part 1 of the Competition Act 1998 (UK domestic law claims) are aimed at preventing abusive behaviour by undertakings who hold a dominant position in a relevant geographic and product market (eg by imposing unfair prices or unfair trading arrangements).

A claim may be for an injunction to restrain an alleged breach or threatened breach of the competition rules, and/or for damages resulting from such a breach. Proceedings frequently involve consideration of economic or technical issues on which expert evidence is called. The procedure is governed by the Practice Direction on Competition Law (See further Ch.29 (7) of the Chancery Guide).

(Note: claims such as those identified above may also be brought in the Competition Appeal Tribunal, whose jurisdiction was expanded by the Consumer Rights Act 2015 to bring it largely into line with that of the High Court. However, by virtue of the 2015 Act the Competition Appeal Tribunal has the exclusive jurisdiction over certain proceedings for collective redress for infringement of the competition rules.)

Although a claim under paragraph 1 of the Practice Direction on Competition Law may be issued in any of the district registries with which it has significant links (see paragraph 7 above), its case management and/or trial will be dependant on the availability of a suitable judge.

(5) Financial List (ChD/Commercial Court - QBD)

The Financial List is a specialist cross-jurisdictional list set up to address the particular business needs of parties litigating on financial matters. Disputes that are eligible for inclusion are those that principally relate to financial disputes of over £50m or equivalent, and which require particular market expertise or raise issues of general market importance. The list can deal with cases:

- generally worth more than £50 million
- which need expert judicial knowledge of financial markets
- which raise important issues for the sector

(6) Insolvency and Companies List (ChD)

This list deals with both personal and corporate insolvency on the one hand, and companies work on the other hand.

Specifically, the work includes:

Insolvency

- applications concerning company voluntary arrangements;
- administration applications and applications concerning administrations;
- petitions to wind up companies and partnerships;
- applications concerning the winding up of companies and partnerships (whether in members or creditors voluntary liquidation or following winding up by the court);
- applications concerning individual voluntary arrangements;
- bankruptcy petitions and applications concerning bankruptcy;
- applications relating to transaction avoidance in both personal and corporate insolvency;
- applications under the Cross-Border Insolvency Regulations

- petitions and applications under the Insolvency Act 2016 or the Administration of Insolvent Estates of Deceased Persons Order 1986.

Directors' disqualification

- claims for the disqualification of unfit directors;
- applications for permission to act as a director after disqualification.

Company law

- unfair prejudice petitions/shareholder disputes;
- applications for the confirmation of a reduction of capital;
- applications concerning schemes of arrangement
- other claims and applications under the Companies Act 2006, FISMA 2000, or the Companies (Cross-Border Mergers) Regulations 2007

This list of examples is not exhaustive.

(7) Intellectual Property List (ChD)

The following matters must be dealt with in either the Patents Court or the IPEC (multi-track):

(1) claims under the Patents Act 1977

(2) claims under the Registered Designs Act 1949

(3) claims under the Defence Contracts Act 1958

(4) claims relating to Community registered designs, semiconductor topography rights or plant varieties

(collectively "registered rights claims")

Claims under the Trade Marks Act 1994 and the other intellectual property claims set out at paragraph 16.1 of Practice Direction 63 (collectively "general intellectual property claims") must be dealt with in either the Intellectual Property List generally or the IPEC.

There is no lower limit on the value of claims that may be commenced in the Intellectual Property List. Where, however, the damages or sums payable on an account of profits are likely to be £500,000 or less, consideration should be given to issuing the claim in the IPEC.

Intellectual property claims outside London

Intellectual property claims may be issued in B&PCs District Registries. However the case management and/or trial of a claim in the Patents Court or the IPEC in the B&PCs District Registry in question will be dependent on an appropriate judge being made available in the district registry in question.

(8) Property, Trusts and Probate List (ChD)

This list covers a large amount of Chancery work which is separate from the Business List. The examples given below are not intended to be a definitive list. The Property list deals mainly with land, and the Trusts list with matters that fall within Part 64 of the CPR, i.e. the administration of estates and the execution of trusts, and with charities. The Probate list covers all matters which fall within Part 57 of the CPR.

Property

Landlord & Tenant residential
Landlord & Tenant commercial
Trespass/squatters
Mortgages

Land Registry
Land – title, easements, restrictive covenants etc
Orders for sale to enforce charging orders
Trusts of Land and Appointment of Trustees Act 1996 (TOLATA)

Trusts

Variation of trusts
Removal of trustees
Claims against trustees for breach of trust
Issues of construction/rectification
Trustees/Personal Representatives seeking directions including Beddoe applications
Disputes about trust property
Applications for prospective costs order
Charities
Applications for administration order

Probate

Contentious Probate claims
Rectification of wills
Substitution or removal of Personal Representatives
Inheritance Act
Presumption of Death Act

(9) Revenue List (ChD)

Claims involving major points of principle relating to taxation where HMRC is a party. (This List does not include claims for the recovery of taxes or duties or where a taxpayer disputes liability to pay tax. Such claims fall within the Business list).

(10) Technology & Construction Court (QBD)

This list can be divided into three areas of work as follows:

(a)   **Adjudication disputes.**

These are claims to enforce or challenges to adjudicators' decisions arising out of the Housing Grants' Construction and Regeneration Act 1996 (as amended).

(b)   **Public procurement.**

This concerns all kinds of public procurement (not limited to construction or engineering projects) and involves, amongst other things, applications to lift the automatic suspension, and challenges to tender evaluations and decisions to award contracts.

(c)   **The General TCC list.**
       This includes:
       • Building and engineering disputes.
       • Claims by and against architects, engineers, surveyors, accountants and other specialised advisors relating to the services they provide.
       • Claims involving issues that are technically complex.
       • Claims relating to the design, supply and installation of computers, software and related network systems.
       • Claims relating to the supply and provision of materials, goods, plant and other services.
       • Claims by and against local authorities relating to their statutory duties concerning the development of land or the construction of buildings.
       • Dilapidation claims as between landlord and tenant.

- Environmental claims, including pollution and reclamation.
- Nuisance claims relating to land use.
- Claims arising out of fires, explosions and other catastrophic events.
- Insurance disputes relating to construction, engineering and technology.
- Contractual disputes involving oil and gas installations, onshore and offshore, and ship building.
- Any arbitration claim under the Arbitration Act 1996, including challenges to decisions of arbitrators in construction and engineering disputes and/or application for permission to appeal and appeals in such cases.

Titles of Claims

15. All claims issued in the Business and Property Courts must be titled as in the following examples:

    IN THE HIGH COURT OF JUSTICE

    BUSINESS AND PROPERTY COURTS OF ENGLAND AND WALES PROPERTY TRUSTS AND PROBATE LIST (ChD)

    or

    IN THE HIGH COURT OF JUSTICE

    BUSINESS AND PROPERTY COURTS IN MANCHESTER BUSINESS LIST (ChD)

    or

    IN THE HIGH COURT OF JUSTICE

    BUSINESS AND PROPERTY COURTS IN WALES TECHNOLOGY AND CONSTRUCTION COURT (QBD)

16. For claims which belong in one of the sub-lists, it is not necessary to include the overarching list/court in the title (although parties can do so if they would prefer to do so). The sub-list title suffices, as follows:

    IN THE HIGH COURT OF JUSTICE

    BUSINESS AND PROPERTY COURTS OF ENGLAND AND WALES LONDON CIRCUIT COMMERCIAL COURT (QBD)

    or

    IN THE HIGH COURT OF JUSTICE

    BUSINESS AND PROPERTY COURTS IN BIRMINGHAM PATENTS COURT (ChD)

    or

    IN THE HIGH COURT OF JUSTICE

    BUSINESS AND PROPERTY COURTS OF ENGLAND AND WALES COMPANIES COURT (ChD)

17. When lodging an appeal to the Technology and Construction Court or the Patents Court, the case should be marked accordingly. For all other appeals to the Business and Property Courts, the title should be as follows:

    IN THE HIGH COURT OF JUSTICE

    BUSINESS AND PROPERTY COURTS OF ENGLAND AND WALES APPEALS (ChD)

    or

    IN THE HIGH COURT OF JUSTICE

    BUSINESS AND PROPERTY COURTS IN BRISTOL APPEALS (ChD)

18. When issuing proceedings, the general rule, which has not changed, is that below the title of the court in which the claim is issued, the title of the claim should contain only the names of the parties to the proceedings. There are however various exceptions. Examples include:

    (i) Proceedings relating to arbitrations

(ii)   Proceedings relating to the administration of an estate should be entitled "In the estate of AB deceased"

(iii)   Contentious probate proceedings should be entitled "In the estate of AB deceased (probate)"

(iv)   Proceedings under the Inheritance (Provision for Family and Dependants) Act 1975 should be entitled "In the Matter of the Inheritance (Provision for Family and Dependants) Act 1975"

(v)   Proceedings relating to pension schemes should be entitled "In the Matter of the [ ] Pension Scheme"

(vi)   Proceedings in the Companies Court should be entitled "in the matter of [the relevant company or other person] and of [the relevant legislation]

(vii)   A claim form to which Section I of Part 63 applies (patents and registered designs) must be marked "Patents Court" below the title of the court in which it is issued (PD 63 paragraph 3.1(a))

(viii) a claim form to which Section II of Part 63 applies (e.g. copyright, registered trade marks, Community trade marks and other intellectual property rights) must, except for claims started in the Intellectual Property Enterprise Court (IPEC), be marked Intellectual Property below the title of the court in which it is issued (PD 63 paragraph 17). Claims relating to trade marks and Community trade marks must state the registration number of the trade mark

(ix)   proceedings under the Presumption of Death Act 2013 should be entitled "In the matter of an application for a declaration of the presumed death of [*name*].

19.   The new headings indicated above should be used throughout the Business & Property Courts for new cases issued after 2nd October 2017. The headings of orders made subsequently to 2nd October 2017 may (but are not required to) refer to the Business and Property Courts and the list or court in which the case would be were it to have been issued on or after 2nd October 2017, or they may continue to refer to the jurisdiction in which they were originally issued. A date will shortly be identified after which the headings of orders will be required to be in the new Business and Property Courts form.

20.   The daily cause list published in the Business and Property Courts will list all the courts and lists in alphabetical order, indicating for each court/list which judge is sitting (in order of seniority), at what time, and in which court room. Those Business and Property Courts centres that operate fewer courts and lists than the Business and Property Courts of England & Wales may list all Business and Property Courts cases in a single daily list, or divide the cases by court/list, as preferred.

21.   Existing claims, issued before 2nd October 2017, will retain their claim numbers. These will not change at any stage.

22.   All claims issued in London on or after 2nd October 2017 are given a claim number with a prefix that reflects the Court, List or sub-list in which they are issued, in accordance with the table below, which can be found on CE-File.

List	Sub-List	Pre-Fix
Admiralty Court	Admiralty Court	AD
Appeals (ChD)*	Appeals (ChD)	CH
Business List	Business	BL
	Financial Services and Regulatory	FS
	Pensions	PE

List	Sub-List	Pre-Fix
Commercial Court	Commercial Court	CL
	London Circuit Commercial Court	LM
	Circuit Commercial Court (other than London)*	CC
Competition List	Competition List	CP
Financial List	Financial List	FL
Insolvency & Companies List	Insolvency List	BR
	Companies Court	CR
Intellectual Property List	Intellectual Property	IL
	Intellectual Property and Enterprise Court (IPEC)	IP
	Patents Court	HP
Property Trusts and Probate List	Property Trusts and Probate	PT
Revenue List	Revenue List	RL
Technology and Construction Court	Technology and Construction Court	HT

*NB: "Appeals (ChD)" is not a list in itself (and indeed does not exist in any centre other than London), but rather an option that can be selected on CE-File to lodge an appeal from Chancery-type cases decided in the County Court. TCC County Court cases will continue at present to be appealed through QBD appeals, although this may change when the centres outside London option an electronic filing system.

*NB: outside London the "Commercial Court" list option will be replaced by the Circuit Commercial Court and no sub list will exist. The Circuit Commercial Court replaces the Mercantile Court, and in London it will be called the London Circuit Commercial Court. On the CE-File system the London Circuit Commercial Court appears as a sub-list of the Commercial Court (although strictly speaking it is not). The prefix for the Circuit Commercial Court other than the London Circuit Commercial Court will in due course be CC.

23.   At present, case numbers in the centres outside London are not changing, and will only change once CE-File is introduced in those centres.

Claim Form marking

24.   All claim forms and all subsequent court documents relating to business or property work issued in the High Court must be marked "Business and Property Courts"; and all such claims issued in the County Court must marked "Business and Property Courts Work" by court staff, for proper triage.

25.   In addition:

•   Claims in the Shorter Trials Scheme must be marked in the top right hand corner "Shorter Trials Scheme".

•   Where the claim is a probate claim, the claim form and all subsequent court documents must be marked at the top "In the estate of [name] deceased (Probate)".

•   A claim form to which Section I of Part 63 applies (patents and registered designs) must be marked "Patents Court" below the title of the court in which it is issued.

Transfer of Proceedings

26. Cases that have specific links with a locality must be capable of being tried in that locality by a specialist judge. Therefore, although the transfer criteria in CPR rule 30.2 (transfer between the County Court and the High Court) and 30.5 (transfer between High Court Divisions and to or from a specialist list) continue to apply, new transfer rules set out in the Practice Direction will also apply alongside the existing criteria for a transfer order in CPR rule 30.3.

27. When considering whether to make an order for transfer between the Royal Courts of Justice and the District Registries when the proceedings are in the Business and Property Courts, the court must, in addition to the criteria in CPR rule 30.3, also have regard to:

    (a) significant links between the claim and the circuit in question, considering the factors listed in paragraph 11 above;

    (b) whether court resources, deployment constraints, or fairness require that the hearings (including the trial) be held in some other court than the court it was issued into;

    (c) the wishes of the parties, which bear special weight in the decision but may not be determinative;

    (d) the international nature of the case, with the understanding that international cases may be more suitable for trial in centres with international transport links;

    (e) the availability of a judge specialising in the type of claim in question to sit in the court to which the claim is being transferred.

28. An application for a transfer from the Rolls Building to or from a B&PCs District Registry or from a B&PCs District Registry to another such District Registry or to the Rolls Building must be made to the court from which transfer is sought and must additionally be discussed with and consented to by the receiving court. It will be sensible practice for the parties to discuss transfer with the appropriate judge at the receiving court before they apply for an order for transfer. If the parties are uncertain about the availability of a specialist judge, they should discuss this with the Listing Manager at the receiving court.

29. In addition to the provisions set out in CPR 30.3, the Business and Property Courts considering whether to make an order for transfer from the Business and Property Courts to a county court hearing centre must have regard to:

    (a) to the nature of the claim, in accordance with guidance as to what business falls within the specialist work of the B&PCs, provided at paragraphs 4.2 to 4.5 of the Practice Direction; and,

    (b) to the availability of a judge specialising in the corresponding type of claim to sit in an appropriate court in the circuit.

30. The following guidelines, which relate to transfers to a District Registry outside London, the County Court, or another Division of the High Court, are still relevant and should also be followed.

    • Only cases which may properly be regarded as being suitable for management and trial in London will be retained there. All other claims will be transferred out. Active consideration will be given at all stages of the management of a claim to the appropriate venue for the claim to be managed and tried. If a case is suitable for transfer, it is generally preferable for it to be transferred before detailed case management has taken place, leaving the receiving court to case manage the claim in accordance with its usual approach.

    • Consideration will be given, where relevant, to:

- PD 29 paragraphs 2.1 to 2.6 which provide guidance for case management within the High Court in London;
- Part 49 and PD 49A and PD 49B – Specialist Proceedings;
- Part 57 – Probate and Inheritance;
- Part 63 – Intellectual Property.

- Under PD 29 paragraph 2.2 a claim with a value of less than £100,000 will generally be transferred to the County Court unless it is required by an enactment to be tried in the High Court, it falls within a specialist list, or it falls within one of the categories specified in the list at PD 29 paragraph 2.6.

- The figure of £100,000 in PD 29 paragraph 2.2 accords with the current minimum value of money claims which may be issued in the High Court. It does not follow that money claims of over £100,000 (or over £200,000 (the value figure beyond which court fees do not increase)) will be retained. The value of a claim is not a consideration which has greater weight than the other criteria set out in CPR rule 30.3(2) but it is likely to be a factor with considerable influence in making a decision about transfer to the County Court or a specialist list. Similarly, for probate and equity claims, the figures of £30,000 and £350,000 respectively are not determinative.

- If the value of the claim is ascertainable, the court will consider the possibility of transferring Part 7 claims with a value of less than £500,000. Factors which may point to retention of such claims in the High Court include complex facts and/or complex or non-routine legal issues or complex relief; parties based outside the jurisdiction; public interest or importance; large numbers of parties; any related claim; and the saving of costs and efficiency in the use of judicial resources.

- The availability of a judge with the specialist skills to deal with the claim is always an important consideration when considering whether or not to transfer it. There are for example two circuit judges at Central London County Court who are specialised in Chancery work, and the waiting times at Central London are likely to be shorter than in the High Court for a trial before a judge. The delay in having a case heard should also be a consideration when deciding whether to transfer a case to the County Court or not and regard will be had to listing information provided by the Central London CC Business and Property Court team. The order for transfer of a claim to Central London County Court, may include a direction that the case is considered to be suitable for trial only by a specialist circuit judge. Such a direction is not binding on the County Court but should be taken into account.

- PD 29 paragraphs 2.6(1), (3) and (7) indicates that professional negligence claims, fraud and undue influence claims and contentious probate claims are suitable for trial in the High Court, but it does not follow that claims within these categories should necessarily remain in the High Court. Less complex and/or lower value claims of these types are suitable for trial in Central London County Court, as Business and Property Court Work. Serious cases of fraud, however, should generally remain in the High Court. Certain professional negligence claims may be better suited to the Queen's Bench Division.

- Part 7 and Part 8 claims may sometimes be dealt with more efficiently by a Master rather than transferring the claim, especially since the amendments to PD 2B which came into effect on 6 April 2015.

- Many claims under the Inheritance Act will be suitable for trial in the County Court and should generally be transferred to Central London County Court, Business and Property Court List unless the Master is willing to try the claim and it is efficient to do so. Inheritance Act claims by a spouse will usually be suitable for transfer to the Family Division. Where there is a related Probate claim, or other Part 7 claim, the overall scope of the issues before the Court should be considered and generally all related claims should either be retained in the High Court or transferred out. The

County Court limit for probate claims is £30,000, but claims well above that figure should be transferred to the County Court nonetheless.

- Most claims relating to joint ownership under the Trusts of Land and Appointment of Trustees Act 1996 will be suitable for transfer to the County Court.

31. An application to transfer a case into the shorter trials scheme may be made to a Judge or, in the relevant list, to a Master.

Sir Geoffrey Vos
Chancellor of the High Court
13th October 2017

Appendix 20

Practice Direction 57AA – Business and Property Courts

Contents of this Practice Direction

Title	Number
Scope	Para. 1
Starting proceedings	Para. 2
Transfers	Para. 3
Specialist work in the district registries and the County Court	Para. 4
Appeals	Para. 5

Scope

1.1 The Chancery Division of the High Court, the Commercial Court, the Technology and Construction Court, the Circuit Commercial Court, and the Admiralty Court located in the Royal Courts of Justice, Rolls Building together with the Chancery Division of the High Court, the Technology and Construction Court and the Circuit Commercial Courts in the District Registries of the High Court in Birmingham, Bristol, Leeds, Manchester and Cardiff together constitute the Business and Property Courts.

1.2 The Business and Property Courts located at the Royal Courts of Justice, Rolls Building, are collectively described as the Business and Property Courts of England and Wales. Those Business and Property Courts in the District Registries of the High Court in Birmingham, Bristol, Leeds, Manchester, and Cardiff, are, respectively, described as the Business and Property Courts in Birmingham, the Business and Property Courts in Bristol, the Business and Property Courts in Leeds, the Business and Property Courts in Manchester, and the Business and Property Courts in Wales. In this Practice Direction the Business and Property Courts in Birmingham, Bristol, Leeds, Manchester and Cardiff are referred to together as the BPCs District Registries.

1.3 The work of the Business and Property Courts is divided and listed into the following courts or lists: the Admiralty Court, the Business List, the Commercial Court, the Circuit Commercial Courts, the Competition List, the Financial List, the Insolvency and Companies List, the Intellectual Property List, the Property, Trusts and Probate List, the Revenue List, and the Technology and Construction Court.

1.4 The courts or lists of the Business and Property Courts include sub-lists, as follows:

(1) The Pensions sub-list and Financial Services and Regulatory sub-list are sub-lists of the Business List;

(2) The Patents Court and the Intellectual Property Enterprise Court are sub-lists of the Intellectual Property List.

1.5 (1) The Business and Property Courts operate within and are subject to all statutory provisions and rules together with all procedural rules and practice directions applicable to the proceedings concerned.

(2) In particular, the following provisions of the CPR apply—

Part 49 (Companies Court)

Part 57 (Probate, Inheritance and Presumption of Death)

Part 58 (Commercial Court)

Part 59 (Circuit Commercial Courts)

Part 60 (Technology and Construction Court Claims)

Part 61 (Admiralty Claims)

Part 62 (Arbitration Claims)

Part 63 (Intellectual Property Claims)

Part 63A (Financial List)

Part 64 (Estates, Trusts and Charities)

Practice Direction – Insolvency Proceedings

Practice Direction: Directors Disqualification Proceedings

Practice Direction PD51O (Electronic Working)

EU Competition Law Practice Direction

1.6 This Practice Direction applies to cases in the Business and Property Courts or cases which are to be issued in those courts. In the event of inconsistency between this Practice Direction and any other Practice Direction the provisions of this Practice Direction shall prevail.

1.7 Parties will also need to give careful consideration to the Chancery Guide, the Admiralty and Commercial Courts Guide, the Technology and Construction Court Guide, the Financial List Guide, the Circuit Commercial Court Guide, the Patents Court Guide, and the Intellectual Property Enterprise Court Guide (where applicable).

Starting proceedings

2.1 Starting proceedings in the Business and Property Courts is subject to CPR Parts 7 and 8.

2.2 (1) A claimant wishing to issue a claim in the Business and Property Courts chooses which court, list or sub-list from within the Business and Property Courts in which to issue its claim, based (subject to sub-paragraph (2)) on the principal subject matter of the dispute.

(The courts, lists and sub-lists are set out in paragraphs 1.3 and 1.4.)

(2) In cases where different aspects of the dispute indicate that the case be issued in different lists, sub-lists or courts, the claimant must consider whether there are aspects requiring the expertise of a specialist judge and choose the list, sub-list or court in which the relevant specialist judges sit.

2.3 (1) Before a claimant issues a claim in the Business and Property Courts, the claimant must determine the appropriate location in which to issue the claim.

(2) With the exception of claims started under Parts 58, 60, 61 and 62, claims which are intended to be issued in the Business and Property Courts and which have significant links to a particular circuit outside the South Eastern Circuit must be issued in the BPCs District Registry located in the circuit in question. If a claim has significant links with more than one circuit, the claim should be issued in the location with which the claim has the most significant links.

(3) A link to a particular circuit is established where—

(a) one or more of the parties has its address or registered office in the circuit in question (with extra weight given to the address of any non-represented parties);

(b) at least one of the witnesses expected to give oral evidence at trial or other hearing is located in the circuit;

(c) the dispute occurred in a location within the circuit;

(d) the dispute concerns land, goods or other assets located in the circuit; or

(e) the parties' legal representatives are based in the circuit.

(4) A claim which raises significant questions of fact or law in common with another claim already proceeding before a B&PCs District Registry may be regarded as having significant links with the circuit in question.

2.4 (1) In a claim issued in London in the following courts, a hearing may, where appropriate, take place in a court in a circuit—

(a) the Commercial Court;

(b) the Admiralty Court;

(c) the Financial List;

(c) the Technology and Construction Court.

(2) A judge of the Commercial Court may, where appropriate and subject always to available judicial resources, be made available to hear a claim issued in a Circuit Commercial Court.

2.5 While any appropriate claim may be issued in any of the BPCs District Registries, the following are circumstances in which case management or trial may instead occur in the Business and Property Courts of England and Wales—

(1) Where a claim is issued in the Revenue List in one of the BPCs District Registries, Her Majesty's Revenue and Customs may nevertheless seek to have the proceedings case managed and/or tried in the Business and Property Courts of England and Wales, in accordance with CPR 30.3(2)(h) and Annex 1 of Practice Direction 66.

(2) A claim meeting the definition established in paragraph 1.1 of the EU Competition Law Practice Direction may be issued in an appropriate BPCs District Registry, but its case management and/or trial in the district registry in question will be dependent on an appropriate judge being made available in the district registry in question.

(3) A claim in the Intellectual Property List, which includes the Patents Court and the Intellectual Property Enterprise Court ("IPEC") (and includes the IPEC small claims track to which rule 63.27 applies), may be issued in an appropriate BPCs District Registry. However the case management and/or trial of a claim in the Patents Court or the IPEC in the BPCs District Registry in question will be dependent on an appropriate judge being made available in the district registry in question.

Transfers

3.1 (1) Subject to CPR 30.2, 30.5 and 59.3, the Business and Property Courts may, having regard to the criteria in 3.1(3), order proceedings in the Business and Property Courts of England and Wales or of a BPCs District Registry, or any part of such proceedings (such as a counterclaim or an application made in the proceedings), to be transferred—

(a) from the Business and Property Courts of England and Wales to the Business and Property Courts in a BPCs District Registry; or

(b) from the Business and Property Courts in a BPCs District Registry to the Business and Property Courts of England and Wales or to the Business and Property Courts in another BPCs District Registry.

(2) An application for an order under paragraph 1(b) must be made to the Business and Property Court from which the transfer is sought, and notified to the intended receiving Business and Property Court at the same time by the applicant, and must be consented to by the receiving Business and Property Court before any order for transfer is made.

(3)   When considering whether to make an order under rule 30.2(4) (transfer between the Royal Courts of Justice and the district registries) when the proceedings are in the Business and Property Courts, the court must also have regard to—

(a)   significant links between the claim and the circuit in question, considering the factors listed in paragraph 2.3(3) above;

(b)   whether court resources, deployment constraints, or fairness require that the hearings (including the trial) be held in another court than the court into which it was issued;

(c)   the wishes of the parties, which bear special weight in the decision but may not be determinative;

(d)   the international nature of the case, with the understanding that international cases may be more suitable for trial in centres with international transport links;

(e)   the availability of a judge specialising in the type of claim in question to sit in the court to which the claim is being transferred.

3.2   In addition to the provisions set out in CPR 30.3, the Business and Property Courts must have regard, when considering whether to make an order for transfer from the Business and Property Courts to a county court hearing centre:

(a)   to the nature of the claim, in accordance with the guidance provided at paragraphs 4.1 to 4.4; and,

(b)   to the availability of a judge specialising in the corresponding type of claim to sit in an appropriate court in the circuit;

3.3   When considering the availability of a judge under paragraph 3.1(e), the listing office of the court to which the claim is being transferred will be consulted before the order is made by the court.

Specialist work in the County Court

4.1   Subject to any enactment or rule relating to the jurisdiction of the County Court, the County Court at Central London, Birmingham, Bristol, Cardiff, Manchester, Newcastle, Leeds, Liverpool, and Preston are appropriate venues for any cases which are suitable to be heard in the County Court which fall within the definition in paragraph 4.2 as the specialist work of the type undertaken in the Business and Property Courts.

4.2   The specialist work of the type undertaken in the Business and Property Courts includes all the work that falls under the jurisdiction of the courts and lists that make up the Business and Property Courts, except for—

(a)   Claims for possession of domestic property and rent and mesne profits, or in respect of domestic mortgages;

(b)   Claims for possession of commercial premises or disputes arising out of business tenancies that are routine in nature;

(c)   Claims falling under the Trusts of Land and Appointment of Trustees Act 1996, unless combined with other specialist claims;

(d)   Hearings of unopposed creditors' winding-up or bankruptcy petitions or applications to set aside statutory demands;

(e)   Building claims, other than adjudication claims, of a value under £75,000;

(f)   Invoice and other straightforward business claims of a value under £75,000;

(g)   Boundary and easement disputes involving no conveyancing issues;

(h)   Claims to enforce a charging order;

(i)   Applications under the Access to Neighbouring Land Act 1992;

(j)   Proceedings under the Inheritance (Provision for Family and Dependants) Act 1975.

4.3   Claims issued in the County Court which are issued in the County Court at the hearing centres defined in paragraph 4.1 and relate to the specialist work of the type undertaken in the Business and Property Courts will be marked "Business and Property work" by the court upon allocation if they have not already been marked in that way by the claimant, and will be managed and heard only by judges specialising in this work.

4.4   Judges specialising in the County Court Business and Property work must spend a minimum of 20 percent of their time handling Business and Property work, either in the Business and Property Courts or in the County Court.

Appeals in BPCs District Registries

5.1   Specific appeal slots will be created in listing in the BPCs District Registries to accommodate blocks of applications for permission to appeal and appeals which are to be heard by a Group A judge (as defined in PD52A) in accordance with that PD52A.

5.2   So far as possible these slots will be concomitant with the slots identified for cases listed in BPCs District Registries requiring a Group A judge as defined in PD52A to hear them and transferred cases referred to in paragraph 3.

Appendix 21

Practice Direction 51U - Disclosure Pilot for the Business and Property Courts

1. General

1.1 This Practice Direction is made under rule 51.2 and provides a pilot scheme for disclosure in the Business and Property Courts. Section I provides a new scheme for disclosure.

1.2 The Commencement Date is 1 January 2019. The pilot applies from the Commencement Date for two years to existing and new proceedings in the Business and Property Courts of England and Wales and the Business and Property Courts in Birmingham, Bristol, Cardiff, Leeds, Liverpool, Manchester and Newcastle. For the avoidance of doubt, it does not apply in the County Court although this may be reviewed in the course of the pilot.

1.3 The pilot shall not disturb an order for disclosure made before the Commencement Date or before the transfer of proceedings into a Business and Property Court, unless that order is varied or set aside. If proceedings are transferred out of one of the Business and Property Courts into a court that is not one of the Business and Property Courts, any order for disclosure made under the pilot will stand unless and until any other order is made by the transferee court.

1.4 The pilot shall not, unless otherwise ordered, apply to proceedings which are—
    (1) a Competition claim as defined in Practice Direction 31C;
    (2) a Public Procurement claim;
    (3) within the Intellectual Property and Enterprise Court;
    (4) within the Admiralty Court;
    (5) within the Shorter and Flexible Trials Schemes; or
    (6) within a fixed costs regime or a capped costs regime.

1.5 In the Patents Court, PD63 paragraphs 6.1 to 6.3 will continue to apply under the pilot with the following modification: unless the court expressly orders otherwise, no provision in this practice direction nor any disclosure order made under this pilot will take effect as requiring disclosure wider than is provided for in PD 63 paragraph 6.1.

1.6 The pilot will continue to apply after the end of the two year period to any proceedings to which it applied at that point.

1.7 For the purposes of the pilot, where the provisions of this Practice Direction conflict with other provisions of the rules or other Practice Directions, this Practice Direction shall take precedence.

1.8 Terms in Section I of this Practice Direction shall have the meaning given to them in the schedule of definitions at Appendix 1.

1.9 Save for those provisions of CPR Part 31 that are set out in Section II, and the related provisions of Practice Directions 31A and 31B, CPR Part 31 and Practice Directions 31A and 31B shall not apply to any proceedings falling within the pilot.

1.10 Save that references in Section II to an Electronic Documents Questionnaire should be treated as references to the Disclosure Review Document, nothing in this Practice Direction is intended to change the application or working of those provisions of CPR Part 31 that are set out in Section II and the related provisions of Practice Directions 31A and 31B, and CPR Part 31 as a whole should still be used to interpret those provisions.

SECTION I

2. Principles, "document", "adverse" and "known adverse documents"

2.1 Disclosure is important in achieving the fair resolution of civil proceedings. It involves identifying and making available documents that are relevant to the issues in the proceedings.

2.2 For the purpose of disclosure, the term "document" includes any record of any description containing information. The term is further defined below.

2.3 The court expects the parties (and their representatives) to cooperate with each other and to assist the court so that the scope of disclosure, if any, that is required in proceedings can be agreed or determined by the court in the most efficient way possible.

2.4 The court will be concerned to ensure that disclosure is directed to the issues in the proceedings and that the scope of disclosure is not wider than is reasonable and proportionate (as defined in paragraph 6.4) in order fairly to resolve those issues, and specifically the Issues for Disclosure (as defined in Appendix 1).

2.5 A "document" may take any form including but not limited to paper or electronic; it may be held by computer or on portable devices such as memory sticks or mobile phones or within databases; it includes e-mail and other electronic communications such as text messages, webmail, social media and voicemail, audio or visual recordings.

2.6 In addition to information that is readily accessible from computer systems and other electronic devices and media, the term "document" extends to information that is stored on servers and back-up systems and electronic information that has been 'deleted'. It also extends to metadata, and other embedded data which is not typically visible on screen or a print out.

2.7 Disclosure extends to "adverse" documents. A document is "adverse" if it or any information it contains contradicts or materially damages the disclosing party's contention or version of events on an issue in dispute, or supports the contention or version of events of an opposing party on an issue in dispute.

2.8 "Known adverse documents" are documents (other than privileged documents) that a party is actually aware (without undertaking any further search for documents than it has already undertaken or caused to be undertaken) both (a) are or were previously within its control and (b) are adverse.

2.9 For this purpose a company or organisation is "aware" if any person with accountability or responsibility within the company or organisation for the events or the circumstances which are the subject of the case, or for the conduct of the proceedings, is aware. For this purpose it is also necessary to take reasonable steps to check the position with any person who has had such accountability or responsibility but who has since left the company or organisation.

3. Duties in relation to disclosure

3.1 A person who knows that it is or may become a party to proceedings that have been commenced or who knows that it may become a party to proceedings that may be commenced is under the following duties ("the Disclosure Duties") to the court—

(1) to take reasonable steps to preserve documents in its control that may be relevant to any issue in the proceedings;

(2) once proceedings have commenced against it or by it and in accordance with the provisions of this pilot scheme, to disclose, regardless of any order for disclosure made, known adverse documents, unless they are privileged;

(3) to comply with any order for disclosure made by the court;

(4)   to undertake any search for documents in a responsible and conscientious manner to fulfil the stated purpose of the search;

(5)   to act honestly in relation to the process of giving disclosure and reviewing documents disclosed by the other party; and

(6)   to use reasonable efforts to avoid providing documents to another party that have no relevance to the Issues for Disclosure in the proceedings.

3.2   Legal representatives who have the conduct of litigation on behalf of a party to proceedings that have been commenced, or who are instructed with a view to the conduct of litigation where their client knows it may become a party to proceedings that have been or may be commenced, are under the following duties to the court—

(1)   to take reasonable steps to preserve documents within their control that may be relevant to any issue in the proceedings;

(2)   to take reasonable steps to advise and assist the party to comply with its Disclosure Duties;

(3)   to liaise and cooperate with the legal representatives of the other parties to the proceedings (or the other parties where they do not have legal representatives) so as to promote the reliable, efficient and cost-effective conduct of disclosure, including through the use of technology;

(4)   to act honestly in relation to the process of giving disclosure and reviewing documents disclosed by the other party; and

(5)   to undertake a review to satisfy themselves that any claim by the party to privilege from disclosing a document is properly made and the reason for the claim to privilege is sufficiently explained.

3.3   The duties under paragraph 3.1 and 3.2 above are continuing duties that last until the conclusion of the proceedings (including any appeal) or until it is clear there will be no proceedings.

3.4   Where there is a known adverse document but it has not been located, the duty to disclose the document is met by that fact being disclosed, subject to any further order that the court may make.

4.   Preservation of documents

4.1   Documents to be preserved in accordance with the duties under paragraph 3.1(1) and 3.2(1) above include documents which might otherwise be deleted or destroyed in accordance with a document retention policy or in the ordinary course of business. Preservation includes, in suitable cases, making copies of sources and documents and storing them.

4.2   The duty under paragraph 3.1(1) and 3.2(1) includes—

(1)   an obligation to suspend relevant document deletion or destruction processes for the duration of the proceedings;

(2)   an obligation to send a written notification in any form to all relevant employees and former employees in accordance with paragraph 4.3 below; and

(3)   an obligation to take reasonable steps so that agents or third parties who may hold documents on the party's behalf do not delete or destroy documents that may be relevant to an issue in the proceedings.

4.3   A written notification under paragraph 4.2 above should—

(1)   identify the documents or classes of documents to be preserved; and

(2)   notify the recipient that they should not delete or destroy those documents and should take reasonable steps to preserve them.

4.4   Legal representatives who have the conduct of litigation on behalf of a party to proceedings that have been commenced, or who are instructed with a view to the conduct of litigation where their client knows it may become a party to proceedings that have been or may be commenced, must within a reasonable period of being instructed—

(1) notify their client of the need to preserve documents and of their obligations under paragraph 3.1 above; and

(2) obtain written confirmation from their client or an appropriate representative of their client that their client has taken the steps required under paragraphs 4.2 and 4.3 above.

4.5 Each party must confirm in writing when serving their particulars of claim or defence (as appropriate), that steps have been taken to preserve relevant documents in accordance with the duties under paragraph 3.1(1) and 3.2(1) above, and as required by paragraph 4.1 to 4.4 above.

5. Initial Disclosure

5.1 Save as provided below, and save in the case of a Part 7 claim form without particulars of claim or a Part 8 claim form, each party must provide to all other parties at the same time as its statement of case an Initial Disclosure List of Documents that lists and is accompanied by copies of—

(1) the key documents on which it has relied (expressly or otherwise) in support of the claims or defences advanced in its statement of case (and including the documents referred to in that statement of case); and

(2) the key documents that are necessary to enable the other parties to understand the claim or defence they have to meet.

5.2 This form of disclosure is known as "Initial Disclosure".

5.3 Initial Disclosure is not required where—

(1) the parties have agreed to dispense with it (see paragraph 5.8 below);

(2) the court has ordered that it is not required (see paragraph 5.10 below); or

(3) a party concludes and states in writing, approaching the matter in good faith, that giving Initial Disclosure would involve it or any other party providing (after removing duplicates, and excluding documents referred to at paragraph 5.4(3)) more than (about) whichever is the larger of 1000 pages or 200 documents (or such higher but reasonable figure as the parties may agree), at which point the requirement to give Initial Disclosure ceases for all parties for the purposes of the case.

Documents comprising media not in page form are not included in the calculation of the page or document limit at (3) but, where provided pursuant to a requirement to give Initial Disclosure, should be confined strictly to what is necessary to comply with paragraph 5.1 above.

5.4 A party giving Initial Disclosure—

(1) is under no obligation to undertake a search for documents beyond any search it has already undertaken or caused to be undertaken for the purposes of the proceedings (including in advance of the commencement of the proceedings);

(2) should briefly describe in its Initial Disclosure List of Documents any searches just mentioned;

(3) should not provide unless requested (but should still list in the Initial Disclosure List of Documents) documents by way of Initial Disclosure if such documents—

(a) have already been provided to the other party, whether by disclosure before proceedings start (see CPR 31.16) or through pre-action correspondence or otherwise in the period following intimation of the proceedings (and including when giving Initial Disclosure with a statement of case that is being amended); or

(b)   are known to be or have been in the other party's possession.

5.5   Unless otherwise ordered, or agreed between the parties, copies of documents shall be provided in electronic form for the purpose of Initial Disclosure. The Initial Disclosure List of Documents should be filed but the documents must not be filed.

5.6   In proceedings where a statement of case is to be served on a defendant out of the jurisdiction Initial Disclosure is not required in respect of that defendant unless and until that defendant files an acknowledgement of service that does not contest the jurisdiction, or files a further acknowledgement of service under CPR 11(7)(b).

5.7   For the avoidance of doubt, Initial Disclosure does not require any document to be translated.

5.8   The parties may agree in writing, before or after the commencement of proceedings, to dispense with, or defer, Initial Disclosure. Each party should record its respective reasons for any agreement, so that those reasons may be available to the court, on request, at any case management conference. The court may set aside such an agreement if it considers that Initial Disclosure is likely to provide significant benefits and the costs of providing Initial Disclosure are unlikely to be disproportionate to such benefits.

5.9   The court shall disregard any prior agreement to dispense with Initial Disclosure when considering whether to order Extended Disclosure.

5.10   If a party is requested but does not agree to dispense with Initial Disclosure, the requesting party may apply to the court with notice to the other party for directions limiting or abrogating the obligation to provide Initial Disclosure if it considers compliance with the obligation will incur disproportionate cost or be unduly complex. Such an application must be made by application notice, supported by evidence where necessary, and, save in exceptional cases, will be dealt with without a hearing or at a short telephone hearing.

5.11   In an appropriate case the court may, on application, and whether or not Initial Disclosure has been given, require a party to disclose documents to another party where that is necessary to enable the other party to understand the claim or defence they have to meet or to formulate a defence or a reply.

5.12   A complaint about Initial Disclosure shall be dealt with at the first case management conference unless, exceptionally and on application, the court considers that the issue should be resolved at an earlier hearing.

5.13   A significant failure to comply with the obligation to provide Initial Disclosure may be taken into account by the court when considering whether to make an order for Extended Disclosure and the terms of such an order. It may also result in an adverse order for costs.

5.14   For the avoidance of doubt, nothing in this paragraph affects the operation of paragraph 7.3 of Practice Direction 16.

6.   Extended Disclosure

6.1   A party wishing to seek disclosure of documents in addition to, or as an alternative to, Initial Disclosure must request Extended Disclosure. No application notice is required. However, the parties will be expected to have completed the Disclosure Review Document pursuant to paragraphs 7 and following below.

6.2   The court will determine whether to order Extended Disclosure at the first case management conference or, if directed by the court, at another hearing convened for that purpose or without a hearing.

6.3 Save where otherwise ordered, Extended Disclosure involves using Disclosure Models (see paragraph 8 below) after Issues for Disclosure have been identified (see paragraph 7 below). The court will only make an order for Extended Disclosure where it is persuaded that it is appropriate to do so in order fairly to resolve one or more of the Issues for Disclosure.

6.4 In all cases, an order for Extended Disclosure must be reasonable and proportionate having regard to the overriding objective including the following factors—

(1) the nature and complexity of the issues in the proceedings;

(2) the importance of the case, including any non-monetary relief sought;

(3) the likelihood of documents existing that will have probative value in supporting or undermining a party's claim or defence;

(4) the number of documents involved;

(5) the ease and expense of searching for and retrieval of any particular document (taking into account any limitations on the information available and on the likely accuracy of any costs estimates);

(6) the financial position of each party; and

(7) the need to ensure the case is dealt with expeditiously, fairly and at a proportionate cost.

6.5 A request for Extended Disclosure must specify which of the Disclosure Models listed in paragraph 8 below is proposed for each Issue for Disclosure defined in paragraph 7 below. It is for the party requesting Extended Disclosure to show that what is sought is appropriate, reasonable and proportionate (as defined in paragraph 6.4). Where Disclosure Model D or E is proposed parties should be ready to explain to the court why Disclosure Model C is not sufficient.

6.6 The objective of relating Disclosure Models to Issues for Disclosure is to limit the searches required and the volume of documents to be disclosed. Issues for Disclosure may be grouped. Disclosure Models should not be used in a way that increases cost through undue complexity.

7. Identifying the Issues for Disclosure

7.1 Within 28 days of the final statement of case each party should state, in writing, whether or not it is likely to request Extended Disclosure to include one or more of Models B, C, D or E (see paragraph 8 below) on one or more issues in the case. At this point it should not particularise the Model(s) or the issue(s) in the case.

7.2 Where one or more of the parties has indicated it is likely to request Extended Disclosure, the claimant must within 42 days of the final statement of case, prepare and serve on the other parties a draft List of Issues for Disclosure unless the equivalent of such a list has already been agreed between the parties (for example, as part of a fuller list of issues). The List of Issues for Disclosure should be set out using Section 1A of the Disclosure Review Document (see further paragraph 10 below).

7.3 "Issues for Disclosure" means for the purposes of disclosure only those key issues in dispute, which the parties consider will need to be determined by the court with some reference to contemporaneous documents in order for there to be a fair resolution of the proceedings. It does not extend to every issue which is disputed in the statements of case by denial or non-admission.

7.4 The claimant should seek to ensure that the draft List of Issues for Disclosure provides a fair and balanced summary of the key areas of dispute identified by the parties' statements of case and in respect of which it is likely that one or other of the parties will be seeking Extended Disclosure.

7.5   In the event that a particular Issue for Disclosure has not been included in the List of Issues for Disclosure, or is described in a manner that is unacceptable to the defendant, using section 1A of the Disclosure Review Document the defendant should provide the claimant with its proposed wording or alternative wording for inclusion in the draft List of Issues for Disclosure as soon as practicable but in any event no later than 14 days after service of the draft List of Issues for Disclosure.

7.6   In advance of the first case management conference, the parties must discuss and seek to agree the draft List of Issues for Disclosure. They should consider whether any draft Issue for Disclosure can be removed. For each Issue for Disclosure that is maintained, the parties should indicate at this point, using section 1A of the Disclosure Review Document, which Model of Extended Disclosure is sought for each party. Where Model C Disclosure is contemplated the parties should discuss the requests that might apply for the purpose of that disclosure (see further paragraph 10.5 below).

7.7   The List of Issues for Disclosure may be revised or supplemented at any time prior to or following the case management conference, including as a result of statements of case or amended statements of case subsequently served or discussions between the parties in relation to the Disclosure Review Document.

7.8   If the parties are (subject to the court) agreed that there are preliminary issues suitable for determination before other issues in the case, or that the case should be divided into stages, the parties may apply to the court before any case management conference for an order for the trial of those issues or for trial in stages (and related directions), and they may agree in writing to limit the work towards disclosure required by this Practice Direction until that application has been heard.

7.9   In an appropriate case where the claimant is acting in person and a defendant is not the court may request the legal representatives of the defendant to lead on the preparation of the List of Issues for Disclosure.

8.   The Extended Disclosure Models

8.1   Extended Disclosure may take the form of one or more of the Disclosure Models set out below.

8.2   There is no presumption that a party is entitled to Extended Disclosure, and in particular to Model D or Model E disclosure. No Model will apply without the approval of the court.

8.3   The court may order that Extended Disclosure be given using different Disclosure Models for different Issues for Disclosure in the case. In the interests of avoiding undue complexity the court will rarely require different Models for the same set of documents. The court may also order that Extended Disclosure be given by only one party, or that different Models are to apply to each party's Disclosure on a particular Issue for Disclosure.

Model A: Disclosure confined to known adverse documents

The court may order that the only disclosure required in relation to some or all of the Issues for Disclosure is of known adverse documents in accordance with the (continuing) duty under paragraph 3.1(2) above.

Model B: Limited Disclosure

(1)   The court may order the parties to disclose (where and to the extent that they have not already done so by way of Initial Disclosure, and without limit as to quantity)—

(a)   the key documents on which they have relied (expressly or otherwise) in support of the claims or defences advanced in their statement(s) of case; and

    (b)   the key documents that are necessary to enable the other parties to understand the claim or defence they have to meet;

and in addition to disclose known adverse documents in accordance with their (continuing) duty under paragraph 3.1(2) above.

(2)   A party giving Model B Disclosure is under no obligation to undertake a search for documents beyond any search already conducted for the purposes of obtaining advice on its claim or defence or preparing its statement(s) of case. Where it does undertake a search however then the (continuing) duty under paragraph 3.1(2) will apply.

Model C: Request-led search-based disclosure

(1)   The court may order a party to give disclosure of particular documents or narrow classes of documents relating to a particular Issue for Disclosure, by reference to requests set out in or to be set out in Section 1B of the Disclosure Review Document or otherwise defined by the court.

(2)   If the parties cannot agree that disclosure should be given, or the disclosure to be given, pursuant to a request, then the requesting party must raise the request at the case management conference. The court will determine whether the request is reasonable and proportionate and may either order the disclosing party to search for the documents requested, refuse the request, or order the disclosing party to search for a narrower class of documents than that requested. Any appropriate limits to the scope of the searches to be undertaken will be determined by the court using the information provided in the Disclosure Review Document.

(3)   For the avoidance of doubt, a party giving Model C Disclosure must still comply with the duty under paragraph 3.1(2) above to disclose known adverse documents; these will include any arising from the search directed by the court.

Model D: Narrow search-based disclosure, with or without Narrative Documents

(1)   Under Model D, a party shall disclose documents which are likely to support or adversely affect its claim or defence or that of another party in relation to one or more of the Issues for Disclosure.

(2)   Each party is required to undertake a reasonable and proportionate search in relation to the Issues for Disclosure for which Model D disclosure has been ordered. Any appropriate limits to the scope of the searches to be undertaken will be determined by the court using the information provided in the Disclosure Review Document.

(3)   The order should specify whether a party giving Model D disclosure is to search for and disclose Narrative Documents. If the order does not so specify, Narrative Documents should not be disclosed.

(4)   For the avoidance of doubt, a party giving Model D Disclosure must still comply with the duty under paragraph 3.1(2) above to disclose known adverse documents; these will include any arising from the search directed by the court.

Model E: Wide search-based disclosure

(1)   Under Model E, a party shall disclose documents which are likely to support or adversely affect its claim or defence or that of another party in relation to one or more of the Issues for Disclosure or which may lead to a train of inquiry which may then result in the identification of other documents for disclosure (because those other documents are likely to support or adversely affect the party's own claim or defence or that of another party in relation to one or more of the Issues for Disclosure).

(2)   Model E is only to be ordered in an exceptional case.

(3)   Each party is required to undertake a reasonable and proportionate search in relation to the Issues for Disclosure for which Model E Disclosure has been ordered. The scope of the search will be determined by the court using the information provided in the

Disclosure Review Document and is likely to be broader than that ordered for Model D Disclosure.

(4)   Narrative Documents must also be searched for and disclosed, unless the court otherwise orders.

(5)   For the avoidance of doubt, a party giving Model E Disclosure must still comply with the duty under paragraph 3.1(2) above to disclose known adverse documents; these will include any arising from the search directed by the court.

9.   Other provisions concerning Disclosure Models

9.1   Where an order for Model B, C, D or E Extended Disclosure is made on one or more Issues for Disclosure, any adverse documents to be disclosed in compliance with the duty under paragraph 3.1(2) above and not already disclosed must be disclosed at the time ordered for that Extended Disclosure.

9.2   In a case where no order for Model B, C, D or E Extended Disclosure is made in respect of a party on any Issue for Disclosure (so that the only disclosure has been Initial Disclosure or Model A Extended Disclosure) that party must within 60 days of the first case management conference provide a Disclosure Certificate certifying that all known adverse documents have been disclosed.

9.3   The provisions of paragraph 8 and this paragraph 9 do not affect the fact that the duty under paragraph 3.1(2) above is a continuing duty as provided by paragraph 3.3 above: if adverse documents in the control of a party come to its knowledge at a later date they must (unless privileged) be disclosed without delay.

9.4   The court may make an order for Extended Disclosure in stages.

9.5   When it is necessary to decide any question of what is reasonable and proportionate under a particular Disclosure Model, the court will consider all the circumstances of the case including the factors set out in paragraph 6.4 above and the overriding objective.

9.6   Where the Disclosure Model requires searches to be undertaken, the parties must discuss and seek to agree, and the court may give directions, on the following matters with a view to reducing the burden and cost of the disclosure exercise—

(1)   that the scope of the searches which the disclosing parties are required to undertake be limited to—

(a)   particular date ranges and custodians of documents;

(b)   particular classes of documents and/or file types;

(c)   specific document repositories and/or geographical locations;

(d)   specific computer systems or electronic storage devices;

(e)   documents responsive to specific keyword searches, or other automated searches (by reference, if appropriate, to individual custodians, creators, repositories, file types and/or date ranges, concepts);

(2)   if Narrative Documents are to be excluded, how that is to be achieved in a reasonable and proportionate way;

(3)   the use of—

(a)   software or analytical tools, including technology assisted review software and techniques;

(b)   coding strategies, including to reduce duplication.

(4)   prioritisation and workflows.

9.7   In making an order for Extended Disclosure, the court may include any provision that is appropriate including provision for all or any of the following—

(1)   requiring the use of specified software or analytical tools;

(2)   identifying the methods to be used to identify duplicate or near-duplicate documents and remove or reduce duplicate documents;

(3)   requiring the use of data sampling;

(4)   specifying the format in which documents are to be disclosed;

(5)   identifying the methods that the court regards as sufficient to be used to identify privileged documents and other non-disclosable documents;

(6)   the use of a staged approach to the disclosure of electronic documents;

(7)   excluding certain classes of document from the disclosure ordered.

9.8   In considering Extended Disclosure as well as when complying with an order for Extended Disclosure the parties should have regard to the guidance set out in Section 3 of the Disclosure Review Document.

9.9   In an appropriate case, the court may order that the question of which party bears the costs of disclosure is to be given separate consideration at a later stage rather than the costs being treated automatically as costs in the case;

9.10   For the avoidance of doubt, Extended Disclosure does not require any document to be translated.

10.   Completion of the Disclosure Review Document

10.1   The Disclosure Review Document is the document by which the parties must identify, discuss and seek to agree the scope of any Extended Disclosure sought of Model C, D or E, and provide that information in due course to the court.

10.2   In a complex case the format of the Disclosure Review Document may be modified as required in order that information is exchanged and in due course provided to the court in an efficient, convenient and helpful format.

10.3   The parties' obligation to complete, seek to agree and update the Disclosure Review Document is ongoing. If a party fails to co-operate and constructively to engage in this process the other party or parties may apply to the court for an appropriate order at or separately from the case management conference, and the court may make any appropriate order including the dismissal of any application for Extended Disclosure and/or the adjournment of the case management conference with an adverse order for costs.

10.4   In the Disclosure Review Document each party should (save as already described for Initial Disclosure: see paragraph 5.4(2) above) describe any searches for documents that it has already undertaken or caused to be undertaken for the purposes of the proceedings (including in advance of the commencement of the proceedings).

10.5   Any party proposing Model C Extended Disclosure must complete Section 1B of the Disclosure Review Document and provide it to the other parties no later than 28 days after the defendant has responded in accordance with paragraph 7.5 above to the claimant's draft List of Issues for Disclosure. Any party provided with a completed Section 1B in this way must respond within 14 days by completing the "response" column either agreeing to the request or giving concise reasons for not agreeing to the request.

10.6   Having agreed the List of Issues for Disclosure and exchanged proposals on Model(s) for Extended Disclosure, the parties should prepare and exchange drafts of Section 2 of the Disclosure Review Document (including costs estimates of different proposals, and where possible estimates of likely amount of documents involved) as soon as reasonably practicable and in any event not later than 14 days before the case management conference.

10.7   The parties must seek to resolve any disputes over the scope of any Extended Disclosure sought in advance of the first case management conference. Any disputes which have not been resolved will normally be decided by the court at the first case management conference.

10.8 A finalised single joint Disclosure Review Document should be filed by the claimant not later than 5 days before the case management conference. Related correspondence and earlier drafts should not ordinarily be filed.

10.9 The parties must each file a signed Certificate of Compliance substantially in the form set out in Appendix 3 as soon as reasonably practicable after the claimant has filed the finalised single joint Disclosure Review Document but in any event in advance of the case management conference.

10.10 In an appropriate case where the claimant is acting in person and a defendant is not the court may request the legal representatives of the defendant to lead on the preparation and filing of the Disclosure Review Document.

11.   Disclosure Guidance Hearings

11.1 The parties may seek guidance from the court by way of a discussion with the court in advance of or after a case management conference, concerning the scope of Extended Disclosure or the implementation of an order for Extended Disclosure, where—

(1)   the parties have made real efforts to resolve disputes between them; and

(2)   the absence of guidance from the court before a case management conference is likely to have a material effect on the court's ability to hold an effective case management conference, or the absence of guidance from the court after a case management conference is likely to have a material effect on the parties' ability to carry out the court's case management directions effectively.

11.2 A Disclosure Guidance Hearing may be fixed by issuing an application notice, before or after a case management conference. The application notice should contain a statement confirming the matters at (1) and (2) of paragraph 11.1 above. Evidence will not normally be required for a Disclosure Review Hearing and an early hearing will be offered where possible. The application will have a maximum hearing length of 30 minutes and a maximum of 30 minutes pre-reading.

11.3 At a Disclosure Guidance Hearing the court will generally expect a legal representative with direct responsibility for the conduct of disclosure to be the person who participates on behalf of each party in the discussion concerning the scope of Extended Disclosure or the implementation of an order for Extended Disclosure.

11.4 The guidance given at a Disclosure Guidance Hearing will be recorded in a short note, to be approved by the court. Whilst the primary function of the Disclosure Guidance Hearing is to provide guidance, for the avoidance of doubt the court may, where appropriate, make an order at a Disclosure Guidance Hearing.

11.5 Unless otherwise ordered, the costs of a Disclosure Guidance Hearing are costs in the case and no order from the court to that effect is required.

12.   Complying with an order for Extended Disclosure

12.1 An order for Extended Disclosure is complied with by undertaking the following steps—

(1)   service of a Disclosure Certificate substantially in the form set out in Appendix 4 signed by the party giving disclosure, to include a statement supported by a statement of truth signed by the party or an appropriate person at the party that all known adverse documents have been disclosed;

(2)   service of an Extended Disclosure List of Documents (unless dispensed with, by agreement or order); and

    (3)   production of the documents which are disclosed over which no claim is made to withhold production or (if the party cannot produce a particular document) compliance with paragraph 12.3.

12.2   The order for Extended Disclosure will not have been complied with until each step specified in paragraph 12.1 has taken place.

12.3   If a party cannot produce a particular document (because the document no longer exists, the party no longer has it in its possession or for any other reason) the disclosing party is required to describe each such document with reasonable precision and explain with reasonable precision the circumstances in which, and the date when, the document ceased to exist or left its possession or the other reason for non-production. If it is not possible to identify individual documents, the class of documents must be described with reasonable precision.

12.4   In the case of a company, firm, association or other organisation, or where the Disclosure Certificate is signed by a party on behalf of other parties, the certificate must—

    (1)   identify the person signing the Disclosure Certificate; and

    (2)   explain why she or he is considered to be an appropriate person to sign it.

12.5   A party may not without the permission of the court or agreement of the parties rely on any document in its control that it has not disclosed at the time required for Extended Disclosure (or within 60 days after the first case management conference in a case where there will be no Extended Disclosure). For the avoidance of doubt the party and its legal representatives remain under the duties under paragraph 3.1 (the Disclosure Duties) and 3.2 above.

13.   Production of documents

13.1   Save where otherwise agreed or ordered, a party shall produce—

    (1)   disclosable electronic documents to the other parties by providing electronic copies in the documents' native format, in a manner which preserves metadata; and

    (2)   (save as provided by paragraph 5.5 above in the case of Initial Disclosure) disclosable hard copy documents by providing scanned versions or photocopied hard copies.

13.2   Electronic documents should generally be provided in the form which allows the party receiving the documents the same ability to access, search, review and display the documents (including metadata) as the party providing them.

13.3   A party should provide any available searchable OCR versions of electronic documents with the original, unless they have been redacted. If OCR versions are provided, they are provided on an "as is" basis, with no assurance to the other party that the OCR versions are complete or accurate.

13.4   A party should not disclose more than one copy of a document unless additional copies contain or bear modifications, obliterations or other markings or features which of themselves cause those additional copies to fall within a party's Initial or Extended Disclosure obligations.

14.   Right to withhold production of documents (other than public interest immunity)

14.1   A person who wishes to claim a right or duty (other than on the basis of public interest immunity) to withhold disclosure or production of a document, or part of a document, or a class of documents which would otherwise fall within its obligations of Initial

Disclosure or Extended Disclosure may exercise that right or duty without making an application to the court subject to—

(1)   describing the document, part of a document or class of document; and

(2)   explaining, in the Disclosure Certificate, the grounds upon which the right or duty is being exercised.

A claim to privilege may (unless the court otherwise orders) be made in a form that treats privileged documents as a class, provided always that paragraph 3.2(5) is complied with.

14.2   A party who wishes to challenge the exercise of a right or duty to withhold disclosure or production must apply to the court by application notice supported where necessary by a witness statement.

14.3   The court may inspect the document or samples of the class of documents if that is necessary to determine whether the claimed right or duty exists or the scope of that right or duty.

15.   Confidentiality

If there are material concerns over the confidentiality of a document (whether the confidentiality benefits a party to the proceedings or a third party), the court may order disclosure to a limited class of persons, upon such terms and subject to such conditions as it thinks fit. The court may make further orders upon the request of a party, or on its own initiative, varying the class of persons, or varying the terms and conditions previously ordered, or removing any limitation on disclosure.

16.   Redaction

16.1   A party may redact a part or parts of a document on the ground that the redacted data comprises data that is—

(1) irrelevant to any issue in the proceedings, and confidential; or

(2) privileged.

16.2   Any redaction must be accompanied by an explanation of the basis on which it has been undertaken and confirmation, where a legal representative has conduct of litigation for the redacting party, that the redaction has been reviewed by a legal representative with control of the disclosure process. A party wishing to challenge the redaction of data must apply to the court by application notice supported where necessary by a witness statement.

17.   Failure adequately to comply with an order for Extended Disclosure

17.1   Where there has been or may have been a failure adequately to comply with an order for Extended Disclosure the court may make such further orders as may be appropriate, including an order requiring a party to—

(1)   serve a further, or revised, Disclosure Certificate;

(2)   undertake further steps, including further or more extended searches, to ensure compliance with an order for Extended Disclosure;

(3)   provide a further or improved Extended Disclosure List of Documents;

(4)   produce documents; or

(5)   make a witness statement explaining any matter relating to disclosure.

17.2   The party applying for an order under paragraph 17.1 must satisfy the court that making an order is reasonable and proportionate (as defined in paragraph 6.4).

17.3   An application for any order under paragraph 17.1 should normally be supported by a witness statement.

18. Varying an order for Extended Disclosure; making an additional order for disclosure of specific documents

18.1 The court may at any stage make an order that varies an order for Extended Disclosure. This includes making an additional order for disclosure of specific documents or narrow classes of documents relating to a particular Issue for Disclosure.

18.2 The party applying for an order under paragraph 18.1 must satisfy the court that varying the original order for Extended Disclosure is necessary for the just disposal of the proceedings and is reasonable and proportionate (as defined in paragraph 6.4).

18.3 An application for an order under paragraph 18.1 must be supported by a witness statement explaining the circumstances in which the original order for Extended Disclosure was made and why it is considered that order should be varied.

18.4 The court's powers under this paragraph include, but are not limited to, making an order for disclosure in the form of Models B to E and requiring a party to make a witness statement explaining any matter relating to disclosure.

19. Restriction on use of a privileged document which has been inadvertently produced

19.1 Where a party inadvertently produces a privileged document, the party who has received the document may use it or its contents only with the permission of the court.

19.2 Where a party is told, or has reason to suspect, that a document has been produced to it inadvertently, that party shall not read the document and shall promptly notify the party who produced it to him. If that party confirms that the document was produced inadvertently, the receiving party shall, unless on application the court otherwise orders, either return it or destroy it, as directed by the producing party, without reading it.

20. Sanctions

20.1 Throughout disclosure the court retains its full powers of case management and the full range of sanctions available to it.

20.2 If a party has failed to comply with its obligations under this pilot including by—

   (1) failing to comply with any procedural step required to be taken;

   (2) failing to discharge its disclosure duties; or

   (3) failing to cooperate with the other parties, including in the process of seeking to complete, agree and update the Disclosure Review Document,

   the court may adjourn any hearing, make an adverse order for costs or order that any further disclosure by a party be conditional on any matter the court shall specify. This provision does not limit the court's power to deal with the failure as a contempt of court in an appropriate case.

21. Documents referred to in evidence

21.1 A party may at any time request a copy of a document which has not already been provided by way of disclosure but is mentioned in—

   (1) a statement of case;

   (2) a witness statement;

   (3) a witness summary;

   (4) an affidavit; or

   (5) an expert's report.

21.2 Copies of documents mentioned in a statement of case, witness evidence or an expert's report and requested in writing should be provided by agreement unless the request is unreasonable or a right to withhold production is claimed.

21.3 A document is mentioned where it is referred to, cited in whole or in part or there is a direct allusion to it.

21.4 Subject to rule 35.10(4), the court may make an order requiring a document to be produced if it is satisfied such an order is reasonable and proportionate (as defined in paragraph 6.4).

22.   Cost

22.1 The parties are required to provide an estimate of what they consider to be the likely costs of giving the disclosure proposed by them in the Disclosure Review Document, and the likely volume of documents involved, in order that a court may consider whether such proposals on disclosure are reasonable and proportionate (as defined in paragraph 6.4). These estimated costs may be used by the court in the cost budgeting process.

22.2 In cases where the cost budgeting scheme applies, if it is not practical to complete the disclosure section of Form H in relation to disclosure prior to the court making an order in relation to disclosure at the case management conference, the parties may notify the court that they have agreed to postpone completion of that section of Form H until after the case management conference. If they have agreed to postpone they must complete the disclosure section within such period as is ordered by the court after an order for disclosure has been made at the case management conference. Where possible the court will then consider (and if appropriate, approve) that part of the cost budget without an oral hearing.

23.   False Disclosure Certificates

23.1 Proceedings for contempt of court may be brought against a person who signs, or causes to be signed by another person, a false Disclosure Certificate without an honest belief in its truth.

SECTION II

31.16.   Disclosure before proceedings start

(1)   This rule applies where an application is made to the court under any Act for disclosure before proceedings have started.

(2)   The application must be supported by evidence.

(3)   The court may make an order under this rule only where—

(a)   the respondent is likely to be a party to subsequent proceedings;

(b)   the applicant is also likely to be a party to those proceedings;

(c)   if proceedings had started, the respondent's duty by way of standard disclosure, set out in rule 31.6, would extend to the documents or classes of documents of which the applicant seeks disclosure; and

(d)   disclosure before proceedings have started is desirable in order to—

(i)   dispose fairly of the anticipated proceedings;

(ii)   assist the dispute to be resolved without proceedings; or

(iii)   save costs.

(4)   An order under this rule must—

(a) specify the documents or the classes of documents which the respondent must disclose; and

(b) require him, when making disclosure, to specify any of those documents—

    (i)   which are no longer in his control; or

    (ii)   in respect of which he claims a right or duty to withhold inspection.

(5)   Such an order may—

    (a)   require the respondent to indicate what has happened to any documents which are no longer in his control; and

    (b)   specify the time and place for disclosure and inspection.

(Rule 78.26 contains rules in relation to the disclosure and inspection of evidence arising out of mediation of certain cross-border disputes.)

31.17.   Orders for disclosure against a person not a party

(1)   This rule applies where an application is made to the court under any Act for disclosure by a person who is not a party to the proceedings.

(2)   The application must be supported by evidence.

(3)   The court may make an order under this rule only where—

    (a)   the documents of which disclosure is sought are likely to support the case of the applicant or adversely affect the case of one of the other parties to the proceedings; and

    (b)   disclosure is necessary in order to dispose fairly of the proceedings or to save costs.

(4)   An order under this rule must—

    (a)   specify the documents or the classes of documents which the respondent must disclose; and

    (b)   require the respondent, when making disclosure, to specify any of those documents—

        (i)   which are no longer in his control, or

        (ii)   in respect of which he claims a right or duty to withhold inspection.

(5)   Such an order may—

    (a)   require the respondent to indicate what has happened to any documents which are no longer in his control; and

    (b)   specify the time and place for disclosure and inspection.

(Rule 78.26 contains rules in relation to the disclosure and inspection of evidence arising out of mediation of certain cross-border disputes.)

31.18.   Rules not to limit other powers of the court to order disclosure

Rules 31.16 and 31.17 do not limit any other power which the court may have to order—

(a)   disclosure before proceedings have started; and

(b)   disclosure against a person who is not a party to proceedings.

31.19.   Claim to withhold inspection or disclosure of a document (public interest immunity)

(1)   A person may apply, without notice, for an order permitting him to withhold disclosure of a document on the ground that disclosure would damage the public interest.

(2)   Unless the court orders otherwise, an order of the court under paragraph (1)—

    (a)   must not be served on any other person; and

    (b)   must not be open to inspection by any person.

...

(8)   This Part does not affect any rule of law which permits or requires a document to be withheld from disclosure or inspection on the ground that its disclosure or inspection would damage the public interest.

31.22.   Subsequent use of disclosed documents and completed Electronic Documents Questionnaires

(1)   A party to whom a document has been disclosed may use the document only for the purpose of the proceedings in which it is disclosed, except where—

(a)   the document has been read to or by the court, or referred to, at a hearing which has been held in public;

(b)   the court gives permission; or

(c)   the party who disclosed the document and the person to whom the document belongs agree.

(2)   The court may make an order restricting or prohibiting the use of a document which has been disclosed, even where the document has been read to or by the court, or referred to, at a hearing which has been held in public.

(3)   An application for such an order may be made—

(a)   by a party; or

(b)   by any person to whom the document belongs.

(4)   For the purpose of this rule, an Electronic Documents Questionnaire which has been completed and served by another party pursuant to Practice Direction 31B is to be treated as if it is a document which has been disclosed.

Index